Far China Station

ROBERT ERWIN JOHNSON

Far China Station

The U.S. Navy in Asian Waters
1800–1898

NAVAL INSTITUTE PRESS

Frontispiece: Commodore Matthew Calbraith Perry landing at Yokohama in 1854. Ships of the East India Squadron are at anchor in the background. Courtesy of Naval Photographic Center.

In memory of
Franz Oscar Johnson
and
Edgar Lawrence Ellis

Contents

List of Illustrations

Preface

The battles with which this book begins and ends, those at Quallah Battoo and in Manila Bay, are fairly well known, as are a number of other events involving the U.S. Naval Forces in the East India and China seas, most notably Commodore Perry's negotiation of the treaty with Japan. While the accounts of these occurrences often indicate that the U.S. Navy maintained a squadron of warships in the Far East as a part of its peacetime organizational structure, it was beyond their authors' purposes to inquire into this squadron's origins, its importance in the implementation of the nation's policies, or such routine matters as logistic support, hazards to ships and men, and relations with officials, American and foreign, and with other naval forces in the region. Indeed, the bulk of the squadron's history has remained concealed in official records and private papers.

Almost a quarter of a century ago, I wrote the story of the U.S. Navy's Pacific Squadron, a work that made me aware of the importance of the Navy's distant-station policy in the nineteenth century and also stirred my interest in the other squadrons. None had a closer relationship to the Pacific Squadron than its neighbor to the westward, and my subsequent research toward a biography of Rear Admiral John Rodgers, whose service included two important commands in Asian waters, whetted my interest even further; nor has that interest been sated by several years spent studying the squadron's records and then writing its history.

I share Justice Holmes's opinion that "a ship is the most living of inanimate things," and the vessels themselves—the majestic *Columbus* and the workhorse *Vincennes*, the famous *Olympia* and the plodding *Palos*, together with all of their sisters—are the real heroines of this narrative.

No one could write a work of this scope without a great deal of help from others. I am especially grateful to the University of Alabama, which granted me two semesters of sabbatical leave and provided financial support both through its Research Grant Committee (this book was Research Project #543) and through its Office of International Studies and Programs. My thanks are also due the following institutions and individuals: The National Archives staff, especially Aloha South, Elaine Everly, and Harry Schwartz of the Old Army and Navy Section, and Elmer Parker, former head of that section; the staff of the Library of Congress Manuscript Division and the officers of the Naval Historical Foundation; Rear Admiral Ernest M. Eller and Vice Admiral Edwin B. Hooper, former directors of naval history, and the staff of the Naval Historical Center, especially Dr. Dean C. Allard and William C. Heimdahl; the Keeper of the Records and the staff of the Public Record Office, especially Commander Michael Godfrey and R. F. A. Saggers; the Director of the British Museum and the staff of the Students' Room; the staff of the Manuscripts and Archives Division, New York Public Library, Astor, Lenox and Tilden Foundations; the staff of the New-York Historical Society Manuscript Section; the United Church Board for World Ministries for permission to use the records of the American Board of Commissioners for Foreign Missions and the staff of Harvard University's Houghton Library, especially Miss Carolyn Jakeman, for assistance in using those records; the staff of the University of Alabama's Amelia Gayle Gorgas Library, especially Mrs. Catherine T. Jones, Derek Milsom, and Dean James Wyatt; Dr. Richmond D. Williams and the staff of the Eleutherian Mills Historical Library for making available copies of Captain Du Pont's letters; Cynthia H. Requardt and other members of the staff of the Maryland Historical Society; Douglas L. Stein and others at the G. W. Blunt White Library, Mystic Seaport, Inc.; Dr. William N. Still, who provided copies of letters from the East Carolina Manuscripts Collection, East Carolina University; and members of the staff of the Peabody Museum. Robert A. Carlisle, head of the Navy Department's Photojournalism and Public Inquiries Branch, and Dr. Philip K. Lundeberg, curator of naval history at the Smithsonian Institution, furnished illustrative material. Mrs. Carolyn C. Sassaman and Mrs. Ruth M. Kibbey typed the manuscript in exemplary fashion. Jan Snouck-Hurgronje has guided me with regard to the policies of the Naval Institute Press, and I am grateful for the editorial assistance given me by Beverly Sopp. I appreciate the interest and encouragement of my good friends John Haskell Kemble and James M. Merrill. Finally, no words can express my gratitude to Vivian; she served as research assistant and perceptive critic and contributed to this book in countless other ways. Not least, she and our late cocker Meg created the setting in which I could work most effectively.

CHAPTER ONE

The *Peacock* and Her Predecessors

In the early morning darkness of 6 February 1832, the small boats of the USS *Potomac* embarked 282 officers and men and pulled for the beach near the Sumatran village known as Quallah Battoo. Splashing through the surf at dawn, the sailors and marines quickly captured three of the village's four forts and set fire to the dwellings from which the inhabitants had fled. Commodore John Downes then recalled his landing force and took the *Potomac* inshore where an hour's deliberate fire from her 32-pounders caused the defenders of the remaining fort to surrender. When the frigate retired to an anchorage a few miles distant, a messenger from Quallah Battoo entreated the commodore to grant its people peace. Downes was willing but warned that future transgressions would be punished with equal severity. So the first U.S. punitive operation in the "East India and China Seas" ended, with an estimated 150 Sumatran fatalities and two Americans dead and eleven wounded.

The *Potomac*'s mission had been necessitated by the seizure and looting of the merchantman *Friendship* of Salem, which occurred off Quallah Battoo a year earlier. Hearing of this incident, master mariners trading to the East Indies had petitioned President Andrew Jackson for naval assistance. They pointed out that, although Americans had been engaged in the pepper trade with Sumatra for more than forty years, no U.S. warship had ever shown the flag in its waters.

In response, the *Potomac*, fitting out for a cruise as flagship of the Pacific Squadron, received orders to proceed to her station by way of the

1

Cape of Good Hope, investigating and punishing the Sumatran offenders en route. In addition, Secretary of the Navy Levi Woodbury recommended that money be appropriated "to provide a sufficient force to visit occasionally the Indian and Chinese seas."[1]

In his next annual report, Woodbury expressed his satisfaction with Downes's action and noted that a detachment from the Brazil Squadron had also been ordered to Sumatra and "such places in India, China, and on the eastern coast of Africa, as may be conducive to the security and prosperity of our important commercial interests in those regions."[2] This detachment, the ship-rigged sloop of war *Peacock* and the new schooner *Boxer*, was fitting out at Boston when Secretary Woodbury offered its command to Master-Commandant David Geisinger, specifying that it must sail before the end of January 1832. But warships of the sailing Navy were rarely ready for sea as early as the Navy Department expected; Geisinger assumed command on 7 February, and a few hours later the "Peacocks" exchanged cheers with the "Boxers" as the schooner got underway for Rio de Janeiro.

During the next month, the sloop of war completed her preparations for sea, and Geisinger acquainted himself with the duties that she was expected to perform. He had a copy of Downes's orders, which he was to carry out if the *Potomac* failed to chastise the *Friendship*'s assailants; more important than Downes's orders, however, was a confidential section of his own orders which directed him to rate one Edmund Roberts as captain's clerk, "to do duty as such, but . . . to be treated as a Gentleman having the confidence of the Government and entrusted with important duties in India, Arabia, and Africa. . . ."[3]

Roberts, a businessman from Portsmouth, New Hampshire, was fluent in French and Spanish, widely traveled, and personally acquainted with Arabia and the east coast of Africa. In short, he was well qualified for the duty of "procuring commercial and political information . . . and learning on what terms our commerce there can be put on the footing of that of the most favoured nations."[4] However, it was Roberts's acquaintance with Levi Woodbury, a "Granite State" senator before joining Jackson's cabinet, that undoubtedly won him the appointment. Roberts had urged such a mission on Woodbury earlier. Learning of the *Friendship* incident, he kept himself free of all engagements in the expectation that it would provide the opportunity he sought.

All was arranged by the beginning of 1832. One-third of Roberts's salary was to be paid by the Navy, and Secretary of State Edward Livingston would provide the remainder from his "contingent fund for Foreign Intercourse." Strict secrecy was enjoined, presumably for political reasons; Roberts agreed to assume the duties and the humble guise of a captain's clerk in an unimportant man-of-war although commissioned a special agent of the State Department empowered to conclude treaties with the governments of Muscat, Siam, and Annam.[5]

When one considers the scope of American trade with the Orient in 1832, it is obvious that the Roberts mission was hardly premature. U.S. merchant vessels had been lured to the Far East soon after the republic had won its independence, and statistics for the year 1831–32 show thirty American merchantmen engaged in trade with China alone. U.S. exports to China during that year were valued at $1,580,522, while imports amounted to $5,344,907. But the China trade was only part of the trade with the Far East; Yankee merchant ships were also familiar with the ports of Indo-China, the Philippines, and the East Indies, while whaling vessels seeking their prey on the "Japan ground" often sought refreshment or succor in harbors of the region.

In spite of the history and value of this trade, it was conducted largely without the formality of treaties or commercial agreements. In the case of China, this was not unusual. The Chinese government of the Ch'ing Dynasty had not extended diplomatic recognition to any Western nation. All trade had to be conducted under strict regulation through the port city of Canton with officially licensed merchants. Americans engaged in this trade generally were treated well by Chinese authorities. Having learned the methods by which some of the restrictions might be circumvented, they evinced no desire for diplomatic or naval protection from the United States. Vessels touching at ports in the Philippines, Dutch East Indies, or India and Ceylon came within the purview of treaties with Spain, the Netherlands, and Britain respectively, but elsewhere they were trading at their own risk.

However, the *Potomac* was not the first U.S. man-of-war to venture into Far Eastern waters. The frigate *Essex*, ordered to Java by way of the Cape of Good Hope to protect trade during the Quasi-War with France, had spent two months in the vicinity of Sunda Strait before departing with a convoy of homeward-bound merchantmen in July 1800. Almost fifteen years later, the sloop of war *Peacock* (whose name Geisinger's command bore) played the opposite role, capturing four British vessels in the same region.

The foreign trade of the United States fell off sharply during the War of 1812 and recovered with almost equal rapidity, while the U.S. Navy emerged from the war with enhanced reputation and a larger number of warships than ever before. Some of these warships found employment when a permanent squadron was established in 1815 to protect commerce in the Mediterranean Sea from the depredations of corsairs and the arbitrary actions of petty rulers. Revolutionary wars on the Pacific coast of

Latin America caused the frigate *Macedonian* to be dispatched in the autumn of 1818 to that area to watch over U.S. interests. Her successors soon acquired the status of a permanent Pacific Squadron, and in 1822 the West India Squadron was established to protect American shipping from privateers and pirates in the waters of the Gulf of Mexico and the Caribbean Sea. Four years later, unsettled conditions in South America's Rio de la Plata region led to the formation of the Brazil Squadron, so-called because it was based at Rio de Janeiro.

A few months after the *Macedonian* had sailed on her voyage to the Pacific, the frigate *Congress* undertook a trade-protection cruise in the Orient. When she arrived off Lintin Island at the entrance to the Canton River estuary (about sixty miles from Canton) on 3 November 1819, Captain John D. Henley received an order from the viceroy at Canton that the frigate was to depart at once "for she is not permitted to linger about here and create disturbance."[6] Henley chose to interpret this as a mere formality and the U.S. consul agreed, albeit hesitantly, fearing that he and his fellow merchants might suffer the results of any Chinese displeasure. After a good deal of difficulty, in the course of which the captain made a visit to Canton, arrangements were finally made to supply the *Congress* with provisions, firewood, and fresh water; but the frigate's defective mizzenmast could not be repaired in the exposed roadstead off Lintin, nor could permission be obtained for her to seek a more protected anchorage.

The *Congress* made sail for Manila in mid-January 1820. Spanish authorities received her very hospitably and offered the facilities of their navy yard for unstepping and repairing the mast. By March she was back in Chinese waters and spent the spring and summer cruising in the South China Sea and in the vicinity of the East Indian straits to the southward. No difficulties were encountered until the frigate returned to Lintin in September; there the usual problems of procuring supplies exasperated Henley to the point that he sailed up the estuary to the Boca Tigris, the navigable entrance to the Canton River. Fearing that the *Congress* was about to emulate HMS *Alceste*, the British frigate that had forced her way within twenty miles of Canton in 1816, the authorities quickly gave permission to furnish her with supplies, after which she dropped down to Lintin and prepared for the long passage home. Captain Henley made known his willingness to escort homeward-bound merchant vessels, but the *Congress* sailed alone. The merchant mariners considered piracy a lesser threat than the possibility of future Chinese retribution—the expulsion or arrest of merchants or the confiscation of goods—for accepting the frigate's protection.

Reports of disturbances at Manila led Henley to touch there; however, the cholera then afflicting the city soon appeared among his ship's company. Cutting short her visit, the frigate fled the pestilential bay and set a course for the United States where she arrived in May 1821.

Although the *Macedonian* was the first of a continuous line of "United States Naval Forces on Pacific Station," the *Congress*, whose cruise was similar in time and purpose, had no successor until 1830 when the sloop of war *Vincennes* paused almost incidentally at Macao and Manila in the course of the first voyage of circumnavigation by a U.S. naval vessel. There were several reasons for this break in continuity: the *Macedonian* was able to render significant services to American-flag shipping on the coasts of Chile, Peru, Ecuador, and Panama, while Captain Henley's efforts to be of assistance were spurned by his countrymen. American citizens trading to Valparaiso, Callao, Guayaquil, and Panama urged that naval forces continue to protect their interests; their counterparts at Canton were embarrassed by the presence of a warship that could only irritate local officialdom without the ability to redress wrongs that they might suffer in China. Twenty-six of some 400 "Macedonians" died of various causes during their vessel's 30-month cruise, while the *Congress* lost 68 men from her company of 350, 26 of them to cholera, in 2 years. Moreover, cordage and canvas were reported to deteriorate rapidly in the extreme humidity of the China Sea's rainy season, and, with the exceptions of Manila and Batavia, both notoriously prone to outbreaks of tropical disease, there was no harbor in the Orient in which the U.S. government could arrange base facilities for its warships. In short, the Far East seemed an unhealthy area where the presence of a naval force was neither necessary nor desired. A Navy Department that had to provide squadrons for the Mediterranean, Pacific, and West India stations was understandably loath to establish another in the depression years following the Panic of 1819.

Nine years after the *Congress* returned to the United States, the *Vincennes* found a different attitude among the American merchants at Canton. They informed Master-Commandant William B. Finch that, although their relationship with Chinese authorities was generally favorable, the periodic presence of a warship would both spare them petty annoyances and vexatious delays and reduce the likelihood of loss to pirates. "The visits would be most beneficial if made annually, and of short stay in the waters of China, visiting Manila and proceeding through the seas and straits usually frequented by our ships."[7] However, it was the *Friendship* incident rather than this change in the China merchants' attitude that brought the next American warships to Chinese waters. En route to her station from Sumatra, the *Potomac* paused at Macao; China was also included in the *Peacock*'s itinerary.

The latter was finally ready for sea on 8 March 1832 and weighed anchor after embarking the chargé d'affaires to the Argentine Republic and his family. The *Peacock* stopped at Puerto Praia in the Cape Verde Islands a month later. Learning that the inhabitants of the neighboring island of Fogo were starving, Captain Geisinger landed a barrel each of beef, bread, and rice, and two of pork at Puerto Praia for them. The *Peacock* then left for Rio de Janeiro, where she was to transship the chargé and his family to another vessel of the Brazil Squadron for trans-portation to Buenos Aires before sailing for the Cape of Good Hope in company with the *Boxer*. But neither the schooner nor any other unit of the squadron was at Rio de Janeiro; as Geisinger learned, the entire force had gone southward. After replenishing provisions and water, the sloop of war was towed to sea by the boats of foreign men-of-war—a pleasant custom in the Brazilian harbor—and made sail for Montevideo. Ascending the Rio de la Plata to Buenos Aires, she found the sloop of war *Warren* and the schooner *Enterprise*, but no *Boxer*. Geisinger landed his passengers and waited two weeks; then, with Roberts's concurrence, he decided to sail and await the schooner off Sumatra.

Beating out of the Plata estuary on 25 June, the *Peacock* made her way across the South Atlantic Ocean. On the Fourth of July, the sloop of war "at Daylight hoisted the Colors at the Peak and fired a gun in honor of the Day."[8] One week later, the watch on deck got a glimpse of Tristan da Cunha, and the *Peacock* continued eastward, past the Cape of Good Hope and into the Indian Ocean. Soon after sighting Amsterdam Island, the warship encountered bad weather. She was running before a gale when a mass of water crashed over her starboard quarter, carrying away the gig and both davits. No more damage was suffered, but frequent heavy squalls kept her men busy shortening and making sail as she headed northeastward. "Land ho!" rang out from aloft on 24 August, and four days later the *Peacock* anchored off Sumatra's southwest coast, sixty-three days out of Montevideo.

Learning that the *Potomac* had dealt with Quallah Battoo, the sloop of war soon departed Sumatra bound for Manila. There, Roberts and Geisinger accepted the American consul's invitation to stay at his resi-dence while their less fortunate shipmates made good the defects resulting from a long ocean passage. Once again Manila took its toll of American sailors—six "Peacocks" died of "Asiatic Spasmodic Cholera" during the month their vessel spent there and another expired soon after her depar-ture.

The *Peacock* anchored in Macao Roads on 7 November and beat up to an anchorage off Lintin two days later. Here she received the usual order to leave Chinese waters forthwith; as usual, it was ignored. Roberts and

Geisinger boarded a "fast boat" of the type plying the Canton River. Passing Whampoa, the merchant ship anchorage twelve miles below Canton, they counted twenty-five vessels flying the U.S. flag. Just outside the Canton city wall, a row of impressive two- and three-story buildings of granite and brick caught their attention. These were the "factories"—combination warehouses and living quarters—where the foreign merchants resided and conducted their business from September to March. During the remainder of the year, they were forced to retire to the Portuguese city of Macao. Geisinger and Roberts spent six weeks at these American factories, no doubt enjoying the luxurious standard of living and the companionship of other Americans. However, if they desired American female companionship, they were disappointed; foreign women were forbidden to reside in the factories or even to visit them.

Just before Christmas, they returned to the Peacock. Although Roberts had been authorized to visit Japan, it was obvious that the sloop of war alone could not bring about a change in the island empire's centuries-old policy of isolation. Therefore, the Peacock made sail for Indo-China. Since wind and current combined to keep her from reaching Tourane Bay, reputedly the best port from which to communicate with Hué, the capital of Cochin-China, she had to drop down to Vunglam, another poorly protected roadstead. There the vessel spent a month while Roberts attempted to negotiate a commercial treaty. He finally concluded that his efforts were in vain, and the ship made sail for the Gulf of Siam.

An eleven-day passage brought her to an anchorage off the Menam (Bangkok) River, and on 24 February 1833 Roberts, Geisinger, and several junior officers traveled the twenty-five miles upstream to the Siamese capital. Their reception was in marked contrast to that in Cochin-China. A house fully staffed with servants was prepared for their use, and they were lavished with attention. After being presented to the king, the naval officers returned to the Peacock, which then had the honor of a visit by the king's brother. Her crew was exercised at the great guns and performed various evolutions for the edification of the royal visitor. Thereafter, the vessel lay idly at her moorings until Roberts finally came on board with the desired treaty on 5 April.

From the Gulf of Siam, the Peacock made her way to Singapore and on to Batavia where the Boxer, which had been detained in South American waters by order of the senior officer on the Brazil Station, awaited her. Ship-sloop and schooner dropped down to Anjer Roads late in July, whence they shaped a course across the Indian Ocean to Cape Guardafui, easternmost promontory of Africa, and thence through the Gulf of Aden and the Strait of Bab-el-Mandeb into the Red Sea.

The sighting of four square-rigged vessels in company off the strait on

27 August caused the sloop of war to beat to quarters and clear for action lest they be a piratical force. The largest of them, a brig, fired two guns; believing this to be a signal, Geisinger ordered the *Boxer* to speak her. In due course, the schooner reported that the stranger was the British East India Company's *Nautilus* with a convoy of merchantmen bound for the Indian port of Surat from Mocha on the coast of Yemen. Since the latter was the American squadron's next port of call, the news that a revolution had occurred there was of some interest.

The *Peacock* and the *Boxer* anchored off Mocha four days later and were received cordially by the rebel Turk who controlled the area. He manifested good will toward American shipping, so the squadron was soon on its way to Muscat on the Gulf of Oman.

U.S. merchants enjoyed an extensive trade with this sultanate, and Roberts had been charged to arrange a treaty with its ruler. The Imam, whose territories extended from the Persian Gulf to Zanzibar, remembered that Roberts had been presented to him in the course of a trading venture several years earlier. He readily agreed to sign a treaty assuring American shipping the same treatment as that of the most-favored nation and providing for the care of shipwrecked mariners until they could be repatriated. After a visit to the *Peacock*, the Imam ordered that both vessels be supplied with firewood and water, for which he refused any payment.

Although the treaty was signed on 21 September, just three days after the squadron's arrival in the Cove of Muscat, the *Peacock* and her consort spent another two weeks there while awaiting the northeast monsoon to assure good weather for the first part of their homeward passage. They weighed anchor on 7 October and, after touching at Mozambique and Table Bay, the *Peacock* stood into Rio de Janeiro on 17 January 1834, two days ahead of the *Boxer*.

No doubt Geisinger would willingly have departed for the United States as soon as possible, but his vessels were assigned to the Brazil Squadron and could not leave the station without orders from the commander in chief, Commodore Melancthon T. Woolsey, who was in the Plata region. Geisinger sent the *Boxer* to report to him at the end of January, and Edmund Roberts took passage in the homeward-bound sloop of war *Lexington* on 1 March. Three weeks later the USS *Potomac*, also homeward bound, came to anchor near the *Peacock*, and Geisinger exchanged experiences with Commodore John Downes. Commodore Woolsey arrived in the sloop of war *Natchez* later the same day and signified that the *Peacock* was to return to the United States as soon as the chargé d'affaires to Brazil was ready to take passage in her. The sloop of war's sojourn at Rio de Janeiro ended on 13 April. In spite of the date, she enjoyed a pleasant passage to New York, coming to anchor off the navy yard on 26 May.

In his notes on the cruise, Geisinger wrote that his vessel had logged 43,150 miles in the 412 days she spent under sail. She had lost 21 men from a company that had numbered 174 originally. Compared to the loss of life during the *Congress*'s cruise of like duration thirteen years earlier, the *Peacock*'s casualty list was rather low. Perhaps one reason for this relatively low figure is that living conditions in the old frigate were probably not as favorable as those in the less-crowded sloop of war.

Diplomatic and naval historians writing about this period have commonly regarded Edmund Roberts's negotiations as the significant facet of the *Peacock*'s first cruise in the East India and China seas. They point out that his treaty with Siam was the first with an Oriental ruler entered into by the United States and that its counterpart with Muscat contained even more favorable terms than the envoy had sought. Although this is true, the importance of the treaties is easily exaggerated. American merchant vessels had been treated informally on the same basis as those of most other Western nations, and there is no reason to believe that they were saved from discriminatory treatment by the negotiation of these treaties. Nor does there seem to have been any marked increase in American trade with the two areas as a result of the newly formalized relationship.

Perhaps the true significance of the *Peacock*'s cruise is that it marked the beginning of an almost constant American naval presence in the Far East, of a separate East India Squadron. To be sure, Master-Commandant Geisinger was not authorized to fly a commodore's broad pennant at the *Peacock*'s main truck. He was merely the commanding officer of the sloop of war and, when the *Boxer* was in company, the senior officer of a detachment of the Brazil Squadron. In actuality, however, he held an independent command during the eighteen months that his ship was absent from South American waters; indeed, she was a part of the Brazil Squadron only at the beginning and the end of her voyage. Except for the formality of a broad pennant, this 1832–34 cruise was markedly similar in purpose to those which followed; each was undertaken for "the protection and extension of our commerce in that quarter."[9] Admittedly, Geisinger was accompanied by Roberts, but so was his immediate successor, and the envoy's diplomatic mission was simply another means to the end. David Geisinger would not hoist his broad pennant as commander in chief of the East India Squadron until 1848, but for all intents and purposes he had held that position as commanding officer of the *Peacock*.

However, Edmund Roberts's role in bringing about the formation of a permanent East India Squadron must not be overlooked. While at Batavia

MAP 1–1. The East India Station

in June 1833, he wrote a formal dispatch urging that several warships be kept in Far Eastern waters for commerce protection. This proposal was a far cry from the occasional visits to that region which Navy Secretary Woodbury had stated as his department's desire in 1831, yet soon after Roberts's return to the United States in the spring of 1834, Woodbury took the first step toward implementing his recommendation by directing that the Pacific Squadron send one of its sloops of war to China and thence to Sumatra, after which she would return home via the southern tip of Africa.

But orders from Washington to the commander in chief of the Pacific Squadron, whether going across the Isthmus of Panama or around Cape Horn, took many months to reach their recipient; additional time then elapsed before he could communicate with the ship chosen for the mission and have her provisioned for such a lengthy cruise. Thus, another naval force destined for the Far East left New York three months before the USS *Vincennes*, under Master-Commandant John H. Aulick, departed Callao, Peru, in July 1835 to carry out Woodbury's orders. However, the *Vincennes* was the first to reach China and to terminate her cruise; therefore, her fortunes will be briefly described before those of the first East India squadron are considered.

The ship-sloop *Vincennes* came to anchor off Lintin Island on 2 January 1836. Aulick communicated with the Canton merchants, ignored the usual order to depart, and replenished his vessel's provisions by purchase from merchantmen in the vicinity. Unfortunately, many of her company, which had been very healthy, contracted what was described as a "violent catarrh." Sixty-two were on the binnacle list at one time, and two men died. These, together with one sailor lost overboard, were the only fatalities in the course of her cruise, but to Aulick they were good reason not to linger.

The *Vincennes* put to sea on 24 January and ran down the South China Sea before the prevailing northeasterly winds to Singapore, thence through Malacca Strait and Great Channel to Quallah Battoo. There Aulick ascertained that, although the town's fortifications had been strengthened since the *Potomac*'s attack, an amicable attitude toward Americans prevailed among its inhabitants. Having heard at Singapore that the *Peacock* and the schooner *Enterprise* were en route to that region, he got the *Vincennes* underway on 19 February and set a course for the Cape of Good Hope.

Meanwhile, the *Peacock* had not been allowed to languish in ordinary for many months after Geisinger decommissioned her at the New York Navy Yard. In January 1835, Secretary of the Navy Mahlon Dickerson wrote Captain Edmund P. Kennedy to offer him command of the sloop of war and the *Boxer's* sister, the *Enterprise*, which were to cruise in "the East Indies and along the coast of Asia." An additional sentence made the offer more attractive: "As this is to be a separate and distinct service from that of any of the Squadrons now employed, the Commander will be allowed to hoist his broad pendant and receive the allowances incident to the command of a Squadron."[10] Kennedy, whose application for command of the West India Squadron had been refused a few months earlier, lost no time in accepting the offer. He thus became the first officer to be recognized officially as commander in chief of the East India Squadron.

Several reasons help to account for this change in attitude toward the East India Squadron only three years after the *Peacock* began her earlier cruise. Roberts's influence was partly responsible; he was to sail in the *Peacock* again to exchange ratifications of the treaties with Muscat and Siam and to make agreements with Cochin-China and Japan. His mission would have greater dignity and thus a better chance of success if he were embarked in a flagship, even if she were but a sloop of war. Nor was this argument valid only in diplomatic negotiations. The U.S. Navy had no rank senior to that of captain, but an officer commanding a squadron was commonly known as a commodore both then and later, flying the blue broad pennant in his flagship and receiving the salutes and other honors accorded officers of that rank in European navies. Needless to say, a commodore would command more respect than the most outstanding captain or master-commandant could, especially in the rank-conscious Orient.

The *Boxer's* experience indicated another reason for not ordering vessels of the Brazil Squadron to cruise in Far Eastern waters—the commander in chief had authority to divert ships of his squadron to duties he considered more important than those to which the Navy Department had assigned them. Of course, he had to justify his action, but with a squadron as chronically understrength as that on Brazil Station, this would seldom be difficult.

The orders under which the *Peacock* sailed on 23 April 1835 required her to touch at Rio de Janeiro, where the *Enterprise*, permanently detached from the Brazil Squadron, would join her. Their route would then lead to Muscat, Sumatra, Siam, Cochin-China, and China, and they were to return to the United States by way of Cape Horn, calling at the principal ports on the west coast of South America en route.

From Rio de Janeiro, Commodore Kennedy reported that his flagship's mainyard was sprung, her jib boom had carried away because of dry rot, her standing rigging was 10 percent tar, and she had to be recaulked. Such a list of defects was quite usual after a month or two at sea. Many commanding officers attributed these faults to the inefficiency or even dishonesty supposedly typical of American navy yards at the time. However, Kennedy was probably correct in suggesting that seams caulked in the cold winter weather of Boston, New York, and the like were bound to gape when the vessels sailed into tropical waters; insufficient appropriations may help to explain the other deficiencies.

The East India Squadron stood into the South Atlantic Ocean on 12 July, and three days later the deeply laden *Enterprise*, unable to keep pace with the flagship, was ordered to proceed independently. The *Peacock* cracked on more sail and was soon out of sight of her consort. After fifty days in "an apparently interminable waste of water,"[11] the ship-sloop made Zanzibar. Her needs were quickly supplied without charge—another example of the friendship of the Imam, whose young son was acting as governor. The *Peacock* spent a week there and then made sail for Muscat.

Although the southwest monsoon was almost at its end, she enjoyed fine weather during the run northward. When the wind moderated off the Gulf of Aden, she set studdingsails alow and aloft and continued to fly along at 9 knots. Her noon reckoning on 21 September put her seventy-two miles to the eastward of the Arabian coast; therefore, it was a shock emotionally as well as physically when the vessel piled up on a coral reef at two o'clock the next morning.

Daylight revealed an island, low and sandy, without vegetation other than a few bushes, 1½ miles ahead. It thus became apparent that the *Peacock* had actually grounded on the Arabian coast in the Gulf of Masira. Boats were quickly lowered and soundings taken. Then anchors were carried out, and the hands were piped to the capstan in an effort to heave off—in vain, for the tide was ebbing and the anchors merely came home.

The *Peacock*'s plight was perilous indeed. Should the sea get up, she would soon be pounded to pieces, her boats could accommodate less than half her company, and those left on the inhospitable shore would be at the mercy of hostile Arabs. Within a short time, obviously piratical craft began to congregate with the clear intention of plundering the stranded warship as soon as others joined them. Kennedy decided that help must be sought from Muscat, and Edmund Roberts volunteered to undertake the four-hundred-mile journey in a twenty-foot boat manned by six sailors and a passed midshipman.

Meanwhile, the ship was being lightened—tackles were rigged from the yardarms and all manner of weighty items were swayed up from the deck or out of the hold and dropped overside. Eleven of the great guns, barrels of provisions, spare spars, chains and cables, even the contents of the spirit room, went over the rail in this fashion—some onto a raft hastily constructed to receive the provisions but most into the depths. The top hamper was struck down from aloft, and two thousand gallons of fresh water were pumped overboard. Hard work at any time, this was the worse because of the Arabian Sea sun blazing down on the sweating seamen and marines, and the pirates lurking malevolently in the distance.

But those in the small boat suffered more: their labors at the oars were at least as arduous; they had no shelter from the sun; piratical craft harassed them; and the boat shipped an occasional sea, so that rowing had to give way to bailing. Nonetheless, they pulled onward steadily and reached Muscat in 4¼ days. The Imam again demonstrated his good will, furnishing refreshment and lodging for the envoy and his fellows and ordering that his own new sloop of war *Sultana* proceed to the *Peacock's* assistance, while a force of Bedouins was sent overland to succor her company if they had to abandon ship.

However, the *Peacock* was saved by the exertions of her own people. After sixty hours of unremitting labor, they hove her off to her anchors, recovered those items of equipment within reach, and then filled away. There was an anxious moment as the vessel passed within one-hundred yards of the reef, but she continued to beat to windward until nightfall when she anchored in six fathoms. Leaking badly, the *Peacock* made sail for Muscat the next morning, meeting the *Sultana* en route.

At Muscat, the Imam continued to be gracious, supplying the wounded warship with fresh provisions and water and doing all in his power to make her company comfortable. Roberts engaged in the ceremonies incidental to his mission, while Kennedy investigated his flagship's faulty navigation. Her chronometers were suspected of error and quickly exculpated. Finally the commodore informed the Navy Department that the Arabian coast was actually thirty miles farther to the eastward than the *Peacock's* charts showed, a fact confirmed by the British survey then being made. That explanation still left the sloop of war forty-two miles offshore at noon; she must have been set that far to the westward by an unknown current in the fourteen hours before her stranding.

This explanation was acceptable to Navy Secretary Dickerson. If the *Peacock* had been lost, however, a court-martial might have been satisfied less easily. To be sure, Kennedy learned that nearly two-hundred vessels had fallen victim to the reefs and inhabitants of that treacherous coast, but the *Peacock* and the *Boxer* had traversed it twice without mishap two years earlier, as had countless other vessels before and after them. Inaccurate charts and unknown currents have explained many maritime disasters, undoubtedly many more disasters than they actually caused.

With his flagship leaking at the rate of fifteen inches an hour, Kennedy was eager to get her to a port where she could be repaired. As soon as Roberts had concluded his mission, the *Peacock* stood across the Arabian

Sea to Bombay, where the British East India Company maintained dockyard facilities and stores sufficient to restore her to full efficiency. The *Enterprise* was already there—Bombay was the second of the rendezvous the commodore had appointed before he left the schooner three months earlier.

A little more than a month sufficed to repair the sloop of war and to dock the *Enterprise*. Even as their ships were being restored, however, American sailors were sickening of "Bombay jungle fever." Almost all hands became ill, but they managed to work the vessels to sea on 4 December. Impure water was thought to be the cause, so the squadron put in at Colombo, Ceylon, to flush out the water casks and refill them with good water. Most of those on the binnacle list improved thereafter, but both ships' companies remained sickly enough so that the commodore accepted the surgeons' advice to forgo the visit to Sumatra's pepper ports.

After a period of recuperation at Batavia while awaiting the diminution of the northeast monsoon, the two vessels made an uneventful passage to the head of the Gulf of Siam. Roberts and Kennedy, accompanied by junior officers and the *Peacock*'s band, ascended the Menam River to Bangkok where the elaborate ceremonies accompanying the exchange of treaty ratifications took place. But this visit was fraught with unexpected danger—illness forced the commodore to return to the flagship prematurely, and by the time the remainder of the party embarked after the ceremonies ended on 14 April, most were suffering from cholera and dysentery.

Ill or not, Roberts was determined to attempt the Cochin-China negotiations, so the vessels went to Tourane Bay. They spent eight days at anchor in the heat and humidity of mid-May, until the envoy reluctantly admitted that he simply was too sick to carry out his mission. From there they sailed to Macao, where they arrived on 25 May with sixty-one men on the binnacle list.

On the surgeons' recommendation, Kennedy rented a house ashore to which the sick were transferred. Roberts, however, was taken to the Macao residence of the American merchant W. S. Wetmore. Most of those prostrated by illness improved rapidly in the relatively spacious and well-ventilated temporary hospital, but the *Enterprise*'s Lieutenant-Commanding Archibald Campbell and Edmund Roberts did not respond to treatment, the former dying on 3 June and the fifty-two-year-old envoy nine days later. Both were buried at Macao; the officers of the squadron provided a monument to Campbell's memory and the American merchants raised a fund to erect one on Roberts's grave.

On the eve of the *Peacock*'s departure from New York, Commodore Kennedy had suggested that he be sent credentials authorizing him to negotiate treaties "in the event of accident to Roberts."[12] No such authority having been received, Kennedy wrote Secretary Dickerson that the squadron's mission had been terminated by Roberts's death and it would sail for the United States as soon as the hospital could be closed and its patients returned to their ships.

After touching at Honolulu and Mexican ports, the East India Squadron met its Pacific counterpart at Callao, Peru, in July 1837. There Commodore Henry E. Ballard convinced Kennedy that the *Enterprise* should remain with the Pacific Squadron. Those of the schooner's company who wished to return home were transferred to the *Peacock*. They replaced some of the *Peacock*'s men who preferred service in Ballard's flagship, the ship of the line *North Carolina*, to a winter passage around Cape Horn in a small sloop of war. The *Peacock* arrived at Rio de Janeiro on 23 August, forty-six days out of Callao, and she anchored in Hampton Roads, Virginia, two months later.

The cruise of the first East India Squadron had been fairly eventful, marked by a stranding and no less than three epidemics by Kennedy's reckoning. Yet it cannot be said to have accomplished a great deal other than exchanging ratifications of the two treaties and showing the flag in Oriental waters for a few months. No significant assistance had been rendered to American citizens or shipping; indeed, much of the time the squadron's personnel were not healthy enough for a punitive force to be sent ashore.

Perhaps the most valuable result of the cruise was the letter containing Kennedy's recommendations for keeping ships' companies healthy in the Orient:

In this region, ships should be kept dry, scrupulously clean, and above all thoroughly ventilated by every possible means. The crew should be shielded as much as possible from the Sun and night dews, by awnings and proper clothing, and the strictest regard should be paid to their personal cleanliness. Their food should be of the best quality. . . . Ardent spirits are never useful and are always prejudicial; indeed I doubt whether their habitual use be ever necessary, under any circumstances, in any climate. . . . A plenty of good water, and an unrestrained breathing of air will be found the greatest prophylactic or preservative of ships' companies in all climates. . . .[13]

This letter reveals Edmund P. Kennedy to have been a man of sound common sense. The Navy Department would have been well advised to require its commanding officers to enforce the measures he advocated, although the spirit ration was specified by congressional action and could be changed only by the same means. Needless to say, his views on ardent spirits did not increase his popularity among some of his fellows!

CHAPTER TWO

The Opium War

Even before the *Peacock's* return to the United States, signs that the East India Station was likely to become permanent were not wanting. Because the nation was prospering economically, the national debt was paid in full in 1836 and a surplus then began to accumulate in the U.S. Treasury. A near approach to war with France over spoliation claims remaining from the period of the French Revolution had focused attention on the paucity of American military and naval strength, especially the latter; as a result, the majority Democratic party began to weaken its traditional opposition to increased naval expenditures. Pointing out that the American merchant marine was second only to that of Britain, a congressional committee emphasized its vulnerability in time of war and asserted that "the interest, the honor, and even the safety of our country" required a sufficient naval force.[1] The committee then recommended the numbers and types of warships that should be assigned to distant stations, including an East India Squadron. To be sure, recommendation and practice are quite different things, and the committee's advocacy by no means guaranteed the permanence of the East India Station. But it was indicative of a favorable climate of opinion, which would facilitate the continuation of the station when a pressing need became apparent in the course of the next squadron's cruise.

Secretary of the Navy Mahlon Dickerson offered the East India command to Captain George C. Read, who had earlier refused the force which sailed under Master-Commandant David Geisinger because it was not suitable for one of his rank. Assured that he would sail as a commodore on this occasion, Read went to Norfolk to prepare his vessels, the new frigate *Columbia* and the sloop of war *John Adams*, for sea. Dickerson had specified that they depart in three months, but nine months elapsed before the squadron sailed.

Two problems contributed to the delay. Commodore Read had great difficulty in manning the *Columbia*—seamen were in short supply in the vicinity of Norfolk, and it may be that stories of the unhealthiness of the Far East gained greater credence after the *Peacock*'s return to the navy yard at Norfolk. The frigate finally received an adequate number of men in January 1838 and dropped down to Hampton Roads preparatory to sailing. Then the discovery of dry rot in her stem forced her to return to Norfolk for repairs, which were slowed by unusually cold weather. So it was that the second East India Squadron did not leave the United States until 6 May 1838, nearly six months after the first had returned.

Having made the usual visits to Rio de Janeiro, Muscat, and Bombay, the two warships were at Colombo, Ceylon, when Commodore Read heard that Sumatrans had recently killed or wounded several seamen on board the American merchantman *Eclipse*, from which they had stolen a large sum in Spanish dollars and several chests of opium. Departing hurriedly on 2 December, the squadron made an eighteen-day passage to the west coast of Sumatra where inquiries revealed that those principally responsible belonged to the town of Mukkee, while others who had been involved resided at Quallah Battoo and Soo Soo.

When the squadron arrived at Quallah Battoo, the village rajah promised to bring the malfeasants on board within two days. He failed to do so, whereupon the *Columbia* and the *John Adams* came to anchor close inshore with springs on their cables. Bringing their broadsides to bear, they celebrated Christmas Day with a thirty-eight-minute bombardment of the forts. After returning the fire with three ineffectual shots, the forts showed the white flag. Read thought it unwise to send a landing party to complete their destruction; but he kept his ships at their anchorage until 29 December lest Quallah Battoo gain an erroneous impression of the efficacy of its defense.

Mukkee was next. The frigate sent an officer to require that the guilty individuals from there be delivered to him within two days, but his efforts were in vain. Indeed, the attitude of the rajahs led Read to believe that they would resist forcibly. On the morning of 1 January 1839, the two vessels were towed and warped into position just off the town, whence they opened a deliberate fire while a landing force prepared to disembark. The *John Adams*'s Commander Thomas W. Wyman led 320 sailors and marines from both companies to the beach where they formed up for an

FIGURE 2-1. The destruction of Mukkee by the *Columbia* (*left*) and the *John Adams*.

assault on the forts. Covered by the ships' fire, they moved forward, only to find the forts and town alike deserted. All were put to the torch, and then the landing force was reembarked.

Soo Soo remained to be punished, but Commodore Read found its people so inoffensive and its fortifications so pathetically weak that he merely exacted a promise that American ships and seamen in the vicinity would be protected. While the *Columbia* was watering ship there, rajahs from other ports came on board to assure the commodore of their friendship and their desire that the pepper trade should continue. Obviously the destruction of Mukkee had made an impression.

The squadron weighed anchor on 7 January and beat through Great Channel into the Strait of Malacca, pausing at Penang and then standing on to Singapore. Here, Commodore Read learned that the China trade had been interrupted, but the news did not cause him to hurry on to Macao. His vessels had spent most of the past nine months under sail, and a mild form of smallpox and dysentery had plagued their companies—indeed, the *Columbia* had lost twenty men since leaving Rio de Janeiro. Thus, Read elected to await the change of monsoon at Singapore, from which his ships finally sailed on 28 March.

Meanwhile, the situation of foreigners in China was becoming critical, due to the traffic in opium. Import of the narcotic had been made illegal by imperial edict in 1800. Nonetheless, because it was one of the few items for which Western merchants could find a Chinese market, the quantity sent to China from India and Turkey grew steadily. Periodic reports that opium importation would be legalized caused its production to be increased; nor was there any inclination to destroy the surplus of opium when the edict was not rescinded. Thus, opium smuggling had become an ever greater part of the China trade. Those involved in this traffic salved their consciences with the arguments that the drug was really no more dangerous to its users than alcoholic beverages were to Westerners and that smuggling could be carried on only with the connivance of Chinese officials, whose responsibility it actually was.

Whether or not the Chinese government agreed, it took a decisive step to end the opium trade early in 1839 by appointing Lin Tŝe Hsü high commissioner for the Canton region with especial powers to suppress smuggling of the drug. Lin proceeded quickly and effectively by demanding that all opium be surrendered immediately, enforcing his demand by stopping trade, ordering Chinese servants to leave the factories, and detaining sixteen foreign merchants as hostages. Meanwhile, the factories were virtually besieged by thousands of Chinese.

The Reverend Dr. Elijah C. Bridgman, who had founded the first American mission in China in 1830, was among those at Canton. He expressed the hope that the traffic in opium would never recover, blaming it for the fact that "our little community here have been held these two months in painful—fearful suspense. Nor does the prospect brighten."[2] His companion, the missionary-printer S. Wells Williams, lashed out at a trade which "was draining the country of its wealth, and giving in exchange death & disease; a drug so noxious that not one of its advocates would consent to use it at all, while they say it does the Chinese no harm."[3]

This was the situation when the USS *Columbia* let her anchors go in Macao Roads on 27 April 1839. Peter W. Snow, U.S. consul at Canton, lost no time in acquainting Commodore Read with the facts, adding that two of the hostages were American citizens. However, Snow urged forbearance because the hostages and the occupants of the factories would almost certainly be killed before the frigate could force her way upstream to rescue them. In short, Read could only await developments and be ready to protect the Americans in Macao should the Chinese attack that city.

In due course, the merchants decided to surrender the opium to Lin, who promptly had it destroyed. The British and most of the other foreigners then withdrew to Macao, but the Americans remained in their factories in the expectation that trade would soon be resumed. However, the Chinese demand that the merchants promise not to engage in opium smuggling on pain of confiscation of ships and cargoes and of death penalties for those involved in such activity, continued to present an obstacle, the last penalty being particularly abhorrent to the Americans.

Commodore Read noted with concern that a number of British merchantmen in Macao Roads had opium in their cargoes, and he was certain that it would be landed somewhere in China, perhaps from ships flying the American flag. How to prevent this, he was not sure—the smuggling vessels could not simply be driven offshore because they would return as soon as the warships left the area. If they were seized, the problem of their disposal would remain, because technically smugglers were not breaking any American law. He could only hope that none of his countrymen were "so wicked" and, if perchance they were, at least that their vessels would show no colors while engaged in smuggling.

So the East India Squadron rode at anchor in Macao Roads, showing the flag and doing nothing more. When a small boat under American colors was attacked without provocation by Chinese in Macao harbor, Read urged Consul Snow to demand that the assailants be punished. The consul demurred on the ground that no American had been killed; the serious injury of several of those embarked did not justify a protest in such uncertain times. Read, powerless because his presence was not recognized by the Chinese, could only observe that "this is a most awkward situation to be placed in. . . ."[4]

The weather was no help. Incessant rain, which began early in June, caused the flagship's binnacle list to soar. Ninety men were ill, many of dysentery, of which eleven had died since the squadron left Singapore. There seems to have been no thought of setting up a hospital ashore; perhaps the fear of spreading the smallpox that had been in the ship since the beginning of the cruise kept the sick from being landed.

Trade began again in July, with the merchants certifying that they would not engage in opium smuggling. The death penalty remained, but Read thought that could be overcome if orders were given to American warships on the scene to retaliate for any such executions—the threat of reprisal alone would be enough to deter the Chinese authorities. He did not condone the opium trade; rather he feared that innocent foreigners would be victims of summary trial and punishment.

Representatives of the American commercial houses had already sent a memorial to the Congress explaining their situation, piously expressing their strong opposition to a renewal of the drug traffic, and asking that their problems be resolved by treaty. They thought a treaty could be obtained easily without resort to force if a fleet of British, French, and American warships were sent to Chinese waters. Should the U.S. government prefer not to become involved in Oriental affairs to that extent, the memorialists submitted the necessity of appointing an agent or commissioner to oversee American interests in China and of maintaining constantly a naval force to protect a commerce of greater importance than that with Latin America.

Meanwhile, the merchants tried to keep the East India Squadron in their vicinity, at least until Anglo-Chinese difficulties had been worked out. Read had written earlier that, if the expected hostilities occurred, it would be well to have a "respectable" number of men-of-war on hand to assure that the United States shared in any commercial benefits accruing to Britain as a result of the conflict, and he was aware that British blockaders had shown slight respect for neutral rights on occasion. But three more of the *Columbia*'s men had died, while another 120 were ill. The plight of the *John Adams* was almost as bad, and the surgeons believed that the ravages of dysentery would cease only when the vessels were well away from Chinese waters. In addition, the commodore had received orders to investigate a disturbance in the Society Islands. Thus, he turned a deaf ear to the entreaties of the merchants and made preparations to sail as soon as a supply of bread could be obtained.

The frigate and sloop of war weighed anchor, homeward-bound on 6 August. Old China hands had assured Read that typhoons were unknown in years as rainy as 1839; therefore, the *Columbia*'s oldest sails had been bent as she prepared for sea. But the old hands were wrong. A "violent tempest" struck just after nightfall, when the squadron was only about thirty miles offshore, blowing the frigate's threadbare sails out of the boltropes before they could be furled and driving her toward the coast at an alarming rate. Although the more weatherly *John Adams* fared better, both vessels welcomed the change of wind direction and force which enabled them to gain an offing after thirty-six hours of buffeting. No more storms were encountered, but the vessels spent ten weary weeks tacking against easterly winds before reaching Honolulu. The meager supply of fresh provisions obtained at Macao was consumed well before that, so scurvy combined with dysentery to claim thirty more men from the two ships' companies in the course of the passage.

From Honolulu, the squadron sailed to Tahiti and thence to Callao, where Read heard that the British had proclaimed a blockade of Canton. Refusing to believe that this blockade would endanger American interests, he took his vessels around Cape Horn and arrived in Boston in June 1840.

One might expect that the news of the Anglo-Chinese conflict popularly known as the Opium War and of the British blockade of Canton would have led the U.S. Navy Department to dispatch additional force to the Far East immediately, especially since the China merchants, heretofore aloof, had urged the necessity of such support. Yet those merchants who had watched the *Columbia* and the *John Adams* stand out of Macao

Roads in August 1839, would wait almost three years before men-of-war flying their country's flag again appeared off the Portuguese city.

This interval can be explained in part by changes in U.S. diplomatic, economic, and political situations. The omens that seemed to augur well for naval expansion during President Jackson's second term had proven false—amicable settlement of the controversy with France removed the principal reason for enlarging the Navy, and the Panic of 1837 converted the Treasury surplus into a deficit within a short time, effectively curtailing naval appropriations. Moreover, President Martin Van Buren was a placid individual once quoted to the effect that the United States needed no navy, while his secretary of the navy, James K. Paulding, enjoyed his greatest reputation in literary circles.

But it was not intended to leave the Far East without a squadron for so lengthy a period. The frigate *Constellation*, at forty-three the oldest ship in the U.S. Navy, and the sloop of war *Boston* were fitting out in the autumn of 1840, the former at the Boston Navy Yard. Commodore John Downes, the commandant of the navy yard, had orders to sail in the *Constellation* as commander in chief of the East India Squadron. Downes was in his fifty-fifth year and his enthusiasm at the prospect of a lengthy cruise in the Far East dwindled, especially after the *Columbia*'s losses to dysentery and other ills became known. He decided to remain at the Boston yard, so Paulding chose a slightly younger man, Captain Lawrence Kearny, then commanding the *Potomac*, the flagship of the Brazil Squadron.

Soon after Kearny hoisted his broad pennant in the *Constellation* at Rio de Janeiro in February 1841, he wrote to complain about his flagship's condition and enclosed a formidable list of defects. George E. Badger, the new secretary of the navy, referred the complaint to Commodore Downes, who responded that the frigate had been prepared for sea under the assumption that he would sail in her ". . . & in my opinion, I never saw a ship better fitted from any of our dockyards, than was the Constellation."[5] Badger had to accept this reply because the *Constellation* was well on her way to the station, but Kearny's experience with her cast doubt upon the validity of Downes's statement.

The flagship lay at Rio de Janeiro for a month while her company made good some of her defects, and then began a leisurely passage which ultimately brought her and the *Boston* to Macao on 22 March 1842, more than a year after she had departed the Brazilian city. The frequent need for repairs explains the delay only in part; Kearny seems to have felt no need for haste despite his orders to the contrary.

Those orders also emphasized that China was the most important part of his station and made the protection of Americans and their property his first responsibility, although the Chinese were to be told that the squadron had been sent to prevent opium smuggling by American citizens or others under the U.S. flag. If Kearny's protestation of friendship for the Chinese led them to seek his support against a legal British blockade, he would reply that he could do so only on direct orders from his government. In fact, international law required the recognition of legal blockades by all neutral shipping; however, if Kearny had been disposed to ignore the blockade, he had to face the reality that his force consisted only of an elderly frigate and a sloop of war, while the British had twenty-three warships in Chinese waters.

At any rate, there was no blockade of Canton when the *Constellation* and the *Boston* stood into Macao Roads, for hostilities in that vicinity had been ended almost a year earlier. Superior weaponry, tactics, and discipline had enabled small forces of Britons to disperse many times their number of Chinese and to destroy the fortifications; trade was then resumed. Even as British units were conducting offensive operations against the Chinese Empire farther northward, merchant vessels under British colors were allowed to trade at Canton without interference or discrimination on the part of Chinese authorities.

Commodore Kearny soon had occasion to implement that portion of his orders relating to the smuggling of opium. A shipping report in the Hong Kong *Gazette* listed an American vessel laden with opium, whereupon Kearny wrote the U.S. consul at Canton desiring him to publicize and make known to Chinese authorities the fact that Americans and their ships seized while engaged in the opium trade could expect no assistance from the East India Squadron because the U.S. government did not approve of the narcotic smuggling. There Kearny stopped—non-interference with the traffic obviously was not the same as its suppression, but more than a year elapsed before he took any further action.

Soon after the squadron came to anchor in Macao Roads, the American vice-consul transmitted a request from several merchants that redress be sought for incidents which had occurred almost a year before. The principal complaint concerned Chinese soldiers firing on a boat belonging to the merchantman *Morrison* while it was en route from the factories to Whampoa. One American had been killed and his fellows were wounded and captured. At least one other case of an imprisoned boat crew was cited—all had been released within a short time, but Chinese officials had ignored all damage claims. The *Canton Register* did what it could to force the commodore's hand by announcing that the *Constellation* and the *Boston* would, if necessary, "vindicate the honor of the U.S. flag by exacting from the Chinese a most heavy retribution for their most treacherous violation of international law."[6] But Kearny would adopt a belligerent stance only as a last resort, nor was he interested in obtaining anything more than a fair settlement.

U.S. warships arriving off Macao or Lintin Island had been accustomed to receive through the consul—and to ignore—orders from Chinese officials to depart forthwith. No such orders were forthcoming for the *Constellation* and the *Boston*, leading Kearny to hope that this might indicate a changed attitude on the part of the authorities—perhaps he would be able to communicate with them directly rather than through the agency of the merchants as his predecessors had had to do. And, since there was no protest against his squadron's presence in the usual anchorage, might it not sail up to Whampoa without arousing Chinese displeasure? The commodore decided to seek an answer to that question by sailing up the Canton River. To indicate that he had no intention of trying to force a passage, he sent the *Boston* to Manila while the frigate alone tested the Chinese disposition.

Receiving Dr. Bridgman on board to serve as interpreter, the flagship weighed anchor on 11 April and stood up the estuary, into the Boca Tigris, past the Second Bar, and on to the First Bar. There she paused while Kearny wrote the consul in Canton, asking him to inform Chinese authorities that the *Constellation* sought an anchorage convenient for replenishing her provisions and communicating with Chinese officials. When no prohibition of further movement was received, the frigate sailed up to the merchant ship anchorage at Whampoa, where she stayed for seven weeks. The *Boston* rejoined the flag early in May, and again the Chinese made no protest.

Understandably elated at his success in gaining an anchorage where foreign warships had never before been permitted, Kearny next tried to open direct communication with Chinese officialdom. His efforts were rebuffed at first, but when he argued that letters delivered by a commissioned officer could be received properly only by another of equivalent rank, the protocol-conscious Orientals had to agree. Thereafter, direct communication became customary.

Chinese amiability extended to the incidents of which the American merchants had complained to Kearny. Explaining that the soldiers involved had thought the American small craft were British boats, the viceroy at Canton asked the commodore to decide the amount of damages to be paid, although payment would have to be made by the Hong merchants who alone were allowed to trade with foreigners. Kearny accepted this duty and did not require that the guilty individuals be punished.

Settlement of the claims was endangered when a Chinese fort fired on one of the *Constellation*'s boats. Kearny's request for an explanation

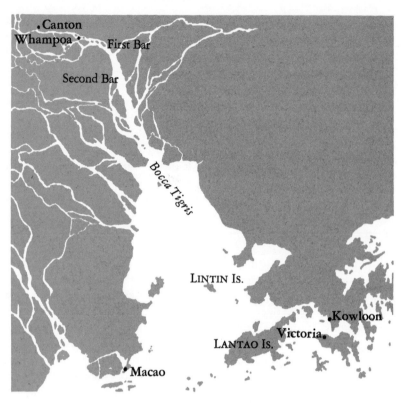

MAP 2–1. The Canton River Estuary

brought the response that the boat was taking soundings in the vicinity of a barrier and that the garrison had tried to warn it off. When the warnings were ignored, the boat had been fired on in the belief that it had no right to show the American flag. The officer in charge of the boat admitted that its approach to the barrier might have been thought provocative; whereupon Kearny reprimanded him and declared the incident closed.

Having no further reason to stay at Whampoa, the squadron dropped down to Macao in June. When sickness appeared in both ships, they ran over to the harbor between the island of Hong Kong and the mainland, some forty miles to the eastward of Macao. This had become the anchorage for merchant shipping when the Canton trade was halted in 1839, and Britons had established a permanent settlement there. Apparently the change of locale was effective, for neither vessel reported any fatalities and both crews were restored to health in a short time.

Commodore Kearny was dubious about the British military situation vis-à-vis China. Sickness had made great inroads into the effectiveness of the 12,000 Britons available for service, and he thought the strategy of dispersing these troops among widely separated points made it unlikely that a significant victory could be won at any one. Moreover, the Anglo-Chinese conflict was proving to be immensely costly; Kearny heard that the East India Company had had to borrow money at 10 percent and was anxious that the war should come to an end.

Come to an end it did. Little more than two weeks after Kearny had expressed his doubts, Sir Henry Pottinger's army moved on Nanking, whereupon the Chinese recognized the futility of further fighting and agreed to negotiations. But the peace treaty was more nearly dictated than negotiated, for the British received virtually everything they wished. Hong Kong was ceded to Britain outright, and five so-called treaty ports—Canton, Amoy, Foochow, Ningpo, and Shanghai—were opened to British trade. A consulate could be established at each, and merchants would be allowed to reside permanently in these ports with their families. Trade could be carried on with any Chinese merchants under a fixed tariff on imported goods. The Chinese had to pay a sum that included the value of the destroyed opium as well as the expenses of the British military expeditions, but the Treaty of Nanking made no reference to the status of the opium trade.

Commodore Kearny obtained three copies of the treaty in late September. Two he sent to the United States by separate messengers taking the overland route to Western Europe; the *Boston* took the third across the Pacific to Mazatlán, Mexico—from there it would be forwarded to Washington.

Meanwhile, the commodore himself undertook to gain rights for American commercial interests that were similar to those won by the British. A brief letter to the viceroy at Canton called the viceroy's attention to Kearny's desire while emphasizing that the naval officer did not wish to force the issue. Nor was it necessary to do so; the viceroy replied promptly that merchants of all nations had received equal treatment at his hands in the past and he had no intention of altering this policy. As soon as the details of a commercial treaty with Britain had been worked out, he would make recommendations to Peking with regard to trade regulations in general and "decidedly it shall not be permitted that the American merchants shall come to have merely a dry stick."[7]

Kearny believed that he could not require any additional assurance. Chinese treatment of Americans as citizens of a most-favored nation could be guaranteed only by treaty, and that he was not authorized to negotiate. He had already urged the dispatch of a commercial agent not connected with any of the commercial houses and supported by an impressive force of warships; until these warships could arrive, the American merchants would have to trade on whatever terms the Chinese saw fit to give them.

Kearny intended to sail on 1 November to visit Australia, New Zealand, and various South Pacific islands in order to show the flag and give any assistance which American whaling ships frequenting those waters might need. Although this "whale fishery protection" duty had been designated an important part of his squadron's mission, second only to that of looking after U.S. interests in China during the Opium War, it was never carried out. The announcement of the *Constellation*'s intended departure brought a strong protest from Consul Snow at Canton, who insisted that the frigate remain in Chinese waters at least until mid-February. "You . . . know the prompt and immediate action by this Govt on communications from the Commander of an American Squadron."[8] The commodore concluded that Snow was correct; since he had no intelligence of conditions requiring his presence elsewhere, he would stay.

Kearny's decision probably did not elicit an enthusiastic response from the *Constellation*'s company, one of whom had just written that "the extremely dull time we have had since we arrived in China has made everyone low spirited."[9] The frigate would spend a week or so at Macao, then run up to the Boca Tigris for a time, thence to Hong Kong; but the movement from one anchorage to another did little to relieve the boredom. Late in November, the flagship went to Manila for a month, which must have been a welcome interlude.

Back at Macao, the commodore received news of a mob attack on the Canton factories and a request from Augustine Heard and Company for assistance in obtaining reparation for damages suffered in the riot. After conferring with Vice-Consul James P. Sturgis at Macao, Kearny took the *Constellation* up to Whampoa, whence he went on to Canton.

During the five weeks he spent there, the commodore got the viceroy's assurance that the damages would be made good, and the latter added that the death of a Chinese official had delayed the formulation of trade regulations. The viceroy suggested that when these regulations had been drawn up, perhaps Kearny would meet with imperial commissioners to decide on the specific rules to govern Sino-American trade. To this, the naval officer could reply only that his government would require terms identical to those given other countries and that, although he was not empowered to negotiate a treaty, the United States doubtless would send an envoy for that purpose should the Chinese be willing to receive him. But the Chinese sought no treaties; the viceroy assured Kearny that they were unnecessary and foreign to Chinese tradition.

By the time the *Constellation* dropped down the Canton River again, mid-February was long past, but she continued her periodic shuttling between Macao, Hong Kong, and the Boca Tigris until late April. Reports that vessels flying the American flag were involved in the revived opium trade led the commodore to seek information on this subject from Sturgis and others. He learned that several schooners, supposedly American, were actually serving British interests, and this news appeared to infuriate him. He prepared a strongly worded statement reiterating his squadron's orders to prevent opium smuggling under American colors and declaring himself ready to enforce those orders.

Nonetheless, Kearny seemingly had no intention of acting. After sending this statement to Sturgis, he sailed for Manila. There he wrote the secretary of the navy that his recent warning would suffice to prevent illegal use of the flag; thus he need not touch at the area where the incidents were reported.

The *Constellation* embarked a five months' supply of provisions from those deposited there for the squadron's use. Unfortunately, cholera was making one of its periodic visitations to Manila, and a few of the frigate's men contracted the malady. The *Constellation* departed in haste, but not before two men had died; two more men succumbed soon afterward.

Her homeward passage was of short duration. The water obtained at Manila proved to be impure, so a fresh supply had to be sought. Macao during the "sickly season" might be fatal to some of those on the binnacle list; therefore, the flagship sailed up to Amoy, southernmost of the treaty ports save Canton.

At Amoy the opportunity to deal a blow to the opium traffic presented itself. The schooner *Ariel*, one of those named by Sturgis as improperly registered, had just landed a cargo of opium. Kearny sent a boarding party to take possession of the vessel, forced her master to discharge the money and camphor he had received in payment for the drug, and ordered him to take her to Macao for further action by Sturgis, explaining that she was so heavily sparred as to be unseaworthy—hence she could not be sent to the United States for trial. It should be noted that the *Ariel* was seized, not because she was a smuggler—no U.S. law forbade smuggling opium into China—but because she had no right to the American flag she was accustomed to fly. The commodore promised the same treatment to any of the schooner's fellows he might encounter—an idle threat because the *Constellation* got underway for Honolulu on 22 May 1843, just three days after ordering the *Ariel* to Macao.

Lawrence Kearny has generally been recognized as an able "sailor diplomat" whose ability as a diplomat was largely responsible for the extension of the commercial advantages obtained in China by the British to other nations. In addition, he has been cited for making the first real effort to suppress opium smuggling. However, one doubts that the commodore himself would have claimed much credit for either. He practiced "jackal diplomacy" to the extent that he requested for his nation a share of the spoils won by the British lion in combat; had Britain or China opposed his request, he was powerless to do more. Kearny had the intelligence to grasp opportunities—he did not create them. His steps to curb opium smuggling were innocuous in the extreme and designed mainly to mislead Chinese officials; but this conduct was in accordance with his orders.

This is not to say that Commodore Kearny deserves no credit. Rather he should be recognized for his feat in keeping his men unusually healthy and reasonably contented during a lengthy cruise on an unhealthy and "very disagreeable station." The commodore attributed their good health mainly "to the plentiful supply of good wholesome water and provisions" and the men themselves expressed their appreciation of Kearny's "mild mode of discipline" which had made the frigate "the happiest ship that ever left the United States."[10]

CHAPTER THREE

A Treaty with China and Visits to Japan

Secretary of the Navy Abel P. Upshur's *Annual Report* for 1842 was
another milestone on the road toward a permanent East India Squadron.
His predecessors had shied away from the title "East India Squadron,"
referring to it instead as "the force employed in the Indian and China
seas" or similarly implying that it was quite different from the longer-
established squadrons. Upshur's report, however, left little doubt that the
Navy Department recognized the East India Squadron as a part of its
permanent peacetime operational organization.

Had there been any strong demurs to this development, news of the
Treaty of Nanking undoubtedly would have overcome them. President
John Tyler and Secretary of State Daniel Webster recommended that a
diplomatic mission be sent to negotiate a commercial treaty with China,
and the Congress agreed. To support this mission and to take the place of
Commodore Lawrence Kearny's squadron in the Far East, the Navy
Department ordered that the frigate *Brandywine* and the sloop of war *St.
Louis* be fitted out at Norfolk.

Commodore Foxhall A. Parker took the *Brandywine* and the *St. Louis*
to sea on 23 May 1843, two days after the *Constellation* had sailed from
Amoy, leaving the Far East devoid of American naval force once more.
His orders required the *Brandywine* to embark former Massachusetts
Congressman Caleb Cushing, who had been appointed to negotiate the
treaty with China, at Bombay and transport his mission to Macao. The
squadron paused at Rio de Janeiro for replenishment and then stood on

toward the Cape of Good Hope. When the vessels were eleven days out, a leak in the *St. Louis*'s bow forced her to turn back. The *Brandywine* continued on alone and reached Bombay after an eighty-day passage, arriving three weeks before Cushing, who had been delayed by the irregularity of the East India mail steamer service from Suez.

Parker noted that American vessels were loading opium quite openly in Bombay. His orders contained the same instructions regarding the narcotic trade that had appeared in Kearny's, and, like Kearny, he knew of no law that would permit him to interfere with Americans engaged in smuggling goods into a foreign country. He could only ask for further instructions; until these were received, "the only course that appears proper for me to pursue is, not to interfere in their favor should they be taken by the Chinese Authorities."[1]

The commodore was disappointed at not receiving any letters from the Navy Department by Cushing (they had been lost in the accidental burning of the paddle frigate *Missouri* at Gibraltar), but the envoy brought the welcome news that the new brig *Perry* had been ordered to join Parker's flag. She would reconnoiter ahead of the larger ships in the event that they would have to enter the poorly charted Yellow Sea; in addition, she would perform other duties for which a small, handy vessel was especially suited.

The *Brandywine* landed Cushing and the members of his mission at Macao late in February 1844 and then ran over to Manila to check on the condition of the squadron's provisions stored at that port. Parker returned to Macao early in April and a week later took his flagship up the Canton River to Blenheim Reach, an anchorage about four miles below Whampoa. From there, he announced his arrival to the Canton authorities, offering to exchange salutes and visits. The Chinese declined on the ground that such formalities were contrary to custom; indeed, the commodore was made to understand that the *Brandywine* ought not to have come beyond the Boca Tigris.

The long-awaited *St. Louis* finally stood into Hong Kong late in May, and the *Perry* made her appearance soon afterward. The commanding officers of both had to return to the United States because of illness, leaving their executive officers to bring the ships to China.

The *Brandywine* was in Macao Roads on 18 June, when the commodore received an appeal for assistance—an American had shot a member of a Chinese mob threatening the factories, and further trouble was anticipated. The *St. Louis* sailed up to Whampoa, whence she sent sixty sailors and marines in small boats to Canton. The Chinese held the area in front of the American factories but had not attacked the buildings when the landing force appeared. Although the situation remained tense for some days, the mob finally dispersed without untoward incident, and Commodore Parker had no doubt that the "St. Louis'" timely arrival had saved lives and property.

Meanwhile, Caleb Cushing had opened communication with Canton to inform the viceroy of his presence at Macao and of his intention to go to Peking to present a letter from President Tyler to the emperor. This began a lengthy correspondence in which the services of the Reverend Dr. Elijah C. Bridgman, a missionary at Canton, were invaluable because of his knowledge of Chinese forms as well as his ability as an interpreter. Ultimately, Cushing realized that an attempt to go to Peking, as his instructions required, would probably defeat his purpose; so he agreed to meet with the Chinese commissioner at Macao. The negotiations proceeded speedily, and the treaty was signed at Wanghia, on the outskirts of Macao, on 3 July. Dr. Bridgman, who had been pessimistic about the prospects, praised the agreement: "If ratified—as it surely must be—this Treaty will secure to the United States no inconsiderable advantages— indeed all that could be asked, under existing circumstances."[2]

Briefly, the Treaty of Wanghia gained for citizens of the United States the same rights in the treaty ports as Britons had received by the Treaty of Nanking. In addition, the principle of extraterritoriality in civil and criminal cases was extended to them, and the United States received most-favored-nation status. Article XXXII referred directly to American naval vessels, specifying that their commanding officers would meet with local officials in their Chinese ports of call on terms of friendship and equality. "And the said ships of war shall enjoy all suitable facilities on the part of the Chinese Government in the purchase of provisions, procuring water, and making repairs if occasion require."[3] Whether Parker had any part in arranging this is not clear. He and some of his officers were frequently in attendance on Cushing during the negotiations, so one may assume that the article had received his approval.

Caleb Cushing stayed several weeks longer to arrange better protection for the American settlement outside Canton and to resolve the problems arising from the shooting incident of mid-June. Then he asked that the Perry be assigned to transport him to Mexico, whence he would return to the United States. Parker agreed readily—the expedition to the Yellow Sea had been made unnecessary when Cushing decided to remain at Macao. He also ordered Captain Isaac McKeever, who had just arrived from the United States, to visit treaty ports to the northward in the St. Louis, while the Brandywine remained at anchor in the Boca Tigris.

Late in July, British Rear Admiral Sir Thomas Cochrane arrived at Hong Kong and introduced himself by letter to Commodore Parker, offering all facilities at his command to assist the Americans in any way "and uniting with you in every measure calculated to strengthen those bonds of union which so happily exist between our respective countries."[4] Parker expressed his thanks and friendship for Britain in more restrained terms, meanwhile making preparations to have his squadron's provisions that were stored at Hong Kong removed to Macao.

Foxhall Parker had definite ideas on logistic support for the East India Squadron. He would have preferred that a storeship be moored more or less permanently in one of the Chinese bays or harbors; she could receive supplies and provisions sent from the United States and distribute them to the warships at need. In the absence of such a vessel, he had arranged with the Portuguese authorities to land stores at Macao without paying any duty on them. For this purpose of landing provisions, Macao was, in his opinion, superior to Hong Kong in most respects. Macao was drier and healthier than Hong Kong during the southwest monsoon; better water was available at Macao; in addition, stores at Hong Kong would be lost at once in the event of an Anglo-American war, as would the East India Squadron were it caught in that confined harbor. With the American-British dispute over the future of the Oregon Country yet undecided, it was well to avoid reliance on a British possession.

The *St. Louis* returned in mid-October, and Captain McKeever reported that gales and adverse currents had slowed her passage northward. Keeping the island-studded Chinese coast close aboard, she had required twenty-seven days to run from Macao to the Chusan Archipelago. Local fishermen might have advised her officers and facilitated her progress, but none of the myriad fishing boats could be enticed to approach the strange warship. The rugged and scenic islands of the Chusan group possessed hazards for the mariner in the form of swift, irregular tidal currents surging through narrow passages and mud-laden waters that effectively concealed submerged rock pinnacles. Approaching her anchorage, the *St. Louis* had made the acquaintance of one of those tidal whirlpools known in pidgin English as "chow chow water"; completely unmanageable for a time, she narrowly escaped grounding.

After this experience, McKeever decided not to take his ship to Ningpo, the treaty port on the mainland opposite the Chusan Archipelago. Instead, he hired a boat and took a party of officers to the ancient city some twelve miles up the Yung River. Ningpo had neither American residents nor commerce, but McKeever was sure that it would become a market for the coarse cotton cloth already finding favor among Chinese farther to the southward. As the first U.S. naval officers to visit the city, McKeever and his party were objects of much curiosity, "annoying, but not uncivil."[5] Returning to the ship two days later, McKeever concluded that she should return directly to Macao—her men were already afflicted with diarrhea and Amoy was said to be unhealthy.

Commodore Parker gave the *St. Louis* two weeks to recover and then directed her to prepare for the cruise that the *Constellation* was to have made to Australia and New Zealand "to protect our lawful commerce, and to assist our whalers should they require it."[6]

In accordance with his orders, the commodore set 1 December 1844 as the date on which the *Brandywine* was to sail for Honolulu. Late in November, representatives of fifteen American commercial houses presented a silver service to him in appreciation for the assistance and protection rendered them without ignoring the rights of "the peculiar people amongst whom we are residing."[7]

Then the *Brandywine* weighed anchor to begin the long voyage home by way of Honolulu, Tahiti, and Valparaiso, Chile. The *Perry* joined her at Tahiti; and off Valparaiso, the *St. Louis* made her number to the flag.

The *St. Louis* had had an interesting cruise. After touching at Manila and Batavia, she spent a stormy six weeks reaching Australia. When celestial observations indicated that Hobart, Tasmania, was near at hand, McKeever decided to put in there. This first American man-of-war to visit the penal colony then known as Van Diemen's Land was cordially received by the authorities and after a few days she went on to Sydney. There she learned that American whalers had recently been exempted from port charges, an exemption soon to be extended to Hobart. Thus, American interests in that quarter needed no assistance from the Navy.

The situation in New Zealand was not as tranquil. When the *St. Louis* stood into the Bay of Islands on 3 March 1845, McKeever found the Maori threatening Kororareka, the settlement composed of survivors of shipwrecks, deserters, beachcombers, and other white men who had made its name synonymous with lawlessness before the British government had extended its control over New Zealand some five years earlier. A number of more respectable inhabitants had arrived since that time. The British sloop of war *Hazard* was lying off the town, and the *St. Louis* chose an anchorage where her guns could cover the only American property, a trading establishment some distance away. Communicating with the British authorities and the principal Maori chief, McKeever announced his intention to pursue an impartial course, at the same time extracting from the Maori a promise to spare the American commercial buildings, the missionary establishment, and all women and children.

The expected attack came at dawn on 11 March. Skillfully pretending that the town itself was the object of their assault, the Maori captured a blockhouse nearby. Following this misfortune, a powder magazine in the town was exploded accidentally with considerable loss to its people. The survivors then abandoned Kororareka and were taken off to vessels in the harbor, with the *St. Louis*'s boats ferrying women, children, and wounded men. By the day's end, the town had been sacked and destroyed, but neither missionary buildings nor the American trading establishment had sustained any damage. In response to a request for medical assistance, McKeever sent his vessel's doctors to the *Hazard*; the next morning he received a similar request from the Maori ashore and responded to it as promptly.

The *St. Louis* then embarked 150 of the now homeless inhabitants of Kororareka while the remainder boarded the *Hazard* and a whaler. The three vessels sailed in company to Auckland, seat of the British government of New Zealand, and, after landing his passengers, McKeever took his ship back to the Bay of Islands to supervise the loading of the contents of the American store into whaleships chartered to return the goods to the United States. Her Majesty's frigate *North Star* arrived at the end of March, whereupon the *St. Louis* made sail for Valparaiso.

The ships designated to relieve Commodore Parker's squadron departed the United States in June 1845 and made Macao late in December, more than a year after the *Brandywine* had left the station. However, the USS *Constitution* spent the summer of 1845 in Chinese waters while on a special service cruise.

The reasons for dispatching the celebrated frigate on this cruise are not apparent. David Henshaw of Massachusetts was acting as secretary of the navy at the beginning of her cruise; perhaps he simply wished to gratify the desire of an old Cape Codder for one last tour of sea duty. At any rate, Captain John Percival's sailing orders required him to look after American commercial interests on the east coast of Africa and in the East Indies, acquiring the knowledge necessary to increase trade with those regions. Borneo was to receive especial attention because of its supposed coal deposits; indeed, Percival was authorized to purchase a coal mine for the United States "at a reasonable compensation."[8]

"Old Ironsides" sailed on her only voyage of circumnavigation in May 1844, touching at a number of ports, including Rio de Janeiro, Majunga Bay, Mozambique, Zanzibar, Quallah Battoo, and Singapore, en route to Borneo. Notwithstanding the importance assigned to this island by her orders, the *Constitution*'s men landed at only two points on its west coast and then she spent two weeks groping her way out of its treacherous waters, keeping her small boats sounding ahead most of the time and kedging frequently as the wind died or shifted foul. The frigate touched bottom on one occasion; on another she suddenly found herself almost surrounded by coral reefs and had to be kedged out by the same channel that had led her into that dangerous predicament.

The *Constitution* arrived in Tourane Bay, Cochin-China, in May 1845. When local officials came on board, one of them stealthily slipped Captain Percival an appeal from a Roman Catholic bishop, Dominique Lefebre, who was among a number of Europeans imprisoned in Cochin-China. Monseigneur Lefebre addressed the senior French naval officer, asking that he demand their release and assurances that henceforth no molestation would be visited on missionaries in the kingdom. A postscript, "I am condemned to death without delay. Hasten or all is finished,"[9] seemed to emphasize the necessity for quick action.

Percival led a landing force ashore and returned with five mandarins who were detained as hostages for Lefebre's safety. Three armed junks believed to be royal property were seized the next day; then the captain dispatched an ultimatum to Hué threatening to fire on Tourane if the bishop was not released within four days. The *Constitution* stood inshore and anchored with a spring on her cable with which to bring her broadside to bear on the town, but the only shots fired were aimed over the detained junks which tried to escape in a squall. Three days after the ultimatum had expired, Percival suddenly released his hostages and sailed soon thereafter, ostensibly because his provisions were exhausted.

At Macao, he notified the French minister of the situation, and in due course that envoy sent his thanks together with the information that Monseigneur Lefebre had been delivered to a French corvette. Forwarding this letter to the Navy Department, the captain stated that his efforts had probably saved the bishop's life and that he would have won the latter's release could the *Constitution* have remained in Tourane Bay a little longer. The secretary's endorsement on this letter reads in part: "Answer at once. The Department wholly disapproves the conduct of Captain Percival as not warranted either by the demands of the Bishop or the Law of Nations."[10]

The *Constitution* spent three months at Macao, Blenheim Reach, and the Boca Tigris, and on 1 September made sail for Manila whence she began her homeward passage. Reporting her return to the United States in the autumn of 1846, Secretary of the Navy John Y. Mason stated that Captain Percival had carried out his orders satisfactorily. This was generous, for the results of the cruise actually seem to have been minimal. The frigate had not even touched at a number of the points named in her sailing orders, and such incidents as her captain's intervention on behalf of Monseigneur Lefebre cannot have enhanced the prospects for American trade.

Meanwhile, Commodore James Biddle had acknowledged the receipt of orders to command the East India Squadron. He hoisted his broad pennant in the USS *Columbus*, the largest American man-of-war yet sent to the station—indeed, she was the only one of the Navy's ships of the line to serve in the Far East. Although one of the more satisfactory ships of that type built for the U.S. Navy, she had made only three cruises since first commissioning in 1819 because it cost so much to keep a ship of the line manned. The other unit of the squadron, the veteran sloop of war *Vincennes*, was seven years her junior and one of the hardest-worked vessels in the service, as familiar with Oriental waters as any.

Commodore Biddle's sailing orders required him to embark Alexander H. Everett, American commissioner to China, who was to exchange ratifications of the Treaty of Wanghia. Because of the diplomatic mission, Everett's needs were to dictate the squadron's movements.

The two vessels took departure from Sandy Hook early in June 1845. In view of the time limit for the exchange of ratifications, Biddle considered sailing directly to Sunda Strait; however, the fleet surgeon counseled against it, since men subsisting on salt provisions and a small allowance of fresh water were likely to contract dysentery. Therefore, the squadron put in at Rio de Janeiro, where Commissioner Everett decided that the state of his health required that he return to the United States. He went ashore after delegating his diplomatic powers and duties to Commodore Biddle, and the warships sailed in mid-August. The flagship reached Macao on Christmas Eve, while the *Vincennes*, having parted from the *Columbus* after leaving Batavia, stood in two weeks later. Unlike the battleship's company, which had been remarkably healthy, the *Vincennes*'s men had contracted dysentery at Batavia and six died before she anchored in Macao Roads.

The *Columbus*'s arrival was timely, for 3 January 1846 was the last date on which treaty ratifications could be exchanged. Leaving the ship at an anchorage off the Boca Tigris, the commodore, accompanied by a number of officers and the missionaries Elijah C. Bridgman and Peter Parker, quickly made his way to Canton. The ceremony took place on 31 December without any difficulty; thereafter, Biddle established the first U.S. legation in China, not in Canton but in the foreign settlement outside the city walls.

Treaty terms required that foreigners be permitted to enter Canton, and the Chinese authorities proclaimed that the city gates would be opened on 14 January 1846. At once the temper of the native population rose dangerously—placards were posted denouncing the officials and promising death to foreigners. Recognizing that the authorities were incapable of restraining the Chinese people should they decide to attack the foreign factories, Biddle ordered the *Vincennes* to transfer her sick to the *Colum-*

FIGURE 3–1. *Left to right:* Lawrence Kearny, James Biddle, and Matthew Calbraith Perry.

bus, receive forty men from the flagship's marine contingent, and come up to Whampoa, from which a landing force could reach the factories within a few hours. No officers were permitted to visit the shore without the commodore's express permission; Biddle feared lest some indiscreet act should ignite an obviously inflammable situation. In the event of a general outbreak against foreigners, Biddle intended to protect all Americans "without giving just cause of offence to the Chinese, or wounding unnecessarily their national pride."[11]

With the Chinese authorities having abandoned temporarily their plans to open Canton, the threat of violence soon passed, and the commodore decided that the *Columbus* should be displayed at Manila as an example of American prowess. Not feeling free to leave the legation, he transferred his flag to the *Vincennes* before the battleship sailed. As so often, a visit to Manila was filled with peril. Not long after the *Columbus* came to her anchors in Manila Bay, Asiatic cholera made its appearance in her formerly healthy company; although the *Columbus*'s stay was cut short, twelve men died before the epidemic was checked. Nonetheless, periodic visits to Manila could not be avoided; the number of American merchantmen trading there had doubled since 1842, with fifty being reported in 1845. Some sought cargoes of rice for delivery to China, and others loaded sugar, coffee, hemp, indigo, hides, and the like for the United States.

By mid-April, Biddle was reasonably certain that affairs at Canton no longer required his presence. He transferred his diplomatic title and duties to Dr. Peter Parker, after which the *Vincennes* beat down the Canton River to join the *Columbus* in Macao Roads.

When the southwest monsoon set in, the squadron sailed northward to visit the treaty ports. Biddle found no American commercial activity at Amoy, and the ships did not stop off the mouth of the River Min, on which Foochow is located, because there was no safe mooring offshore at that season for a ship of the *Columbus*'s size. She was left at an anchorage in the Chusan Islands while the commodore visited Shanghai and Ningpo in the sloop of war. Shanghai had already attracted a good deal of American trade, but Ningpo was almost devoid of foreign commerce.

Having exchanged treaty ratifications, opened a legation, and called at the treaty ports, James Biddle had fulfilled the duties entrusted to his squadron so far as they pertained to China. But his sailing orders also required him "to ascertain if the ports of Japan are accessible."[12] On 7 July 1846, the East India Squadron sailed from its anchorage in the Chusan Islands to make the U.S. Navy's first attempt to open communications with the Japanese government.

Biddle's knowledge of the situation in Japan was hardly extensive. For more than two centuries, the Netherlands alone had been allowed contact with the island empire and that contact had been limited by restrictions that made pre-1842 China seem liberal by comparison. Nagasaki was the Japanese equivalent of Canton—the Dutch factory was located on Deshima, an artificial island off the city itself, and the few Dutchmen attached to it were virtual prisoners therein. Although their trade with Japan was limited to one or two ships each year, the Dutch guarded their monopoly jealously.

Other nations had made sporadic attempts to open trade to no avail. In 1837, the unarmed American *Morrison*, trying to return a number of shipwrecked Japanese to Edo, the political and administrative capital of Japan, was fired on and driven away. Eight years later the whaleship *Manhattan* succeeded in landing Japanese mariners whom she had rescued, but her master was made to understand that henceforth shipwrecked Japanese must be repatriated only by Dutch vessels trading to Nagasaki.

Commodore Biddle knew that Nagasaki was the only Japanese port in which foreign ships were permitted; he was also aware that officials there would have to send his proposals to Edo and that months might elapse before a reply was received. Moreover, he suspected that the Dutch at Deshima would do their utmost to thwart his mission if he took his ships to Nagasaki; therefore, Biddle took his squadron to Edo Bay.

As the two vessels stood into the bay on 20 July, the *Columbus* was boarded by a Japanese officer accompanied by a Dutch interpreter, through whom he queried Biddle's motives. The commodore responded that he wished to know whether Japan's ports had been opened to foreign shipping; if so, he was desirous of negotiating a commercial treaty. Higher authority would have to decide, he was told; meanwhile, supplies and water would be furnished the ships' companies, but no one was permitted to go ashore.

When the men-of-war anchored off Uraga, a village just inside the channel leading to Edo Bay and some thirty miles from the capital itself, they were surrounded by guard boats whose men were soon clambering on board the flagship in considerable numbers. No attempt was made to restrain them, for Biddle wished to exhibit the friendly disposition of his squadron as well as its force.

An officer of higher rank came on board the next day with information that the commodore's letter had been sent to the emperor, and, since the emperor was not at Edo, no reply could be expected in less than five days. The Japanese officer also demanded that the ships' guns and small arms be landed in accordance with Japanese law. Biddle brushed this requirement aside as applicable only to merchant vessels and asked why the guard boats continued to encircle the warships. To be ready to tow them if necessary, said the Japanese; Biddle did not believe this, but, in keeping with the pacific nature of his mission, he took no steps to have them dispersed.

When no reply to his communication was forthcoming after five days, the commodore expressed his impatience and asked that the governor of Edo be told that he wanted an answer. Two days later, he received it.

A junk bearing an official party approached the *Columbus* on the morning of 27 July, and Biddle was told that he must board her to receive the emperor's reply. This affront to the flag officer's dignity was promptly rejected. Biddle demanded that the communication be delivered to him in his flagship. Thereupon, the Japanese agreed, adding that Biddle's note had been handed to a Japanese officer on board the *Columbus*, so it seemed proper that the emperor's letter should be given the American on board a Japanese vessel. This appeared to be a reasonable argument, and the interpreter was told that the commodore would accede to the original Japanese request.

Commodore Biddle, in full uniform, embarked in his barge an hour later and was pulled over to the junk. As he boarded her, a Japanese standing on her deck pushed him rudely back into the boat. Furious at this insolent gesture, the commodore ordered the interpreter to have his assailant seized and then returned to the *Columbus*. Apologetic Japanese officials followed to explain that the man was no more than a common soldier and to ask how Biddle wished to have him punished. "According to the laws of Japan," said the commodore, adding that the officials themselves were responsible because they should have been awaiting him at the junk's side.[13] To this, they responded that they had understood that they were to bring the letter to him in the flagship and so did not expect him. Ultimately, Biddle decided that an error on the interpreter's part was responsible for the contretemps. Emphasizing his great forbearance, he accepted the explanation and the letter.

As translated by the Dutch interpreter, this missive stated that Japan could trade only with the Netherlands and China and that everything concerning foreign countries must be arranged at Nagasaki—"therefore you must depart as quick as possible, and not come any more in Japan."[14]

That was definite enough. The commodore reiterated that his purpose was to seek a treaty with Japan; since Japan did not wish a treaty and had not opened her ports for trade, his squadron would sail on the morrow, weather permitting. Baffling winds detained the ships another day, but on 29 July they weighed anchor and stood out of Edo Bay, towed by the guard boats which supposedly had been waiting ten days for that privilege.

Commissioner Alexander H. Everett, his health restored, arrived at Canton in time to read the report Biddle had sent Dr. Peter Parker in the *Vincennes*. The commissioner held that the naval officer's mishandling of the mission had diminished the chances of reaching an accord with Japan, and historians since have criticized Commodore Biddle's conduct, sometimes in scathing terms. He erred in receiving officials of inferior rank and in permitting Japanese to board his ships without restraint. Above all, his decision to go to the junk to receive the reply to his letter was a mistake, leading to the humiliating encounter with a common soldier. Finally, he had accepted a document bearing neither address, date, seal, nor signature.

In making these judgments, the more recent critics cannot escape comparison of Biddle's behavior with that of Commodore Matthew Calbraith Perry, who succeeded in a similar mission less than a decade later. They overlook the fact that the Japan mission was only of secondary importance to Biddle, who, unlike Perry, had neither a letter from the president to the emperor nor a draft treaty. The lack of an interpreter for the earlier mission was of special importance, and Biddle could hardly be blamed for it. While the Reverend Dr. Charles Gutzlaff of the Netherlands Missionary Society had obligingly translated the commodore's diplomatic accreditation, he would not permit either of the *Morrison* castaways who had become his assistants to accompany Biddle and no other interpreter was available. Thus, for all interpretation and translation, the commodore was dependent on an absolute stranger to whom neither English nor Japanese was a native language and who was in Japanese employ.

James Biddle had carried out his orders. Having ascertained that Japan had not opened her ports and did not desire a treaty, he withdrew. His actions were not impressive to the Japanese, but he did nothing to arouse in them any intense hostility toward the United States. He failed, as had the French Rear Admiral Jean-Baptiste Cecille at Nagasaki in the preceding month, because the time was not right. Nonetheless, Commodore Perry's success owed much to his predecessor's experience.

Upon leaving Japanese waters, Biddle's warships separated, the *Vincennes* returning to Hong Kong while the *Columbus* set a course for Honolulu, homeward bound. The sloop of war was ordered to New York before the end of 1846. Due mainly to the Mexican War, well over a year again elapsed before the next squadron arrived on the East India Station. In October 1847, Captain David Geisinger received orders to report to

Commodore Thomas ap Catesby Jones for transportation to the Pacific Station in Jones's flagship *Ohio* and, upon joining the squadron, to take command of the frigate *Congress* as commander in chief of the East India Squadron. Almost seven months later, Geisinger reported from Mazatlán that the *Congress*'s crew was in no condition for a cruise on an unhealthy station after prolonged service ashore in California and Mexico. In the frigate's place, the captain accepted Jones's offer of the sloop of war *Preble* to take him to his station.

The *Preble* was one of five third-class sloops of war built in 1838–39. Good sailers and economical cruisers, they were handicapped somewhat by their inability to stow provisions and stores ample for extended voyages. The same criticism did not apply to the second ship of the squadron, which was coming out by the Cape of Good Hope route. The USS *Plymouth* was also a sloop of war, one of seven near-sisters built a few years after the *Preble*. In these vessels, the sloop-of-war type reached its highest point of development by the U.S. Navy. Big ships, almost as large as frigates, they carried their batteries easily, performed very well on almost any point of sailing, stowed supplies sufficient for a prolonged cruise, and—perhaps most important for service in Oriental waters— provided relatively spacious and well-ventilated quarters for their men. Six of them—the *Plymouth, St. Mary's, Saratoga, Germantown, Portsmouth,* and *Jamestown*—served in the Far East; the seventh, the *Albany*, was lost with all hands in 1854, probably the victim of a West Indian hurricane.

The *Plymouth* reached Macao in mid-August 1848, transporting John W. Davis, newly appointed commissioner to China. Geisinger arrived in the *Preble* six weeks later, to learn that Davis was dissatisfied with his reception by Chinese authorities. After transferring his flag to the *Plymouth* in Blenheim Reach, the commodore took a party of officers to the legation, and within a few hours the commissioner had established a much friendlier relationship with his Chinese counterpart.

Commodore Jones had directed that the *Preble* be returned to his squadron; but news of peace between the United States and Mexico led Geisinger to keep her, at least until the brig *Dolphin* joined him. His decision did not win the Navy Department's approval, but it was correct nonetheless. The *Dolphin* encountered very heavy weather off the Cape of Good Hope during the antipodean winter and, after eighteen days of battering by wind and sea, sought refuge at Mauritius. Repairs there required almost a month, and then she had to make her way to the station against the northeast monsoon. The brig arrived at Whampoa late in February 1849; thus, if the *Preble* had returned to the Pacific Squadron as ordered, the *Plymouth* would have been the only U.S. warship on the station for five months.

The two sloops of war were at Whampoa early in 1849, when Commodore Geisinger received a letter from Commissioner Davis informing him that a number of American castaways were imprisoned in Japan. The Dutch superintendent at Deshima had interviewed these men when they were brought to Nagasaki in September. They claimed that in June the whaleship *Lagoda* of New Bedford had grounded in dense fog in the Sea of Japan and was abandoned by her company when she began to break up. Two of her boats had been swamped; those in the boats, including the master and mates, had been lost. The survivors had landed in Japan, where they were quickly apprehended by the authorities.

Davis and Geisinger agreed that they must be rescued, so Commander James Glynn was ordered to take the *Preble* to Nagasaki and arrange their release. In the event that they could not be freed without an order from Edo, the sloop of war would proceed to the capital and "make a firm, temperate, and respectful demand."[15]

Ostensibly, the *Preble*'s was strictly a rescue mission—Glynn's orders from Geisinger contain no mention of establishing an American consulate and a coaling station in Japan. Yet Dr. Gutzlaff, who translated Glynn's orders into Japanese, is said to have forwarded to British authorities copies of a letter to that effect, and the British commissioner reported to the Foreign Office at Whitehall that the commander was expected to make strenuous efforts to gain such concessions.[16] If Glynn did so, however, no mention of it appears in his official report.

The *Preble*'s orders were dated 31 January 1849, but smallpox among her crew detained her until 21 March. She anchored in Nagasaki's outer roads on 18 April, and Glynn soon obtained permission to take her into the harbor.

Aware of Commodore Biddle's experience, the commander was authoritative and aloof, refusing to reveal the purpose of his visit to the interpreter until he had ascertained that the Japanese boarding officer was of sufficient rank to receive such information. A letter was dispatched to the governor of Nagasaki. When only vague promises of a response were forthcoming, Glynn indicated that the *Preble* would depart as soon as the castaways had been delivered to him—"if I am unsuccessful in getting them, then I am ordered by my superior officer 'to do something else.'"[17]

Thanks to the intercession of the Dutch superintendent, an officer arrived on the morning of 26 April with news that the men would be sent to the ship that day. When Glynn asked for a copy of Japan's laws so that merchant seamen would know what to expect if wrecked on her shores, his request was denied; but within a few hours two Dutchmen brought an "Extract from the Laws of Japan" on board. As translated from the Dutch, it read: "Shipwrecked seamen of other countries, who are cast upon the shores of Japan, having no means to reach their homes, will remain in Japan and be treated well, and sent in the first opportunity, in the Dutch ship to Batavia, or the Chinese ship to China."[18] The translator also asked that American ships not sail so close to the Japanese coast.

Thereafter, fourteen seamen were brought on board. Thirteen admitted to Glynn that they had actually deserted from the *Lagoda*, while the other, Ranald McDonald, had shipped in another whaler for the express purpose of being set adrift just off the Japanese coast in order that he might learn something of the empire. The *Lagoda*'s men, half of whom were natives of the Hawaiian Islands, averred that they had been treated very harshly, but McDonald had no complaint. He reported that the warship's arrival had led to a general mobilization in the Nagasaki vicinity, with some 6,000 troops coming from the surrounding area to protect the city.

From Nagasaki, the *Preble* ran over to Shanghai where she spent the first week in May. As she stood down the Hwangpoo River en route from Shanghai to Macao, she met the *Plymouth* coming upstream and Glynn made a verbal report of his mission's success. The two vessels met again in Macao Roads at the end of May, and there the liberated Americans quickly found berths in merchant ships while the Hawaiians were sent to San Francisco in the *Preble* when she sailed to rejoin the Pacific Squadron in mid-June.

Commodore Geisinger had not undertaken the Japan mission himself because of the unsettled situation at Canton. The *Dolphin* spent several days off the factories in March—even the Chinese authorities were thought to approve her presence—and, when the tension eased, she returned to Whampoa while Geisinger visited the treaty ports.

When the *Plymouth* got back to Macao in May, the *Dolphin* was ordered to inquire into the possibility of obtaining coal from Formosa for the use of transpacific merchant steamers. The brig spent a month at Keelung, the principal village, where the Chinese mandarins assured Lieutenant-Commanding William S. Ogden that the mines were in the vicinity of the burying place for native Formosans, "a fierce, cruel and vindictive people," who would take offense if foreigners approached their ancestors' graves.[19] Samples of the coal burned well in the *Dolphin*'s forge, but Ogden was pessimistic about the accessibility of any quantity.

The brig returned from Formosa with half of her crew prostrated by dysentery and fever. Although most recovered at a temporary hospital in Macao, Geisinger advised his superiors that vessels such as the *Dolphin* were utterly unsuitable for the East India Station because of their limited accommodation.

Most of the "Dolphins" were fit for duty when, in August, the Portuguese governor of Macao was assassinated. The authorities asked that the brig land an armed force to reassure the foreign residents who feared that the assassination portended a Chinese attack on the city. Two British warships came over from Hong Kong, and Geisinger brought the *Plymouth* down from Whampoa, stating his readiness to do anything necessary to protect American citizens and to offer asylum to other foreigners. However, the destruction of the Chinese fort nearest Macao by Portuguese troops seemed to end the danger, so the *Dolphin*'s men were reembarked.

During the summer, piracy had become a serious problem in the waters around Macao. As might have been expected, the Royal Navy was most active in its suppression, and the American commander in chief regretted that the lack of a steamer kept him from cooperating "in the laudable endeavor to exterminate these outlaws; Sailing vessels being wholly unsuited to the service on account of the shoals and intricate passages where the Pirate junks take refuge."[20] The *Dolphin* and armed boats from the flagship did capture several supposed pirate-junks and their victims during the autumn. Most of the former had to be released for want of evidence, while the latter were returned to their English owners.

By this time, the commodore had heard that his relief, Captain Philip F. Voorhees, was on his way to the station by way of Cape Horn and San Francisco. Voorhees reached Macao at the end of January 1850 in the sloop of war *St. Mary's* which was on her homeward passage from the Pacific Squadron. Commodore Geisinger quickly exchanged ships with his successor and sailed home to receive the congratulations of the Navy Department for his conduct of affairs on the East India Station.

Commodore Voorhees's tour of duty on the station was devoted almost entirely to one mission, that of conducting a diplomatic agent, Joseph Balestier, on a round of visits to Cochin-China, Siam, and Borneo. It was not a happy cruise. The commodore himself seems to have been aggrieved at having to undertake it, and he did not get along with Balestier, whose conduct he described as "singularly strange, unreasonable, irritable & captious—so as to have made it a most painful & anxious time for me."[21] With some satisfaction, one suspects, he forwarded a communication from the commissioner of Siamese naval forces complaining of the agent's impatience, rudeness, and lack of dignity.

Matters were not improved when Voorhees decided that the *Plymouth* could not take Balestier to Batavia, Bali, Sumatra, and Penang because of the change of monsoon. The flagship's men were showing the effects of their third summer in the Far East, and the fleet surgeon thought it unwise to expose them further "under a nearly vertical sun."[22] So back to

Macao, the *Plymouth* sailed, arriving on 9 July after an absence of more than four months.

American interests in the vicinity of Canton had been left in the care of the *Dolphin*, which was relieved by the *Preble*'s sister *Marion* in June. Voorhees sent the *Marion* to search for possible victims of a typhoon early in August, and then, leaving orders for her commanding officer's future guidance with the U.S. consul at Macao, he sailed for the United States in the *Plymouth*.

Secretary of the Navy William A. Graham was astounded to hear that the commander in chief of the East India Squadron had arrived at Norfolk in January 1851. He required that Voorhees provide a detailed explanation of his departure from his station without being recalled or relieved. In response, the commodore cited his poor health and that of the flagship's captain and the fact that the East India Station had not been considered "a regular relief station" in the past. Graham cannot have found these reasons very convincing, especially in the absence of a medical survey. On the other hand, the navy secretary was aware that Philip F. Voorhees had mustered sufficient political support a few years earlier to reverse a court-martial's sentence that he be dismissed from the Navy. The Navy Department took no further action in the matter, but Commodore Voorhees was never employed again.

◉

CHAPTER FOUR

The Most Frustrating Cruise

The decade following Commodore Philip F. Voorhees's premature departure from the East India Station was the most significant in its history, witnessing the introduction of steam-propelled warships, the opening of Japan, a civil war and a foreign war in China, and the squadron's involvement in belligerent operations at Canton. Ironically, at the end of the decade the East India Squadron itself virtually disappeared when its vessels were called home to participate in the internecine strife that threatened the very existence of the United States.

Although steam propulsion for ships had become practical early in the nineteenth century, navies were reluctant to adopt it. Even as late as 1851, the U.S. Navy had only a half-dozen steamers in commission, one of which, the new paddle frigate *Susquehanna*, was ordered to the East India Station.

On few stations was steam so important. The activities of sailing vessels in the Far East had always to be planned with the monsoon season in mind, for prevailing unfavorable winds could lengthen a ship's passage by months. With the growing importance of the treaty ports, most of which were located on rivers and were some distance from the sea, a warship able to make her way against the current in the absence of a fair wind was obviously desirable. And, as Commodore David Geisinger had pointed out, effective action against the piratical craft infesting the Canton River estuary and contiguous waters was almost impossible without shallow-draft steamers.

FIGURE 4–1.   The paddle frigate *Susquehanna.*

But steam brought its own problems of maintenance and supply. The sailing warship was wonderfully self-reliant. Serious indeed was the materiel casualty that her own company could not cope with, and the only fuel she required was firewood for culinary purposes. Repairs to engines, boilers, and paddle wheels or screw propellers, on the other hand, too often required the facilities of well-equipped machine shops and perhaps even foundries, facilities that the United States did not possess in the Far East. An even greater problem was posed by the steamers' insatiable furnaces. The quest for adequate and assured supplies of reasonably priced steam coal would occupy much of the attention of successive commanders in chief until late in the century.

However, both the British and French navies had used steamers in Chinese waters before 1850, and steam-propelled commercial vessels were plying the Canton and Yangtze rivers by that time. Privately owned facilities and dockyards to service these were being developed at Hong Kong, Whampoa, and Shanghai, while cargoes of coal for their use were arriving with increasing frequency. Thus, the problems attendant on steam propulsion were not insoluble.

Captain John H. Aulick, the first commander in chief to grapple with these problems, was in his sixty-fourth year when he received orders to command the East India Squadron in February 1851. Early in May, he learned that seventeen Japanese mariners, driven far offshore, had been picked up by an American bark and brought to San Francisco. At once

Aulick suggested that their repatriation might lead the Japanese government to grant the desired commercial concessions to the United States. In spite of all the evidence to the contrary, Secretary of State Daniel Webster agreed, as did Secretary of the Navy William A. Graham who ordered that the Japanese be sent to Macao in a vessel of the Pacific Squadron. Webster drafted a letter to the Japanese emperor for President Millard Fillmore's signature and gave Aulick full powers to negotiate with persons possessing similar authority from the emperor.

As the *Susquehanna* was fitting out, the commodore was informed that Minister to Brazil Robert A. Schenck and the chargé d'affaires to the Argentine Republic were to sail to Rio de Janeiro in her. A week later, the passenger list was enlarged by the addition of the Chevalier S. de Macedo, former Brazilian minister to the United States. The paddle frigate had not been designed to accommodate so many distinguished passengers, so Commodore Aulick and Captain William Inman, "neither being remarkable for patience or amiability," had to share a small cabin.[1]

Arriving at the Brazilian capital, the vessel landed her passengers and Aulick asked that Commodore Isaac McKeever of the Brazil Squadron order a survey of her masts and engines. The boards recommended rather extensive alterations, so the *Susquehanna* was taken into the Brazilian navy's dockyard where her masts were unstepped and her paddle wheels and air pumps were removed for repair and modification. By mid-September, the frigate was ready for a trial run, and Commodore Aulick reported that she performed very well.

The weeks of inactivity at Rio de Janeiro exacerbated the tense relationship between Aulick and Captain Inman. The two seem to have been at odds even before leaving the United States, and the intimacy enforced by the *Susquehanna*'s crowded officers' quarters must have made matters worse when she put to sea. The commodore suspected the captain's seamanship—Inman had not actually served at sea since 1837—and the captain resented his superior's supposed interference in matters of routine. Each wrote letters to the Navy Department complaining of the other's behavior, and Aulick recommended that a commander be sent out to relieve Inman. Finally the commodore addressed a formal letter to his subordinate, pointing out that their respective views on almost any subject differed so widely as to make cooperation and the preservation of discipline impossible. Therefore, Captain Inman was detached and ordered to return to the United States. Secretary Graham received the letters from both officers and held them jointly responsible. He refused to order Inman's detachment, but by that time the captain was already on his return to the United States and his former command was bound for Cape Town. The *Susquehanna* had a stormy passage across the South Atlantic, but her spars, engines, and paddle wheels stood the strain, thereby justifying the recent expenditure on them in the commodore's view. At the Comoro Islands and Zanzibar, Aulick was called on to settle controversies between local officials and American merchants; he reported that he had done so to the satisfaction of all. The *Susquehanna* then went to Ceylon and on to Penang. When coal could not be purchased at Penang, the commodore borrowed 400 tons from the British Peninsular and Oriental Steam Navigation Company's agent. After calling at Singapore, the frigate kept on her way, reaching Macao on 4 February 1852.

The USS *Marion* was at anchor in Macao Roads with many of her crew sick, so Aulick lost little time in ordering her home. The large sloop of war *Saratoga* was also on the station and joined the *Susquehanna* at Hong Kong within a week.

Since his Japanese mission could not be undertaken until the rescued mariners were delivered to him, Aulick decided to show his flagship at Whampoa where merchants and Chinese alike would be impressed by the appearance of the new steam frigate. But before he could carry out his intention, he received letters from the United States which effectively cancelled his freedom of action and cast a pall over his entire period of command.

Six weeks after his refusal to permit Captain Inman's detachment, Secretary of the Navy Graham had occasion to write an even harsher letter to Commodore Aulick. The State Department had sent him a communication from Minister Schenck to the effect that Aulick had led the Chevalier de Macedo to believe that he personally was paying all of the Brazilian's expenses on board the *Susquehanna*. The chevalier's passage was said to have been marred by "discomforts and annoyances," and the commodore was accused of transporting his son in the frigate without authorization. Graham demanded "a prompt and full explanation," and a day later at President Fillmore's direction, he ordered that the commodore keep the *Susquehanna* at Hong Kong or Macao until an officer arrived to relieve him of command of the East India Squadron.[2]

Aulick responded that the principal charge with regard to Macedo was absolutely untrue and that he could not "understand how it can have even the shadow of truth for its foundation, as nothing of the kind ever entered my mind." He enclosed letters from his officers in support of this statement. So far as annoyances were concerned, Aulick had heard that Macedo had had some difficulty with a hired boat at Funchal, but that had occurred ashore and could hardly be attributed to him. The discomforts were simply those incidental to sea travel and so were unavoidable. Aulick's son had accompanied him in the hope of finding a commercial situation in South America or China, but all of his expenses had been paid by Aulick. Such an arrangement commonly did not require permission from the Navy Department. Finally, the anguished commodore questioned the propriety of condemning him without awaiting his explanations.[3]

One can only speculate as to the reasons for Fillmore's and Graham's peremptory action. The latter had been exasperated by what he considered Aulick's undignified behavior with regard to Inman, and the Bureau of Construction and Repair had held that the expensive alterations to the *Susquehanna* at Rio de Janeiro had been unnecessary. Thus, he was prepared to accept accusations, especially when they came from an influential Whig politician such as Schenck. The motives of the latter in forwarding an unsubstantiated account of apparently trivial misdeeds cannot be divined. Perhaps some earlier animosity between Schenck's elder brother, who was a naval officer, and Aulick led to this action; or an irascible act on the commodore's part may have alienated the minister.

No matter what the reasons may have been, Secretary Graham acted unwisely. He assured Aulick that his relief would "proceed by the most speedy conveyance,"[4] yet Commodore Matthew Calbraith Perry was not officially appointed to the command until 24 March 1852, and his flagship finally departed the United States more than a year after Graham had written his assurance of a speedy relief for Aulick. Meanwhile, the commodore was virtually confined to the Canton River estuary, and his position became even more difficult when reports appeared in the press to the effect that his impending relief was due to some misconduct on his part.

The *Plymouth*, the *Marion*'s relief, arrived at Macao in April, and Commander John Kelly reported that she had grounded twice in East Indian waters on her way to the station. Contact with a coral reef off Batavia had removed most of the copper from her keel, while she had had to jettison 600 round shot to get off a sand spit near Banca Strait. Kelly doubted that the sloop of war had sustained any serious damage, but docking at Whampoa seemed desirable.

The *Plymouth* was not yet ready for service when, in early May, Aulick received news of an atrocity in the American ship *Robert Bowne*. The merchantman had sailed from Amoy bound for San Francisco with 410 Chinese coolies embarked. Allegedly to ensure cleanliness, her master ordered many of his "passengers'" pigtails cut off and his seamen scrubbed the protesting Chinese in cold sea water with cane brooms. The coolies endured it for a time, but ten days out, they armed themselves with belaying pins, boarding pikes, and the like, and rose against their tormentors. The master, both mates, and four seamen were killed, and the remainder of the seamen saved themselves by climbing aloft. The coolies offered to spare them if they would sail the ship to Formosa. They agreed, but none of them could navigate, so the *Bowne* made Ishigaki Jima to the eastward of Formosa instead. Two seamen, who escaped in the longboat, were picked up by a British schooner, and their fellows recaptured the vessel after most of the coolies had gone ashore.

When news of the "mutiny" reached Amoy, British authorities, believing that many of the culprits would probably escape before Commodore Aulick could be informed, sent small vessels of the Royal Navy to apprehend them. As soon as Aulick learned of the occurrence, he ordered the *Saratoga* to Amoy to procure information so that a search could be undertaken.

While the *Saratoga* was at Amoy, HMS *Lily* stood in with twenty-one coolies who had been taken in the *Robert Bowne*. Commander William S. Walker took them, together with five of the *Bowne*'s men and an interpreter, into the *Saratoga* and sailed for Ishigaki Jima. Resident magistrates there informed him that almost 300 coolies were on the island and that the expense of feeding them was becoming a burden. The *Saratoga*'s landing parties rounded up fifty-five coolies before a typhoon and incessant rains made further pursuit pointless.

The question of how to deal with these Chinese was perplexing. About ninety were ultimately confined on board Aulick's vessels, an expense that he too was anxious to be freed of. British officials were sympathetic, but one of their courts had ruled that coolies who had robbed and murdered in similar circumstances could not be treated as pirates under international law; thus, they had no jurisdiction. Finally, Aulick, Chargé d'Affaires Dr. Peter Parker, and the American consul agreed that a consular court should identify the leaders and turn them over to the Chinese commissioner at Canton to be dealt with according to Chinese law. The remainder were sent back to Amoy in the *Saratoga*, there to be released.

Even that mission of clemency was not devoid of hazard. As the sloop of war was standing out of Amoy under all plain sail late in June, an error on the part of the Chinese pilot put her on a reef off Seao Tan Island. Throwing the sails aback failed to free her, so they were furled. The tide was ebbing rapidly; as she settled, the *Saratoga* heeled far over to starboard. Her topgallant masts and upper yards were sent down, and then Commander Walker had eight guns of the starboard battery buoyed and thrown over the side while Chinese lighters came alongside to receive the shot and other weighty objects. As soon as the American was seen to be aground, the East India Company's *Semiramis* in the inner harbor was ordered to raise steam and go to her assistsnce. After eight hours of labor, the "Saratogas," aided by the *Semiramis*, were able to float their vessel at high water. Walker reported no apparent damage. When the *Saratoga*'s guns were recovered the next day, however, one gun simply could not be

FIGURE 4–2.   The *Saratoga* in heavy seas.

located; another, which had been cracked by striking a rock, had to be discarded.

The sloop of war *St. Mary's* reached Macao from San Francisco early in May, and Commodore Aulick had the Japanese mariners, whom he was to have repatriated, transferred to the *Susquehanna* to await the Navy Department's pleasure. The *St. Mary's* was not joining the East India Squadron, but the commodore assigned her a mission to be carried out on the way home.

Some two weeks earlier, Aulick had received a letter from the Dutchman who was acting as U.S. consul at Batavia; enclosed was another letter from Walter M. Gibson, master of the American merchant schooner *Flirt*. Gibson claimed that, while intoxicated, he had unwittingly promised to aid the sultan of Djambi, who was leading a revolt against the Dutch colonial government in Sumatra. A letter to this effect bearing Gibson's signature, had fallen into Dutch hands, whereupon the *Flirt* was seized and her people imprisoned without trial. Aulick had no vessel to send to Batavia until the *St. Mary's* arrived, so her commanding officer, George A. Magruder, was directed to do what he could for Gibson and his men.

When the sloop of war departed Macao at the end of May, the southwest monsoon caused Magruder to take the easterly route through Mindoro Strait, the Sulu and Celebes seas, and Makassar Strait. During a passage of thirty-seven days of squalls, calms, variable breezes, and heavy rains, the *St. Mary's*, by unceasing vigilance and a constant readiness to let an anchor go, avoided the countless reefs and shoals threatening her much of the time.

Commander Magruder was received courteously by the Dutch authorities at Batavia, who explained that the *Flirt's* men had been released for want of evidence while Gibson was still held—he could not be tried because necessary witnesses were fighting the rebellious Sumatrans. Magruder emphasized his government's interest in the case and assured himself that Gibson was confined in relative comfort—beyond that, he could do no more. The Sumatran revolt was put down quickly, but Gibson's trial dragged on for months and was ended only by his escape from Java, an outcome that owed nothing to Magruder's efforts.

There was an ironical sequel to the Gibson affair. During the Civil War, Secretary of the Navy Gideon Welles sent confidential orders to the senior naval officer at Hong Kong to arrest the notorious friend of Brigham Young and Confederate sympathizer, Captain Gibson, "who mixes the business of making Mormon converts and Rebel adherents." Gibson was believed to be seeking a vessel in which to cruise against Union commerce, and, if he were apprehended, his career could be terminated speedily by turning him over to the Dutch colonial authorities at Batavia.[5]

Meanwhile, the *Plymouth* was looking after American interests in Shanghai. Commander Kelly reported that he had landed his marine guard in July to restore order at Woosung where American seamen were fighting Chinese. The conflict resulted in two Chinese fatalities. American sailors involved in the fighting were confined in the warship until a consular court ruled that it lacked sufficient evidence for their conviction. However, someone evidently did not agree; within a few days, an alleged murderer was found dead in a nearby field.

In the autumn of 1852, the *Saratoga*, disguised as a merchant vessel, put out to search for pirates who had chased an American clipper ship off Hainan. She found no pirates, but a rapidly falling barometer presaged the approach of a much more dangerous foe. Her company sent down light yards and topgallant masts, secured guns and boats with extra lashings, and took other precautionary measures in ample time, yet the full fury of the typhoon ripped away three boats with their davits and gear, blew out most of her close-reefed storm canvas, and did a good deal of damage to her rigging. But her cruise was not entirely in vain. Two weeks later, she removed six Chinese from a dismasted fishing boat; with neither water nor food, they would soon have died if the *Saratoga* had not rescued them.

Commodore Aulick could send his vessels on various missions; he could not go himself. The weary months of waiting for his relief passed slowly. On 6 November, he received by Commander Franklin Buchanan an order to turn command of the squadron over to its bearer, but the mails which arrived on that day included a more recent letter ordering the commodore not to leave the station until regularly relieved. Thereupon, Aulick made Buchanan captain of the *Susquehanna* and retained the squadron command himself. Buchanan's displeasure with this decision did not make Aulick's situation any easier.

Orders releasing the commodore and his flagship from their confinement finally arrived, and mid-December brought news of riots in Amoy, with attacks on British commercial houses that were thought by the Chinese to be kidnapping coolies for transportation abroad. No Americans resided in Amoy except two missionary families and a vice-consul who was employed by one of the British companies, and there had been no American trade with the city since the *Robert Bowne*'s ill-starred venture. Nonetheless, Aulick decided to go there in the *Susquehanna* to make sure that the U.S. flag was not being used improperly.

His visit was uneventful. The missionaries explained that the Chinese brokers through whom the coolies were engaged were the probable malefactors. Aulick frankly told the vice-consul that a building belonging to a foreign firm of questionable reputation was not the proper location for the American consular flag, and, in the absence of a suitable house, the flag should not be displayed at all. If his advice were ignored, the commodore promised to recommend that the vice-consulate, for which there was no apparent need, be discontinued.

Aulick then went to Manila, whose American residents had been urging that the *Susquehanna* be shown there. Aulick reported that American trade with Manila had increased markedly since California had become a part of the United States, to which the bulk of Philippine hemp, sugar, and indigo was exported. American merchant vessels were always to be found in Manila Bay; six of them were there during the frigate's visit.

Flagship and flag officer alike suffered breakdowns in the course of this cruise. The *Susquehanna* limped back to Hong Kong at the end of January 1853 with Aulick so ill that the surgeons doubted his ability to survive the homeward passage. Five weeks later, however, his health had improved so he accepted the advice of the fleet surgeon and Dr. Parker that he return by the overland route to Europe and thence to the United States.

Leaving orders for Commander Kelly, the senior officer, to act in his stead until Commodore Perry arrived, Commodore Aulick departed Hong Kong on 10 March, ending what surely must have been one of the most frustrating periods of command ever experienced by a senior officer of the U.S. Navy. Throughout, John Aulick seems to have borne his tribulations with a dignity that belied earlier reports of his irascibility. It is satisfying to note that he survived the homeward journey by twenty years and that Navy Secretary Graham's Democratic successor believed him guiltless of any misconduct.

CHAPTER FIVE

The Most Important Cruise

Commodore Matthew Calbraith Perry, seven years Captain John Aulick's junior, was nonetheless his senior in the Navy. Nor was this Perry's only advantage: he was the younger brother of Oliver Hazard Perry, the War of 1812 hero of the Battle of Lake Erie; he was related by marriage to the Rodgers family, among the foremost of the American naval aristocracy; and his own marriage to Jane Slidell of New York had brought him into an influential Democratic kindred. In addition, Perry's own abilities had won him a considerable reputation in the Navy.

The commodore seems to have desired the Mediterranean Squadron, but, upon being assured that the mission to open Japan would be entrusted to him, he accepted the East India command instead and began gathering all available information on Japan. The Navy Department promised him twelve vessels—three times the number any of his predecessors had commanded—and permitted him to select many of his subordinates. Preparations were interrupted in the summer of 1852 when Perry had to spend a month helping to settle a long-standing controversy concerning American fishing rights in the waters of Britain's Maritime colonies of Nova Scotia, New Brunswick, and Prince Edward Island. Thereafter, he helped to prepare his orders and sailed in the paddle frigate *Mississippi* on 24 November; the vessels which were to have accompanied him were delayed by engine trouble or other causes.

The *Mississippi* reached Hong Kong less than a month after Aulick's departure and found most of the squadron—the *Plymouth*, the *Saratoga*, and the storeship *Supply*—awaiting the commodore. The *Susquehanna* was at Shanghai, to which city she had conveyed the recently arrived U.S. commissioner to China, Humphrey Marshall.

One of the first matters to attract the new commander in chief's attention was the location of his squadron's supply depot. Commodore Foxhall Parker had arranged to have stores landed at Macao, and the U.S. government was paying $800 per annum rent for a storehouse, or "godown," there. Robert P. DeSilver, U.S. consul at Macao, had received an official appointment as naval storekeeper, and to him Commodore Aulick had turned when Secretary of the Navy William A. Graham forwarded a proposal that Hong Kong be made the squadron's headquarters. DeSilver responded that the British colony's fine harbor was its only advantage—its atmosphere was "mouldy" and unhealthy during the rainy season, storehouses would have to be built and maintained at great expense, and the white ants infesting the area were very destructive to buildings and stores alike. So long as the Portuguese kept a sufficient military force in Macao, it was the best location for the squadron's stores.

But Macao's importance was diminishing even as Aulick accepted DeSilver's advice. The *Saratoga*'s Lieutenant John R. Goldsborough wrote his elder brother, who had served on the station earlier, of "the wonderful and rapid improvement going on at Hong Kong, and the gradual decaying of Macao."[1] The coming of steam navigation accelerated that process. Macao's great disadvantage was its lack of a harbor. Vessels of any size had to anchor in an open roadstead three miles from the city, with the result that all supplies had to be lightered from the storeships to the godown and from the godown to the warships at considerable expense. Moreover, this transshipping was interrupted whenever the wind sprang up, since the lighters could not lie alongside the ships if even a good topgallant breeze were blowing. The difficulty of moving hundreds of tons of coal to or from the shore under these conditions was a convincing argument in favor of Hong Kong as the location of the squadron's stores. At Hong Kong, large ships could anchor within a thousand yards of the shore and discharge or receive supplies in almost all weathers.

Commodore Parker had preferred Macao in large part because of the uncertain state of Anglo-American relations in the mid-1840s. By 1853, however, those relations were so amicable that Commodore Perry anticipated no danger whatsoever if he shifted the depot to Hong Kong; indeed, he thought that the Chinese in Macao were a greater threat to the squadron's stores. Accordingly, he located a suitable building in Hong Kong and rented it for the government at $480 per annum, spending another $90 to construct a small pier nearby. DeSilver approved Perry's decision —he "had no idea Hong Kong could provide so commodious & advantageous a site."[2] Perry directed that storeships coming from the United States henceforth deposit their cargoes at the Hong Kong depot and that the stores at Macao remain there until all had been issued to the warships.

Somewhat as an afterthought, the commodore sought the approval of the British colony's governor, who replied that the arrangement was very satisfactory to his government. Well it might have been—so long as Hong Kong remained the East India Squadron's principal base, U.S. naval forces operated in Far Eastern waters only with Britain's tacit consent.

Perhaps Commodore Perry recognized that complete reliance on British goodwill was unwise, for Shanghai also received some consideration as a potential base site. In Perry's opinion, however, one visit to Shanghai was enough to disqualify it. Located on the narrow Hwangpoo River which flows into the Yangtze Kiang estuary, Shanghai was difficult of access because of the hazardous entrance to the estuary. Perry described it succinctly: An outer bar with but twenty feet depth at low water and an entrance channel only 1½ miles wide with dangerous shoals on either hand; a coast too low to be seen from the outer bar; no lighthouses, beacons, or buoys; the tidal currents notorious for their velocity and irregularity. The *Susquehanna, Mississippi,* and *Plymouth* had all touched on the south shoal while crossing the outer bar, and the *Supply,* unable to obtain a pilot, grounded on the north shoal, from which she was refloated with some difficulty.[3]

In spite of its hydrographic drawbacks, Shanghai was already beginning to surpass Canton as the focal point for trade with China. Its position as the natural outlet for the vast and heavily populated Yangtze Basin made this development inevitable, and it was hastened by the fact that its inhabitants were generally friendly to foreigners, in marked contrast to the Cantonese, who had so far resisted successfully all efforts to open their city to Europeans and Americans. The international settlement that had risen beside Shanghai on a spacious tract made available for that purpose by the imperial government, contained consulates and the buildings of the major commercial companies as well as luxurious dwellings, clubs, a race course, and even Christian churches.

It was here that Commodore Perry met Humphrey Marshall, U.S. commissioner to China, and, through Marshall, encountered difficulties which threatened the Japan mission. The envoy was determined to present his credentials at Peking; since his efforts to communicate with the imperial court had been unproductive, he wanted a warship to convey him to the mouth of the Pei Ho, the river on which the imperial capital was situated. None of Marshall's predecessors had insisted on being received at Peking, but he felt that the Chinese government would not risk a war with the United States by refusing him.

Marshall's certainty was founded on the Taiping Rebellion, the civil war that was to ravage parts of China for more than a decade. The revolt against grinding oppression by corrupt and inefficient imperial officials was led by a Chinese who had some acquaintance with Christian doctrine. Claiming to be a son of God, he announced his intention to drive the usurping Manchu from the Chinese throne and establish the "Heavenly Dynasty of Perfect Peace."

The rebels had captured Nanking, which was proclaimed "the Heavenly Capital of the Heavenly Dynasty," and imperial forces seemed powerless to stop their advance. Under these circumstances, it was natural that the Chinese government should seek assistance wherever it might be found. Perry responded to its officials' overtures with a statement that he had no authority to intervene in a domestic insurrection and that, even if he had, he would not intervene because Marshall had not been allowed to present his credentials.

The demand of the leading American merchants at Canton and Shanghai that their property be protected by the squadron was a more serious matter. Marshall left it to the commodore to decide whether American interests in China justified keeping all or a part of his force there; the commissioner, of course, wished to have a warship stationed in each of the treaty ports.

Perry was not to be dissuaded so easily. Commander John Kelly, who had been directed to investigate charts and sailing directions for the Yellow Sea and the Gulf of Pechihli, reported that hydrographic knowledge of these bodies of water was vague and incomplete, and at that season strong currents and dense fogs would make their navigation even more hazardous for a large vessel. This bolstered Perry's opinion that any effort to reach Peking would be unwise as well as unnecessary—the United States already had the same commercial relationship with China as the other leading maritime powers and sought no exclusive rights, so Marshall's projected course would be more likely to harm the American position than to improve it. So far as the rebels were concerned, Perry thought their danger to Shanghai was exaggerated. He would leave the *Plymouth* to reinforce temporarily the three British and two French warships moored there; thereafter, his vessels would be within three days' steaming from Edo Bay should conditions deteriorate.

Rumors that the Japanese were busily strengthening their coastal defenses increased the commodore's anxiety to be off. He had transferred his broad pennant from the *Mississippi* to the larger *Susquehanna*, and completed with stores, provisions, and coal. On 17 May, the two paddle frigates, the *Supply* and the chartered American bark *Caprice*, dropped down the Hwangpoo, negotiated the estuary channel, and set a course for Okinawa in the Ryukyu Islands.

Perry had decided to utilize Okinawa's Naha harbor as a base where his steamers could replenish their coal supplies from chartered colliers; to this end, he spent several days arranging a visit to the royal palace. This turned out to be a useful exercise in diplomacy, for the Okinawans were almost as adept as their more powerful neighbors at procrastination and postponement. Meanwhile, the commodore's subordinates busied themselves surveying the harbor and making an excursion to the island's interior. When the *Saratoga* stood in from Macao, the *Susquehanna* joined her for a visit to the Bonin Islands, which Perry also was considering as the site of a future coaling station. On his return to Okinawa, he found that the *Plymouth* had arrived from Shanghai and that two chartered colliers were waiting for him. When both steamers' bunkers had been filled with coal, the chartered vessels were ordered back to Shanghai for more of the essential fuel. The *Supply* was directed to remain in the vicinity of Naha, and the squadron got under way for Edo Bay on 2 July, with the steamers towing the sailers to ensure a uniform rate of progress.

Little less than seven years earlier, Commodore James Biddle had departed the Chusan Islands bound on a similar mission. He had failed to open Japan; why should Commodore Perry have hoped to succeed? The reasons are several: the responsibility had been thrust on Biddle unexpectedly by Everett's illness, while Perry knew from the outset that the mission was his alone and had devoted some months to the study of Japan and the ways of its inhabitants. More information was available to him, including the records of the Biddle and Glynn visits. He had his own interpreters—a Japanese-speaking Dutchman, who signed on at Shanghai, and S. Wells Williams, although the latter's knowledge of Japanese was very limited. The State Department had made ample preparation, so that Perry's instructions, which he had had some voice in drawing up, authorized a much wider range of action and were accompanied by the necessary documents, including a letter from the president and a draft treaty. The Japanese had never seen steam-propelled vessels; thus, the *Susquehanna* and the *Mississippi* would make a great impression as well as permit a freedom of movement denied Biddle's sailing ships.

These advantages were known to Perry; he did not know that conditions within Japan were somewhat more favorable as well. Some discontent with the oppressive policy of seclusion enforced by successive shoguns for more than two centuries was beginning to be manifested, and the incumbent shogun, one of the weaker members of the Tokugawa family, was even less effective because of ill health. In addition, prior to Perry's visit, a shipwrecked Japanese, who went to school in Massachusetts before returning to Japan, had brought a good deal of information about the United States, including an account of its easy success in the Mexican War and its supposed lack of territorial imperialistic desires in the Far East. Thus, circumstances favored Perry much more than they had Biddle. But favorable circumstances do not guarantee success—a commander less able than Matthew Calbraith Perry would almost certainly have encountered much greater difficulty and might very well have failed entirely.

The events of Perry's visits to Japan have been described so often and in such detail that there is little point in repeating them here. Suffice it to say that the four ships of the East India Squadron anchored off Uraga on 8 July, triggering a mobilization of Japanese defense forces and the usual foray of guard boats which soon surrounded the warships. The commodore assumed an imperious attitude, permitting only officials and interpreters to board the flagship, refusing to meet with anyone not his equal in rank, threatening to drive the guard boats off if they were not withdrawn, and ordering that neither food nor water be accepted by his squadron unless he was allowed to pay for it. While awaiting someone of sufficient rank and authority to receive the documents pertaining to his mission, the commodore had the squadron's boats employed sounding the anchorage. To encourage prompt Japanese action, the boats, escorted by the *Mississippi*, began to take soundings farther up Edo Bay on 11 July. Guard boats, apparently bent on preventing this brazen violation of Japanese waters, gave way before the approaching paddle frigate, and the surveys continued.

After almost daily negotiation with a Japanese official, Perry's representatives—and Perry—found the credentials of the dignitaries appointed to receive the documents satisfactory and agreed that the presentation would take place on 14 July at the village of Kurihama, just below Uraga. The Japanese chose that date because their mobilization was essentially completed; they selected Kurihama because of its location and its level ground on which thousands of soldiers could be mustered. Perry accepted both—his provisions and water would not last indefinitely, and his warships could anchor within easy gunshot of Kurihama.

Americans and Japanese seem to have striven to outdo one another with regard to the pageantry of the occasion, and each group was impressed by the appearance and bearing of the other. No untoward event marred the dignity of the ceremony; the American documents were presented to the noblemen serving as co-governors of Uraga and their receipt was received by Perry, who presently informed his hosts that his squadron would depart within a few days, to return in the spring of 1854 for the Japanese response.

To demonstrate that he was not leaving under duress, the commodore boarded the *Mississippi* the next day and in her stood up the bay almost to Edo's outskirts, ignoring Japanese pleas that he turn back. Having made his point, he arranged an exchange of gifts with the emissary through whom most of the negotiations had been conducted. The squadron then weighed anchor on 17 July; the *Saratoga* was bound for Shanghai, the other vessels for Okinawa.

Having coaled at Naha, the steamers departed for Hong Kong, leaving the *Plymouth* with orders to sail to the southernmost group of the Bonin Islands as soon as the typhoon season had passed. Commander Kelly was to survey these islands and take possession for the United States, which he did to no avail, since the United States made no effort to retain them.

En route to Hong Kong, Commodore Perry fell in with the sloop of war *Vandalia*, which was just coming from the United States, and his squadron was further increased by the arrival of the *Susquehanna's* sister *Powhatan* and the sailer *Macedonian* before the end of August. The *Vandalia* and the *Macedonian* were in good condition; indeed, the latter, rebuilt as a frigate in 1832 and cut down to a sloop of war twenty years afterward, was praised as "the most Magnificent Ship that had ever been in these seas."[4] The *Powhatan*, on the other hand, had been plagued by engineering casualties on the way out. Since the *Susquehanna's* engines were still infirm as a result of her breakdown en route to Manila some eight months earlier, two of Perry's three steamers had to be considered unreliable.

Nonetheless, he refused to send the flagship home until he had visited Japan again. He was determined to appear in Edo Bay with greater force, and the newcomers had brought word that neither the ship of the line *Vermont* nor the steamers *Allegheny* and *Princeton* would join the squadron—the first was too expensive to man, and both steamers had been relegated to harbor service because of defective engines. So the Navy Department's promise of twelve ships was not kept, to Perry's disappointment, but two more storeships, the *Southampton* and the *Lexington*, were on their way to the station. When they arrived, the East India Squadron was the largest seagoing command in the U.S. Navy.

However, there was no assurance that all or even most of the vessels would reach Japan. Humphrey Marshall refused to agree that the Japan mission was important enough to lure Perry's warships away from the Chinese coast. The State Department had informed the commissioner that the squadron would be devoted to the protection of American interests in China. Therefore, Marshall desired the commodore to send vessels to the various treaty ports, although he would allow Perry to decide which ships should be sent, adding "I have not the slightest wish to encroach upon *your privilege,* as an officer."[5]

To this, Perry replied that he would cooperate with Marshall as he saw the need, but so far as he knew, no foreigner had been molested during his time on the station. The *Supply,* one of the two ships that could reach Canton, was to remain there for the time being. She had touched at Amoy on her way from Okinawa and reported that, although the rebels held the city, the three American residents were in no danger nor was there any foreign trade to be protected. Shanghai also was in rebel hands, but no threats against foreigners or their property had been reported. The *Saratoga* was there for repairs, and her company was ready to act in defense of Americans in the international settlement. Neither Ningpo nor Foochow had any American residents or trade, so there was no reason to heed Marshall's request that ships be sent to those ports.

The commissioner's efforts to gain recognition at Shanghai or Peking having come to nought, Perry sent the *Mississippi* to bring him back to Canton. Marshall fared no better there, and by late December he was planning drastic action—American merchants would cease to pay duties on cargoes entering and leaving the port of Shanghai, of which imperial forces had regained control. Marshall expected that the Chinese would endeavor to collect the duties forcibly, so it would be necessary for Perry to send more warships northward. The envoy also wished to visit Nanking to open communication with the Taiping rebels, implying that this would be a first step toward U.S. recognition of their government.

Commodore Perry's response was worded very plainly. His plans for the second visit to Japan had been completed, and some of his vessels were already en route to the appointed rendezvous; therefore, he could not send additional ships to Shanghai. Heretofore, it had not been his place to comment on Marshall's policy, but the commissioner's demand for naval support made it the commander in chief's business. Briefly, Perry thought that it would be politic to await the outcome of the Taiping Rebellion before attempting to negotiate with either of the Chinese governments. Needless to say, Humphrey Marshall did not accept the naval officer's right to pass judgment on his actions. He responded hotly that the whole matter would be left for the president to decide, leaving no doubt regarding his own opinion that the decision would be in his favor.

Unknown to either, the impasse had already been resolved. Robert M. McLane had been appointed to replace Marshall, and the former's instructions stated specifically: "The President does not propose to subject [the commander in chief of the East India Squadron] to your control, but he expects that you and he will cooperate together whenever, in the judgment of both, the interests of the United States indicate the necessity of such cooperation."[6] Perry could have asked no more.

The commodore's insistence on the overriding importance of the Japan mission was due in part to rumors that others were trying to share the credit for opening the island empire. Arriving at Shanghai in November after his small squadron had spent three fruitless months at Nagasaki, the Russian Vice Admiral E. V. Putiatin wrote Perry to ask that some coal be lent him from the latter's supply, adding that "I trust when we meet we shall by mutual cooperation attain more easily the end, that both our Governments have in common."[7] The French admiral was also supposed to be desirous of joining forces with Perry. Only the British seemed disposed to allow Perry to go it alone. Flag officers commanding their East Indies Station had standing instructions to regard the protection of British subjects and property on the coast of China as their primary responsibility; with the Taiping Rebellion and a possible war with Russia to threaten these British interests, Vice Admiral Sir Fleetwood Pellew had little inclination to divert vessels to a project in whose beneficial results, if any, Britain would probably share in due course even without direct effort on his part.

Perry's relationship with his foreign counterparts was generally amicable, but he was most friendly toward the British. The Royal Navy's storehouses at Hong Kong were opened to his squadron, which accepted only some lime juice for use as an antiscorbutic. Since a lack of ships to bring coal from Europe had resulted in a general shortage on the station, Perry offered to share his own ample supply with Pellew, to be repaid within a specified time. French and Russian applications for coal were turned down, however, on the ground that those admirals could not replace any which might be supplied them—a reasonable argument for keeping from them the commodity without which they could not go to Japan.

No matter how anxious Commodore Perry was to return to Edo Bay, he could not do so until the storeship *Lexington* had joined him because the gifts intended to impress upon the Japanese the technological attainments of American civilization had been embarked in her. The sailing qualities of this notoriously slow sloop of war had not been improved by conversion to a storeship—she spent more than six months on her passage from New York.

All was in readiness early in January. On the advice of leading American merchants at Canton, Perry had chartered a new shallow-draft paddle steamer, the *Queen*, from her British owners at $500 per month. Manned by twenty sailors and ten Chinese, armed with four small guns, and commanded by the *Mississippi*'s Lieutenant Alfred Taylor, the 150-ton *Queen* was to protect American interests at Canton, and the commodore grudgingly ordered the *Plymouth* to remain at Shanghai to placate his countrymen there. On the eve of his departure from Hong Kong, he received orders from the Navy Department to place a steamer at the disposal of Commissioner Robert McLane. But Perry would tolerate no further weakening of his squadron at that time; he replied that a vessel would be sent to Macao as soon as she could be spared from the force in Edo Bay.

With too few steamers to tow all of his sailers, Perry sent three of the latter in advance of their fellows. The paddle frigates stood out of Hong Kong on 14 January 1854, the *Mississippi* and the *Powhatan* towing the storeships *Lexington* and *Southampton*. They went first to Okinawa, where the commodore spent several days in an effort to assure that American whalers and merchantmen calling at Naha would be able to procure provisions and water, while the sailing vessels were ordered on to Japan.

On the morning of 11 February, the *Southampton*, which had outsailed her consorts, arrived at the so-called American anchorage above Uraga. Not long afterward, the *Macedonian*'s navigator identified a small cove some miles to the westward as the entrance to Edo Bay, and the sloop of war was soon aground on a coral reef jutting offshore. The *Vandalia* and the *Lexington* were in sight—the *Macedonian* signaled her plight to the former and hoisted out her boats to sound around the stranded vessel and carry out kedge anchors. The *Vandalia* anchored within a mile and sent her launch to assist, to no avail. Thereupon, the "Macedonians" began to lighten ship, heaving coal, shot, and other easily jettisoned articles over the side and shifting the big guns in an effort to trim her more favorably. The weather deteriorated as the day wore on, with squalls and cold rain, and the ship's thumping on the reef gave added proof of her precarious position. Fortunately, the coast gave some shelter, so she sustained no apparent damage before she was kedged off the following afternoon, several hours after the three paddle frigates had reached the scene from Okinawa. The *Mississippi* towed her to a safe anchorage, and Captain Joel Abbot explained to the commodore that an inaccurate chart had caused his vessel's mishap. Perry generously accepted the explanation; he might have pointed out that the other ships, with identical charts, had had no difficulty. The remainder of the day was devoted to getting the *Macedonian* shipshape again, and on 13 February the squadron steamed through Uraga Channel to join the *Southampton* in Edo Bay.

Commodore Perry had left Japan less than seven months earlier, after informing the Japanese that he would return in the spring. However, his premature arrival caused little perturbation at Edo. The ailing shogun had died in the interim, and under his successor a reevaluation of Japanese policy had been undertaken. Advice from the daimyo (hereditary noblemen) ranged from outright rejection of all foreign demands to an immediate opening of trade, but the general attitude seemed to be that Japan should continue to resist intercourse with foreigners while recognizing that a foreign war would be disastrous. Thus, while some concessions might have to be made if a conflict were to be avoided, they should be kept to an absolute minimum. This decision made, the Japanese were ready to receive Perry whenever he arrived.

Japanese officials boarded the flagship soon after she anchored to arrange the site for the negotiations. They suggested Uraga or a town below it; Perry's representatives insisted on Edo. The Japanese were adamant—foreigners must not enter Edo—and so was the commodore, who went so far as to endanger the mission by taking his vessels up the bay to a point whence the capital city could be seen. After a week and more had brought no agreement, the Japanese offered Yokohama, a fishing village some eighteen miles from Edo, and Perry accepted. A treaty house was erected there; having sent an officer to ascertain that it was satisfactory, the commodore moored his eight vessels—the *Saratoga* had arrived from Shanghai early in March—so that their guns could command the site, and he set 8 March for the beginning of negotiations.

Perry's first visit had convinced him that ceremony was invaluable when dealing with the Japanese, and his landing on 8 March was marked by even greater pomp than that on 14 July 1853. Five-hundred officers and men and three ships' bands disembarked from twenty-seven boats to form two lines reaching from the shore to the treaty house. Promptly at noon, the commodore entered his barge as the flagship *Powhatan* fired the seventeen-gun salute due the diplomatic representative of the United States. The bands played while Perry, resplendent in full dress, led a retinue of officers between the files of seamen and marines to the treaty house where he was received by the four imperial commissioners, to whom the boat howitzers boomed out a seventeen-gun salute after first firing twenty-one shots to the emperor of Japan. The commodore's subsequent landings were much less ceremonious, but the first had made an indelible impression.

The Japanese were prepared to alter their usual policy to the extent of promising kind treatment to castaways and opening a harbor of refuge, but they would not consider entering into a trading agreement. In due course, Perry decided that a limited treaty was better than none—he would not insist on a commercial pact if the Japanese would open two ports to American shipping and allow a consulate to be established at one. Selection of the ports required more deliberation. The Japanese offered

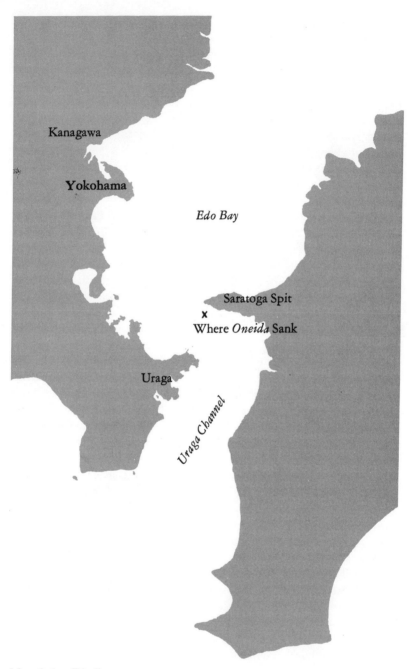

Kanagawa

Yokohama

Edo Bay

Saratoga Spit

✗
Where *Oneida* Sank

Uraga

Uraga Channel

MAP 5–1.   Edo Bay

Nagasaki, but the commodore would not accept that symbol of foreign inferiority. Ultimately, Hakodate, on the northern island later called Hokkaido, and Shimoda, on the tip of the Izu Peninsula southwest of Edo Bay, were chosen. Perry accepted the former at once—it was located on Tsugaru Strait which links the Pacific Ocean with the Sea of Japan—but sent the *Vandalia* and the *Southampton* to reconnoiter Shimoda, which was completely unknown to the Americans. Their commanding officers, possibly overwhelmed by the magnificence of its scenery, reported favorably; therefore, the commodore agreed to it. Then the negotiators addressed themselves to the question of whether liberty should be granted the seamen of ships entering the harbors, and, once that had been settled, to Perry's desire for a consulate at one port. To the Japanese, a consul was necessary only if trade were permitted; Perry denied this, holding that a consul would be needed to settle disputes between seamen and townspeople. Having won this point, Perry got the Japanese to agree that both ports would be opened to American shipping in three months' time and that he could visit both ports immediately after the treaty had been signed.

Meanwhile, the squadron's small boats were kept busy surveying the western side of Edo Bay, and officers were allowed to go ashore at Yokohama when off duty. Relatively lavish entertainments on shipboard and ashore accompanied the negotiations, with alcoholic beverages helping to convince the Japanese that Western civilization was not entirely devoid of desirable products. The gifts brought out in the *Lexington* were landed and assembled: A miniature railroad with locomotive, tender, and a passenger car which could accommodate a small child; a telegraph line which was placed in operation between Yokohama and a nearby village; a lifeboat, firearms, implements, clocks, books, assorted wines and liquors, and various other items. In return, an assortment of Japanese gifts was presented to the commodore for President Franklin Pierce, himself, and his officers and men. Everything went so well that Perry dispensed with his armed guard and even his own sidearms for his visits ashore.

The completed Treaty of Kanagawa, named for the prefecture in which Yokohama was located, was signed on 31 March 1854. It provided for a perpetually amicable relationship between the two nations and their peoples, the opening of the two Japanese ports of refuge and the right of Americans to purchase needed supplies through local officials at prices to be set later, the establishment of a consulate at Shimoda, the return of castaways to either of the two ports, most-favored-nation status for the United States, and an exchange of ratifications within eighteen months. The *Saratoga*, homeward bound, embarked Perry's fleet captain with the American copy of the treaty and sailed on 4 April, while the commodore himself visited Shimoda and Hakodate and sent his other vessels on various missions. He finally departed Japanese waters on 28 June, stopped at Okinawa to conclude the Treaty of Naha, which was similar to that of Kanagawa, and returned to Hong Kong in the *Mississippi*, ordering the *Powhatan* to visit Ningpo, Foochow, and Amoy before rejoining him.

Matthew Calbraith Perry had been a naval officer too long to expect any respite simply because he had achieved partial success in his main object, but he cannot have anticipated the problem which awaited him at Hong Kong. During his absence in Japan, ships of another American squadron had arrived, and he was confronted with two requests. Its senior officer requested that a general court-martial be convened to try its second-ranking officer; the second-ranking officer requested that a board of medical survey determine whether the senior officer was insane. To make matters worse, the junior officer was Perry's near-connection by marriage.

The East India Squadron's diplomatic mission had a hydrographic counterpart—charts and sailing directions for Japanese waters were necessary if American vessels were to avail themselves of the refuges that were to be opened to them. To provide these and to make other surveys, the Congress had authorized the formation of the North Pacific Surveying Expedition composed of five vessels: the *Vincennes*, the screw-steamer *John Hancock*, the brig *Porpoise*, the schooner *Fenimore Cooper*, and the storeship *John P. Kennedy*. Commander Cadwalader Ringgold commanded the *Vincennes* and the squadron, while Lieutenant John Rodgers, the second-ranking officer, was captain of the *John Hancock*.

This squadron had come out by way of the Cape of Good Hope; the *Vincennes* and the *Porpoise* visited Australia en route to Hong Kong, while the other vessels surveyed Gaspar and Karimata straits north of Java before joining them at the end of May. Ringgold had found the merchants at Canton alarmed at the approach of the Taiping rebels, and he doubted the *Queen's* ability to protect them. His orders stated specifically that nothing was to interfere with the surveys; nonetheless, he had the *Hancock* and the *Cooper* moored off the factories at Canton, while the *Vincennes* lay at Whampoa. The *Kennedy* and the *Porpoise* stayed at Hong Kong where the latter received extensive repairs preliminary to operations against Chinese pirates. The brig cruised in the Canton estuary without success for several weeks, and early in July she rescued 520 Chinese survivors of shipwreck on Pratas Shoal.

Meanwhile, Ringgold had been prostrated by illness at Macao and later at Canton. When Vice-Consul D. N. Spooner asked that an armed boat take him upstream from Canton to check on the rebels' advance, the commander's doctor would not permit Ringgold to be disturbed, so Lieutenant Rodgers turned to Lieutenant Taylor of the *Queen*, who readily gave his permission to the excursion. Two boats took Rodgers and Spooner to the outskirts of Fatshan from which they fell back after exchanging fire with rebel sentries. When Ringgold heard of this, he was furious, charging Rodgers with disobedience which had endangered the lives of all foreigners resident in Canton's vicinity. For his part, the lieutenant came to agree with a number of his fellows that the commander's erratic behavior was due to insanity.

This was the situation confronting Perry when he returned to Hong Kong. Taking note of the fact that the surveying expedition seemed on the verge of dissolution owing to the demoralizing effects of liquor and disease among officers and men condemned to months of idleness by Ringgold's policy, the commodore risked the charge of nepotism by ordering a medical survey of the commander. When, after a cursory examination, the surgeons reported that he was permanently insane, Perry dismissed the charges against Rodgers and appointed him to command the North Pacific Expedition in Ringgold's place.

The new senior officer reorganized his command thoroughly (no easy task because both squadrons were short of officers) and turned the storeship *Kennedy*, so rotten as to be worthless for anything but duty as guardship at Canton, over to Perry. When his remaining vessels were ready for sea, they sailed to undertake detailed surveys of Shimoda and Hakodate and a running survey of the Japanese coast. The *Porpoise* went missing with all hands south of Formosa, probably the victim of a typhoon in October, but her consorts carried out their mission, then reconnoitered in the Sea of Okhotsk, the Bering Sea, and the Arctic Ocean before meeting at San Francisco in October 1855. There Rodgers learned that the funds allocated to his command had been exhausted, so the North Pacific Surveying Expedition was disbanded.

Even as he was grappling with the Ringgold-Rodgers problem, Perry had reports from Commander Kelly of the *Plymouth* pertaining to occurrences at Shanghai to consider. During February 1854, the imperial forces in that vicinity had begun to harass foreigners. Protests to the authorities elicited the response that the officers commanding these forces could not control them, so the foreigners would have to fend for themselves. Kelly became involved when the imperial warship *Sir Herbert Compton*, manned largely by foreign adventurers, seized a pilot boat under American colors and confined its Chinese crew. Lieutenant John Guest was sent to the *Compton* with an armed boat crew and freed the prisoners without firing a shot although he and his crew were greatly outnumbered. Commander Kelly demanded that the *Compton* hoist an American flag and fire a salute to it as an apology for the insult. Thirteen days passed without compliance; then the *Plymouth* weighed anchor and stood up to the imperial fleet anchorage to enforce the demand. Kelly was promptly informed that the salute would be fired—when it had been, the sloop of war dropped back down to her mooring off the American consulate.

About two weeks later, imperial troops encamped near the international settlement's race course began to tear down a building. When its owner remonstrated, more soldiers arrived, some of whom attacked a foreign couple walking nearby. This brought a few Royal Marines to the scene, where they too were fired on. The situation seemed ominous indeed—marines and sailors from the British men-of-war *Encounter* and *Grecian* were joined by the *Plymouth*'s landing party, and together they drove the imperial troops back to their camps. That night a conference of consuls and commanding officers agreed to demand that all Chinese forces be withdrawn from the vicinity of the race course. The time limit expired without a response, so Britons and Americans, reinforced by Shanghai Volunteers from the international settlement, and merchant seamen, launched an assault on the imperial encampment on the afternoon of 4 April. Kelly's men on the left wing shelled the forces confronting them with three fieldpieces and then charged, only to be halted under fire by a deep ditch extending across their front. Thereupon, the commander ordered a flanking movement to gain cover whence enfilading volleys could be directed against the Chinese, who soon fled from the field. The British force on the other wing, having destroyed the camp it had attacked, came up behind the American target and leveled it as well. The total British and American casualties were three killed and seven wounded, of whom one of the dead and three of the wounded belonged to the *Plymouth*. After this chastisement, the imperial forces caused no more difficulty to foreigners. The *Vandalia* relieved the *Plymouth* in mid-June, and the commodore gave his hearty approval to Kelly's course of action.

With the pressing problems disposed of, Perry gave thought to his own situation. Almost two years had elapsed since his departure from the United States, the arthritis from which he had suffered intermittently for years had troubled him of late, and he could expect continued frustrating involvement with merchants, consuls, and Commissioner McLane, all of whom would be likely to wish intervention by his vessels to an impractical extent. He had earlier indicated his desire to relinquish his command on completion of the Japan mission; now he was anxious to find someone to write its narrative under his supervision, which would be impossible until he reached the United States. And he wished to return home by the European route to join his family in The Hague, where his son-in-law was serving as U.S. minister to the Netherlands.

Having turned over command of the squadron to its senior captain, the

Macedonian's Joel Abbot, Commodore Perry sailed from Hong Kong on 11 September 1854 in a steamer operated by the Peninsular and Oriental Steam Navigation Company. The *Mississippi*, laden with the records, collections, and memorabilia on which the narrative of the Japan mission was to be based, sailed for the Atlantic coast by way of Cape Horn soon afterward. With her departure, the most important single cruise in the history of the East India Squadron had come to its end.

CHAPTER SIX

Piracy and the Affair at the Barrier Forts

The East India Squadron, largest in the U.S. Navy under Commodore Matthew Calbraith Perry, quickly reverted to something approximating its more usual strength under his successor. Within two months, all vessels except the *Macedonian*, *Vandalia*, and *Powhatan* had sailed for the United States. The *Macedonian* was at Hong Kong, virtually immobilized by the detachment of seamen and marines from her company to man the *Queen* and the *John P. Kennedy* off Canton, while the *Vandalia* remained at Shanghai and the *Powhatan* was kept in readiness to exchange ratifications of the Treaty of Kanagawa.

Perry had cited his indifferent health as a reason for transferring his command to Joel Abbot; the latter might well have refused to accept it on similar grounds. A digestive complaint forced him to attend to squadron affairs from his bed during most of the autumn of 1854, and, although his health improved somewhat for a time thereafter, he was never really in good physical condition. But Abbot insisted that he had no right to leave the station until properly relieved or so ordered by higher authority, nor did he do so.

Piracy was the most urgent problem immediately confronting Abbot. The unsettled conditions in China had led to a proliferation of lawlessness generally, and the thriving commerce of the Canton River estuary attracted the attention of numerous armed junks. Reports of attacks on ships carrying goods of American ownership caused the *Queen*, now commanded by Lieutenant George H. Preble, to be sent to Hong Kong in October

76

1854. Operating from there, she cooperated with small British vessels in searching for survivors of piratical forays and then attacked a pirate fleet moored in Lantao Island's Taiho harbor. The *Queen* steamed in boldly and forced two of the junks to retire, but shoal water prevented her from closing the others and she lacked the means to carry them by boarding. Preble then sought assistance from Rear Admiral Sir James Stirling at Hong Kong, who gladly ordered HMS *Encounter* and armed boats from his larger vessels to join the *Queen*. Standing into Taiho harbor, the *Encounter* opened fire with her 10-inch gun, scoring several hits and causing the hasty abandonment of the junks and of the nearest village. Boarding parties took possession of all; after the junks had been examined for proof of piracy, their guns were removed and seventeen were burned. During the night, Chinese fishermen entered the bay to attack pirates attempting to escape in small craft, and the next morning local officials thanked the British and American officers for ridding them of the marauders.

This very satisfactory engagement led Admiral Stirling to plan a much larger operation against Khulan, a notorious pirate lair on an island nearby. Lieutenant Preble agreed to participate, and on 11 November the *Encounter* led seven men-of-war, some extemporised, to an anchorage near Khulan, whence the light-draft steamers, including the *Queen*, towed the heavier vessels' boats close inshore to attack junks and shore batteries. Casting off her tow, the *Queen* steamed toward the nearest junk, maintaining a steady fire from her howitzer until she ran aground. When it became apparent that the little paddler's light guns were ineffectual, Preble joined the landing force with the four men of his gig's crew. By the time the boats were recalled, fifty junks, three villages, and three shore batteries had been destroyed. Ninety pirates were thought to have been killed, and, as usual in these affrays, losses to the assaulting force were incredibly light, with a seaman from the *Macedonian* the only American fatality.

Abbot commended Preble and his little *Queen* for their vigorous part in these effective actions against the pirates, but, on learning that the steamer's charter had been renewed, Secretary of the Navy James C. Dobbin wrote Abbot that no money had been appropriated for that purpose. "It is for Congress to increase the Navy, not the Department."[1] And, despite the fact that Abbot had acted on the advice of Perry and Commissioner Robert McLane in rechartering the *Queen*, the U.S. government persisted in charging the amount paid her owners to Commodore Abbot's estate after his death.

Fleets of imperial and rebel war junks clashed in Whampoa Reach on 29 December in full view of the *Macedonian* and Admiral Stirling's flagship. The imperial forces lost the fight and withdrew through the line of foreign merchantmen in the anchorage, with the rebels in pursuit. Although the merchant vessels suffered no loss, the American vice-consul wrote a condemnatory letter to Abbot the next day, charging that he and Stirling had shirked their duty by refusing to intervene and stating that the foreign merchants were justifiably alarmed at their inactivity. Defending his policy in a dispatch to Navy Secretary Dobbin, Abbot expressed the belief that the merchants were conspiring to use the British and American squadrons to prevent a rebel attack on Canton. Such an action would be unneutral and, the commodore thought, unwise: "For I believe that China will never be improved until it is completely revolutionized." However, he and Admiral Stirling had made the preparations necessary to protect the foreigners and their property in any eventuality; indeed, the cooperation between the two commanders in chief was "most friendly and harmonious," their views of their respective responsibilities being virtually the same.[2]

Disagreements between merchants and naval officers continued so long as Canton was threatened by the rebels, but that threat disappeared suddenly in the spring of 1855 when division of the Taiping forces enabled their imperial foes to defeat them decisively.

A cordial relationship existed between the British and American naval forces at Shanghai as well. Captain John Pope of the *Vandalia* reported that the situation in the vicinity of that city was very confused and that French sailors and marines appeared to be cooperating with the imperial troops against the rebels still holding Shanghai. When a joint attack was repulsed, the international settlement seemed to be endangered so the *Vandalia* and the British men-of-war in the Hwangpoo landed almost all of their men, and Pope called on the North Pacific Expedition's *John Hancock* and *Fenimore Cooper*, also moored there, to contribute to the settlement's defense. The tense situation was eased when the rebels evacuated the city during the spring.

With the situation at Canton no longer requiring his presence, the commodore sailed up to Shanghai, whence in June he sent the "most excellent and valuable" Preble with an armed party in the towboat *Confucius* to visit Foochow and Ningpo.[3] In the course of this cruise, the *Confucius* helped to escort a convoy of 250 junks laden with timber to Ningpo and participated in the destruction of five pirate vessels. A month later, Preble in the *Confucius* joined British vessels for an anti-pirate cruise in the Yellow Sea. This foray ended prematurely when the coal brig *Clown* foundered in heavy seas. Her men were picked up, but the force had to return for want of coal after touching at Weihaiwei and Chefoo. No pirates were encountered.

However, Lieutenant Preble was not the only pirate-hunter in the East

India Squadron. HMS *Rattler* stood into Hong Kong early in August, and Commander William A. Fellowes requested assistance in attacking a pirate fleet that he had chased into Khulan. His screw-sloop drew too much water to get within range of the anchorage, and she had too few boats to carry an adequate assault force. The *Powhatan* promptly dispatched 100 seamen and marines in three boats, each mounting a howitzer, under the command of Lieutenant Robert B. Pegram. The *Rattler* towed the boats to Khulan, then manned her own, and the small English steamer *Eaglet* took them all in tow. When the pirate fleet was sighted, it opened an ineffectual fire which the *Eaglet* answered with five rockets. Thereupon, thirty-four junks made sail to escape and five boats cast off, their crews pulling lustily in pursuit and firing shrapnel from their howitzers as they came into range. Round shot and grape splashed around them, but the pirates' fire was typically inaccurate and did no harm. The *Powhatan*'s Lieutenant Henry Rolando took first honors, hoisting American colors in a large junk with a loud cheer. Fellowes and Pegram boarded another junk simultaneously; then Fellowes, who had only five musketeers in his gig, tackled a third. Rolando came to help him. As they boarded, the junk's magazine exploded, blowing the two officers and a number of "Powhatans" overboard and capsizing the gig. Rolando's boat picked them up while the others, undeterred by the mishap, continued the engagement. When the action ended, nine pirate junks and a like number of their prizes were in Anglo-American hands; of an estimated 1,000 pirates, about half were thought to be casualties. The junk explosion made this operation more costly than usual for the attackers—the *Powhatan* counted five dead and eight wounded, while the *Rattler* had four fatalities and seven wounded.

Such operations convinced Abbot that at least one small steamer should be attached to the squadron permanently; he thought a vessel such as the *Confucius* would contribute more to the protection of American interests in China than all of the Navy's frigates and ships of the line. Having heard that U.S. relations with Spain had been strained by the obvious desire of the Franklin Pierce administration to annex Cuba, he added that his squadron would do very well to capture Manila, which he was prepared to undertake, but even for that operation, a light-draft steamer would be very useful.

The commodore had hoped to visit Japan during the summer, but his business at Shanghai was not concluded until September, by which time a cholera epidemic had begun. The *Macedonian* had several deaths from cholera and dysentery, and, with a binnacle list numbering seventy, Abbot decided that Japan was out of the question. As soon as the spring tide enabled her to cross the bar, the flagship proceeded to an anchorage near the Saddle Islands and there she spent several weeks while her men recuperated in the sea air. She went on to Hong Kong in late October, where the *Powhatan*, ordered home, embarked those of her invalids condemned by medical survey.

Commodore Abbot himself was so ill that the surgeons held out little hope of his recovery and that only if he departed the station as soon as possible, which he would not do until relieved. Through November, his condition worsened steadily. Early in December he was moved to Storekeeper Robert DeSilver's residence in Hong Kong's Spring Gardens area, whence he continued to devote himself to squadron affairs.

On 13 December 1855, Joel Abbot dictated his last letter to the Navy Department. The consul at Manila wished him to send a warship to investigate the suffocation of 200 coolies in a vessel's hold, but the dying commodore could do no more than report the request.

He died the next morning, and on 16 December his remains, sealed in a lead coffin, were escorted to the pier by a guard of Her Majesty's 59th Regiment, sent by Governor Sir John Bowring, and by Royal Marines from Admiral Stirling's squadron. As the coffin was embarked in the commodore's barge, the *Macedonian* began to fire the thirteen minute guns due his rank; when her guns fell silent, the final salute was taken up by a British shore battery and then by HMS *Winchester*, a gesture of respect which ended only when the coffin was hoisted on board the *Macedonian*.

By this time, the squadron consisted of only two vessels, the *John P. Kennedy* having been sold in November. Captain Pope assumed command of the *Macedonian* and sent the *Vandalia* to Manila in response to the consul's request.

The latter's commanding officer could do nothing beyond reporting the facts of the case. The master of the ship *Waverly* had died at sea, so her mate took her into Manila. There the coolie passengers were said to have risen against the crew, who then drove the Chinese into the hold. According to the *Waverly*'s men, the Spanish authorities directed that the coolies be kept there until arrangements could be made for landing them. When the ship's hatches were opened, 251 coolies were found dead, whereupon the officers and men were imprisoned and held without trial.

Upon the *Vandalia*'s return to Hong Kong, Pope took the *Macedonian* to Singapore to await the arrival of Commodore James Armstrong who was coming out in the screw-frigate *San Jacinto*. It proved to be a lengthy wait, for the *San Jacinto* had to repair storm damage at Simonstown, the Royal Navy's South African dockyard, and engine trouble delayed her at Penang. Townsend Harris, who had been appointed to negotiate a more satisfactory treaty with Siam and to open the U.S. consulate at Shimoda, joined the ship there. The screw-frigate reached Singapore early in April, two weeks after Captain Pope had begun to fear that some accident had befallen her. The "Macedonians" gave their relief a hearty welcome—now they could begin their homeward passage—but the *San Jacinto*'s company cannot have found much comfort in the report that the *Macedonian* had lost 105 men to dysentery, cholera, and other illnesses during a commission of more than three years.

From Singapore, the *San Jacinto* proceeded to the anchorage at the head of the Gulf of Siam, whence Harris, Armstrong, and a retinue of officers ascended the Menam River to Bangkok. Six weeks sufficed to conclude the diplomat's business there; then the flagship sailed for China.

The sloop of war *Levant*, the *Vandalia*'s relief, saluted the commodore's broad pennant when the *San Jacinto* stood into Hong Kong in mid-June, but the third vessel assigned to the squadron, the larger sloop of war *Portsmouth*, was still on her outward passage—she would arrive in August. Armstrong ordered the *Levant* to Shanghai with Dr. Peter Parker, now U.S. commissioner to China, while the flagship's engineers put her temperamental engines in condition to take Consul General Harris to Japan.

The *San Jacinto* got underway on 10 July, but, when her engines were reversed, the blades of her propeller struck the rudderpost violently and she had to anchor again. A diver reported that the screw, which apparently had worked loose on the shaft, was resting against the rudderpost, so that the vessel was disabled. Two days later, towboats took her up to Whampoa for docking. Hulks were brought alongside, and, in spite of a driving rainstorm, coal and stores were discharged into them until the ship was light enough to enter the dock. When the dock was pumped out, closer inspection showed that the diameter of the propeller shaft had been reduced by galvanic action to the extent that the screw was free to slide between sternpost and rudderpost.

During the next two weeks, First Assistant Engineer Andrew Lawton and his men worked to key the screw securely to the weakened shaft, while other members of the black gang fitted new pump strainers and overhauled the engines generally. The chief engineer was seriously ill with dysentery, and the absence of his authority was very noticeable. Some of the junior engineers, dissatisfied with their inferior social status, quarters, and, most of all, their pay (they could have earned two or three times as much had they been civilians in Hong Kong), had tried to resign their commissions earlier, but Armstrong had refused to accept them because replacements were not available. One of them, "a very insubordinate, disrespectful, discontented, and unhappy tempered man," preferred charges against Lawton after the latter had reprimanded him for dereliction of duty; again, the commodore took no action because a trial would deprive the vessel of indispensable engineers for some time.[4]

Indeed, the weeks in dock were trying for everyone. The fleet surgeon condemned Whampoa as "a miserable, marsh-surrounded, pestilential anchorage," although the incessant rain was credited with keeping the miasma arising from the marshes to a minimum.[5] But the rain also kept the men wet much of the time, a condition they tried to alleviate by immoderate consumption of the whiskey that was smuggled on board in quantity despite the most rigorous efforts to prevent such smuggling. It is not surprising that the binnacle list increased alarmingly under these conditions.

Her repairs completed, the San Jacinto dropped down to Hong Kong to fill her water tanks and embark Townsend Harris. She put to sea in mid-August, weathered a gale two days later, and then succored some of its victims. The first of these gale victims was a single Chinaman on a bamboo raft, the sole survivor of a junk that had foundered with thirty-six of his fellows. Later that afternoon, four dismasted junks were sighted. Three were provided food, water, and such articles of equipment as would permit them to reach port, while the fourth, a war junk, was leaking so badly that her fifty-three officers and men were taken off during the night and she was burned.

At Shimoda, it took the threat of the San Jacinto's double-shotted guns to persuade the Japanese that Consul General Harris should be allowed to establish himself ashore. An unused temple was provided for him to reside in, and the frigate's sailors erected a flagstaff so that the consular flag might be displayed properly. Thereafter, Townsend Harris signified his willingness to dispense with the warship's protection, so she sailed for Shanghai early in September, leaving him to endure a year of virtual isolation.

Upon the San Jacinto's arrival at Shanghai, Commodore Armstrong sent the Levant to Hong Kong with orders for Commander Andrew H. Foote to bring his command, the Portsmouth, to Shanghai. However, the Portsmouth was at Whampoa when the Levant reached Hong Kong, and Foote, who was guarding the American factories at Canton with eighty of his men, declined to depart. Instead, he ordered the Levant's Commander William Smith to come up the river with reinforcements from his ship's company as soon as possible.

The difficulty that had caused Commander Foote to ascend the Canton River was the beginning of a second Anglo-Chinese War. A piratical lorcha known as the Arrow had been seized by Chinese forces and her crew imprisoned. British Consul Harry Parkes protested that the lorcha had been registered in Hong Kong; therefore, she was a British vessel and the crew should be delivered to him for investigation and for punishment if he found them guilty. Finally, Chinese Commissioner Yeh Ming-chin yielded the prisoners under protest, but he refused to apologize for the insult to the British flag. In reality, there had been no insult because the lorcha's British registry had expired some weeks before she was seized, yet Governor Bowring supported Parkes's demand on the ground that the *Arrow*'s captors could not have been aware of her registry's expiration; if their action were condoned, a harmful precedent would have been set. British forces were ordered to advance on Canton, and U.S. Consul Oliver H. Perry, the commodore's son who had been appointed to his post through family influence, requested a guard for the American factories.

Foote, who arrived on 23 October, lost no time in organizing his forces and choosing positions whence his men could defend the area, including the French vice-consulate which adjoined the American grounds. Commander Smith reached Canton on 27 October with 69 men and the *Levant*'s boat howitzer, giving Foote more than 150 officers and men and 2 field pieces. By this time, the situation had become more serious; British warships and troops under Rear Admiral Sir Michael Seymour were attacking Chinese fortifications, and the American steamer *Cum Fa* reported that she had been fired on by the Chinese while traversing the Macao Passage a short distance from the factories. Commander Foote held daily battalion drills before crowds of interested Cantonese, many of whom probably welcomed the spectacle as a novel form of entertainment, although others doubtless considered the drills provocative.

Two days after the arrival of the "Levants," Seymour's assault force fought its way through Canton's wall which had been breached by naval gunfire. The Britons were accompanied by a few Americans, who brazenly displayed their nation's flag on the city wall. Foote promptly condemned this action as unneutral and ordered that it not be repeated; since Commissioner Yeh made no protest, he hoped that the flag had escaped Chinese notice. A few days later, random shots in the vicinity of American sentries caused the commander to order that the Chinese responsible be fired on, although no casualties seem to have resulted. Yeh overlooked this incident also; indeed, Foote reported that the commissioner was very courteous to Americans. He asked, however, that the commander and his countrymen leave Canton for their own safety. Nothing was further from Foote's mind—he urged Perry to send Yeh an ultimatum demanding satisfaction for the firing on the *Cum Fa* within forty-eight hours, but the news of Commodore Armstrong's presence at Hong Kong prevented this precipitate act.

The flagship anchored in Whampoa Reach on 12 November. Commander Foote came down to Whampoa two days later, and, after conferring with him and with representatives of the merchant and missionary communities, Armstrong decided that the force at Canton constituted a provocation that the Chinese could not ignore indefinitely. Therefore, it should be withdrawn and the *Levant*, the squadron's smallest unit, was to be towed to an anchorage off the factories where she could provide a refuge for those American citizens remaining in the vicinity.

Foote left the flagship on 15 November to arrange the withdrawal, but that evening he returned to report that the Chinese "Barrier Forts" halfway between Whampoa and Canton had fired five rounds at his boat in spite of the American flag clearly visible at its stern. No damage had resulted, but such an affront could not be excused. Commander Foote and the *San Jacinto*'s Commander Henry H. Bell were sent to procure steamers to tow the sloops of war and to bring most of the men back to their ships, leaving Commander Smith with a small force to defend the consulate.

Sunday, 16 November 1856, was clear and pleasant, with light airs barely ruffling the river's surface as an armed cutter from the flagship pulled upstream to sound the channel leading to the offending forts. These opened fire when she had approached within a half mile, and the boat retired after her coxswain had been killed by a projectile as he was heaving the lead. Meanwhile, the *Cum Fa* had towed the squadron's boats down from Canton by another passage. The men of the landing force were reembarked, but the boats were not hoisted to their davits lest they be damaged by Chinese fire when the ships came into range. The *San Jacinto* drew too much water to participate in the operation, so the bulk of her company was divided between the *Portsmouth* and the *Levant*, with the commodore hoisting his broad pennant in the former while Bell assumed command of the *Levant* in Smith's absence.

At 3 P.M. both ships were cleared for action and their men went to battle stations. The *Portsmouth* took a hawser from the American steamer *Willamette*, while the *Levant*, towed by the *Cum Fa*, followed the temporary flagship upstream.

An old adage holds that ships cannot fight forts successfully without overwhelming superiority of firepower, and certainly the odds were all on the side of the latter on this occasion. These were not the traditional Chinese fortifications, of which it was said that the dragons depicted on their walls were intended to frighten enemies away, but four formidable bastions of European design, mounting 176 guns, some of which were 8 inches or more in caliber. The *Portsmouth*, on the other hand, had been rearmed with sixteen new Dahlgren 8-inch shell guns before commissioning for the East India Squadron, while the slightly older *Levant* mounted eighteen short 32-pounders and four of the new Dahlgrens. Further, the

FIGURE 6–1. The *Portsmouth* in action against the Barrier Forts.

narrow channel precluded any effort at evasive maneuvering; the ships would have to fight at anchor, presenting stationary targets to the Chinese gunners. But the odds were apparent only, for neither forts nor ships can be more effective than the soldiers and sailors who man them. The Chinese were courageous and fought better than they had in the Opium War; but they were to prove no match for Americans who were thoroughly disciplined, well acquainted with their weapons, confident of their superiority, and ably led.

Standing upstream, the *Cum Fa* and the *Levant* had the misfortune to stray from the channel. The sloop of war grounded out of range of the forts and could not be refloated before nightfall. The *Willamette*, conned by her imperturbable civilian master, Captain William Curry, towed the *Portsmouth* to an anchorage 500 yards from the nearest of the forts, all of which opened a well-aimed fire as the vessels approached. A number of projectiles passed through the warship's rigging, and an occasional crash indicated those that hit her hull. When Commander Foote gave the order to commence firing, his men sprang to the task with a will, serving their big smoothbores with a rapidity and precision their opponents could not rival. Repeatedly the Chinese fire slackened under the pounding of the

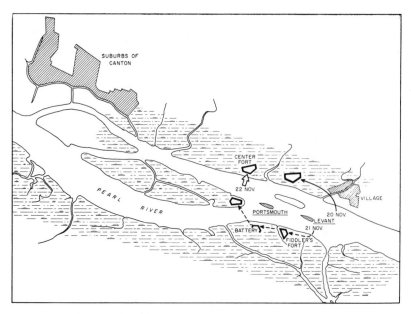

MAP 6–1.   The Affair at the Barrier Forts

Portsmouth's guns, only to renew its intensity whenever the Americans' firing slowed. By the time increasing darkness made it difficult to discern targets, however, the nearest fort had been silenced while the fire of the other forts was said to have "languished." The warship's executive officer reported that her hull had sustained six hits, only one of which, through a stern frame, was at all serious; her one casualty, a marine, had been wounded badly by the same projectile.

During the night, the *Levant* was towed into range and the *Portsmouth* kedged closer to the forts, but a fresh north-northwesterly wind caused the latter to drag into shallow water where the ebbing tide left her aground. The forts' garrisons showed no desire to resume the action, so a rainy Monday passed without a shot being fired. When the flood tide floated the temporary flagship in the course of the afternoon, she sought a more secure anchorage and warped her port broadside to bear on the nearest fort. Soon afterward, Commodore Armstrong returned to the *San Jacinto* to begin a correspondence with Yeh, hoping to reach an understanding which would make further hostilities unnecessary.

Meanwhile, the sailing warships kept their guns trained on the forts and rowed guard by night to minimize the danger of a surprise attack. Commander Smith rejoined his ship from Canton, relieving Bell who went to the flagship in the *Cum Fa* during the afternoon of 19 October with a communication from Foote to the effect that the Chinese were busily strengthening the forts and showed no sign of pacific intent. This news might well have brought Armstrong back to the *Portsmouth*; instead, he wrote Foote, authorizing him to use his own discretion, even to the extent of capturing the forts if the commander thought it necessary.

The bellicose Foote needed no urging. Both vessels opened fire on the two nearest forts the next morning. The Chinese responded vigorously five minutes later; when their fire slackened noticeably after more than an hour, three columns of boats pulled toward the north shore, each of the three commanders leading the contingent from his ship. The accidental discharge of a minié rifle killed two apprentice boys as the force landed, but the 285 officers and men remaining quickly fell into formation for a flanking march across rice fields and a creek to attack the fort from the rear. Some opposition was encountered in a village through which the force had to pass, but a few shots from the howitzers dragged along by sailors cleared the way. The marines led the assault on the first fort. Its garrison departed under their fire, and the American flag was soon displayed above its ramparts. An artillery duel between this fort and the next then ensued, with the latter having the worst of it although one of its shots sank the *Portsmouth*'s launch before it was silenced. When a sizable Chinese force was reported approaching from Canton, Captain John D. Simms led his marines to meet it; this and subsequent attacks were repulsed with ease by the greatly outnumbered "soldiers of the sea." Meanwhile, sailors were spiking guns and destroying their carriages. Toward the end of the day, Commanders Foote and Smith returned to their vessels, leaving all of the marines and most of the sailors with Bell to hold the fort.

The so-called "Fiddler's fort" on the south shore opened fire on the *Portsmouth* in the early morning darkness of 21 November, scoring an 8-inch hit near her waterline. Two rounds from her own 8-inch guns ended the exchange, after which Bell and his men were recalled and at first light the *Cum Fa* towed the *Levant* as close to the barrier as the latter's draft would permit. Both ships then directed their fire against the Fiddler's fort while the little steamer towed the lines of boats, carrying about the same force as on the preceding day, to the beach. Forts on the north shore and on an island in midstream kept the warships and the boats under fire; one of their shots struck the *San Jacinto*'s launch, killing three men and wounding seven. Again, the Chinese garrison fled as the assault party approached, so the Fiddler's fort was soon firing on its island neighbor while American sailors and marines disabled its other guns. A howitzer did good service lobbing shells into the island fort, which was abandoned during the afternoon and occupied some time later, after a battery between the two forts had been carried.

The remaining fort on the north shore was captured in the same fashion the next morning. Its defenders poured a hail of fire on the approaching boats, but, by "the merciful interposition of a kind Providence," thought Foote, no one of the attack force was hit.[6] The fort was abandoned by its captors after its guns had been disabled.

Commander Foote boarded the *Portsmouth* later in the morning. His men greeted him with six cheers, and, after refreshing himself, he departed for Whampoa in the *Cum Fa* which towed a boat containing the remains of those who had been killed during the operation. Commodore Armstrong received him with congratulations, and the two officers agreed that the forts should be demolished as thoroughly as their means would permit.

This task required another two weeks of hard labor. During this time, a demolition mine exploded prematurely, killing two and wounding a like number, and a number of men had to be returned to their ships because of illness. A Chinese surprise attack on the night of 26 November, which was repulsed without loss, proved to be the last exchange of fire connected with "the affair at the barrier forts."

The final cost to the attackers was reckoned at ten men dead and twenty-five wounded. The *Portsmouth* was hit twenty-seven times in hull and rigging, while the *Levant*, which was not engaged on 20 November, counted twenty-two hits. Both vessels had completed repairs before they left the river. The Chinese loss was reckoned by some to amount to 500, but Commander Foote thought half that number a more realistic estimate.

Meanwhile, Commodore Armstrong had been carrying on an exchange of views with Commissioner Yeh in a correspondence which was characterized by the usual circumspection and which gave no hint that Americans and Chinese were engaged in combat even as it was in progress. Yeh indicated his belief that the Americans were practically looking for trouble, citing the presence of those with Admiral Seymour's assault force on 29 October. The commissioner held that there was no reason for any Sino-American difficulty—let the Americans withdraw from Canton until the problems with the British had been solved and all would be well. The commodore refused to agree to this because two European consulates remained unmolested; why should not the Americans be treated as well? The correspondence came to a close in mid-December with Yeh requesting a description of the American flag so that no future mistakes would be made. Armstrong replied that the flag was well known and could be seen at the American consulate; nonetheless, he appended a description and asked that Yeh issue a proclamation commanding all Chinese to show

FIGURE 6–2.   The *Cum Fa* towing the landing force to the shore while the *Portsmouth* (*foreground*) and the *Levant* fire on the Barrier Forts.

that flag due respect. The commodore also promised that his forces would take care not to get involved in belligerent operations.

U.S. Commissioner Peter Parker, reviewing the whole matter, concluded that it had been handled well and that Armstrong should not press for an apology. "To have stopped short of the point you did had been an error, now, without fresh reasons, to pursue it farther inexpedient."[7] And Secretary of the Navy Dobbin agreed: "Had the offensive act been temporarily submitted to and referred to the tardy process of Chinese explanations, this trifling with our flag would probably have been repeated and led to still more serious consequences." Dobbin went on to praise the "gallantry, good order and 'intelligent subordination' displayed by all in the various conflicts." He added: "But, Sir, I cannot permit myself to let this occasion pass without impressively assuring you of the earnest anxiety of your Government and our Countrymen to cultivate and maintain friendly relations with the people and Government of China."[8]

Not all contemporaries agreed. The *Portsmouth*'s Lieutenant Henry K. Davenport, who had been with Foote at the factories, firmly believed that the affair at the barrier forts had been entirely unnecessary. In his view, a marine guard in the U.S. consulate at Canton would have maintained the dignity of the flag without provoking the Chinese. He accused Commander Foote of exhibiting his force in a deliberately provocative manner, hoping to incite hostilities in which he might distinguish himself. Davenport reported that there was practically no property to protect in the factories, since trade had been halted, and that American civilians remaining there were simply waiting "to 'see the fun.'" The lieutenant further charged that Foote had sited his sentries and howitzers in locations whence they provided assistance to the British forces operating against the city. He denounced Commodore Armstrong as "Aunt Sally," an "old woman" who was completely under his vigorous subordinate's domination and who would not even stay at the scene of action.[9]

Complaints by junior officers against their seniors cannot be accepted without some support, but Davenport's accusations ring true at least so far as Foote's actions are concerned. The commander's own reports reveal that he enjoyed "playing soldier" at Canton, and the commodore's decision to withdraw the force indicates that it was unnecessary and provocative in his view. The lieutenant's account of the dearth of property and the motives of the Americans there is borne out by the fact that they left the factories readily soon after the forts had been destroyed. Andrew Hull Foote won deserved praise for his conduct of the attack on the barrier forts; he should have been censured for his role in making the attack necessary.

In retrospect, however, James Armstrong seems to have been a stronger commander in chief than Davenport thought. The incident of 15 November, stemming from Foote's course of action before the commodore arrived, made some punitive action mandatory, but Armstrong kept it within certain bounds, issuing strong orders forbidding retention of any articles taken from the captured forts and prohibiting any foraging whatsoever. Sir Michael Seymour, whose force was not adequate to protect its line of communications and launch an effective attack on Canton simultaneously, suggested that the Americans join the British to guarantee passage of the river. The commodore refused, reluctantly to be sure, but when Foote urged the same cooperation, he too received a negative reply.

Armstrong had to withstand pressure from others as well. Former Vice-Consul D. N. Spooner, returning to the United States after twenty years with Russell and Company at Canton, denounced the East India Squadron's inactivity and threatened to undertake a newspaper campaign exposing its failure to protect American citizens from "insult, injury, and hazard."[10] Other merchants tried to get the U.S. naval force involved against the Chinese in their own interest, to no avail. Consul Perry, himself a former naval officer, wrote Peter Parker that the graves of sailors and marines killed at the barrier forts had been desecrated by the Chinese (Admiral Seymour later ascertained that this report was false), adding the hope that Armstrong would "rouse himself up and assume *some responsibility*, sufficient at least to protect American lives and defend them, so far as his present force will admit, against insult and murder."[11]

Following the demolition of the forts, the *Portsmouth, Levant,* and *Cum Fa* dropped down to Whampoa; however, the *Portsmouth* grounded on the way and spent some twenty hours on a shoal before she could be kedged off at high water. On 12 December, Commodore Armstrong had the *Levant* towed to an anchorage off Canton; she was withdrawn a week later after all U.S. citizens, including the consul, had departed and the factories had been burned by the Chinese. Thereafter, the squadron dropped down to Hong Kong, where the commodore agreed to the request of American shipmasters, forwarded by Governor Bowring, that its boats row guard around the merchant ship anchorage at night.

The *San Jacinto* and the *Levant* were still at Hong Kong when, in mid-January, an apparent plot to poison the entire foreign community resulted in the illness of some 500 people, including Commander Smith and several of his officers. A Chinese baker was charged with including arsenic in the ingredients of his bread; although Britons and Americans alike were convinced of his guilt, a British jury found the evidence insufficient to convict him.

The *Levant* embarked the *San Jacinto*'s invalids in late February and sailed to Manila in the hope of finding a homeward-bound merchantman in which they could be embarked. At Manila, Commander Smith conferred with the U.S. consul and Spanish authorities about the unfortunate *Waverly* seamen who were still in prison. He learned that a Spanish marine court had sentenced them to imprisonment in Morocco and that a superior court would consider their appeal within a short time. Having ascertained that the men were confined in comfortable quarters, Smith could do no more than to wish them well before he departed for Shanghai.

A visit to Manila remained a perilous venture; smallpox made its dread appearance among the *Levant*'s crew after she put to sea. By the time she reached Shanghai, four men had died and twenty-seven were ill. The sickbay was overcrowded, so the most severe cases were lodged under the forecastle where they were "exposed to a continuance of cold and rainy weather, while their quarters were deluged and cots soaked by the water rushing in through the hawseholes and the bow and bridle ports."[12] Apparently the less-seriously ill received better treatment because their chances of survival were greater. Upon reaching Shanghai, Smith rented a house ashore where those suffering from smallpox could receive more adequate care; only one man died there.

The *Levant* had been ordered to Shanghai for docking to repair the bottom damage sustained when she grounded off the barrier. Her experience was an example of the disadvantage of reliance on a commercial dock—a merchant vessel was in the dock when she arrived, another was waiting her turn, and Smith thought the *Levant* would follow her. But then Russell and Company's *Antelope* steamed up the Hwangpoo, and the commander learned that she too had a prior claim to be docked. Thus, the *Levant*'s Shanghai visit lasted several weeks longer than expected.

The flagship remained at Hong Kong. In March, Dr. Parker wrote from Macao to inform the commodore of a reported plot to destroy all of the merchant steamers plying the Canton estuary and to ask that the *San Jacinto* be moored in the passage where the attacks were supposed to occur. Armstrong refused; so far as he could learn, the Chinese had no inimical intent toward Americans.

Three leading commercial houses—Russell, King, and Augustine Heard —received a similar response two weeks later when they suggested that the East India Squadron take steps to prevent other vessels from sharing the fate of the small steamers *Thistle* and *Queen*. The commodore pointed out that both had been captured by Chinese embarked in them; thus, owners could provide for the safety of their craft by hiring only European or American crew members and by arming their officers.

A problem not connected with the Chinese situation must have been almost welcome to Commodore Armstrong. The master of the American merchantman *Coeur de Lion* reported that British officials at Singapore had deprived her company of salvage by transferring the Dutch merchant bark *Henrietta Maria*, which she had saved from stranding, to a warship sent from Batavia. The *Portsmouth* had come in from Amoy by this time, and Foote was ordered to take her to Singapore to investigate the incident. The commander found the British apologetic, and the governor accepted full responsibility, whereupon Foote entered a formal protest against his action. Four months later, British law officers agreed that the governor had acted illegally in depriving the bark's salvors of their reward; therefore, salvage would be paid the *Coeur de Lion*'s company by the colonial government at Singapore.

Consul Robert C. Murphy at Shanghai had been regarded highly by naval officers; thus it was disappointing to learn in May that he had written the State Department to complain that "it has been the habit of the China portion of our squadron to remain at anchor at Hong Kong more than half their cruise, coming to Shanghai only when they want money."[13] The commodore defended the disposition of his squadron— with no more than three vessels, he could not keep the treaty ports constantly under surveillance; furthermore, the Canton region was generally the most turbulent while that about Shanghai was remarkable for its tranquility. Moreover, Hong Kong was the most conveniently located for the receipt of dispatches, whether from the United States or from other parts of the station. This explanation satisfied the Navy Department, but Murphy was only the first of the consuls to complain about the squadron's lack of attention to Shanghai.

By mid-June, the *San Jacinto* had been in the Canton estuary for seven months. Surprisingly enough, most of her men remained in good health, but Commodore Armstrong and a number of the older officers were noticing the effects of the climate, so he decided that a visit to Shanghai might be beneficial. On ascending the Yangtze estuary, the flagship encountered the *Levant*, aground on a bank off Woosung. The sloop of war had taken the ground at noon on 19 June; since that time, her company had lightened ship and were laying out kedge anchors when the *San Jacinto* stood into sight. The latter furnished such assistance as she could, and the *Levant* was refloated, apparently undamaged, at high water on 22 June. The commodore sent her to Woosung to replenish her fresh water, which had been pumped overboard, and then to Hong Kong.

The *Portsmouth*, which had paid a visit to Siam after departing Singapore, reached Shanghai in July. She was docked to replace the copper lost in the Canton River; then Foote was ordered to Japan, which had been entirely neglected by the East India Squadron for more than a year. The *Portsmouth* was received properly by the Japanese and very cordially by Townsend Harris. The latter had put his year of isolation to good use by winning the confidence of the Japanese and negotiating a convention which enlarged American rights in the open ports and extended the principle of extraterritoriality to both signatories. Since its completion, he had been working on a commercial agreement which he hoped might be concluded in Edo, as it was in March 1858.

After a week at Shimoda, the *Portsmouth* went on to Hakodate. Here, in the absence of a consul, her commanding officer had to deal directly with the Japanese. He did so in characteristically brusque fashion, asserting the warship's right to ignore certain port regulations and acquiring a supply of fresh beef for her sailors by threatening to use force.

Following this "amicable" visit to Hakodate, the *Portsmouth* returned to Hong Kong, to which, on 6 November 1857, she and the *Levant* welcomed the USS *Minnesota*, harbinger of a new East India Squadron.

CHAPTER SEVEN

The Treaty of Tientsin and the Squadron's Termination

The Anglo-Chinese conflict was developing into a full-scale war as 1857 came to an end. Lord Palmerston's government in Britain held that Sir John Bowring's policy vis-à-vis the *Arrow* incident could not be reversed without an intolerable loss of British prestige in the Far East; nonetheless, the governor was recalled for his mishandling of the incident, and his successor, the earl of Elgin, was empowered to make war or peace according to his appraisal of the situation. A third power became involved when the Emperor Napoleon III of France decided to seek redress for the murder of a Roman Catholic priest in China. The Sepoy Mutiny in India delayed the increment of British forces, but, by the end of the year, Elgin was in a position to demand satisfaction from Chinese Commissioner Yeh Ming-chin. When this was not forthcoming, Britain and France declared war on the Chinese Empire.

Six months earlier, Secretary of the Navy Isaac Toucey had written Commodore James Armstrong that the new screw-frigate *Minnesota*, the *Mississippi*, and the sailing sloop of war *Germantown*, all nearly ready for sea, were to join his flag. However, this reinforcement was more apparent than real, for the time was approaching when the *San Jacinto*, *Portsmouth*, and *Levant* would have to leave the station because their crews' enlistments were expiring. Moreover, the *Minnesota*, the squadron's most powerful unit, was to be kept at the disposal of William B. Reed, the first U.S. diplomat since Caleb Cushing to be accredited to the Chinese government with the rank of envoy extraordinary and minister plenipoten-

95

tiary. Indeed, the minister had some control over the entire squadron, for the commodore was directed to heed his wishes even to the extent of concentrating all of the warships at any point that Reed might designate.

Another communication informed Commodore Armstrong that the Congress had finally moved to establish a naval rank senior to that of captain, "commodore" being merely a courtesy title. Unwilling to accept any of the various grades of admiral with their supposedly aristocratic connotations, the congressmen settled on the cumbersome appellation "flag officer," to be borne by each captain commanding a squadron for the duration of that command. A square, blue flag at his flagship's mizzen truck replaced the traditional broad pennant at the main, but the flag officer remained a commodore so far as most of his subordinates were concerned.

Canton fell to Anglo-French forces in January 1858, and Commissioner Yeh was sent to exile in India by his British captors. A lull followed, during which Flag Officer Josiah Tattnall reached Hong Kong to relieve Armstrong, who hauled down his flag on 29 January.

Tattnall's first task, to procure a small steamer for Reed's use, was not easy. Several of these vessels had been lost during the difficulties with the Cantonese, and the owners of those available expected to realize sizable profits as the Canton trade revived. Tattnall's orders specified that the steamer must be chartered for a short term and at the lowest rate; Toucey must have been unpleasantly surprised to learn that the 450-ton propeller *Antelope* had been hired from Russell and Company for six months at almost $6,000 per month.

Meanwhile, the ministers of Britain, France, Russia, and the United States, having learned at Shanghai that no direct negotiation with the imperial court at Peking could be permitted, had agreed that they should proceed to the mouth of the Pei Ho in order to present their demands more forcefully at a point only some 120 miles from the imperial capital. Minister Reed had to sail in the *Mississippi* because the *Minnesota's* rudder was being repaired, but the screw-frigate, the largest man-of-war yet seen in Chinese waters, resumed her role of legation afloat late in April.

When Chinese commissioners arrived at Taku, a village just above the fortifications guarding the Pei Ho mouth, the four ministers landed to begin negotiations. Embarrassingly enough, the *Antelope* drew too much water to cross the Taku Bar, formed by silt deposits off the river mouth, unless her boilers were emptied. Reed had to accept the offer of Admiral Putiatin, the Russian minister, that his little steamer *America* (built in New York) tow her to an anchorage inside the bar. During the next three weeks, British and French men-of-war concentrated off the Pei Ho to impress the Chinese with the ability of Britain and France to gain their ends by force if necessary. The Chinese commissioners, however, professed to believe that the forts on both sides of the river would repel any invaders capable of getting across the bar. Putiatin, who like Reed had firm instructions to remain absolutely neutral in the event of hostilities, assured them that they were in error. Indeed, Putiatin was meeting with the Chinese as the first British and French gunboats crossed the bar, and the *Minnesota*'s commanding officer, Captain Samuel F. Du Pont, gave him credit for convincing the commissioners that the forts should not fire on the approaching vessels.

Du Pont, who was on very friendly terms with Sir Michael Seymour and a number of his officers, found the British gunboats interesting indeed. Drawing only about seven feet of water, the first group of these small screw-steamers had been designed for service in the shallow waters of the Baltic Sea during the Crimean War, but most had not been completed in time for that conflict. Each carried one or two heavy guns, a complement of forty to eighty officers and men, and light sail rig, although they were usually towed on lengthy passages at sea. The gunboats frequently were manned from larger warships, to which they were attached for victualling and the like, being incapable of carrying food and water for more than a few days. Their ability to take heavy guns into waters that no regular warship dared approach made them instrumental in extending British influence in China and elsewhere, and officers of the U.S. Navy were frankly envious of them.

When the negotiations brought a negative response from Peking, Lord Elgin and the French minister, Baron Gros, agreed that the time had come to force the issue. Du Pont and several of his officers joined Minister Reed in the *Antelope* to witness the bombardment and storming of the forts on the morning of 20 May. In spite of the brisk Chinese fire, some shots of which splashed near the American steamer, only a few casualties had occurred in the attacking vessels by the time the fighting ended with the Chinese in full retreat. However, after the French had scaled the walls of the fort assigned to them, a series of explosions killed and wounded numerous Frenchmen, and this unfortunate aftermath gave the Americans their sole opportunity to assist. When a boat bringing powder-burned men out to the improvised hospital ship fouled a junk, Du Pont quickly sent one from the *Antelope* to tow it clear and help it on its way. Returning to the *Minnesota* late in the day, he took the opportunity to give Elgin and Gros their first information regarding the outcome of the attack.

After clearing ineffectual barriers from the Pei Ho, the gunboat flotilla steamed up the river to Tientsin, where Admiral Seymour moored his flag vessel opposite the entrance to the Imperial Canal to symbolize his ability to cut Peking off from its riverine artery. Elgin and Gros signified their wish to reopen negotiations there, while Putiatin and Reed came upstream in the *America* so that they could share the benefits of the Anglo-French victory.

Flag Officer Tattnall in the *Powhatan* arrived off the Pei Ho on 8 June, having left the *Germantown* to look after U.S. interests in the vicinity of Canton, and ordered the *Mississippi* to fill up with provisions at Hong Kong. Thereafter, the latter was to embark 800 tons of coal which had been contracted for at Nagasaki—Tattnall feared lest it be commandeered by a British or French warship.

In order to communicate with Reed at Tientsin, Tattnall sent Du Pont up in the British gunboat which made semi-weekly runs between the city and the anchorage. The ascent of the tortuous Pei Ho was an interesting experience, not least because HMS *Slaney* had to anchor for the night en route. Her commanding officer, by now an old river hand, did not bother to check the vessel's heading by compass when she got underway at daylight the next morning. She continued to steam upstream, or so he thought, assuming that she had been riding to an ebb tide when her anchor was weighed. In fact, the tide was flooding, and the *Slaney* stood downstream through the flat, almost featureless landscape for some twenty-five miles before a passing junk confirmed growing suspicions that the river was becoming wider instead of narrower.

By this time, serious negotiations were being held between the Chinese commissioners and the individual ministers. Admiral Putiatin was the first to sign a satisfactory treaty and his fellows were reporting progress, although spontaneous attacks on foreigners occasionally threatened to disrupt the proceedings.

Captain Du Pont himself became involved when he learned that the Chinese servant who had accompanied him from the *Minnesota* had been abducted while walking in the city. Summoning twelve marines of Reed's ceremonial guard, he set off to the rescue. The small force attracted the attention of a growing crowd as it proceeded along Tientsin's streets, until a mandarin appeared to request that Du Pont march the marines into the courtyard of his yamen while they conferred. When the gate was closed, the crowd became uproarious. As the captain learned, the mandarin was none other than the senior Chinese commissioner and the people quite naturally assumed that the force of armed foreigners must have entered the yamen to seize him! Presumably the Occidentals had no way of knowing whether they were being encouraged or threatened. Du Pont was assured that the servant would be restored to him at Reed's temporary residence if he would return there; he agreed, promising to come back to the yamen with a larger force should the servant not be found. All ended well. The abducted man was returned, and Lord Elgin expressed his belief that the American's prompt show of firmness would hasten the conclusion of the treaties.

The Sino-American Treaty of Tientsin, signed on 18 June 1858, was as similar to its Sino-British counterpart as the Treaty of Wanghia was to that of Nanking. Eleven Chinese ports were opened to American trade and residence; the U.S. minister should be allowed to reside at Peking so long as any other foreign power had a minister resident there; and protection was assured Christians, whether foreigners or Chinese. Article IX referred specifically to U.S. warships; it repeated Article XXXII of the Treaty of Wanghia, adding "national vessels of the United States . . . cruising . . . for the advancement of science" to those engaged in commerce protection, and recognizing the responsibility of American men-of-war to pursue pirates who had pillaged merchantmen under their flag, with those captured to be turned over to Chinese officials for trial and punishment.[1] Subsequent negotiations at Shanghai in the autumn of 1858 established a tariff schedule and legalized the opium trade, although the drug was to be sold by foreigners in treaty ports only, its traffic in the interior being restricted to Chinese.

The *Powhatan* and the *Minnesota* departed the Yellow Sea early in July, the flagship bound for Japan and the screw-frigate for Woosung. At Nagasaki, Tattnall found the *Mississippi* with her crew quite sickly so he ordered her to the cooler climate of Hakodate before going on to Shimoda in the *Powhatan*. There he found that Consul General Townsend Harris had succeeded in negotiating the greatly desired commercial treaty, but its formal signing was not to occur until 1 September. The flag officer, aware that Lord Elgin and Admiral Putiatin would soon reach Japan to conclude similar agreements, convinced Harris that his treaty should be signed first, whereupon the consul general informed the authorities at Shimoda of his intention to go to the capital in the *Powhatan*. As the paddle frigate stood into Edo Bay, the inevitable guard boats put out from the shore; Tattnall simply ordered full speed and the boats were left in her foaming wake. There was little delay. Harris sent a messenger to Edo as soon as the flagship had anchored off Yokohama, the shogun's commissioners arrived in a Japanese steamer the next day, and the Treaty of Edo was signed on board the *Powhatan* on 29 July 1858.

This agreement opened the ports of Nagasaki, Yokohama, and Hakodate to American trade without any Japanese governmental intervention at once and provided that other ports would be opened in several years. The rights of diplomatic and consular representation and of American citizens to reside in Edo after 1 January 1862 and in Osaka a year later, were granted. A fixed tariff was established, and Americans in Japan would enjoy extraterritoriality in civil and criminal cases. The treaty specified that ratifications were to be exchanged in Washington, so Tattnall and Harris thought it well to offer one of the East India Squadron's steamers to convey the Japanese diplomatic mission across the Pacific.

From Edo Bay, the *Powhatan* took Harris back to Shimoda, where her chaplain held Sunday services in the consul general's residence for a congregation made up of sailors and marines from the flagship and the *Mississippi*. "Thus the first public renewal of Christian worship since the expulsion of the Jesuits two hundred and forty years since, has been under our flag and in a heathen temple," wrote Tattnall.[2]

The flag officer's secretary was entrusted with the signed treaty, and the *Powhatan* took him to Shanghai whence he would sail in the mail steamer, bound for the United States by way of Europe. Touching at Nagasaki on the way, she found the *Minnesota*; Captain Du Pont reported that an outbreak of cholera in which nine of the screw-frigate's company had died, had induced him to leave Woosung. Within a week after the *Powhatan* had anchored in the Hwangpoo, she counted three deaths from cholera, but the disease was brought under control thereafter.

The *Minnesota* returned to the Yangtze Kiang to embark Minister Reed and then began her homeward passage, touching at Bombay so that the diplomat could board a P & O steamer bound for Aden and then calling at Muscat. That sultanate had received little attention from vessels of the East India Squadron for some years, and Du Pont's report indicated that its importance had waned markedly. Thereafter, the Arabian Sea virtually ceased to be a part of the station.

February 1859 brought a request from the Japanese government that Tattnall send a steamer to embark the diplomatic mission to the United States. The *Mississippi* was ordered to Shimoda to prepare for this purpose, and the flag officer would have followed had the mails not brought an order from the Navy Department that he meet John E. Ward, the newly appointed minister to China, at Singapore. Ward was to exchange ratifications of the Treaty of Tientsin at Peking, and Tattnall was directed to offer support. "Without intending to interfere with the command of your Squadron, the Department desires that you will consult freely with the Minister as to its movements, and to pay the highest regard to his wishes."[3]

That order cancelled the *Mississippi*'s Japanese assignment, for in her absence Tattnall would have only his flagship with which to escort Ward to the mouth of the Pei Ho. The *Germantown* was directed to carry new orders to the *Mississippi* while the *Powhatan* steamed southward to meet the minister. The sloop of war's men must have welcomed this assignment, for she had spent her entire time on the station, almost a year, in the Macao-Whampoa-Hong Kong vicinity.

Owing to the northeasterly monsoon, the *Germantown* had rather a difficult passage, but she encountered more favorable weather to the eastward of the Ryukyu Islands. On the morning of 23 March, Kikai Shima was ahead. The sloop of war approached to within two miles of the island and then came about, expecting to weather it with ease. A cast of the lead showed twenty-seven fathoms, no outlying dangers appeared on the chart, and the ship was standing offshore making 6 knots under topgallant sails when she struck an uncharted reef and was fast aground before her commanding officer could reach the deck. Leadsmen reported deep water ahead and astern, so there could be no thought of kedging off, yet she obviously could not endure the pounding for many hours as the heavy swell alternately raised and dropped her. Concluding that his vessel's only chance lay in sailing over the reef, Commander Richard L. Page had her yards braced to obtain the maximum force from the wind and then mustered all hands forward as human ballast to trim her by the head. He considered jettisoning the aftermost guns to lighten her aft, but the danger that the ship might be bilged on one of them as she pounded on the reef made that a last resort. Wind and swell were driving her ahead. The *Germantown* struck one last time and then floated free, apparently undamaged except that her rudder was unshipped and hanging by its iron tiller.

The commander climbed to the fore crosstrees to con his vessel, and, steered by her sails, she crept inshore to anchor in twenty-five fathoms. Yard and stay tackles hoisted the rudder to the deck where its pintles were straightened, but inspection showed that the gudgeons were also bent, so temporary repairs ultimately required two days. While the carpenter and his mates were working on the rudder, Page sent a boat to chart the reef, from which the sloop of war had been very fortunate to escape.

The *Germantown* made Shimoda on 31 March, and there her mission was found to have been unnecessary. Because the Japanese government had decided to postpone its diplomats' departure until February 1860, there was no need for the warship to have left Whampoa. But at least the reef off Kikai Shima was less dangerous for shipping since its existence and location were now known.

The *Powhatan* brought Minister Ward to Hong Kong in May, and Tattnall sought a light-draft steamer for the diplomat's use. Only two were available, both profitably employed, so the owners could drive a hard bargain. The flag officer reluctantly chartered the little English-owned paddler *Toey-wan* (ex-*Eaglet*) for five months at $9,000 per month, an amount which should have convinced the Congress that it would be cheaper to build such vessels than to charter them.

The *Mississippi* and the *Germantown* had already been ordered to Shanghai, where the *Powhatan*, towing the *Toey-wan*, joined them at the end of May. Ward had intended to go directly to Peking by way of the Pei Ho, but the Chinese commissioners responsible for the exchange of ratifications signified that they must await the arrival of Sir Frederick Bruce, the British minister, at the port city. When Bruce reached Shanghai a few days later, he refused to conduct any business there because the Sino-British treaty specified that the exchange must take place in Peking.

Minister Ward saw no necessity to take the entire squadron into the Gulf of Pechihli, so the flagship and her tender departed Shanghai on 17 June, anchoring off the mouth of the Pei Ho four days later. Here they found that the Taku forts had been rebuilt and the river obstructed. A sizable force of British and French naval vessels, which had accompanied their respective ministers, was anchored off the bar. Communicating with them, Tattnall and Ward learned that the Chinese were now insisting that the Pei Ho actually emptied into the Gulf of Pechihli some ten miles to the northward, to which point the ministers must go. Sir Frederick Bruce had refused; if the barriers were not removed by 25 June, the date set for the formalities, the gunboats would force their way upstream.

Since Ward had no official knowledge of this latest Chinese mandate, he and his suite embarked with Tattnall in the *Toey-wan* to undertake an ascent of the river. The little paddler crossed the Taku Bar on 24 June and steamed past the thirteen gunboats anchored just out of range of the forts, taking care not to exchange signals with them. Strangely enough, the forts seemed to be deserted—no gun muzzles protruded from the embrasures and not a flag was flying—in marked contrast to their appearance in May 1858.

Approaching the first barrier, before which the flag officer intended to anchor, the *Toey-wan* grounded. Her situation was precarious indeed, for she had run onto a steep bank and was in danger of rolling over and filling as the tide ebbed. Moreover, she was within easy range of the forts. Rear Admiral Sir James Hope promptly sent HMS *Plover* to pull the *Toey-wan* off the bank, but the "sixty horsepower" gunboat succeeded only in parting the towline. Thereupon, Hope suggested that Tattnall transfer to another British gunboat in which he could hoist the U.S. colors and his own personal flag. This offer was declined with thanks, nor was any assistance needed. The *Toey-wan* floated off on the flood tide at sunset.

In the course of the afternoon, a small boat had taken Tattnall's flag lieutenant and interpreters to the shore to explain the steamer's mission. In response, they were informed that, although the forts were poorly manned by country militia, their guns would fire on anyone attempting to remove the river barriers. The Chinese officer thought that preparations for the ministers' reception had been made at Pehtang, a village near the northern mouth of the Pei Ho.

As soon as the *Toey-wan* was afloat once more, she left the river. The allied gunboats were seen to be preparing for action, and Tattnall took care to select an anchorage where his vessel's lights could not possibly be confused with their signals.

Sir James Hope's battle plan was based on that which had been so successful thirteen months earlier. That unlucky number of vessels, of which one was French, steamed in to attack the forts in mid-afternoon the next day, while a force of seamen and marines, embarked in several junks, awaited the signal to board their small boats and carry the forts by storm. But the despised Chinese had a surprise in store for the Royal Navy. Hardly had the *Plover*, flying the admiral's flag, entered the narrow channel before the forts on both banks opened a deadly fire, directed low so that the projectiles ricocheted from the water's surface against the gunboat's frail planking. So effective was the Chinese fire that one officer noted that "everyone supposes that there are foreigners, probably Russians, in the forts."[4] The little warship's men stood to their guns courageously, but heavy casualties among them soon reduced the rapidity and accuracy of their shooting. The *Plover* settled into the mud, so HMS *Cormorant* became the flag vessel and a principal Chinese target.

Meanwhile, Flag Officer Tattnall and Minister Ward were interested onlookers from the deck of their unarmed steamer. Tattnall soon concluded that the gunboats were in serious difficulty and that their crews could not be reinforced by the sailors in the junks, for the latters' boats could not be rowed against the ebb. Realizing that the tide would probably turn too late to help Admiral Hope, Tattnall conferred with Ward about the propriety of towing the boats in with the *Toey-wan* as a gesture of appreciation for Hope's efforts to assist him on the preceding day. The minister agreed that he could do no less. Soon thereafter, the British admiral sent a messenger to report on the situation, whereupon the flag officer insisted that Ward and his suite board one of the junks while the steamer's men passed hawsers to the boats. When all was ready, the *Toey-wan* headed into the fray with six boats in tow. Shot and shell splashes rose all around her, but the Chinese gunners were less adept when firing at a moving target and she sustained no damage. Casting off her tow close aboard the *Cormorant*, the "neutral" flagship withdrew to an anchorage out of gunshot, whence Tattnall embarked in his barge to visit Sir James Hope, who had been reported to be seriously wounded. As the boat approached the British flag vessel, a shot struck it, killing the coxswain and doing such damage that the boat sank as its crew clambered on board the *Cormorant*. The American flag officer found the British admiral suffering from a severe thigh wound and several broken ribs; nonetheless, he was intent on continuing the action. After a period of time variously described as ten minutes to ninety minutes, during which members of his barge crew were reported to have helped to serve one of the *Cormorant*'s guns, Tattnall hailed a passing British boat which took the Americans back to the *Toey-wan*.

The *Cormorant* grounded later, so the paddle steamer *Coromandel* became Hope's third flagship of the afternoon. His second-in-command directed that an effort be made to carry the nearest fort by storm—to no avail, for the assault force found itself mired in the mud flats exposed at low tide and had to retire after sustaining heavy losses. Thereafter, the surviving gunboats sought a position nearly out of range of the forts, from which they kept up a desultory fire during the night.

Flag Officer Tattnall decided to return to the *Powhatan* the next morning. Before doing so, he took leave of the British and French flag officers, both of whom were prostrated by battle wounds. From the former, he learned that the British had lost six gunboats by sinking or grounding, although three were subsequently recovered. Total allied casualties amounted to some 450 officers and men killed or wounded, of whom 12 were French. In response to Admiral Hope's request, the *Toey-wan* towed two boatloads of wounded men out to the larger vessels of the British fleet anchored beyond the bar, after which Tattnall sent her in once more under command of the flagship's senior lieutenant "with orders to remain at the mouth of the harbor, out of fire, and to afford all aid consistent with our neutrality."[5]

After a time, the battered Anglo-French forces retired to Shanghai to lick their wounds, while the *Powhatan* steamed up to Pehtang whence Minister Ward and his suite were conveyed to Peking. While there, according to Tattnall, they were treated well (other accounts, however, indicate that they were virtually prisoners); but Ward's refusal to make the customary gestures of obeisance to the emperor kept him from obtaining an audience. The exchange of ratifications of the Treaty of Tientsin took place in Pehtang in mid-August, after which the Chinese stated that they held a young American who had been captured on 25 June. Ward said that this could not be true—no Americans had landed or taken any part in the action except those involved in the *Toey-wan*'s service as a towboat. The Chinese produced a sailor who admitted that he was a Canadian serving in the Royal Navy; he had claimed American citizenship with the hope of receiving better treatment from his captors. Nonetheless, the Chinese insisted on releasing him to Ward as an expression of good will, and in due course he was sent to Admiral Hope, whom Tattnall had earlier promised: "Should I ascertain that the Chinese hold any of your men prisoner, I need not add that I will look out for them."[6]

Josiah Tattnall's peculiar concept of neutrality, which he supposedly justified on the ground that "blood is thicker than water,"[7] apparently had no deleterious effect on Sino-American relations. The Chinese did not assert the right to confiscate the *Toey-wan*, as they might properly have done under Article XXII of the Treaty of Wanghia: ". . . the [American] flag shall not protect vessels engaged in the transportation of officers or soldiers in the enemy's service . . . all such vessels so offending shall be subject to forfeiture and confiscation to the Chinese Government."[8] Nonetheless, Secretary of the Navy Toucey and President James Buchanan approved of Tattnall's conduct.

While the flag officer was in the Gulf of Pechihli, Captain William C. Nicholson of the *Mississippi* served as senior officer at Shanghai. He offered his ship's medical facilities to aid in the treatment of British casualties of the Taku attack, and early in August helped to quell a disturbance growing out of rumors that a French merchant vessel was embarking kidnapped coolies. The *Mississippi* was anchored off Shanghai's international settlement and sent a landing force ashore; quiet was restored without resort to arms.

The *Germantown* was at Nagasaki, where there had been trouble between Japanese and American merchant seamen. The British consul felt that his own authority, as well as the safety of all foreigners, was assured by the sloop of war. When he heard that she was about to depart for Hong Kong to await her relief, he urged Admiral Hope to send a vessel to take her place, for "the benefit of the [*Germantown*'s] presence cannot be overestimated."[9]

One other U.S. naval vessel was in Japanese waters during this period, but she was not attached to the East India Squadron, and her presence was of slight value to anyone. Lieutenant John M. Brooke, astronomer of the North Pacific Surveying Expedition, had been sent to complete the expedition's work by surveying potential steamer routes in the schooner *Fenimore Cooper*. While she was lying off Yokohama, a gale struck the anchorage and drove her ashore without loss of life. It seemed that she might be salved without difficulty, but a survey revealed that her frame timbers were rotten. Commodore A. A. Popoff of the Imperial Russian Navy, whose advice Brooke sought, recommended that the schooner be sold because of the uncertainty that extensive rebuilding at a reasonable cost was possible in Japan. Tattnall later concurred in this opinion, so the former New York pilot boat ended her days as a Japanese coaster. Within a few months, Lieutenant Brooke and his men returned to the United

States in the *Kanrin Maru*, the first Japanese steamer to cross the Pacific Ocean.

Minister Ward having concluded his business at Pehtang, the flagship weighed anchor on 18 August and towed the *Toey-wan* back to Woosung. A week after her arrival in the Yangtze, the little paddler dragged ashore in a gale. She was refloated without damage, but Tattnall, anxious to be rid of a costly encumbrance, had the *Mississippi* take the *Toey-wan* to Hong Kong to be returned to her owners, while the *Powhatan* made the circuit of Japanese ports during the autumn.

Steaming into Hong Kong on 20 November, the flagship encountered a newcomer flying the American flag. She proved to be the screw-sloop *Hartford* with Flag Officer Cornelius K. Stribling on board. Tattnall lost no time in transferring command of the East India Squadron to his relief, after which the *Powhatan* steamed to Yokohama to embark the Japanese diplomatic mission to the United States for its passage across the Pacific.

Flag Officer Stribling, who had commanded the East India Squadron's first flagship, the *Peacock*, almost a quarter-century earlier, was charged with the usual duties of protecting American citizens and their interests and of helping to increase trade "with China, Japan, and the Isles of India."[10] Because of the number of ports open to American trade, the flag officer had greater responsibilities than any of his predecessors, yet his squadron was to consist only of his flagship, one sailing sloop of war, and the shallow-draft side-wheel steamer *Saginaw*, when she was commissioned.

Quite naturally, Stribling wanted more ships. He argued that, if six vessels were assigned to the squadron, danger to their crews' health could be avoided by frequent change of station; he also maintained that the Navy Department's frequently expressed desire that warships be employed in cruising as much as possible would be more likely to be realized with a larger force. The flag officer concluded his appeal by pointing out that the East India Squadron was too distant from the United States to be reinforced rapidly in time of need.

Stribling's request that six vessels be assigned to his command seems modest when one considers the station's geographic extent and the fact that the U.S. Navy had enough warships in commission to send at least that number to each of its six permanent squadrons. But the Navy Department apparently had more pressing needs to consider. Notwithstanding the frequently stated importance of American interests in "the East India and China Seas," only the Brazil Squadron usually was composed of fewer men-of-war. While the expense of maintaining warships in the Far East cannot be discounted as a factor contributing to the squadron's small size, the paramount reason was the lack of any evidence that a larger force was required. British naval officers had never hesitated to extend assistance to U.S. officials or private citizens in the absence of American warships, just as the latter were ready to protect Britons should the situation be reversed. So long as the Royal Navy found it possible to keep a fleet numbering thirty vessels or more in Oriental waters, American interests were protected as well as if the same number of warships flying their flag had been present. To be sure, it was somewhat embarrassing for those patriotic individuals who still looked on Britain as the traditional enemy to have to appeal for British assistance, but neither congressmen nor secretaries of the navy worried unduly about this—the Canton River and the Yangtze Kiang were a long way from the Potomac.

Stribling's flagship, the *Hartford*, was on her maiden voyage. One of a class of five, of which three others—the *Brooklyn, Lancaster*, and *Richmond*—would also serve in the Far East, she was slightly smaller than the paddle frigates which had preceded her on the station, although larger than the *San Jacinto*. Of relatively shallow draft for their size, she and her sisters were not very weatherly under sail, but they had a fair turn of speed off the wind and were good steamers for their day.

His second ship, the *John Adams*, had been ordered to join the squadron as expeditiously as possible. However, her commanding officer seems not to have desired a cruise in the Far East at all, for he put in at Rio de Janeiro on the pretence that the old sloop of war was so rotten as to be unseaworthy. When this news reached the Navy Department, Toucey ordered a board of survey to examine the ship thoroughly. The survey revealed a "moderate leak," which could easily be stopped if the vessel were hove down, and a few small spots of decay which could be repaired by her carpenter. The commanding officer, suspected of trying to impede the survey, was found unfit for duty and returned to the United States. Repairs to the sloop completed, her senior lieutenant took her to Hong Kong, which she reached in April 1860, eleven months out of Norfolk.

The squadron's third vessel, the *Saginaw*, was the first warship built on the Pacific coast of the United States and the first designed especially for service in the Far East. Toucey hoped that she could "be particularly useful in suppressing piracies, as her light draught will enable her to reach the retreats of those who commit them."[11] She was much larger than the British gunboats, being an ocean-going vessel in every respect. The *Saginaw* steamed up the Hwangpoo to Shanghai in May.

Stribling began a series of visits to treaty ports during the spring of 1860, but a resurgence of the Taiping threat to Shanghai caused the *Hartford* to spend the month of June there. The landing of a sizable force of British and French troops led the flag officer to remark on the paradoxical situation in which the allies were supporting the imperial administration in Shanghai even as they were preparing to fight imperial armies farther to the northward.

The flagship took Minister Ward to the Gulf of Pechihli in July. The *Saginaw* overtook her, bringing an appeal for protection signed by the leading foreigners in Shanghai. Ward transferred to the side-wheeler to continue his observation cruise while the *Hartford* steamed back to the threatened city. There she found that the danger had already passed, the rebels having been repulsed by Anglo-French forces, although the international settlement had not actually been attacked. Soon afterward, the *Saginaw* returned with news that the Taku forts had fallen to a combined attack by troops and gunboats. A few weeks later, the defeat of a Chinese army brought the "*Arrow* War" to an end.

Meanwhile, the *Saginaw* was put to good use, conveying Ward to treaty ports and occasionally searching for pirates. One such mission resulted from a report that an American bark had been captured and nine of her company killed. The gunboat returned with two wounded men, survivors of six deserters from merchant vessels at Chefoo. Heading south in a stolen boat, they had landed to obtain food and four had been killed in a clash with Chinese. The flag officer saw no reason for punitive action: "It appears that they were the only pirates and deserve much greater punishment than they received at the hands of the Chinese."[12]

However, the side-wheeler was very wet, and sickness among her men threatened to curtail her usefulness. Stribling thought she had too many officers and not enough seamen; he had no authority to change her complement, but he directed Commander J. Findley Schenck to hire ten coolies to relieve her seamen of small boat work and other tasks entailing extensive exposure. Although Chinese had earlier been employed as cooks and officers' servants, the *Saginaw* seems to have been the first vessel of the East India Squadron to ship them for duties customarily performed by seamen.

The *Hartford* went to Nagasaki early in October and proceeded from that port to Yokohama by way of Japan's Inland Sea, which had not been used by foreign shipping before 1860. The flag officer's report made no mention of the beauty of one of the world's most scenic water passages, but he did predict that it would become a favorite route for steamers when the ports of Hiogo and Osaka were opened to trade.

Yokohama also received a visit by the screw-frigate *Niagara* in the autumn of 1860. She conveyed the Japanese diplomatic mission returning from the United States and brought an array of gifts in the care of Lieutenant Henry A. Wise. Among them were various types of firearms and the machinery for making ammunition. Wise, an ordnance specialist, had volunteered to instruct the Japanese how to use the firearms and machinery. But the Japanese were not desirous of having a foreign naval officer in their midst; after watching him operate the machinery on board the *Niagara*, they were sure that further instruction was unnecessary, especially since it would detain Wise so far from his native land.

The *Niagara* was not attached to the East India Squadron, but she went to Hong Kong from Yokohama to embark the squadron's invalids and time-expired men for return to the United States. She also transported Minister Ward to Aden, whence he traveled home by the more rapid route through the Mediterranean.

Flag Officer Stribling became chargé d'affaires to China when Ward departed, an additional responsibility that he did not relish. However, he had the consolation of knowing that his squadron was to be reinforced by the screw-sloop *Dacotah* and the old sailer *Vandalia*. The former reached Hong Kong in January 1861, and Commander William Radford reported a list of defects that had revealed themselves on the long passage to the station. Most serious was the fact that only twenty-two days of steaming had corroded her boilers to the extent that they required immediate repair. But at least the *Dacotah* reached the station. The *Vandalia* did not. News of the outbreak of the Civil War overtook the old sloop of war on her way out, and she returned to the United States.

When ready for service, the *Dacotah* went to Shanghai, where Commander Radford collected hydrographic information pertaining to navigation of the Yangtze and arranged a supply of coal for the squadron's steamers. The *Hartford*, which had gone to Manila to inquire into the detention of an American merchantman whose mate was charged with murder, joined the *Dacotah* and the *Saginaw* a few weeks later, and the three began the ascent of the Yangtze Kiang on 30 April. The *Susquehanna* had steamed as far as Wuhu with Commissioner Robert McLane on board seven years earlier, but no U.S. warship had ever shown the flag beyond that point. Stribling thought it prudent to leave the *Hartford* at anchor forty miles farther upstream, and the *Dacotah* remained at Hankow while the flag officer continued on in the *Saginaw*. After steaming a short distance into Tung Ting Lake, some 700 miles from the Yangtze mouth, the side-wheeler stood back downstream. The squadron reached Shanghai on 28 May, and Stribling reported that, except for one difficult stretch fifty miles above Woosung, the Yangtze was an easy stream to navigate—an opinion that many of his successors would not share.

In June, the flag officer received an order to inquire into the fate of the company of the American bark *Myrtle*, reported lost on the Cochin-Chinese coast a year earlier. The *Saginaw* went to Qui Nhon harbor to seek information, and Commander Schenck had a white flag run up to his vessel's foretruck as the anchor was let go. Nonetheless, before any at-

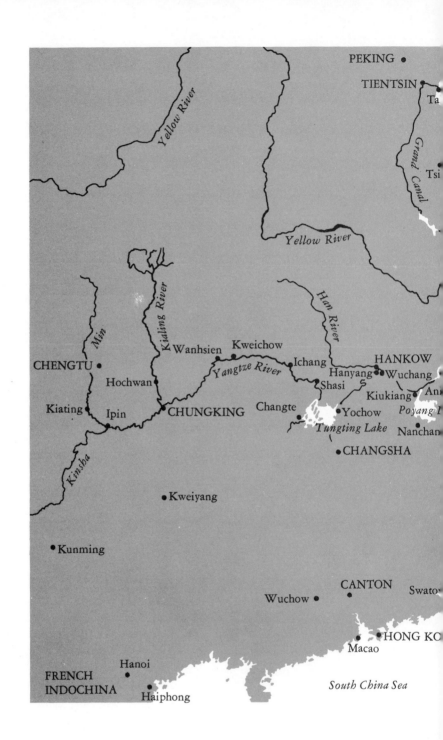

nwangtao

•Port Arthur

of Chihli

•Chefoo

KOREA

•TSINGTAO

Yellow Sea

JAPAN

•Nagasaki

Chinkiang

ANKING

ow   •SHANGHAI

ıu

East China Sea

Ryukyo Retto

ochow

•Taihoku

Amoy

TAIWAN   *Pacific Ocean*

•Tainan

MAP 7–1.   The Yangtze Kiang

tempt to communicate with the shore could be made, a nearby fort fired a shot at the ship. As the commander sent his men to the windlass, another projectile passed over the vessel, and a third splashed nearby soon after the anchor was aweigh. Hauling down the white flag, the *Saginaw* opened fire with her 32-pounder at 900 yards. The first shell exploded directly over the fort, causing an explosion which may have been that of a magazine and silencing its guns. The 32-pounder continued a deliberate fire until Schenck concluded that the fort had been abandoned, after which the *Saginaw* returned to Hong Hong because she had too few men to constitute a landing force.

Forwarding Commander Schenck's report, Stribling commented that, since the Cochin-Chinese had been constantly at war with France for some time, during which they had had little contact with Americans, it was hardly surprising that the *Saginaw* had been fired on. He asked the French admiral at Saigon to make inquiries about the *Myrtle*'s survivors; beyond that, no action could be taken.

During the *Saginaw*'s brief cruise to Qui Nhon, the flag officer had received dispatches that left no doubt as to the nature of the domestic crisis in the United States. Well aware that the next mail might bring news of the dissolution of his country and of the service in which he had spent nearly fifty years, Stribling requested the continued loyalty of his officers and men in a general order which, for simple dignity and nobility of sentiment, could hardly have been improved. When some of the junior officers from seceding states wished to resign their commissions, he refused to allow them to leave the station until their resignations had been accepted by the Navy Department.

Flag Officer Stribling himself was a South Carolinian, a fact which he must have known would make him suspect in the eyes of Secretary of the Navy Gideon Welles. On 22 July, Captain Frederick Engle arrived at Hong Kong with orders to relieve Stribling of his command, and soon thereafter the flag officer departed for the United States by the overland route. This, however, was an unnecessary precaution, for Cornelius Kincheloe Stribling's loyalty to the United States never wavered.

Captain Engle had been sent out to supervise the dissolution of the East India Squadron. The *John Adams* had already sailed for home, and the two screw-sloops departed Hong Kong early in August, leaving the *Saginaw* because Engle did not think her worth the expense of the coal she would burn on the homeward passage.

So the side-wheeler remained on the East India Station, but Commander Schenck and his officers grew increasingly restive as the months passed. Their fellows were winning fame and promotion in combat while they made the circuit of treaty ports. in Japan and China. Schenck's patience reached its limit in December; on his own authority, he engaged passages to San Francisco for himself, seven officers, and forty-two men in an American merchantman.

On 3 January 1862, the USS *Saginaw*, described as "completely rotten and condemned as unseaworthy," was placed out of commission at Hong Kong.[13] Leaving one officer and six enlisted men to look after the vessel, Commander Schenck and the remainder of her company sailed for California the next day. With their departure, the U.S. Navy's East India Squadron ceased to exist.

CHAPTER EIGHT

Japanese Rebels and Rebel Raiders

By the end of 1861 U.S. naval forces had been withdrawn from all distant stations to participate in the nation's internal conflict. The *Saginaw* was one of three vessels remaining abroad—the others were cruising off Africa and Brazil—and even she was ordered to San Francisco in mid-1862. After nine months of rebuilding at the Mare Island Navy Yard, the side-wheeler joined the Pacific Squadron, with which she spent the remainder of her career.

But the Far East was not destined to be devoid of American naval forces for long. Receiving news of a Confederate privateer off the China coast, Secretary of the Navy Gideon Welles directed the Mare Island commandant to hasten repairs to the Pacific Squadron's screw-sloop *Wyoming*, fit her for thirty months' service, and send her directly to Manila. She arrived in the Philippines in August 1862, and Commander David S. McDougal commenced an investigation which ultimately indicated that the commerce raider was a figment of someone's imagination. A few months later, however, Welles ordered the *Wyoming* to intercept the celebrated CSS *Alabama* at Sunda Strait.

While these orders were en route, the *Wyoming* touched at several Chinese ports for the dual purpose of showing the flag and seeking information pertaining to Confederate activities. Standing into Swatow in March 1863 with a pilot on board, she had the misfortune to strike a pinnacle rock while steaming at 8 knots. Water poured into the vessel more rapidly than pumps and the bilge injection could eject it, so

114

FIGURE 8–1.   The screw-sloop *Wyoming*.

McDougal ran her aground. After discharging stores and ammunition into a chartered schooner, the *Wyoming*'s men plugged the leaks sufficiently for her to reach Amoy, where she was docked for permanent repairs. A month after her mishap, the screw-sloop was ready for sea, and McDougal prepared to comply with Welles's Sunda Strait order. But before she could sail, dispatches from Japan and news that the *Alabama* was actually in the West Indies caused the commander to set a course for Yokohama instead.

Isolated instances of violence against foreigners in Japan had been reported almost since the beginning of foreign intercourse with the island empire, but only gradually did Westerners become aware that these were manifestations of a more serious danger. The emperor himself and a number of the most powerful daimyo, including the princes of Choshu and Satsuma, were strongly opposed to the abandonment of seclusion and saw in the new policy an opportunity to oust the government of the Tokugawa shogun.

In the autumn of 1862, a retainer of the daimyo of Satsuma killed an Englishman whom he thought had insulted his prince near Yokohama. The British government made this and earlier incidents the occasion for demanding a sizable indemnity from the Japanese government and a smaller sum from Satsuma, over whom the shogun was said to have little control. The French minister at Edo assured British Rear Admiral Augustus Kuper that his government would support Whitehall's demand, and the senior Netherlands naval officer offered his cooperation. This matter, which had not been settled when the *Wyoming* arrived, did not involve the United States, but on 25 May the American legation at Edo was burned and a short time afterward Minister Robert H. Pruyn and the consul at Kanagawa were advised to withdraw to Yokohama because the Japanese government could no longer guarantee their safety.

The situation assumed a more serious aspect a month later, when the shogun suddenly denounced the promise of his minister that the indemnity would be paid to Britain. Thereupon, the British chargé d'affaires turned matters over to Admiral Kuper to be settled by force. Since the latter thought his warships too few to protect the foreign settlement at Yokohama and to collect the indemnity at the same time, he declined to take any action until the foreign residents had had an opportunity to leave Japan. Within a few days, the Japanese paid the indemnity, but the payment was coupled with an order that all foreigners depart, so the outlook remained ominous.

Nonetheless, the *Wyoming* was preparing to return to the United States in obedience to orders from the Navy Department when letters from Shanghai informed Commander McDougal that the American steamer *Pembroke,* plying between Yokohama and the Chinese port, had been fired on by armed vessels in the vicinity of the Strait of Shimonoseki, western exit from the Inland Sea. The *Wyoming's* destination was changed at once.

Arriving off the town of Shimonoseki on the morning of 16 July 1863, McDougal identified a bark and a brig, of European origin but flying the banners of Japan and Choshu, as the *Pembroke's* assailants. An armed steamer displaying identical flags was anchored nearby. Taking advantage of a favorable tide, the *Wyoming* hoisted her colors and stood in with her men at battle stations. As she neared the town, six batteries at various points along the shore took her under fire. The vessels were McDougal's primary targets, and shells from the *Wyoming's* two 11-inch Dahlgren guns seem to have been very effective against them as she closed the range. The steamer weighed anchor, but a gush of smoke and steam following two shellbursts indicated serious damage to her boilers. She drifted ashore, and the brig, also hard hit, was seen to be settling. The bark too was reported to have suffered severe injury, but the batteries were another matter, keeping up a steady fire to which the *Wyoming* could make little effective reply because of their number and elevation. McDougal's conning of his vessel was made the more difficult by strong currents and the lack of hydrographic knowledge, his pilots being "completely paralyzed and apprehensive of getting on shore."[1] After touching bottom once, the screw-sloop broke off the action. During seventy minutes under fire, she had received eleven shots in her hull while others had damaged her smokestack and rigging. Four of her men had been killed instantly and seven wounded, one fatally. Commander McDougal made no estimate of the Japanese loss, but he was sure that his attack had eliminated the danger from Choshu's warships; the batteries, on the other hand, could be dealt with only by a sizable landing force.

When the *Wyoming* returned to Yokohama, her men learned that she was not the only vessel bearing wounds inflicted by Shimonoseki's guns. The Dutch screw-corvette *Medusa*, en route from Nagasaki to Yokohama, had steamed through the strait under fire from batteries and men-of-war a few days before the *Wyoming*'s punitive action, and even as that action was beginning, French Rear Admiral C. Jaurés departed Yokohama with two warships to avenge an attack on a dispatch boat flying the tricolor.

French soldiers were embarked in the flagship *Sémiramis*, for Jaurés intended to destroy the offending batteries. When he found that his vessel drew too much water to come within range, the admiral landed the troops under the fire of the smaller *Tancréde*'s guns to attack a fortification to the eastward of the strait itself. This was quickly carried and, together with its magazine, destroyed. After burning a nearby village, the force was reembarked. Jaurés's operation was conducted smartly, but, as Admiral Kuper remarked, it had done little to assure free passage of the strait.[2]

When the French vessels returned to Yokohama, the diplomatic representatives of the foreign powers met to discuss the Japanese situation. They quickly resolved that the naval forces of their respective nations should cooperate to protect foreign rights in the treaty ports and to reopen the strait. The senior foreign naval officers, meeting on board HMS *Euryalus* soon thereafter to consider the diplomats' resolution, concluded that no belligerent action should be undertaken, or even planned, until they had been assured that the shogun's government was unable or unwilling to control the daimyo in whose principalities the treaty ports and the strait were located. No reason for this decision was given; presumably the naval officers wished to avoid responsibility for extensive military involvement in Japan so long as there was any possible alternative. Commander McDougal also had to keep in mind that his primary mission was the pursuit of Confederate commerce raiders—should the *Wyoming* suffer serious damage or deplete her ammunition supply, no replacement was at hand.

On the next day, however, another U.S. man-of-war stood into Edo Bay. The sailing sloop of war *Jamestown* had reached Macao from the Atlantic coast by way of the Cape of Good Hope on 1 June. After filling her storerooms with provisions that the naval storekeeper at Macao had purchased for her in Hong Kong, she had touched at Woosung where Captain Cicero Price learned of the threatening state of affairs in Japan.

Although the *Jamestown*'s dependence on the winds practically limited her to duty as a guardship in one or another of the treaty ports, she could contribute sailors and marines to a force which would be landed from other vessels in the event of hostilities. But the arrival of a single obsolete warship did not suffice to change the attitudes of the senior naval officers, and Captain Price concurred in their decision.

Recognizing that the desired international naval cooperation was unlikely to be realized in the near future, the British chargé d'affaires persuaded Admiral Kuper to take unilateral action against the daimyo of Satsuma to force payment of the indemnity. Seven steam-propelled British warships, led by the screw-frigate *Euryalus*, bombarded the fortifications at Kagoshima, Satsuma's capital city, on 15 August. Heavy seas whipped by typhoon-force winds and frequent accidents that befell the squadron's breech-loading Armstrong guns limited the effect of the bombardment, but buildings in Kagoshima were seen to be in flames before the warships sought a sheltered anchorage in which to repair their damage and bury their thirteen dead. The batteries and the daimyo's palace were shelled again as the squadron steamed out of Kagoshima Bay, and none of its vessels were hit by the feeble return fire. Nonetheless, Satsuma could boast that the British had been driven off without collecting the indemnity.

While the bombardment of Kagoshima had no direct effect on the American situation in Japan, it did show clearly that even a more formidable fleet was unlikely to be successful against Japanese fortifications unless troops could be put ashore in strength to destroy the batteries after they had been silenced by naval gunfire. And troops were not available, for Kuper's application to the major general commanding British forces in China had received a flat refusal. Thus, the Strait of Shimonoseki remained closed to foreign shipping.

The threat of Confederate commerce raiders in the Far East seemed likely to materialize in the autumn of 1863 when the CSS *Alabama* was reported to be at Cape Town, where she had armed and commissioned one of her prizes as a cruiser. McDougal took the *Wyoming* to Macao for coal and then stood south to patrol Sunda Strait. After cruising in its waters for a month, the commander received information apparently originating with the U.S. consul at Melbourne, to the effect that a supply of coal for the *Alabama*'s use had been landed on uninhabited Christmas Island, some 200 miles to the southward of Sunda Strait. The *Wyoming* set out to investigate immediately and found no evidence of any coal having been put ashore; indeed, McDougal reported that the waters around the island offered no anchorage where a vessel might be unloaded.

Perhaps the report had been designed to lure the Union warship away from Sunda Strait, for the *Alabama* was actually nearby. She had destroyed a prize off Sumatra's south coast on 6 November and steamed through the strait on the tenth, the day on which the *Wyoming* departed for Christmas Island. Commander McDougal later calculated that the two warships must have passed about twenty-five miles from each other, but by the time the Confederate burned another prize early the next morning, her enemy was too far to the southward to sight the blaze.

The *Wyoming* returned from her wild-goose chase a week later, to learn that the *Alabama* had indeed entered the Java Sea, but McDougal could obtain no information as to her whereabouts after 11 November. Five days were spent searching the waters in the vicinity of Anjer, after which the commander set a course for Bangka Strait, bemoaning the state of his vessel's boilers which could no longer steam at full pressure. The *Wyoming* was off Singapore at the end of November, and there had the unusual experience of being mistaken for her prey—a native boat brought out a packet of papers and a letter for Commander Raphael Semmes. This evidence that the *Alabama* was expected caused McDougal to await her off Singapore, but the raider was more than 500 miles to the northward and did not reach Malacca Strait until late December, by which time the *Wyoming* was well on her way to Manila, whence she went to Whampoa for boiler repairs.

The screw-sloop dropped down to Macao on the completion of her repairs, and the *Jamestown* joined her early in February 1864. Captain Price had received a report that the *Alabama* was bound for Whampoa or Amoy to be docked, so he had left Yokohama late in December, disregarding the protests of American merchants and mariners who were sure that the Confederate would steam into Edo Bay at any moment. The sailing warship had battled boisterous winds for nearly a month to reach Amoy, whence she escorted a merchantman to Hong Kong. Price and McDougal agreed that the *Alabama* was no longer likely to appear in the China Sea, especially since she was reported to have been spoken off India's Coromandel coast early in January. Nonetheless, the *Wyoming* was preparing to return to Sunda Strait when, in mid-February, Captain Price ordered her to Foochow in response to the vice-consul's plea that a warship touch there.

At Foochow, Commander McDougal found that churches belonging to English and American missionary establishments had been damaged by a Chinese mob a month earlier. The vice-consuls of both nations had demanded reparation; compensation required by the Briton was paid promptly—because he was supported by a gunboat, according to McDougal. This view was probably valid, for, upon the *Wyoming*'s arrival, the American claim was satisfied as well. At an interview with the governor, the two vice-consuls, accompanied by the commanding officers of the USS *Wyoming* and HMS *Bustard*, were assured that the guilty individuals would be punished and that foreign property would be protected in the future.

Her Foochow mission successfully concluded, the *Wyoming* returned to Macao to await the mails and then proceeded to Batavia. All information indicated that the *Alabama* was no longer in the Indian Ocean, so the Union warship made her way to Philadelphia in accordance with earlier orders. The information was correct; the *Alabama* was sunk off Cherburg, France, by the USS *Kearsarge* while the *Wyoming* was still on her homeward passage.

Meanwhile, the *Jamestown* remained in Chinese waters until June, when Minister Pruyn asked that she return to Yokohama, both to provide a naval escort when he resumed his residence in Edo and to participate in an effort to reopen the Strait of Shimonoseki. The former mission was completed without incident, but August brought reports of another outrage in the district of the daimyo of Choshu. The American steamer *Monitor*, her passage from Hakodate to Nagasaki prolonged by head winds, had been fired on when she sought fuel and water in a bay on Honshu's northwest coast.

Preparations for a movement against Choshu, whose domain included the northern shore of the Strait of Shimonoseki, were well-advanced when news of the supposedly unprovoked firing on the *Monitor* reached Yokohama. An ultimatum to the daimyo had been answered unsatisfactorily, whereupon the treaty powers' diplomatic representatives concluded that a military-naval expedition should be sent to the strait. Their recommendation to this effect was discussed by the senior naval officers, who agreed to the proposed operation with the proviso that they be relieved of all responsibility for defense of the foreign settlement at Yokohama while it was in progress.

The role of the *Jamestown* received serious consideration. Everyone recognized that her lack of motive power amounted to a complete disability so far as the proposed expedition was concerned, yet the ministers were insistent that American sailors participate. Admiral Kuper offered one of his steamers to tow the sailer to the scene, but, as she would be very difficult to control in the strong currents of the strait, he thought it better for her to remain in Edo Bay where her presence would help to ensure tranquility. Thereupon, Captain Price chartered the American merchant steamer *Ta-Kiang* at $9,500 per month, put seventy men and a Parrott rifled gun into her, and ordered her temporary commanding officer, Lieutenant Frederick Pearson, to operate under Admiral Kuper's direction, towing boats inshore, evacuating wounded men, and otherwise rendering such service as he could without exposing the *Ta-Kiang* unduly. The fleet which sailed from Yokohama late in August consisted of eight British warships, of which a screw-propelled ship of the line and two screw-frigates were the largest, three French vessels, including the screw-frigate *Sémiramis*, four Dutch screw-corvettes, and the *Ta-Kiang*, flying the U.S. ensign. A battalion of Royal Marines and a detachment of sappers were embarked in the larger British vessels. Another of Admiral Kuper's screw-sloops was escorting colliers laden with coal for the fleet from Shanghai to the Inland Sea, while a gun vessel would join from Nagasaki, bringing an interpreter and a pilot.

This array of eighteen vessels was thought to be large enough to open the strait with ease, thus proving to the emperor, the shogun, the daimyo, and other Japanese the folly of any attempt to cut off trade or to eject all foreigners. The ministers, according to Britain's Sir Rutherford Alcock, believed that a decisive blow against Choshu, reputedly the strongest of the daimyo, would encourage his more moderate fellows to adhere to a peaceful course. Indeed, they hoped that it might result in a settlement of the rivalry between the shogun and his opponents. Lest the shogun be tempted to move against the foreign settlement at Yokohama, the *Jamestown* and five small British men-of-war remained at anchor in Edo Bay, while a number of troops were stationed ashore.

Approaching their objective on 4 September, the ships of the combined fleet were formed into three columns according to nationality, with the *Ta-Kiang* steaming humbly at the rear of the French line. That afternoon they anchored within sight of the Choshu batteries, which Admirals Kuper and Jaurés reconnoitered in person and then agreed that the attack should be launched on the first favorable tide.

HMS *Euryalus* made the signal for the engagement to begin on the afternoon of 5 September. The vessels weighed anchor and formed into advanced and light squadrons, the first of which steamed into a bay within easy range of the batteries while the lighter ships took up positions from which they could direct a flanking fire against the same works. The two flagships and the cumbersome ship of the line lay farther out. There was no sign of Japanese activity as the warships maneuvered into position, but when the *Euryalus*'s bow guns fired the first rounds, eight batteries responded smartly. The action then became general, with even the *Ta-Kiang*'s Parrott rifle contributing eighteen rounds to the bombardment. Some three hours later the batteries had been silenced, but the admirals agreed that it was too late in the day to put a landing force ashore.

The Japanese opened the engagement on the morrow, scoring several hits on two vessels of the advanced squadron before fire from the fleet silenced the batteries once more. Soon thereafter, eight of the smaller ships, of which the *Ta-Kiang* was one, towed boats carrying about 1,000 men from the British, French, and Dutch warships toward the beach. The landings were made without accident, but HMS *Perseus*, providing covering fire, was swept ashore by a strong eddy. The landing force encountered little opposition as it overran the batteries in succession, after which their guns were dismounted and spiked and their magazines blown up. This work of destruction completed, Admiral Kuper ordered the force to reembark. The French and Dutch contingents were already in their boats when a group of Japanese soldiers burst out of a valley to the rear of a battery to attack a party of British seamen who had not yet been marched to the beach. The marine battalion quickly arrived on the scene to help repulse the attackers, who were pursued to a stockade which they defended for a time before being dislodged and dispersed. Thereafter, the stockade was burned and the British force reembarked.

The next day, 7 September, was devoted to the embarkation of the captured guns, the senior officers having agreed that their removal would be the best guarantee of Choshu's good behavior, and to measures to refloat the stranded *Perseus*. By midnight, she had been lightened sufficiently to be towed off by a consort at high water. On the eighth, Admirals Kuper and Jaurés boarded the gun vessel *Coquette*, which led four screw-sloops in to attack the two batteries which had not been destroyed. No return fire was noted, so a landing party removed the guns and leveled the works.

The combined fleet's operation was completed by sundown, 10 September. Sixty-two pieces of ordnance had been embarked, ten batteries and their equipment destroyed, and Vice Admiral Sir Augustus Kuper wrote his superiors: ". . . I have satisfied myself, by personal examination of the entire Straits, that no batteries remain in existence in the territory of Prince Choshiu, and thus the passage of the Straits may be considered clear of all obstructions."[3]

It had been a smartly conducted operation. The leadership of Admirals Kuper and Jaurés seems to have been judicious and decisive, while the officers and men under their joint command worked together with little evidence of friction or misunderstanding. Nor was the American contribution entirely negligible—the *Ta-Kiang* enjoyed the distinction of being "mentioned in dispatches" for her services as gunboat, towboat, and hospital ship—the twenty-three wounded men, with a surgeon and attendants to care for them, were embarked in her for transportation to Yokohama.

Lieutenant Pearson and his men who served in the *Ta-Kiang* must have been envied by their fellows, for they were the only members of the *Jamestown*'s company to experience the excitement of active service while in Japanese waters. After they returned to the sloop of war, her vigil off

Yokohama continued its uneventful pattern through the remainder of 1864 and into 1865.

As the *Jamestown* rode at anchor in Edo Bay, other U.S. warships were en route to the Far East. Three screw-sloops, the *Iroquois*, *Wachusett*, and *Wyoming*, had orders to seek the Confederate raider *Shenandoah* in East Indian waters during the spring of 1865. Only the *Iroquois* actually arrived before the war's end; she spent two months cruising in the vicinity of Sunda Strait before returning home. The *Wachusett* was so unfortunate as to lose a topmast and then to run aground in West Indian waters, while the *Wyoming* did not steam into the Indian Ocean until August, by which time the elusive raider, disguised as the British merchantman she had been originally, was well on her way toward Cape Horn from her Bering Sea hunting ground.

The *Jamestown*'s sojourn in Japan came to an end when Minister Pruyn was finally able to dispense with her support early in April. Captain Price took his command to Macao, where he found orders to sail across the Pacific to Mare Island. The sloop of war stood out of Macao Roads on 17 June 1865, and her departure marked the disappearance of the sailing warship from the East India Station. To be sure, sailing storeships would continue to serve the U.S. Navy in the Far East for almost a decade longer, but they assumed warship duties only in cases of pressing emergency. Thus, as the *Jamestown*'s seamen loosed her sails and hove up the anchor, as Captain Cicero Price directed his navigator to set a course across the South China Sea to the Bashi Channel, an era was coming to an end. Undoubtedly it would have ended earlier but for the American Civil War; the commanding officer of the *Vandalia*, on her never-completed passage to the East India Station early in 1861, had reported from the Cape Verde Islands a conversation with foreign naval officers which indicated that his sailing man-of-war would be the only one in the Far East.

CHAPTER NINE

The Squadron Reestablished and Renamed

As the flames of civil strife flickered out in the United States, Secretary of the Navy Gideon Welles addressed himself to the question of employment for the greatly reduced naval force that would compose the Navy's peace establishment. It does not seem that the problem perplexed him unduly, for the solution he chose was a return to the distant-station policy of ante bellum years. Explaining his decision, he wrote: "The commerce and the navy of a people have a common identity and are inseparable companions. Each is necessary for the other, and both are essential to national prosperity and strength. Wherever our merchant ships may be employed, there should be within convenient proximity a naval force to protect them and make known our national power."[1]

Welles was not merely offering a defense of his policy; he was also making a strong argument in favor of an invigorated American merchant marine. Although the country's mercantile tonnage had more than doubled in the fifteen years before 1861, signs of a relative decline were not wanting by the time the Civil War began. The next four years had seen this gradual diminution give way to a decrease of catastrophic proportion as some 200 vessels fell victim to Confederate raiders and eight times as many were transferred to foreign registry to avoid the high insurance rates engendered by the danger of capture. The foreign trade of the Northern states had increased steadily in the course of the Civil War, yet by 1865 the United States no longer could be ranked among the leading mercantile marine nations. Secretary Welles could not anticipate that his country would be content henceforth to have the bulk of its foreign trade carried in ships registered abroad, but so it proved to be.

Restoration of the distant stations began with the formation of the Brazil Squadron in March 1865. Apparently Welles thought that the presence of a naval force might help to bring about a closer diplomatic and commercial relationship with Brazil and the Rio de la Plata region, especially since the former had been alienated by the *Wachusett*'s capture of the CSS *Florida* at Bahia in brazen disregard of Brazil's dignity as a sovereign nation.

During the war, the Navy Department had found it necessary to station a number of warships in European waters in an effort to counter the Confederate policy of having men-of-war built in English and French shipyards. A European Squadron was established early in June 1865 to include those vessels. The mission of this force was largely diplomatic—showing the flag in foreign ports—and its officers were to take advantage of every opportunity to gather information pertaining to naval policies and practices of European nations.

The East India Squadron was the third to be reestablished. On 31 July 1865, Secretary Welles sent final orders to Commodore Henry H. Bell, newly appointed to command U.S. naval forces on a station "extending from the Strait of Sunda to the shores of Japan." After listing the vessels that were to compose the squadron initially—the *Wachusett*, the *Wyoming* and the storeship *Relief*—Welles wrote: "Keep always in mind the leading objects in view, viz, to guard with jealous care the honor and interests of your flag and country, defend the citizens of the United States, and protect and facilitate the commerce thereof within the limits of your command."[2]

Commodore Bell, now in his fifty-seventh year, was an obvious choice for this assignment. He had commanded the *San Jacinto* throughout her 1856–58 cruise as flagship of the East India Squadron. During the war, he had served as fleet captain and division commander under Flag Officer David G. Farragut in the operation which won New Orleans for the Union. His flagship also was a veteran of a cruise in the Far East and had gained fame at New Orleans; indeed, the screw-sloop *Hartford* had flown Farragut's flag in all of the battles which proved him the greatest naval leader of the war.

The problem of relationship between senior officers of the Army and the Navy, together with the desire to recognize the victor of New Orleans, had led the Congress to the long overdue creation of proper flag ranks for the naval service. Farragut and eight fellows were promoted to the rank of rear admiral in July 1862, while Henry Bell was one of eighteen officers who attained the official title of commodore at the same time. In the course of the war, it had become customary for squadron commanders to be made acting rear admirals should they not already hold that rank, and the custom was continued afterward. Welles directed Commodore Bell to hoist his two-starred flag as soon as the *Hartford* dropped the pilot off Sandy Hook.

The flagship arrived in Macao Roads on 4 February 1866, and Admiral Bell wrote Welles: "I regret to say that we have seen but one merchant vessel, under United States colors, between the Cape of Good Hope and Macao, although we have encountered many of them under the flags of other nations."[3] The *Relief* was at anchor in the Taipa anchorage just to the southward when the *Hartford* stood in, and the *Wyoming* steamed over from Hong Kong to join the flag a few days later. The *Wachusett*, still on her way to the station, had sailed from Table Bay in company with the flagship and had been lost to sight in an Indian Ocean gale.

Bell's orders permitted him to choose Macao or Hong Kong to be his squadron's headquarters. He had no doubt as to the latter's superiority—it retained all the advantages that Commodore Perry had noted thirteen years earlier, bread and coal were always available there, and in addition, Hong Kong had become the communication center for the entire coast of China, receiving mails from all points a day before they reached Macao. On the other hand, the memory of Britain's rather unfriendly neutrality during the Civil War died hard; moreover, recent news from the United States indicated the possibility of war with France over the latter's Mexican adventure, and Hong Kong would almost certainly be unavailable to the squadron in the event of hostilities. So the *Relief* remained at anchor off Macao while the *Hartford*, having replenished her supplies from the storeship, went over to Hong Kong for coal and repairs to her engineering plant.

On the anniversary of George Washington's birthday, British warships joined the *Hartford* in dressing ship and firing salutes, signifying their friendliness. A month later, Bell applied to the governor of Hong Kong for permission to moor a storeship in the harbor for his squadron's use. The request was referred to Vice Admiral Sir George St. V. King, who saw no objection, recommending only that the harbor master assign an anchorage in an area clear of that reserved for the Royal Navy's use. Soon thereafter, the *Hartford*'s officers surveyed the contents of the storehouse at Macao; in May, Bell rented a godown in Hong Kong from Augustine Heard and Company for $200 per month and the payment of taxes. Thus, the British colony again became the base for the U.S. naval forces on the East India Station.

Meanwhile, other ports on the station could not be neglected. In mid-February, Commander John P. Bankhead was ordered to visit the Chinese treaty ports between Hong Kong and Shanghai in the *Wyoming*. A sharp lookout for pirates was to be kept, and those captured would be turned over to consuls who in turn were to deliver them to Chinese authorities for punishment.

The *Wyoming*'s cruise to the northward was eventful, but not because of pirates. During the evening of 17 March, she was groping her way toward Ningpo through a dense fog when contact with a small boat or a fishing stake caused the engine to be stopped. Shortly thereafter, land was sighted just off the port bow. Shouts of "Hard aport!" and "Full speed astern!" were followed by sounds of the bowsprit and head rigging striking a rock which projected from the shore, while the vessel "took the ground lightly, but without any shock."[4] She backed off immediately, but water gushing into the bilge beneath the port boiler indicated serious damage. Bankhead called all hands to quarters and had the boats stocked with extra food and water; fortunately, the pumps were able to keep the water level down while the *Wyoming* steamed back to Foochow for docking. From there the commander reported that the southwesterly wind had affected the monsoon current to an unexpected degree so that the screw-sloop had grounded on an island south of the group known as the White Dogs off the Min River. Inspection of the damage revealed that frames apparently rotted by the heat of the boiler had given way; otherwise she would have escaped with only the loss of some copper. Two weeks in dry dock sufficed for repairs, after which the *Wyoming* continued her cruise.

The long-awaited *Wachusett* reached Hong Kong early in March, a year after she had left Boston. Commander Robert Townsend explained his lengthy passage by pointing out that his vessel's light spars and aged canvas made her a poor sailer. Moreover, while at Batavia he had heard that the U.S. consul to Borneo had arranged for a cession of land in the northern part of the island to the American Trading Company of Borneo, whose president had assumed sovereign powers as the rajah of Ambong and Marudu. Since the consul was said to have claimed secret authority from the U.S. government, Townsend decided that he should inquire further. The *Wachusett* touched at Ambong Bay and saw no evidence of the projected American colony, but when she stopped at Manila to repair her fresh water condenser, her commander found the Spanish authorities concerned because Balabac, southwesternmost island of the Philippine archipelago and site of a Spanish penal colony, was reported to have been included in the American Trading Company's grant.

Admiral Bell had no trouble in pursuing the matter because the consul and the "rajah" were in Hong Kong trying to raise capital for their venture, which they asserted was commercial only. The latter tried to interest Bell in Ambong Bay as a base for the East India Squadron, but the admiral rejected it as likely to be inconvenient and expensive, noting that coal mined in Borneo was "very inferior, dirty and liable to spontaneous combustion."[5]

In mid-April, the *Wachusett* was ordered to Newchwang, a treaty port on the north shore of the Gulf of Pechihli, to investigate an incident involving the U.S. consul. It transpired that a Chinese servant in his employ had been abducted by some "sword racks" who later fired on the consul's party when the consul sought redress, wounding him and several others. When the authorities seemed powerless, further fighting occurred, in which four of the Chinese ruffians were killed. Upon the *Wachusett's* arrival, Commander Townsend landed an armed party which apprehended the principal offenders. The Newchwang magistrates hesitated to try them, so the commander suggested that he take them to Taku whence they could be sent to Peking for trial. Thereupon the local authorities accepted the responsibility, and the *Wachusett* sailed.

Admiral Bell had directed Townsend to inquire into the reported molestation of missionary graves at Tengchow. Landing there with an escort of one-hundred armed men, the naval officer demanded the arrest of the perpetrators, an indemnity for the missionary community, and a guarantee of protection from further outrage. When the Chinese prefect ignored his demands, Townsend appealed vainly to officials at Chefoo and then referred the matter to the American chargé at Peking.

Bell approved his subordinate's course of action at Newchwang, but that at Tengchow and Chefoo earned his reproof. However, no action could be taken against Townsend. After leaving Chefoo, the *Wachusett* had replenished her coal and provisions at Shanghai and then steamed up the Yangtze. Her officers and men found the summer heat very trying, and on 15 August, off Chinkiang, Commander Robert Townsend succumbed to "apoplexy produced by the heat of the sun."[6] The ship returned to Shanghai, where her late commanding officer was buried, and then went on to Japan, where Commander Robert W. Shufeldt boarded her from the flagship to assume command.

The Japanese government had assigned lots at Yokohama for the use of the various foreign naval forces at low rents. The British and French admirals took advantage of these, using Yokohama as their Japanese base, but Bell thought it unsuitable, being too far from the center of the station and to windward of most other ports between October and May. He preferred Nagasaki, which was centrally located and could assure provisions, good water, native coal of fair quality, a readily accessible harbor, and a healthy climate during most of the year. Holding this view, the American admiral was glad to sublet half of the U.S. Navy's Yokohama lot to the Pacific Mail Steamship Company, which had been granted a subsidy by the U.S. government to operate a regular steamship service between San Francisco and Oriental ports.

While at Yokohama in August 1866, Admiral Bell acknowledged a Department circular "establishing names and limits of 'permanent Squadrons.'" By this directive, six stations were established: North Atlantic, South Atlantic, North Pacific, South Pacific, European, and Asiatic. The last would encompass "the eastern coast of Africa and Asia and the islands which stud the seas and ocean eastward of the Cape of Good Hope."[7] Even without the Antipodes, which became the responsibility of the South Pacific Squadron, the new Asiatic Station seemed likely to provide an ample cruising ground for the warships assigned to it.

Meanwhile, the problem of piracy in Chinese waters demanded Bell's attention. The British Foreign Office had been urging the Admiralty to take more effective measures for coping with the pirates and it sought international cooperation to the same end. In response to British overtures, Welles ordered Bell to confer with Admiral King on the subject, which he did when the two flagships met at Nagasaki.

It was rather a discouraging conference for the American admiral, for as usual the Royal Navy seemed to have a plenitude of resources while he had virtually none. In 1864, the Admiralty had redrawn the limits of its China Station to exclude the Indian Ocean and all other waters south of 10° south latitude. Nonetheless, Admiral King's command included forty-three vessels of all types, of which eight were cruising warships and twenty-eight were gunboats. The latter were manned from the larger vessels as necessary; when not employed, they were laid up at Hong Kong which now had the dry docks and engine- and boiler-works necessary to maintain the entire squadron in a state of repair. Indeed, the gunboats were not intended to return to home waters; they were kept on the China Station until lost or sold out of the service.

In spite of his means, Admiral King had not yet developed a system capable of stamping out piratical activity. He told Bell that his gunboat commanding officers, usually dashing young lieutenants eager for reputation and prize money, had captured seventy-five pirate-junks in an eight-month period, without noticeable effect on the prevalence of piracy. Moreover, it was almost impossible to detect the pirates—at sea, their junks appeared to be armed cargo-carriers or fishing boats, of which there were so many frequenting the coast that individual inspection was impossible. Thus, paid informers and spies had to be relied on to identify the marauders.

Pirates struck the American brig *Lubra* becalmed off Hong Kong in September, killing her master and three crewmen. She was set afire, but survivors quenched the blaze and sailed her back to the harbor. When word of this reached Bell, he sent the *Wachusett* to Hong Kong, whence Commander Shufeldt reported that the attack must have been planned there—the pirates had known that the brig had opium on board and even where it was stowed. The murders were thought to have been in reprisal for the recent execution of fourteen pirates. Shufeldt believed that "so long as Hong Kong is made a huge smuggling mart for the whole coast of China it must attract the rascals and desperadoes of a superabundant & not over scrupulous population."[8]

The change of monsoon brought a temporary lull in piratical activity in November, and the *Wachusett* went to Amoy to support the consul's effort to gain satisfaction for the destruction of an American missionary's furniture by Chinese soldiers at Changchow. Reporting that not long ago a similar incident had occurred at Amoy, Commander Shufeldt considered it "a matter of regret that these missionaries, preachers of a gospel of peace, should seem so often to need the interpretation of a Gunboat, in order to make the heathen understand them."[9] Nonetheless, he admitted that both incidents were clearly in violation of Sino-American treaty provisions.

In December, Admiral Bell ordered the *Wachusett* to Korea to ascertain the fate of the American merchant schooner *General Sherman*. According to a report said to have originated with the schooner's Chinese pilot, she had been stranded in the Taedong River while on a trading mission a few months earlier, after which the Korean regent had ordered her burned and her company, which included three Americans, put to death. The story was the more plausible because the Korean government, attempting to maintain the "Hermit Kingdom's" isolation from foreign influence, was known to have executed a number of Roman Catholic priests earlier in 1866. In retaliation, French Rear Admiral Pierre G. Roze had blockaded the Salee River and seized Kangwha Island, whence his forces were dislodged by a greatly superior number of Koreans in the autumn. On the other hand, the crew of the merchant vessel *Surprise*, wrecked on the northwest coast of Korea during the spring, insisted that Korean authorities had treated them kindly before sending them through Manchuria to China.

While Bell doubted the legality of the *Sherman*'s attempt to force her way up the river, he came to fear that the reported fate of her company would be shared by the survivors of all vessels wrecked on Korean shores while passing on their lawful occasions. Therefore, he recommended to Welles that his squadron be reinforced by shallow-draft steamers from the North Pacific Squadron and by 1,500–2,000 troops. If such a force were sent quickly, the admiral had no doubt of his ability to capture Seoul, the

Korean capital, before the French renewed their operations in the spring of 1867. As soon as the Korean monarch acceded to American demands, the troops and gunboats would be returned to California, leaving foreign capitals, including Peking and Edo, suitably impressed by the United States' might and lack of territorial ambition. One suspects that Henry Bell was carried away with his own exuberance; after all, he still had no more than an unsubstantiated report of the murder of the *Sherman*'s men.

The *Wachusett* left Hong Kong on 29 December, touched at Shanghai for coal, embarked the *Sherman*'s former pilot and a missionary-interpreter at Chefoo, and then proceeded on her mission. Accepting the pilot's assertion that drifting ice made the Taedong River mouth inaccessible during the winter, Commander Shufeldt landed at a fishing village some distance to the southward to seek information. Its inhabitants, who seemed friendly although fearful of government reprisal for contact with foreigners, told him that bands of Chinese raided the Korean coast regularly and that the *Sherman*'s twenty-nine men, some of whom were Chinese, had perished in a fight with the local populace which suspected that they too were robbers. A Korean messenger summoned a dignitary from the provincial capital, but Shufeldt's interview with this "haughty & imperious . . . most perfect type of a cruel and vindictive savage" was very unsatisfactory. The *Wachusett* weighed anchor after a week, with her commanding officer observing that the Hermit Kingdom must be taught that it could not continue its "contemptuous exclusiveness."[10]

Standing to the southward, the screw-sloop paid a visit to Port Hamilton in the Kŏmun Do, off the south coast of Korea. Admiral Bell hoped that this anchorage might serve as a squadron rendezvous and sanatorium as well as a haven for American merchant vessels in time of danger. Shufeldt was enthusiastic about its potential, so the admiral suggested that it be acquired by the United States, adding that Port Hamilton was conveniently located to support operations against Korea, should Welles agree that the safety of mariners traversing its waters must be guaranteed. The naval officers' arguments failed to find favor in Washington at the time, but the U.S. Navy's—and Robert W. Shufeldt's—involvement in Korean affairs had just begun.

The iron gunboat *Ashuelot* joined the Asiatic Squadron in mid-January 1867. One of a class of side-wheel double-enders designed for service in inshore waters of the Confederacy, the new arrival bore little similarity to the British gunboats, being a much larger vessel in every regard. Nonetheless, she was quite suitable for riverine service, to which much of her sixteen years on the Asiatic Station would be devoted.

The *Ashuelot* was a welcome addition to Bell's command, but the arrival of another vessel at Hong Kong two weeks later seemed to be more significant to the Asiatic Squadron. The Pacific Mail Steamship Company's *Colorado*, which stood in on 31 January, 29½ days out of San Francisco, was the initiator of a monthly steamship connection between San Francisco and the Orient. Admiral Bell, whose flagship greeted the newcomer with a twenty-one gun salute, was quick to realize the importance of this service to his squadron—personnel could be sent out or home much more quickly than they could previously and at no greater cost, and the monthly steamer could also transport urgently needed items of equipment for his vessels. When the *Colorado* began her homeward passage two weeks later, she numbered among her passengers twenty of the squadron's invalids, twelve time-expired men, and two unfortunates whom general courts-martial had sentenced to confinement at Mare Island's naval prison.

Soon after the *Colorado*'s departure, the screw-sloop *Shenandoah* fired a salute to Bell's flag, and at the end of March, the *Ashuelot*'s sister *Monocacy* steamed into Hong Kong. The arrival of another American gunboat attracted little attention—no one could have foreseen that the venerable side-wheeler would still be showing the flag in Oriental waters as the twentieth century began.

En route to Yokohama early in April, the *Hartford* touched at Amoy, where Commander George E. Broad of HMS *Cormorant* informed the admiral of the loss of the American bark *Rover* off the south coast of Formosa. Two boatloads of survivors were said to have got ashore, where all except one Chinese sailor had been murdered by the "aboriginals." Learning of the incident at Takao, Broad had sent an offer of ransom for any other survivors and then took his vessel to the scene. When a landing party was fired on, the Briton recalled his boats, and the *Cormorant* shelled the bushes whence the fire had come before she returned to Amoy.

Expressing his appreciation to Commander Broad, Admiral Bell ordered the *Ashuelot* from Foochow to investigate further. Her commanding officer reported that Chinese authorities on Formosa had confirmed the fate of those in one of the *Rover*'s boats and thought that their fellows in the other boat, landing nearby, had also been killed. Thereupon, Bell decided that punitive action was required.

The *Hartford* and the *Wyoming* coaled at Shanghai and sailed for Formosa early in June. At Takao, the flagship embarked the British consul and an interpreter, while preparations for a landing were made. The punitive force, led by the *Hartford*'s Commander George E. Belknap, was to consist of both ships' marine contingents, eighty sailors from the

FIGURE 9–1. The double-ender gunboat *Monocacy*.

flagship armed with muskets or rifles, forty riflemen from the *Wyoming*, and the *Hartford's* light howitzer with a crew of five.

On the morning of 13 June 1867, the two vessels reached the site of the reputed massacre and came to anchor close inshore. As the boats were lowered and the 181 officers and men of the landing force donned their accouterments, those scanning the shore through long glasses could discern "Savages dressed in clouts and their bodies painted red" gathering in small groups on cleared hills a short distance inland.[11] Obviously, the Formosans were not to be taken by surprise.

Belknap's force landed and began its advance into the hills in mid-morning, to be received by fire from unseen enemies whose agility and familiarity with the terrain enabled them to slip away before American detachments could reach their places of concealment. After several hours of ineffectual pursuit, the sailors and marines stopped to rest, only to be harassed by shots from the stealthy Formosans. Seeking to dislodge the snipers, a company of sailors charged into an ambush in which its leader, Lieutenant Commander Alexander S. Mackenzie, was fatally wounded. By this time, another enemy was taking its toll—a number of men had already suffered sunstroke; continued efforts to pursue the Formosans would endanger their comrades, probably to no avail. So Commander Belknap, himself prostrated by the oppressive heat, ordered his men to retire to the beach, whence they were reembarked.

Realizing that any attempt to renew the assault must have a similar outcome and fearing lest a typhoon strike his vessels should they linger in their exposed anchorage, the admiral decided to return to Takao, where, in the absence of a public cemetery, Mackenzie's corpse was interred in the garden of the British consulate.

In his report to Welles, Bell stated that only the maintenance of a Chinese military force in the vicinity could guarantee the safety of mariners cast away on Formosa's south coast.[12] During the autumn of 1867, the governor of Fukien province, within whose jurisdiction Formosa lay, was induced to order 1,000 troops to accompany General Charles W. LeGendre, U.S. consul at Amoy, to the southern part of the island. On their approach, the chief of the tribe responsible for the deaths of the *Rover's* men signified his willingness to negotiate with the consul if the Chinese were kept out of his territory, and he ultimately promised that henceforth strangers would not be molested by his people. After having a temporary fort erected in an adjoining area, LeGendre returned to Amoy, whence he wrote Bell that his apparent success was due to the admiral's demonstration of "the power of our arms in Formosa in June last."[13]

Meanwhile, a period of relative tranquility during the summer of 1867 allowed Admiral Bell to direct his attention to other matters. The commanding officer of HMS *Serpent*, who was responsible for establishing aids to navigation on the portions of the Chinese coast that were most important to foreign commerce, had been informed that he could look to the French and American naval forces for assistance. Bell knew nothing of such an arrangement and regretfully declined to help in this work without specific direction from the Navy Department, to which he wrote: "Nearly every chart used by our Ships in these Seas are those issued by the British Hydrographic office . . . the assistance thus rendered to navigation is incalculable, and the comparative safety, with which the China Seas may now be navigated, is owing chiefly to their efforts."[14] As usual, however, the United States evinced no desire to share in a labor which the Royal Navy was performing so efficiently.

Britain also wished international cooperation toward the suppression of piracy. The new commander in chief of the China Station, Vice Admiral Sir Henry Keppel, wrote Bell to ask his opinion of a program toward this end. Briefly, Keppel wished to outlaw the arming of trading junks so that, after a specified period, any carrying ordnance could be seized and turned over to Chinese authorities, and to persuade the Chinese government to establish a register of trading junks, issuing a register number to each. Recognizing that foreign warships would have to assume greater responsibility for the protection of the unarmed junks, he believed that rigid enforcement of his program would soon bring an end to piracy in Chinese waters.

Admiral Bell agreed that the disarmament of junks was extremely desirable and recommended that they be forbidden to carry small arms as well, for the pirates usually overwhelmed Occidental merchantmen by the use of armed boarding parties. However, Bell believed that the enforcement of such a prohibition by visit and search must be left to Chinese officials. He suggested that piracies against foreign vessels within 30 nautical miles of the Chinese coast or within 3 nautical miles of Macao or Hong Kong be defrayed from the Imperial Customs treasury at the nearest treaty port after investigation by a mixed commission. This policy might lead the Chinese themselves to adopt effective police measures.

Keppel responded that Prince Kung, leader of the dominant faction at the Chinese court, had promised to put his program into effect. Rapid action by the Ch'ing court was not to be expected, and the Keppel program underwent considerable modification. Nonetheless, the reported incidents of piratical attacks on foreign merchant vessels seem to have diminished markedly in the next few years, while European admiralties ultimately came to recognize that the protection of Chinese commerce from Chinese pirates was properly the responsibility of the Chinese government.

Late in the summer, Bell's squadron was reinforced by two small gun-boats, the *Aroostook* and the *Unadilla*, but the admiral learned that a third, the *Penobscot*, had proven to be unseaworthy and returned to the United States, where she was decommissioned and sold. These were ves-sels of the "ninety-day" type, schooner-rigged screw-steamers hastily built for service in the Civil War. Some years earlier, they would have been a valuable addition to the squadron; now they were virtually worn-out.

By this time, the *Wyoming* had been ordered home, and Admiral Bell, knowing that the screw-sloops *Iroquois* and *Oneida* were en route to the station, decided that the *Wachusett*, which required major engine repairs, should return also. The two departed Hong Kong on successive days in mid-September, a perilous time to sail because September was notoriously the worst month for typhoons in the South China Sea. But the homeward-bound vessels were more fortunate than the *Monocacy*, which had re-turned to Hong Kong in disabled condition little more than a week before they sailed.

The side-wheeler had stood out for Shanghai on 7 September, and the next day "hurricane force winds" caused her to heave to under storm sails and steam. A boat was lost and the steering gear carried away, but she rode the heavy seas buoyantly while repairs were made. The violence of the gale increased as the evening wore on—"it seemed to strike the vessel with the force of a heavy, solid body, and it was a matter of wonder that anything could resist its terrible force." Not everything did—another boat was swept away and both topmasts and the fore topsail yard were snapped off. Preventer tackles were set up when the stack guys began to give way, but two hours later the stack toppled across a fore brace, carrying the fore yard with it. Deprived of the funnel's draft, the boiler fires burned low and steam pressure fell rapidly. The storm mainsail had blown out, but the gunboat was kept under control by loosing a corner of the mainsail. Although the wind moderated before midnight, the seas continued to run high, driving her farther inshore. Fortunately, the *Monocacy* was on soundings when land was sighted before dawn; she anchored until day-light enabled her to limp into Mirs Bay, picking up three Chinese from floating wreckage on the way. After the chief engineer had contrived a jury stack by fitting four fireroom ventilators together, the side-wheeler made her way back to Hong Kong, where Commander Samuel P. Carter credited her survival to "the special Providence of the Supreme Ruler of the Universe."[15] Some other observers felt that it was attributable to her sturdy iron hull. Repairs to the gunboat required two months.

As winter approached, the foreign flag officers made preparations for a mass demonstration off the ports of Hiogo (Kobe) and Osaka on Hon-shu's south coast. These were to be opened to foreign trade on 1 January

1868, and, while Bell reported that no trouble was anticipated, he felt that the presence of foreign warships would help to restrain the turbulent daimyo whose retainers were encamped in the vicinity. The *Shenandoah* brought Minister Robert B. Van Valkenburgh from Yokohama, to which the *Monocacy* was sent, while the *Hartford, Oneida, Iroquois,* and *Aroostook* stood in from Nagasaki. But this sizable U.S. naval force, the largest to be assembled in Japanese waters since Commodore Perry's day, was dwarfed by the British array—twelve warships headed by the massive ship of the line *Rodney*, flying Sir Henry Keppel's flag, and the powerful ironclad *Ocean*.

On 1 January, the men-of-war off Hiogo and Osaka dressed ship with the shogun's flag at the main and fired simultaneous twenty-one gun salutes at noon. Japanese warships and batteries responded promptly, saluting the Royal navy's white ensign first in deference to the ranks of the British plenipotentiary and Vice Admiral Keppel. On the next day, Bell received charts of the newly opened ports from the British naval officer who had conducted the survey.

Some days after the ports had been amicably opened for foreigners, Admiral Bell took four of his vessels to an anchorage off Osaka, some twelve miles from Hiogo. Unlike the latter, which provided a sheltered bay in which vessels could lie close to the town, Osaka was situated six miles above the mouth of a river, with the anchorage an open roadstead some distance off the bar at the river's mouth. Within a short time, a westerly gale began to lash the area and heavy surf made the bar impassable, to Bell's disgust, for he had planned to make a final visit to Van Valkenburgh at Osaka before sailing to meet his relief at Singapore in March. The gale had moderated somewhat by the morning of Saturday, 11 January, but the surf continued to run high on the bar. Nonetheless, the admiral ordered his barge manned and, accompanied by his flag lieutenant, shoved off for Osaka. In all of his vessels, anxious observers followed the barge's progress, and those with long glasses saw distinctly the "three heavy rollers" which "broke over her in quick succession."[16] The barge broached, throwing her occupants into the icy surf. Immediately boats cast off from all four warships and pulled to the scene with little regard for their own safety. That from the *Hartford* picked up two seamen and the *Aroostook*'s boat rescued a third, but Rear Admiral Henry H. Bell, Lieutenant Commander J. H. Reed, and ten seamen were drowned, the bodies of all being washed ashore during the next two days.

Obsequies for the victims of Bell's rash decision to go ashore were held at Hiogo on 14 January. A funeral train composed of thirty-two boats from American and British warships departed the *Hartford* with the flag-draped coffins and mourners embarked, and, as the lead boat pulled away from the flagship, the latter fired the first of thirteen minute guns. As she concluded her salute, that from the *Shenandoah* began, to be followed in turn by the *Oneida* and the *Iroquois*. Meanwhile, the boats reached the shore and several hundred British and American sailors formed a cortege, the former marching on the left in blue and the latter, attired in white uniforms, on the right. Both columns followed the twelve coffins borne shoulder-high to the graves dug in the foreign cemetery whose site had been chosen by Admiral Bell only a few days earlier. Flags flew at half-mast until sunset; then all were two-blocked after which the *Hartford* fired a final salute and the admiral's flag was hauled down.

No satisfactory explanation of this tragedy has ever been presented. There appears to have been no pressing need for Admiral Bell to go to Osaka at that time, and there is ample evidence that some of his sub-ordinates thought the attempt foolhardy. Apparently even routine precau-tions were ignored—the commanding officer of the *Oneida*, off Hiogo at the time, wrote that they had no life preservers. The author of a recent account of Bell's cruise in the Far East believes that the decision to go to Osaka regardless of the condition of the bar "marks the Admiral with the same determination, courage, and devotion to duty" that he had demon-strated below Canton in 1856, and in the capture of New Orleans.[17] One cannot agree—there seems to be nothing to admire in Bell's obstinate refusal to recognize the hazards of the passage and his disregard for the lives of those who perforce accompanied him or manned the boats which sought to succor them.

On this occasion there was a flag officer on hand to succeed to the command. The *Shenandoah*'s John R. Goldsborough had received news of his promotion to the rank of commodore some weeks earlier, and at the end of the month, he broke his broad pennant in the *Hartford* at Nagasaki. He did not, however, adopt the style of commander in chief; in the absence of formal orders from the Navy Department, he was simply the senior naval officer, Asiatic Squadron.

From Nagasaki, Commodore Goldsborough returned to Hong Kong, leaving the *Oneida* and the *Iroquois* to observe events in the newly opened ports, while the *Shenandoah*, under Commander John C. Febiger, was ordered to Korea to seek further information regarding the *General Sherman* and her company. Goldsborough arranged to have the remains of Bell, Mackenzie, and Reed exhumed and sent home in the storeship *Supply*, and early in March went to Canton to urge that the viceroy prohibit fishing junks from embarking arms and extra men. The Chinese official promised to issue a proclamation to that effect, and the com-modore hoped that it might be extended to the entire coast of China.

Meanwhile, he assured Secretary Welles that the British and American gunboats patrolling coastal waters seemed to be keeping potential pirates in check.

The *Hartford* reached Singapore at the end of March, and Commodore Goldsborough forwarded to the Navy Department letters from his subordinates in Japanese waters that indicated that the harmony reported by the late Henry H. Bell had not long survived the admiral himself. Quite clearly, the new commander in chief would have an interesting cruise.

·

CHAPTER TEN

Peace in Japan and Perils of the Sea

The new commander in Chief, Rear Admiral Stephen Clegg Rowan, had last been in the Far East thirty-eight years earlier, when he was a midshipman in the *Vincennes* on her first voyage of circumnavigation. Three years older than his predecessor, Rowan remained on active duty at sixty-two because, as an officer who had received the thanks of Congress for his Civil War service, he was exempt from statutory retirement.

His flagship, the *Piscataqua*, was a new screw-frigate of a class designed for belligerent service against Britain. Long, narrow, and lightly-sparred, "she had many bad qualities, but no good ones," and her name, respectable as it may have been in New England, made her the butt of seamen's ribald remarks.[1]

The *Piscataqua* arrived at Singapore on 18 April 1868, and Rowan took command of the Asiatic Squadron the same day. He found nothing to detain him at Singapore; although the port was crowded with merchant shipping, the American flag was nowhere to be seen and the spice trade with the United States was reported to be carried almost entirely in foreign vessels.

Admiral Rowan had assumed command of a sizable force—a screw-frigate, three screw-sloops, two paddle gunboats, two screw-gunboats, and two storeships—and another gunboat joined his flag in May. The last, the *Maumee*, was a slightly larger, ship-rigged version of the *Aroostook* and the *Unadilla*. Like them, she was in bad condition on arrival, the demand for gunboats during the Civil War having far exceeded the supply of

140

seasoned ship timber. Why the Navy Department considered such vessels as these fit for cruises on a distant station passes understanding.

Needless to say, the Asiatic Squadron was not concentrated when Rowan reached Hong Kong. Two sloops and the two side-wheelers were in Japanese waters and the two "ninety-dayers" were stationed on the Chinese coast to cruise against pirates—the *Unadilla* had burned two piratical junks off Hainan early in May—while the *Shenandoah* returned from her visit to Korea at the month's end.

Commander John C. Febiger's report on the *Shenandoah*'s visit was hardly encouraging. He had received a formal Korean reply to the earlier inquiry of Commander Robert Shufeldt. The Koreans had attributed the blame for the *Sherman*'s destruction to the schooner's company. Febiger had spent several days surveying the Taedong River. While engaged in the survey, the *Shenandoah* had been fired on by a shore battery without sustaining any damage. Admiral Rowan considered the report of the *Sherman*'s fate probably authentic, although he questioned its justification and thought the insult to the flag demanded a formal apology. "If [Japan] becomes settled before the close of the season, so that vessels can be spared, a force will be sent to Corea for that purpose."[2]

The outbreak of fighting in Japan resulted directly from the abolition of the shogunate and the assumption of authority by the youthful emperor, Mutsuhito, who adopted the reign name of Meiji. The Tokugawa and a number of their subordinate daimyo, realizing that the powers controlling the emperor consisted largely of their traditional opponents—especially Choshu, Satsuma, Tosa, and Hizen—resisted, and a battle was fought near Kyoto, the imperial capital, twenty miles northeast of Osaka, late in January 1868.

The *Iroquois* was anchored in the roadstead off Osaka at the time, and on the night of 31 January furnished asylum to the shogun and several of his adherents after the defeat of their forces. The Japanese were sent to one of their own vessels the next day, not long before Minister Robert B. Van Valkenburgh, accompanied by his counterparts of Prussia, Italy, and the Netherlands, came on board and requested Commander Earl English to take them to Hiogo. There the diplomats were established in the customhouse with a small force of marines to protect them. The British and French ministers were already in their respective consulates, each with his own guard.

Violence struck Hiogo on 4 February when soldiers of the daimyo of Hizen, exuberant over their victory, made an apparently unpremeditated attack on the foreigners. One of the *Oneida*'s boats was at the beach; its crew fled to the customhouse, dragging a wounded comrade with them. The fifteen U.S. marines, soon joined by fifty British troops, members of the French legation guard, and a landing force numbering 150 men with howitzers from the *Oneida* and the *Iroquois*, quickly drove the Japanese soldiery into the mountains. Thereafter, defenses were erected around the foreign settlement while armed boat crews took possession of four Japanese steamers in the harbor. Within a few days, the ministers' demand for satisfaction had been satisfied by the imperial government, so the town and vessels were restored. On 2 March the officer responsible for firing on the foreigners committed hara-kiri in the presence of officials from the several legations, with the *Oneida*'s commanding officer attending as a naval representative.

Nonetheless, the danger to foreigners had not passed. A midshipman and ten sailors manning a boat from the French corvette *Dupleix* were victims of an attack near Osaka later in March; twenty-two Japanese were sentenced to death for that outrage, but the French admiral asked that the executions be stopped after eleven had been beheaded.

The *Piscataqua* arrived in Japanese waters in June, touching first at Nagasaki and then going on to Yokohama. The situation at the latter port was tense, for the fighting between Tokugawa and imperial forces was continuing in the interior of Honshu and there were occasional disturbances in nearby Edo. To complicate matters further, the former Confederate ironclad ram *Stonewall* had reached Yokohama from the United States during the spring. She had been sold to the shogun's government after being turned over to the United States at the war's end, and Commander George Brown of the U.S. Navy had been granted leave to deliver her. Both emperor and former shogun claimed her; Minister Van Valkenburgh directed that she be turned over to neither until the struggle for power had been concluded. Her civilian crew received such high wages that it was paid off to save money, a detachment from the *Monocacy* taking its place until relieved by men from the flagship.

Soon after Rowan's arrival in Yokohama, reports of menacing forces of Chinese rebels gathering in the vicinity of Tientsin led him to order the *Ashuelot* there from Nagasaki, while the *Monocacy* was sent to Shanghai. The *Shenandoah*, replenishing at Hong Kong, had orders for Yokohama, as did the *Maumee*, which had been cooperating with a British gunboat in an anti-pirate sweep off the Chinese coast.

July brought some excitement but no action. The *Piscataqua* prepared to weigh and steam up to Edo when a large fire was seen in its vicinity. Van Valkenburgh, however, reemphasized American neutrality vis-à-vis the Japanese conflict. Two weeks later, rumors of an attempt to carry the *Stonewall* by boarding caused Rowan to have her machinery dismantled and to call the flagship's company to battle stations at midnight. If such an attack had been planned, the precautionary measures proved sufficient to dissuade those involved.

A much more serious matter came to Rowan's attention in September. Two of the *Oneida*'s midshipmen with four of like rank from the French ironclad *Belliqueuse* had become involved in a row with Japanese police in a disreputable district of Hiogo. With unusual forbearance, the Japanese had substituted bamboo rods for their razor-edged swords and administered a sound thrashing to the intoxicated youths, who responded with revolver shots before fleeing to the U.S. consulate. Their protest of "police brutality" brought armed boat crews from the *Oneida* and the *Iroquois*; when an investigation revealed the facts of the case, the French and American commanding officers, accompanied by the U.S. consul, made formal apology to the Japanese governor. Admiral Rowan was especially concerned because the midshipmen had fired. In the event of a policeman's death, the Japanese might well have demanded the malfeasant's execution—"we taught the Japanese the demand of a life for a life in the case of the French boat crew at Osaka."[3] Fortunately, the Hiogo affair had no fatal outcome.

From Hiogo, the *Piscataqua*, with the *Iroquois* in company, went to Nagasaki, where the admiral found the *Ashuelot*, the *Maumee*, the homeward-bound *Shenandoah*, and the *Idaho*. The last of these vessels had been built as a fast commerce raider; when she failed to reach her designed speed by a wide margin, her engines and boilers were removed and she was sent to the Asiatic Station for service as a hospital and storeship. On Admiral Bell's recommendation, the *Idaho* had been ordered to Nagasaki, which he thought should be the squadron's Japanese base. His successor did not agree. The British, French, and Dutch maintained hospitals ashore at Yokohama, and there the *Idaho* should be stationed. Further, Rowan held that Yokohama had become the commercial and communication center of Japan, while Edo, the political capital, at which the ministers of foreign powers must reside, was but a short distance away. One cruising vessel would have to be kept at Yokohama; her medical officers could assist those of the *Idaho* if the latter were there.

On arriving at Nagasaki, Admiral Rowan professed to be shocked to learn that more than half of the sick in the *Idaho* were suffering from various forms of venereal disease. He immediately ordered that Nagasaki be off-limits to the companies of his vessels and later decreed that anyone sent to the *Idaho* for treatment of secondary syphilis be reduced in rate until returned to duty or discharged from the service. However, Nagasaki was not the only Japanese city in which venereal disease might be contracted. Little more than two months after he had joined his ship at Yokohama, the junior medical officer of the *Iroquois* wrote: "For a victim of 'Miss Placed Confidence' in Japan is the worst kind of victim. She plays the d—l with the generative organs of the guilty Lords of Creation that worship at her shrine. For particulars consult daily sick lists on board the English, American and French men-of-war in the harbor of Yokohama, Japan."[4]

While venereal diseases were probably accepted as a part of his life by the typical nineteenth-century seaman, it is clear that their prevalence and virulence among the officers and men of warships in Japanese waters were a cause for concern. Moreover, most navies, including that of the United States, had adopted somewhat more generous policies with regard to liberty for their enlisted men as the years passed, thereby increasing Jack's opportunity to make the acquaintance of "Miss Placed Confidence."

In December 1868, Vice Admiral Sir Henry Keppel wrote his fellow commanders in chief of his efforts to cope with the problem, efforts which presumably had their origin in his government's program to eliminate the evil in the Royal Navy's home ports and in the vicinity of British military bases. Keppel had helped authorities in Yokohama to establish a hospital where native women could be inspected and treated during the past summer; six months later, local opposition to the policy had diminished markedly and some Japanese were seeking assistance voluntarily. Surgeons' reports indicated a diminution in the number of new cases in Her Majesty's vessels, and Keppel hoped that other squadrons had shared the benefit. But all was not yet well. From Japan, HMS *Rodney* had sailed to Hong Kong, where "public women" had for some time been obliged to register and submit to periodic physical examination. Within a few days of the British flagship's arrival, a great increase in the number of venereal cases ashore was reported. Keppel concluded that the inspection of liberty men before they left their ships was the only solution, and he asked that his foreign counterparts join him in issuing orders to this effect.

Admiral Rowan responded that he would support the Briton in this "wise and humane" policy "with much real pleasure."[5] His general order adopted the wording of the British regulations which required that all unmarried, non-rated men under the age of thirty-five be examined before going on liberty, with the stipulation that "the medical inspection of each man must be private; and must be conducted so as not to wound the most sensitive."[6] No liberty would be granted any sailor found to be infected while he was under treatment and for two weeks thereafter. Petty officers known to be suffering from venereal disease were subject to the same regulation. The efficacy of this order was obviously reduced by its naive assumption that husbands, older men, and officers were either chaste or immune to infection; medical logs reveal that all too frequently they were neither, as the admirals were well aware.

Meanwhile, the fighting in Japan continued. From Nagasaki, Rowan reported that he expected the shogun to reassert his erstwhile political control, leaving the emperor, as formerly, to exert a vague spiritual influence from Kyoto. This was probably wishful thinking on the admiral's part, for his compatriots favored the shogun, thinking him "progressive and a friend to foreigners, particularly Americans."[7] Britons and Frenchmen, on the other hand, preferred the emperor, in whose cause the Britons had a definite financial interest.

On 24 October 1868, the *Iroquois* departed Nagasaki for Sado Island near Niigata on the northwest coast of Honshu, where rival forces were confronting one another. After observing the military operations there for a short time, the screw-sloop stood on to Hakodate to look into the mystery surrounding a bark manned entirely by Chinese coolies, which had sailed into the Japanese harbor in August with neither documents nor flag. She was apparently of American origin, so Consul Elisha E. Rice had boarded the vessel. He found her in disarray with some indication that her company had met a violent end. Although it appeared that she was actually the Peruvian *Cayolte*, Rice had requested the assistance of a warship to undertake a thorough investigation.

Commander English and the consul spent four days interrogating the coolies. When stories conflicted, the Americans resorted to fairly extreme measures including the denial of food and drink to the leaders and nooses placed about their necks and hauled taut whenever they were suspected of lying. Such methods were denounced by some, but Rice was able to reconstruct the events of the *Cayolte's* cruise. Briefly, she had sailed from Callao bound for other Peruvian ports at which the coolies were to have been landed to work on nearby plantations. Three days out, the Chinese had overpowered and killed the vessel's small crew, sparing the master's life on receiving his promise that he would navigate her to China. After he managed to escape, the bark blundered into Ichiura Wan, whence a Japanese pilot conned her to Hakodate. Although Admiral Rowan denounced the seizure of the *Cayolte* by the coolies as an act of piracy, his government disagreed. No American interest was involved, and no action was authorized. Ultimately the bark was sold at her owner's direction, while the coolies were left to make the best of their situation.

As his first year on the station ended, Rowan had cause to be embarrassed about the physical state of the U.S. Asiatic Squadron. In addition to his flagship, of which no one thought highly, he had two serviceable screw-sloops, both of which were due to return to the United States within a year; two iron double-enders, which he considered useless as cruisers because of their heavy coal consumption, lack of sail-power, and paddle wheels; and three smaller gunboats, of which none could be expected to weather even a moderate gale. And when the *Iroquois*, one of the two "serviceable" vessels, got underway for Swatow early in March, the crown sheet of her port boiler gave way, necessitating a month's inactivity for repairs. Not without reason, one of the *Unadilla*'s engineers wrote: "A North German frigate came in today . . . it is a very nice looking vessel, in fact she looks more like a Man of war than any vessel we have on this station."[8]

By this time, however, the Asiatic Station was enjoying an unusual tranquility. Admiral Rowan reported the triumph of the emperor's forces on Honshu on 24 February 1869, and the *Stonewall* was duly delivered to them within a month to become the *Kotetsu* (later the *Azuma*), the first unit of Japan's armored navy. A portion of the former shogun's force, commanded by his admiral, Enomoto Idzumi no kami, continued to hold Hakodate, against which the emperor's ships prepared to move during the spring. A gallant attack by Enomoto's paddler *Eagle* against the *Kotetsu* helped to delay the imperial offensive for some weeks, but the outcome could not be deferred for long. Aided by British and French merchantmen which transported coal, supplies, and troops, the emperor's forces closed Hakodate, destroyed Enomoto's small squadron in a naval battle on 20 June, and besieged the rebels in their fortifications. These capitulated with the honors of war on 26 June, marking the end of the civil war in Japan.

When fighting appeared imminent in May, the *Aroostook* had been ordered to Hakodate, to be joined within a short time by the *Oneida* and then by the *Iroquois*. Van Valkenburgh had adjured Rowan to follow a course of strict neutrality, and so the warships did, offering asylum to all American residents there and assuring that merchant vessels under the U.S. flag rendered no assistance to the combatants.

British support of the imperial forces caused some hard feeling, but relations between personnel of the British and American warships in the Far East remained relatively good throughout the period, even when baseball teams from the *Piscataqua* and the British China Squadron met in a fifteen-inning, five-hour contest from which the Americans emerged victorious by the score of 66–28. To be sure, some took offense when on 5 July 1869 (the Fourth fell on Sunday) the companies of British warships at Yokohama dressed ship at 8 A.M. while those of other nations showed this mark of respect to the United States at sunrise. The muttering over this supposed slight increased markedly when, on 29 August, the globe-circling British frigate *Galatea* stood into the harbor, saluting the flag of Admiral Keppel and ignoring those of the French and American admirals. This snub was especially apparent because the *Galatea* was commanded by Captain Prince Alfred, the Duke of Edinburgh, Queen Victoria's second son. The duke called on Rowan the next morning and was received with the honors due his naval rank; when the admiral returned the call, he was not saluted, nor did his French counterpart fare better. The *Galatea* hoisted the royal standard the following day and all warships fired the appropriate salute, but Admiral Rowan signified his desire that his subordinates ignore the duke's invitation to attend a levee at the British legation. Within a short time, a British officer brought assurances that the *Galatea* would salute Rowan's flag on 1 September, and the impasse was broken. Nonetheless, when the British ships sailed on 16 September, the captain's clerk in the American flagship expressed his opinion: "Mr. Prince Alfred goes with [Keppel], very good riddance [;] his visit here has been a fizzle as it has been in every other place he has visited and even his own countrymen are ashamed of such a man."9

Disagreeable as the Duke of Edinburgh may have been, his visit had a significance which cannot be overlooked—as a member of a foreign royal family, he was received by the Japanese emperor. Henceforth, diplomatic representatives, naval commanders in chief, and distinguished visitors to Japan would be accorded the same treatment as a matter of course.

A spate of orders from the Navy Department began to reach the Asiatic Station during the summer of 1869. These resulted from the election of General Ulysses S. Grant to the presidency in 1868. His first appointee to the Navy Department, Adolph E. Borie, held office for only four months and during that period, Vice Admiral David D. Porter actually executed the secretary's duties. Borie, however, did interest himself in renaming naval vessels, particularly those which reflected Gideon Welles's propensity for names of New England Indian origin. Sailors generally believed that to change a ship's name was to invite disaster, but when the Department ordered that the *Piscataqua* henceforth be known as the *Delaware*, there were few objections.

Other orders directed that all warships be fitted with full sail rigs and enjoined the strictest economy in the consumption of coal—toward this end, vessels were to cruise under sail alone, raising steam only in cases of emergency and then utilizing no more than half their boiler power. To those familiar with the monsoons and tidal currents of the Asiatic Station, these orders must have seemed highly unrealistic, for even a full head of steam was often insufficient to counter these at their maximum velocities. These regulations were not enforced stringently under Borie's successor, George M. Robeson, but the various fleets were allowed so little money for the purchase of coal that steam was not often used.

Porter was desirous of ridding the Navy of the war-built gunboats, many of which were unsuitable for cruising under sail. Among these were the *Aroostook*, *Maumee*, and *Unadilla*, all of which had been condemned by survey. Admiral Rowan had already requested authority to sell the vessels at public auction on the station because their badly rotted hulls could hardly survive the long passage home. All were sold during the autumn of 1869 to private bidders, and for a time it seemed that the *Ashuelot* and the *Monocacy* might also be offered for sale. The double-enders were especially desirable for mercantile service on the Yangtze because of their paddle wheels, speed, and iron construction, and Rowan considered them "worthless as cruisers," but their sale would have reduced the squadron to two warships, a force he thought inconsistent with the nation's "honor and interest."[10]

The proper role for the *Idaho* had continued to engage the admiral's attention, and he had finally recommended that "a small unpretending hospital on our lot on the heights overlooking Yokohama" be built to care for the squadron's invalids.[11] Released from this duty, the fast-sailing *Idaho* would serve as a transport and supply ship, crossing the Pacific to Panama with time-expired men and returning with new personnel, provisions, and supplies for the squadron. The *Idaho* departed Nagasaki for Yokohama in August and while south of Kyushu was quite shaken by the outskirts of a typhoon which also imperilled the *Oneida* and the homeward-bound *Iroquois*.

Despite this experience, Commander Bushrod B. Taylor was ordered to take the *Idaho* to sea on 20 September, the month in which 50 percent of the typhoons annually occurring in Japanese waters could be anticipated. At sunset the next day she encountered another severe typhoon. The *Idaho* was directly in the track of this storm, which tore her sails from the yards and then snapped yards and masts alike. Completely dismasted and pinned on her beam-ends by the violence of the wind, the helpless hulk seemed doomed—and then the gale gave way to the dead calm typical of a typhoon's eye. Freed of the leveling force of the wind, the seas rose to mountainous heights, imparting to the *Idaho* an indescribable combination of rolling, pitching, lurching motions and immersing her decks under masses of green water. Timbers, stanchions, and bulwarks carried away, but miraculously her hatches did not. By the time she entered the other side of the storm, there was literally nothing left to destroy except the ship herself, and she proved indestructible.

As the wind's force diminished, the *Idaho*'s battered company, hardly able to believe that their vessel had actually weathered the typhoon, began to clear away wreckage and devise a jury rig. The French gunboat *Aspic*, searching for typhoon victims, sighted the *Idaho* and offered every assistance within her power. That did not include towing; the little *Aspic* steamed off to summon a ship capable of that. She directed the Pacific Mail Company's steamer *America* to the *Idaho*, but the *America*'s master merely promised to inform Admiral Rowan of the disabled vessel's condition and position on his arrival at Yokohama. The *Delaware* spent three days searching and returned to port on 29 September to find that the *Idaho* had made her way back to Yokohama under jury rig.

Following a survey, Rowan ordered that the *Idaho* receive only those repairs required to make her habitable; she would serve as a stationary store and receiving ship until the Navy Department ordered her sold. Commander Taylor's report that prisoners embarked in the *Idaho* had been instrumental in saving her led the admiral to recommend that their sentences be remitted, and Robeson concurred.

As 1870 began, Admiral Rowan was able to report that on his station "peace and quietness now appear to be the rule, with an occasional exception, such as the depredations of pirates on the coasting junks and other petty piracies on the rivers on other smaller boats, and the murder of a missionary now and then." Under the circumstances, he thought that "two reliable sea-going vessels for the coast of Japan, and two for the coast of China," in addition to the flagship and a smaller ship to attend her would be an ample Asiatic Squadron.[12] This estimate may be contrasted with the force which Admiral Keppel had been informed would constitute the British China fleet: an armored battleship to carry the flag, four corvettes, sixteen gun vessels, and four others. Vessels assigned to survey duty were not included in this number. As it developed, however, even Rowan's modest proposal was larger than the force which the United States would be willing to assign on occasion.

The second of the Asiatic Squadron's two "serviceable" vessels, the *Oneida*, got underway from Yokohama en route to Hong Kong and thence to the United States late in the afternoon of 24 January 1870, receiving the cheers with which foreign warships on the station traditionally bade farewell to their homeward-bound fellows. As the lightship off the anchorage fell astern, the *Oneida* was put under plain sail in order that the brisk northeasterly breeze might assist her engines. Then the sea watch was set and the watch below piped to dinner.

Winter darkness came early in those waters; there was no moon, but the starlit night was perfectly clear so those on the screw-sloop's bridge had no difficulty in conning her down Tokyo (formerly Edo) Bay. Soon a steamer's masthead light was sighted on the starboard bow, causing no particular concern, for the *Oneida*, on the port tack, was well over toward the eastern shore of the bay, which was more than three miles wide at that point. The approaching vessel's lights drew farther to starboard for a

FIGURE 10–1. The luckless *Oneida* drying sails and hammocks.

time, but then it became apparent that she was turning toward the *Oneida*. The latter's officer of the deck ordered the helm hard astarboard and sent a messenger to summon his superiors; before they could reach the bridge, the screw-sloop reeled under the impact of a larger steamer's iron stem cleaving through her starboard quarter. As the smitten warship began to settle, all hands were called and Commander Edward P. Williams tried to sail her ashore, failing because her steering gear had been carried away. Unfortunately, the three boats which the *Oneida* had lost in the typhoon of the preceding August had not been replaced, her gig was smashed in the collision, and another boat was crushed by her smokestack, which fell as the vessel heeled. Thus, only two boats could be lowered, nor did the stranger delay to offer assistance in spite of the *Oneida*'s distress signals. Some fifteen minutes after the collision and little more than two hours after she had left Yokohama, the stricken vessel sank in twenty fathoms of water, carrying with her Commander Williams and 114 of his officers and men.

The *Oneida*'s minute guns had been heard in Yokohama, some ten miles away, and when an officer of the Peninsular and Oriental Steam Navigation Company's newly arrived iron steamer *Bombay* stated rather casually that the *Bombay* had collided with another ship while standing up the bay, fears for the American warship began to mount. Nonetheless, nothing had been done when the *Oneida*'s surgeon, her senior surviving officer, reached Yokohama early the next morning. Upon receiving his report, Lieutenant Commander Horace E. Mullan of the immobile *Idaho* requested that foreign men-of-war undertake a search for survivors. The senior British naval officer present lost no time in ordering the survey steamer *Sylvia* and a steam launch to the scene and asked that the *Bombay*, the only ship with steam up, assist as well. Her master, Arthur W. Eyre, refused on the ground that the extent of the *Bombay's* damage had not yet been ascertained, but an order from the P & O agent sufficed to get her underway a short time afterward. British, French, and Russian vessels participated in the search, to no avail, for the *Oneida's* only survivors were the four officers and fifty-seven men saved in her two boats.

Meanwhile, Lieutenant Commander Mullan had chartered the former USS *Aroostook* from her civilian owners to undertake his own search. The *Idaho* had no engineering personnel and few of the *Oneida's* had survived; to fill this need, Captain Dmitry Mikbayloff of the Russian man-of-war *Vsadnik* volunteered the services of six officers and firemen from his ship. For more than a month, these Russians kept the old gunboat steaming in search of survivors and the remains of victims, as willingly as if one of their own vessels had been lost.

Three days after the disaster, John F. Lowder, the British consul at Yokohama, convened a court to inquire into the circumstances of the *Oneida's* loss. It consisted of Lowder himself as president, two commanders from HMS *Ocean*, and the masters of two British merchant vessels. The court spent two weeks interrogating those in the *Bombay* and the American survivors, after which it concluded that responsibility for the collision rested with the *Oneida* but that Eyre had "acted hastily & ill-advisedly, in that instead of waiting and endeavouring to render assistance to the *Oneida*, he, without having reason to believe that his own vessel was in a perilous position, proceeded on his voyage."[13] For this, his master's certificate was suspended for six months.

The flagship of the Asiatic Squadron was at Manila in late January, whence she proceeded to Hong Kong. There Admiral Rowan received news of the disaster and as soon as possible the *Delaware* departed for Yokohama. An engineering casualty en route forced her to return to Hong Kong for repairs, but Commander Francis A. Roe, Rowan's fleet captain, boarded a passing mail steamer bound for Yokohama, where he convened a naval court of inquiry. A less exhaustive investigation was undertaken—the *Bombay* had already sailed—and, unlike the British consular court, the naval court of inquiry found the P & O steamer solely responsible for the collision. Admiral Rowan, reviewing the reports of both inquiries, agreed that the British verdict was erroneous.

Perhaps these conclusions were to be expected given the composition of the courts, yet the evidence seems to support the American finding. And Arthur W. Eyre, master mariner, was extremely fortunate to escape with a mere six-months suspension—which he appealed on the apparently valid ground that a court of inquiry had no power to punish. Public feeling in the foreign settlement ran high against him, although he was supported by his countrymen residing there, and some thought that the "Delawares" would have taken matters into their own hands had they found the *Bombay* in port when the flagship finally reached Yokohama.

The bodies of four of those lost in the *Oneida*, including that of Commander Williams, were recovered and interred in the foreign cemetery after a funeral which British military and naval officers attended en masse. Roe reported the great courtesy shown him by Vice Admiral Sir Henry Kellett, who had relieved Keppel, as an indication of the official British desire to maintain a close relationship with the Americans. In May, officers of the U.S. Asiatic Squadron met in the *Idaho* and resolved to raise a granite column over the graves of the *Oneida*'s dead in memory of all lost in the unfortunate vessel. One-thousand dollars for this purpose was subscribed at once.

However, the final memorial service was held almost twenty years later. On 4 May 1889, Rear Admiral George E. Belknap, commander in chief of the Asiatic Squadron, and officers and enlisted men from the flagship *Omaha* and the *Monocacy* attended a Buddhist ceremony at the temple of Ikegami near Omori, in whose garden a stone shaft bearing the *Oneida*'s and Commander Williams's names and the date of their loss had been erected. Seventy-six priests decked in elaborate robes intoned prayers to the accompaniment of drums and reed instruments for those who had perished in the vessel. Meanwhile, Japanese divers, who had been engaged for ten years in removing everything of value from the wreck, acted as kinsmen of the dead sailors, for the repose of whose souls they burned incense at the altar. Admiral Belknap reported that he had been "informed on good authority that this is the first ritual held by the Buddhist sect in Japan as connected in any way with the decease of Christians."[14]

The *Delaware* hoisted her own homeward-bound pennant, presented by the American residents of Hong Kong, on 18 June and got underway for Singapore, where Admiral Rowan would await his relief. The flagship's departure left only the *Monocacy*, the *Ashuelot*, and the hulk *Idaho* in Oriental waters; it was hoped that additional vessels would reach the station from the United States before the need for their services became pressing.

The *Colorado*, the new flagship, finally reached Singapore in mid-August, and Rowan lost no time in turning the command over to his successor. Before the two parted company, however, it was necessary to have a boat race. The *Delaware*'s barge had held the championship of the foreign squadrons in the Far East during Rowan's cruise, and the *Colorado* had a new boat called the *Daring* of which great things were expected. The latter won the four-mile race by twenty seconds, whereupon the "Delawares" delivered their silver-banded oars and black game-cock to the new champions.

Admiral Rowan had asked to be allowed to return home by way of the recently opened Suez Canal, but the Navy Department directed that the *Delaware* take the Cape of Good Hope route. As she stood up New York Bay after an excellent passage, an outward-bound warship fired a vice admiral's salute to Rowan's flag, his first intimation that he had been promoted to that rank. It was also a valedictory salute, for neither Stephen C. Rowan nor the *Delaware* ever went to sea again.

CHAPTER ELEVEN

An Effort to Open Korea

Admiral Rowan's successor, Rear Admiral John Rodgers, had also received the thanks of Congress for his Civil War Service. Fifty-eight years of age when he assumed the Asiatic command, Rodgers was a single-minded individual whose vigor and tenacity had earned him the respect of his contemporaries.

His force was to consist of six vessels: the screw-frigate *Colorado*; the new screw-sloops *Alaska* and *Benicia*, handsome, bark-rigged two-stackers thought to compare favorably with the best of their type in any navy; the *Ashuelot* and the *Monocacy*; and the iron screw-gunboat *Palos*, which had been completed as an ocean-going tug in 1865. The screw-sloops had preceded the flagship to the station, and the *Palos* was coming out by way of the Suez Canal, through which she steamed on 11 and 12 August, the first U.S. naval vessel to use the canal.

Rodgers arrived on his station to find the Tientsin Massacre, in which ten French nuns and twelve other Europeans had perished in June 1870, a major topic of conversation. Nervous foreigners suggested that warships, including the *Ashuelot*, be ordered to winter at Tientsin, but Rodgers reacted unfavorably, insisting that the vessels would be relegated to the role of "blockhouses" with garrisons too small to oppose a horde of Chinese. However, Frederick F. Low, U.S. minister to China, pointed out that symbols of authority were held in great esteem by the Chinese, and Rodgers admitted that it would be much safer to bring the double-ender south in the spring than to do so when she might encounter a winter monsoon gale. So the *Ashuelot* became the first of the Asiatic Squadron's vessels to be frozen in for the winter in a northern Chinese port, a practice which soon became quite common.

During the autumn of 1870, the *Alaska* made a cruise up the Yangtze, which her Commander Homer C. Blake believed very beneficial because it demonstrated the ability of the squadron's larger ships to steam to the scene of any outrage perpetrated on Americans plying the river or residing on its banks. He found the channel changed markedly by the rapid current, but the navigation of the river was actually easier, thanks to beacons which had been erected during the past few years. Since the large and increasing trade on the Yangtze was dominated by Americans, the commander ventured "the opinion that no more important duty could be performed by one of the smaller vessels of this Squadron, than to be employed cruising in the river."[1] He added that three English gunboats were the only men-of-war to which foreigners could look for protection at the time.

The end of the year found the *Colorado* in Japanese waters, but reports of smallpox at Yokohama, where the *Benicia* was showing the flag, caused the admiral to visit only Kobe and Nagasaki before going to Hong Kong. There he devoted most of his attention to planning a full-scale expedition to Korea for the purpose of negotiating a treaty which would guarantee the good treatment of shipwrecked seamen and which might result in the end of Korean isolation.

Admiral Rodgers, whose interest in Korea had been kindled by rumors of the *General Sherman*'s fate, had made the conclusion of a treaty with the "Hermit Kingdom" his goal. He thought originally of opening Korea to trade, but George F. Seward, who saw Rodgers in Washington while on leave from his consulate general in Shanghai, convinced him that it would probably attract little foreign commerce. Thereupon, Rodgers wrote George M. Robeson, Secretary of the Navy, to urge the desirability of an agreement for the protection of mariners in distress. Less than a month later, Secretary of State Hamilton Fish directed Minister Low in Peking to negotiate such a treaty, in which endeavor he would be supported by the Asiatic Squadron. While the diplomat was to be responsible for conducting the negotiations, he would "maintain entire frankness and unreserve with Admiral Rogers, conferring freely with him in every stage of the negotiations."[2]

After talking with Low in November 1870, the admiral decided that the Korean expedition should sail in May 1871. There was no attempt to conceal the preparations; since rumors of an imminent American effort to open Korea had been circulating for well over a year, it would have been pointless. However, foreign naval commanders showed no inclination to take part, and Rodgers was able to obtain a copy of the chart depicting the approaches to the Salee River that French Admiral Pierre Roze had had prepared.

The *Colorado* and the *Palos* proceeded to Woosung in April, there to be joined by Minister Low and his suite and the newly refitted *Monocacy*. Rodgers welcomed on board five Korean survivors of a shipwreck, hoping that their return would help to convince Korean officials of the sincerity of the American desire for peaceful negotiations. But the Koreans were so fearful that they would be executed if they accompanied the expedition that Rodgers turned them over to Japanese authorities at Nagasaki a month later.

The *Ashuelot* proved another disappointment. She limped into the Hwangpoo with the *Palos*'s assistance at the end of April, and a board of survey found her unfit for service without extensive repairs to hull, boilers, and engines, no less than four years having elapsed since her last major overhaul. Rather than wait until the *Ashuelot* was ready to accompany him, Rodgers had all but twenty of her company distributed among the other vessels of the squadron and left her in dockyard hands.

The flagship and the two gunboats joined the *Alaska* and the *Benicia* at Nagasaki on 12 May, and there last-minute preparations were made. Opinions as to the likelihood of success varied. Frederick F. Low was pessimistic, in part because his efforts to communicate with the Korean government through that of China, its nominal suzerain, had been virtually fruitless. The Chinese held that Korea, although subordinate to their emperor, had complete control of her foreign relations; hence it would be improper for them to forward Low's letter. His remonstrances finally led the Chinese to dispatch it to Seoul, but they gave little hope that a reply would be received. Rodgers, on the other hand, believed that the time had come when the Koreans must make a treaty; habitually optimistic on the eve of any operation whose outcome was in doubt, he hoped strongly that this one would be successful.

On 16 May, the five ships stood out of Nagasaki harbor to steer westward across the East China Sea and then northward in the Yellow Sea. The *Monocacy* suffered some damage in a gale one day out, so she was ordered to steam ahead to the rendezvous off the west coast of Korea to effect repairs. Her consorts joined her on 19 May, but thereafter dense fogs delayed progress so that the first anchorage shown on the French chart, called Roze Roads by Rodgers, was not reached until five days later. There the four larger vessels waited while their steam launches, with the *Palos* in support, surveyed and sounded the channel leading to an anchorage off the mouth of the Salee River.

Meanwhile, those remaining on board ship were exercised at infantry

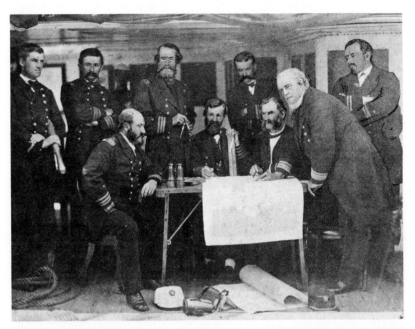

FIGURE 11-1. Council of War on board the flagship *Colorado* before the attack on the Korean Forts. *Standing, left to right:* Master John E. Pillsbury, signal officer; Commander Lewis A. Kimberly, commanding the *Benicia*; Commander Homer C. Blake, commanding the *Alaska*; Lieutenant Commander William K. Wheeler, flag lieutenant; Rear Admiral John Rodgers (*leaning on table*); Lieutenant Charles H. Rockwell, commanding the *Palos*; *sitting, left to right:* Commander Edward P. McCrea, commanding the *Monocacy*; Captain George H. Cooper, commanding the *Colorado*; Commander Edward T. Nichols, chief of staff.

drill and small arms firing, as much to keep them occupied as to improve their soldierly proficiency. Captain McLane Tilton, commanding the squadron's marines, wrote his wife that all were "quite jolly" in spite of stories about the Korean habit of cutting up and pickling or skinning and crucifying unwelcome visitors. "Whether this is positively true or not I can't say; but you may imagine it is not with a great pleasure I anticipate landing with the small force we have, against a populous country containing 10,000,000 of savages!"[3]

The local inhabitants displayed natural curiosity at the presence of the foreign warships. Once their initial timidity had been overcome, they seemed friendly enough, so Low prepared an informal statement of the expedition's purpose for transmission to the local authorities.

The *Palos* and the launches returned after four days to report that the channel was negotiable even for the *Colorado*. However, fog kept the vessels from reaching the Boisee anchorage (later known as Chemulpo and still later as Inchon) until 30 May. There a junk brought news that Low's message had been delivered and that three emissaries had been appointed to confer with him. The minister set the following day for their reception and, like Perry, declined to meet them personally until he had assurances as to their rank. When it became apparent that they were inferior officials, Low's secretary informed the Koreans that the Americans had no hostile intention and that negotiations could be carried on only with diplomats of the first rank. He also explained that it would be necessary for boats from the squadron to survey the Salee River; when the Koreans did not demur, the secretary requested that their forces on both sides of the river be instructed that the surveying party should not be molested.

After waiting a day in order that this information might be disseminated to Korean military commanders, the survey vessels, commanded by the *Alaska*'s Homer Blake and supported by the gunboats, left the squadron at noon on 1 June. They steamed in on a flood tide and had great difficulty in maintaining the low speed required for accurate surveying and sounding. As the launches approached the seaward end of Kangwha Island, those in them made out a line of fortifications apparently fully manned, with flags flying. Directly beneath the loftiest, a ledge of rocks formed a strong eddy in the river, and when the surveyors began to negotiate this hazard, the Korean batteries opened fire without warning. The launches quickly manned their light howitzers and commenced to shoot back, while the *Palos* and the *Monocacy* brought their heavier guns into action as they came up. Within a short time, the current had swept the vessels past the forts, whose guns could not be trained, and Blake ordered all to anchor. The Americans continued to fire until the forts had been abandoned.

Consulting his subordinates, the commander learned that the launches had expended most of their ammunition, while the *Palos*'s light bulwarks had been damaged by the muzzle blast and recoil of her guns. The *Monocacy*, which had been swept onto an uncharted rock by the current, was leaking badly. Only two men had suffered any injury, but Blake concluded that he was justified in disregarding his orders to continue the survey even if fired on. As his vessels steamed back downstream, they took the forts under fire once more; the lack of any response confirmed the belief that their garrisons had fled.

Minister Low and Admiral Rodgers agreed that immediate, punitive action was mandatory. The *Monocacy* was quickly repaired by the expedient of running her onto a mudbank—when the tide ebbed, a temporary patch was placed over the hole, and she was ready for service on the next flood. But by that time Low and Rodgers had had second thoughts. Perhaps the firing on the survey flotilla had been ordered by an officer without direction from the Korean government. If so, continued efforts to negotiate might avert the necessity for an attack. Even if these failed, the delay would have given opportunity to prepare the landing force for its mission, and in ten days the spring tides which made the Salee currents so turbulent would have given way to more moderate neap tides.

During the next few days, the admiral and his staff decided the composition of the landing force and drew up the plans for its use. They recognized the desirability of putting ashore the largest number of men possible, but enough hands had to be retained to protect the warships from surprise attack and to work them back to friendlier waters should disaster befall the landing force. Since the *Monocacy* and the *Palos* would furnish supporting fire, the three wooden ships had to provide the men for an infantry battalion, a battery of artillery, and pioneer and hospital parties. In all, 542 sailors and 109 marines were assigned to the landing force with another 118 bluejackets to serve in the four steam launches or as boatkeepers. Blake was named to command the entire expedition, with the *Benicia*'s Commander Lewis A. Kimberly to take charge of the landing force. Meanwhile, rations were cooked, ammunition was readied for use, and units were assigned to the small boats which would ferry them ashore. In order to provide heavier covering fire, the *Monocacy* was called alongside the flagship to receive two of the latter's 9-inch smoothbores.

During this period, troop movements were observed in the vicinity of the forts, and an exchange of messages was carried on with local officials through the medium of a pole on an island near the anchorage. The Koreans insisted that any relationship between countries so distant from one another as Korea and the United States was impossible and that the attack on the surveying flotilla had been justified as a defensive measure. The Americans, on the other hand, emphasized the peaceful and unselfish purposes of their mission and urged the Koreans to agree to negotiations before 10 June.

The *Palos*, which had been sent to Chefoo with dispatches on 3 June, returned to the squadron five days later laden with coal and provisions. She also brought the master and six seamen of the German schooner *Chusan* whom she had picked up from a small boat after their vessel had been wrecked on Taechong Do, an island off the Korean coast. While the *Palos*'s deckload of coal was being transferred to the *Monocacy*'s bunkers, alterations were made to the former to permit her six 24-pounder howitzers to be trained more easily.

No satisfactory reply to the last American message had been received by the morning of 10 June, so Commander Blake in the *Palos* ordered the punitive expedition to get underway. The *Colorado's* two steam launches sounded ahead, followed by the *Monocacy*, which was prepared to clear the way with her big smoothbores. Next came the *Palos*, towing the twenty-two small boats in which the landing force was embarked, while the *Alaska* and *Benicia* launches, designated to assist any boats that got into difficulty, brought up the rear.

The *Monocacy* opened the action by lobbing a few shells into a battery just before noon. It was deserted, so she stood onward, taking the lowest fort, Ch'o ji jin, as her next target. The Koreans replied vigorously as the double-ender passed within 300 yards of their position, but their fire was high and did only minor damage to her standing rigging. Commander Edward P. McCrea brought his ship to anchor above this fort, which was quickly silenced by her brisk fire.

According to Rodgers's orders, the battalion was to be landed directly in front of Ch'o ji jin after it had been silenced. The Korean fire, however, had been heavier than Blake had expected and he feared that it might be renewed in spite of the *Monocacy's* efforts. Moreover, the tide was about to turn; within a short time the ebb would expose mud flats almost impassible for howitzers if not for men. A plain at the water's edge 800 yards below the fort seemed a likely landing place, so the *Palos* dropped anchor, cast off her tows, and in company with the launches, opened a covering fire from her howitzers. Strong arms in the small boats made short work of the distance to the shore, carefully maintaining the order of beaching required by the admiral's instructions.

No doubt the officers and men of the landing force appreciated Blake's departure from his orders as they pulled toward the shore, for the point of disembarkation was on the fort's flank. But then the boats grounded—in soft mud! As marines and sailors jumped over the gunwales, they sank to

FIGURE 11–2. The *Palos* towing the squadron's boats up the Salee River.

their knees, or deeper, and what was to have been a rapid advance turned into a mud-slogging ordeal under the hot summer sun. To add to their difficulty, the "plain" was traversed by deep gullies which were invisible from the river. Nonetheless, Captain Tilton got his marines formed into a rough skirmish line; and, as it reached firm ground, the few Koreans manning Ch'o ji jin departed with celerity. The sea soldiers occupied the deserted work until the naval infantry approached and Tilton was ordered to push on toward the next fortification, Tokchin. After ascertaining that a road suitable for the artillery led to it, the marines bivouacked in their advanced position, a half-mile ahead of the main body.

Meanwhile, the sailors were getting the artillery ashore, and one may imagine that uncomplimentary remarks were made about Homer C. Blake and his choice of a landing area, as the howitzers were dragged through mud in which they sank to their axles. Kimberly detailed four companies of infantry and the small party of pioneers to help the artillerymen; with seventy-five or eighty men on the traces of each, the seven 12-pounders were got ashore, but the sticky mud retained various items of apparel—shoes, stockings, leggings, and even some trouser legs.

Commander Kimberly decided against advancing farther that evening because it was late and his men were exhausted. One howitzer was moved up to support the marines, and a messenger departed to inform Blake of the situation ashore.

After seeing the small boats well on their way inshore, the *Palos* weighed and stood upstream to bring Tokchin within range. The inadequacy of the survey of 1 June was revealed suddenly when she steamed onto an uncharted rock in midchannel and remained fast as the tide ebbed. Realizing that she could not be refloated until high water, Commander Blake directed Lieutenant Charles H. Rockwell to use every means to free his ship and ordered the *Benicia*'s launch to stand by her before calling his own steam launch alongside to take him to the *Monocacy*. The double-ender, meanwhile, had ceased firing when Tilton's marines approached Ch'o ji jin; and, after being assured of its capture, she steamed toward Tokchin. Its guns opened fire as she closed, but her own shooting was equal to the occasion. As before, Commander McCrea anchored his gunboat within 500 yards, and the accuracy of her fire elicited Blake's highest praise.

Darkness found the *Palos* still impaled on the rock and heeled well over, but she was warped off on the flood tide that night. With her rudder jammed and her steam pumps barely able to keep her afloat, the *Palos* obviously could have no further part in this operation. A few hours later the *Monocacy* had a narrow escape when her anchors dragged. She

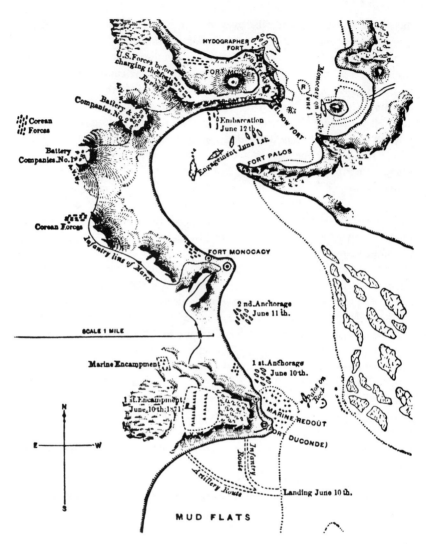

MAP 11–1. The Attack on the Korean Forts. Fort McKee was Kwangsong-chin, Fort Monocacy was Tokchin, and Fort Duconde was Ch'o ji jin.

drifted some distance before another anchor brought her to, and then her iron hull rasped against submerged rocks as she swung to the tide, but no damage was sustained.

The Americans encamped on Kangwha Island awakened to the drumbeat of reveille at 4 A.M. on Sunday, 11 June. Officers and men ate a hasty, cold breakfast and then completed the demolition of Ch'o ji jin. Commander Kimberly then signaled the *Monocacy* for orders, and Blake replied: "Go ahead and take the forts."[4] As infantry and artillery began their march, the gunboat steamed upstream to fire on the remaining forts and on groups of Koreans apparently moving out to dispute the American advance.

Tilton's marines occupied Tokchin without opposition, thanks to the *Monocacy's* fire, and quickly demolished it while their naval comrades continued the advance. From the summit of a prominent hill, the sailors sighted a considerable force of Koreans atop a high ridge beyond howitzer range. In spite of the difficult terrain, Kimberly was able to choose a parallel ridge which would bring the Americans within range and would also lead to the expedition's ultimate objective, Kwangsongchin, whence the first shot was said to have been fired on 1 June. The marines resumed their position as skirmishers, and the advance began again.

As before, progress was slow and after a half-mile had been covered, the marines protecting the left flank came under fire from the ridge above. Wheeling his skirmish line, Tilton led his men up the slope and, upon reaching the top, saw Koreans on an elevation opposite from which they "blazed away at us with their gingalls or matchlocks, their black heads popping up and down the while from the grass, but only one spent bullet struck us, without any injury."[5] The Koreans were quickly scattered by a few shells from a howitzer which sailors had almost to lift to the crest.

A third of a mile farther along, Kimberly called a halt in order to rest his men, who were exhausted by their exertions under the scorching June sun. When the battalion moved on, five howitzers supported by three companies of sailors were left to guard the left flank of the main body against the threat of Koreans massing in that vicinity. As the main body marched forward, it attracted a hail of fire from Kwangsongchin; and, taking advantage of the fact that most of the Korean weapons seemed to be single-shot, sailors and marines made a dash for the last hill short of their goal. Here occurred the first American casualty, Private Dennis Hanrahan, but five companies of naval infantry and two of marines, supported by two guns, had won a position only 150 yards from the stronghold.

Shortly after noon, sailors and marines, 350 in number, raced down the hill to the bottom of the ravine and up the other side. The Koreans in

Kwangsongchin kept up a steady and inaccurate fire, exposing themselves recklessly, until there was no longer time to reload. Singing melancholy songs, they resorted to hurling stones at the Americans scrambling up toward them. The slope was steep, and the attackers would have had difficulty finding footholds had not the earth been torn up by the shellfire from ship and shore. Seth Allen, a landsman from the flagship, was the first to approach the parapet, and he paid for his temerity with his life, while Lieutenant Hugh McKee, who entered the fort before any of his fellows, was felled by gunshot and spear wounds.

A furious hand-to-hand struggle ensued as small groups of sailors and marines scrambled over the parapet. The Koreans fought with desperate courage, but their spears, swords, and stones could not match the cutlasses, bayonets, clubbed rifles, and revolvers of their opponents. They broke and ran. Master Thomas C. McLean, whose company had been on the American left, rallied thirty of his men across the path of the fleeing Koreans, while McLane Tilton led a group of his marines around to the right of the citadel and fell on the fugitives from that direction. Those who survived had to run the gauntlet of fire from two howitzers on the hill whence the attack had come.

While their comrades were swept up in the fury of the assault on Kwangsongchin, the detachment left to secure the flank faced the major Korean force. The five guns kept this at a distance until they ran short of ammunition. The *Monocacy* was then signaled for help and she responded with a boatload of shells for the 12-pounders, which easily repelled two tentative approaches by Koreans estimated at four or five thousand strong. This force retreated when it was apparent that the fort had fallen, and its retirement was hastened by howitzer shells.

The *Monocacy*'s men were interested spectators as Kwangsongchin was taken, and the appearance of the stars and stripes above the parapet was hailed by three hearty cheers. These were cut short, however, when a battery on the opposite shore opened fire. Earlier, it had been temporarily silenced by the gunboat, but now its guns could menace the Americans in the fort. The *Monocacy* gave her full attention to this battery until the surviving members of its garrison were seen fleeing over the hills to the eastward. Soon thereafter, the forces ashore signaled the double-ender to send her boats for the wounded. These numbered eleven, of whom Lieutenant McKee died not long after he was brought on board. The *Monocacy* herself had no battle casualties, although five of her men suffered sunstroke as did several of Kimberly's command.

The cost to the Koreans was not so light. A total of 243 corpses were counted in and around the various forts, and it was impossible to know how many fell under the fire of the *Monocacy*'s great guns and the howitzers on the left flank, or drowned in the Salee River while fleeing from Kwangsongchin. Lieutenant Commander Winfield S. Schley, who served as Kimberly's adjutant, thought that the Korean loss may have reached 350.[6] The Americans captured about twenty Koreans, a number of whom were wounded. Three forts had been captured and demolished, forty-seven flags and standards had fallen into the victors' hands, and significant quantities of military stores had been destroyed.

A number of factors contributed to the cheap American victory. The Korean arms were almost fantastically ineffective—many of the guns were crude imitations of French pieces, presumably those lost by Admiral Roze's men nearly five years before, and others were centuries old. The Koreans fought with heroic bravery, but they were practically a mob contending with a force that was well trained, thoroughly disciplined, and capably led. However, in spite of these disadvantages and that conferred by the superior small arms with which the Americans were equipped, it seems likely that sheer weight of numbers must have prevailed had the thousands of Korean troops present on Kangwha Island closed with the landing force. That they did not is attributable to the guns, the *Monocacy's* heavy pieces and especially the 12-pounders ashore, which held the Koreans at such a distance that an attack en masse was practically impossible.

During the afternoon, Admiral Rodgers was informed of the success of the operation. He ordered that Kwangsongchin be held overnight to demonstrate to the Koreans the ability of the landing force to do so; thereafter Kimberly might embark his men for the return to their ships as soon as he wished.

At dawn on 12 June, the steam launches began to bring the small boats up from their mooring farther downstream. All were beached at low tide and the embarkation began. Little more than an hour later, the last boats were pulling toward the *Monocacy*, where hot coffee awaited the enlisted men and doubtless something stronger their officers.

The gunboat weighed anchor as the tide made and steamed downstream with the boats in tow. As she passed the *Palos*, that vessel also got underway, and the expedition returned to the squadron after an absence of forty-eight hours. Officers and men were sent back to their own ships, and boats were hoisted and secured. Later in the day, the captains mustered all hands to offer their congratulations on the successful outcome of the punitive operation and to read a general order wherein: "To one and all the commander-in-chief expresse[d] his thanks, and the pride he [felt] in commanding such a body of officers and men."[7]

During the week following the expedition's return, a correspondence was kept up with the local prefect via the pole to which messages were affixed. It was of little use, however, for he persisted in the quite natural view that had the Americans not attempted to force the entrance to the Salee River, no trouble would have occurred. Low prepared a lengthy letter explaining the entire situation to the king and requested that the prefect forward it, only to have it returned with a note to the effect that so great was the monarch's wrath against the Americans, he dared not send any communications from them to the court.

Meanwhile, the *Palos* was secured alongside the *Alaska* in order to transfer her coal to the screw-sloop. When the bunker floor was taken up, the extent of her bottom damage was clearly apparent—the leaks could be plugged temporarily, but only docking could make the gunboat fit for service. At the end of June, a launch from the German frigate *Hertha*, anchored in Roze Roads, steamed up to inquire into the Americans' fate. A rumor to the effect that Admiral Rodgers's squadron had been destroyed had reached Chefoo, and the *Hertha* had come to succor the survivors, should there be any need.

The failure to establish communications with the Korean government finally convinced the Americans that their continued presence off the Salee River was pointless. The captive Koreans were put ashore, and a message explaining to the prefect that Minister Low was withdrawing "temporarily to some other point on the coast of Corea or China" to await instructions from his government, was affixed to the pole.[8] The vessels weighed anchor and set a course for Chefoo on 3 July.

Two days later, Admiral Rodgers expressed his thoughts on the Korean situation to Secretary of the Navy Robeson. After explaining that his force could not undertake further operations until the *Monocacy* and the *Palos* had been repaired, he predicted that only the occupation of Seoul would lead the king to admit defeat. For this purpose, 3,000 good soldiers, "such as our army furnished at the conclusion of the late war," would be sufficient—5,000 would be better because the Koreans, expecting no quarter, would probably give none. "Ill success therefore should be the more guarded against."[9]

Even as he wrote this letter, however, John Rodgers knew that such an expedition almost certainly would not be undertaken. The benefits which might accrue to the United States from a treaty with Korea could hardly justify the expenditure, and the Civil War had sated the American public's desire for military adventure for some time to come. The administration which attempted to find support for a war against Korea could be sure that the opposition party would reap the maximum political benefit from its bellicosity in the 1872 presidential election campaign. Within a few months, the admiral received official notification that the U.S. government planned no further action with regard to Korea.

So the largest U.S. military operation against an Oriental nation in the nineteenth century ended, apparently in failure. However, the purpose of the fighting on 10 and 11 June had been punitive—to exact revenge for the "unprovoked" firing on the surveying flotilla nine days earlier. Admittedly, the act of surveying within a nation's territorial waters without formal permission from its government could be considered provocative in the extreme, yet foreign navies had long been accustomed to survey at will in Far Eastern waters and had few doubts as to their right to do so. Westerners generally believed that not to have carried out the punitive action would have led to an intolerable loss of American—and European—prestige throughout the Orient, while Low and his subordinates in the Peking legation felt that Chinese respect for the United States had been enhanced by the "chastisement" of the Koreans. Indeed, from the military point of view, it had been a smartly conducted affair—even if the rumor that "some of the heaviest fighting seems to have been amongst their [the Americans'] own men, who got drunk on Korean wine and fought among themselves," had any validity.[10] After reading the expedition's reports, Admiral David D. Porter, the U.S. Navy's senior officer, stated the Navy's opinion in a letter to Rodgers: "Your squadron seems the most efficient afloat. I cannot pay you a higher compliment."[11]

And there was some evidence that the Korean attitude toward Westerners had not become one of unmitigated hostility as a result of the punitive operation. Within a month, Chefoo heard a rumor that the purchasers of the wreck of the *Chusan* had been killed by Koreans. HMS *Ringdove* was sent to investigate, and the two Britons involved were quickly sent on board the gunboat reporting that they had been treated very well.

With the Korean venture abandoned at least temporarily, Admiral Rodgers turned his attention to his other responsibilities. The damaged gunboats were ordered to Shanghai for docking and repair, the *Alaska* and the *Benicia* remained in northern Chinese waters for the time, the *Ashuelot* was directed to Foochow where disturbances were expected, and the flagship sailed for Yokohama in August.

The *Colorado* was steaming through Shimonoseki Strait with an experienced pilot at the conn when suddenly she struck a rock ledge to which she clung momentarily before the tidal current wrenched her off. The frigate, out of control, swung broadside to and was slammed against perpendicular rocks, from which she defied all efforts to move her until the flood tide gave way to slack water, when she backed off easily. In spite of the two heavy shocks, the vessel made no water, but divers reported extensive damage to her copper. The admiral and the fleet captain, who were on the bridge at the time, concluded that the mishap had been caused by the standard compass sticking and giving an erroneous bearing on a buoy.

The flagship continued on her course to Yokohama and several weeks later stood down Tokyo Bay to Yokosuka, where the government had constructed a dry dock, the first installation in what was destined to be Japan's principal naval dockyard. The *Colorado* was a big ship for this facility; she had to land guns, ammunition, boats, topmasts, and lower yards before entering the dock. Her damage 'was more serious than had been thought, requiring sixteen days to repair.

Meanwhile, Rodgers attended to one of the station's pressing problems —that of a hospital in Japan. Agreeing with Rowan that Yokohama must be the center of the squadron's activities in Japanese waters, he had plans prepared for a building which would be erected on the lot assigned to the Navy's use there. He thought the United States fortunate to have this location, holding that Admiral Bell's action in subletting a portion of the lot to the Pacific Mail Steamship Company was contrary to the terms of the agreement with Japan and that the rent had not been paid regularly. Since the company no longer used its facility, it agreed to have its lease voided, the more readily because Rodgers recommended that the Navy buy its coal sheds. Construction of the two-story hospital building was begun within a few weeks.

Rodgers thought that Westerners in Japan felt perfectly safe; in China, on the other hand, "a sense of impending danger keeps every one generally in a state of uneasiness."[12] In part, this was due to reports of floods which had inundated the area around Tientsin with disastrous consequences for the population. Fearing that lawless bands of marauders would threaten the foreign settlement during the winter, Minister Low requested that a warship be kept at Tientsin. The *Palos* was selected for this duty.

Lieutenant Rockwell's orders from the admiral emphasized that the gunboat's mission was "to protect the persons and property of the foreign residents without regard to nationality." Rodgers hoped that the foreigners would organize to defend themselves, but if they were threatened by danger with which they could not cope, the *Palos* was to send armed men ashore to act in concert with those from other foreign warships. Rockwell was cautioned that any landing party must be conducted in such a way as to make it appear to be "the action of the United Western Nations, rather than of the United States alone."[13]

The *Palos* bumped across the Taku Bar late in November and soon was snugly moored and housed over at Tientsin in company with two British and two French gunboats. Obviously, their combined forces would be dwarfed by the 30,000 troops from the south of China at the disposal of the reputedly anti-foreign provincial governor, but Rockwell thought mob violence the only danger. In the event, it failed to materialize.

The flagship sailed to Hong Kong in December, and Rodgers made a sightseeing tour of Canton. On his return, he met Vice Admiral Charles F. A. Shadwell, newly arrived to relieve Sir Henry Kellett. Shadwell, a rear admiral, had received an acting appointment to the higher rank for the period of his command, and this led the American rear admiral to explain the advantages of such a practice to Secretary Robeson, with especial emphasis on the fact that Orientals were impressed by rank and so tended to consider Britain first among Western nations. Since Robeson had earlier assured the Congress that the peacetime Navy had no requirement for ranks above rear admiral, Rodgers's observations had no effect on the Navy Department's policy.

Admiral Rodgers's tenure of command ended somewhat prematurely when his flag was hauled down in the *Colorado* at Yokohama on 15 May 1872. During the preceding autumn, he had become aware of difficulty involving his brother-in-law, and, since affairs on the station seemed likely to remain tranquil, the admiral decided that his proper place was with his family. His relief, Rear Admiral Thornton A. Jenkins, reached Yokohama in the Pacific Mail steamer from San Francisco on 1 May, and Rodgers sailed in the vessel on her return passage.

While the Korean expedition must naturally dominate any account of John Rodgers's command of the Asiatic Squadron, one other development was to attain greater significance with the passage of time. The extension of a telegraph line from Vladivostok via Nagasaki to Shanghai in 1871 made possible rapid communication between the Navy Department and the most remote of the distant stations. The dispatch reporting that the Koreans had fired on the squadron's surveying boats, which the *Palos* delivered to a Shanghai-bound steamer off Chefoo on 5 June 1871, seems to have been the first to be telegraphed from the station by the U.S. commander in chief.

CHAPTER TWELVE

Leaky Boilers and Infirm Admirals

In his 1871 report to the secretary of the navy, Admiral David D. Porter commented on the Asiatics' recent "unfriendly disposition toward European nations." He was especially concerned about the Chinese, who were establishing arsenals at Shanghai and Tientsin and a dockyard near Foochow. The first, the Kiangnan Arsenal, had built several vessels to European designs, and, while certain fittings had had to be imported for all, it seemed obvious that the Chinese would be able to manufacture hulls, boilers, machinery, ordnance, and ammunition with equal facility before many years had passed. To meet the threat posed by a Chinese fleet of modern warships before it could materialize, the admiral wished to reinforce the Asiatic Squadron, "since a crisis is evidently impending in that quarter, in which all European nations will have to unite in self-defense."[1]

Although Porter's recommendation was carried out only in part, Rear Admiral Thornton A. Jenkins welcomed five vessels during his first year in command of the station. Three of the newcomers—the screw-sloops *Hartford*, *Iroquois*, and *Lackawanna*—were to relieve the *Colorado*, *Alaska*, and *Benicia*, while the gunboats *Saco* and *Yantic*, longer-lived sisters of the late *Maumee*, were reinforcements. However, the *Saco* had to spend her first ten months on the station undergoing boiler repairs at Shanghai, and the *Iroquois*'s passage out was prolonged by the need for machinery overhaul at Gibraltar, Malta, Port Said, Suez, and Aden, which did not augur well for her future usefulness.

The admiral went to Singapore, where he intended to meet the *Hartford*, in the autumn of 1872. Finding that the veteran flagship had not yet arrived, he transferred his flag to the *Lackawanna*, which had accompanied him from Yokohama, and sent the *Colorado* home.

At Singapore, Jenkins received information from the U.S. consul regarding American vessels engaged in the carriage of coolies, three of which had arrived from Swatow, whence they had sailed with the approval of Chinese authorities and the American consul in spite of the fact that they were clearly overloaded with human and general cargoes. The admiral, who had passed close aboard one of the ships in Singapore Road, expressed the opinion that "the law was grossly violated in every respect by her, & that not only the law, but every consideration of decency & humanity was put aside by the persons who were engaged in loading and despatching her from Swatow."[2] All three vessels possessed the necessary documents, so Jenkins had to content himself with transmitting the information to Minister Frederick F. Low in Peking, hoping that the diplomat might take steps to force a closer adherence to the law on the part of the consul at Swatow.

The spring of 1873 brought rumors of Sino-Japanese rivalry on Formosa and anti-foreign feeling in the vicinity of the Pei Ho. There were six American warships at Shanghai; their presence, however, was directly related to neither the rumors nor the anti-foreign feeling but resulted from a more mundane cause—the necessity to provide a sufficient number of officers to form several general courts-martial, two of which were convened to try the commanding officers of the *Yantic* and the *Palos* on charges of habitual drunkenness and conduct unbecoming officers. General courts-martial were hardly unusual in any of the squadrons of the U.S. Navy on distant stations, and in the Asiatic Squadron the tedium of lengthy periods in ports which offered little in the way of recreational opportunity provided a temptation for officers to indulge freely in herculean drinking bouts either ashore or on shipboard. Nor was the temptation removed when the ships paid visits to more sophisticated cities such as Shanghai, for the residents of the foreign settlements vied with one another to extend hospitality to naval officers, and hospitality invariably included a princely selection of alcoholic beverages. For the enlisted men, of course, the temptations were fewer because Navy Regulations forbade them to drink on board ship and they were permitted to go ashore much less frequently than their officers. Yet sailors managed to obtain liquor, usually of the most potent and revolting sort, with which to drink themselves into oblivion on every possible occasion, smuggling it on board when returning from liberty or buying it from the bumboats which flocked around the vessels anchored in almost any Far Eastern port.

The courts-martial convened by Admiral Jenkins detained the ships of his command, except the *Ashuelot* and the *Idaho*, at Shanghai for almost two months. The court-martial trying the *Yantic*'s captain sentenced him to be suspended from the Navy for two years while the *Palos*'s commanding officer was simply dismissed from the service. Like a number of other officers leaving the station, the latter left unpaid creditors in several Chinese ports. Had these presented their bills before his departure, he might have been detained until all had been paid; as it was, the admiral could only follow the usual practice of forwarding them to the Navy Department and advising the creditors that payment should be sought through the civil courts of the United States.

Adjournment of the courts-martial in July permitted the American warships to escape Shanghai's oppressive heat. With the exception of the *Saco*, ordered to relieve the *Ashuelot* at Tientsin, the vessels made northern cruises for their crews' benefit. Thereafter, the *Lackawanna* visited Vladivostok, site of a new Russian naval base; the *Iroquois* ascended the Yangtze to Chinkiang, there to remain during the annual student examinations at nearby Nanking; and the three iron gunboats were ordered to Yokosuka for docking and overhaul.

FIGURE 12–1. The *Hartford* at Hong Kong, with the *Iroquois* off her port quarter.

The *Hartford* and the *Yantic* sailed to Nagasaki, where Admiral Jenkins had concluded that the Asiatic Squadron's principal base should be established. His decision was based on the same arguments which Rear Admiral Henry H. Bell had put forward some six years earlier: Nagasaki's good harbor accessible at all seasons, its central location with regard to the station generally, its salubrious climate, and the coal available from nearby mines. Jenkins had also cited the fact that the Japanese were constructing a naval dockyard, including a dry dock, at Nagasaki, but this project had been abandoned before the *Hartford*'s arrival. To support the admiral's contention that Yokohama was unsuitable, the *Idaho*'s commanding officer had reported that she probably could not ride out a gale in her exposed anchorage there, so arrangements had to be made to have her moored at Yokosuka during typhoon season.

Charles E. DeLong, U.S. minister to Japan, preferred that Yokohama remain the squadron's Japanese base, probably because this would help to guarantee the presence of U.S. warships within a short distance of his legation, but the naval officer's mind was made up and the Navy Department concurred. Before the end of the year, Jenkins forwarded to Washington a ten-year lease on premises rented in the foreign allotment at Nagasaki and described arrangements for transferring the squadron's stores from Yokohama and Hong Kong to the new depot. A stock of coal would be kept at Hong Kong for the use of vessels touching there on the way out from the Atlantic coast of the United States or in the course of visits to the more southerly waters of the station, but all else, including those stores embarked in the *Idaho*, would be landed at Nagasaki.

The *Idaho* herself was destined to be sold, a survey having revealed that she required extensive repairs. She would be missed especially in her role as a prison for the squadron's malfeasants, and Jenkins recommended that one of the old sailing sloops of war laid up at Mare Island be sent out to serve in this capacity. His suggestion found little favor in the Navy Department, which inquired about the possibility of confining prisoners in consular prisons. To this the admiral replied that consulates were usually private residences; because of their temporary character, construction of cells adjacent would be unwise. He added that the confinement of foreigners in Japanese prisons could not be contemplated because of the brutal treatment accorded their inmates. Thus, prisoners would have to be incarcerated on board their vessels, which Jenkins thought a most undesirable practice.

And prisoners there would be. The U.S. Navy, always dependent on foreigners to make up a part of its warships' companies, had had to rely on them increasingly since the Civil War because Americans were even less inclined than before to turn to the sea. Vessels commissioning in the

United States could recruit their crews from the immigrants arriving in the nation's seaports in large numbers, but the Asiatic Squadron's two double-enders and the *Palos* had been exiled for life, as it were, and Admiral Jenkins's request that drafts of men be sent out for them received the response that crews for the three iron gunboats and the *Saco* should be recruited on the station. When he ventured to ask that petty officers at least be sent out from the United States, the Bureau of Equipment and Recruiting informed him that it had neither the personnel nor the money with which to transport them.

The practice of enlisting seamen on the station to fill vacancies in the squadron's complements antedated the Civil War, but recruiting entire crews was another matter. Most of the merchant vessels employed in the Far Eastern trade in 1873 were steamers manned largely by Chinese and Malays, who were not desired as men-of-warsmen. The admiral described those men who did volunteer as "the refuse of the merchant marine" and urged that eighty-five marines be sent out to bring his ships' complements up to their authorized strengths: "With such men as we are obliged to ship, discipline and good order are not easy to maintain even with an efficient police, and without it the difficulties are greatly augmented."[3] His appeal had little effect; almost a year later another commander in chief asked for one-hundred marines, stating that the flagship could not turn out a respectable guard to honor visiting dignitaries.

The arrangements necessary to establish the squadron's supply depot at Nagasaki were nearing completion by early October, so Jenkins sailed across the East China Sea in the *Hartford* and steamed up the Yangtze to Hankow "to show the Chinese that a large ship of war could go up the river if necessary, and that their towns in the interior, as well as on the sea were open to the force of such ships, and not to small gunboats alone."[4] The admiral believed his flagship the largest man-of-war to ascend the river to Hankow, but no navigational difficulties were encountered, in part because she anchored every night.

After four days at Hankow, the *Hartford* stood downstream to Shanghai, whence she sailed to Hong Kong to meet Jenkins's relief. Rear Admiral Enoch G. Parrott had just arrived in the mail steamer from San Francisco when the flagship steamed into Hong Kong, and on 12 December, one day after Thornton Jenkins's sixty-second birthday, Parrott assumed command of the squadron. His predecessor, having reached the statutory retirement age, returned to the United States in the same steamer.

Admiral Parrott had insisted on assuming the command as soon as possible, just in time to be confronted by a series of engineering casualties in vessels of his squadron. The *Iroquois* anchored close aboard the flagship on 13 December and soon afterward reported her boilers leaking so badly as to flood the fireroom. A survey concluded that she could not put to sea without extensive—and expensive—repairs. A week later, the *Monocacy* was getting underway for a visit to Bangkok when a portion of her steam chest was blown out, scalding three men and immobilizing the double-ender for a month. And on 23 December, the *Palos* limped in from Nagasaki with engines deranged and water spewing from her boilers as a result of her hull working in heavy seas. The *Ashuelot* was still in dockyard hands; thus, within eleven days of assuming the command, Admiral Parrott had only half his warships available for service.

Perhaps this run of casualties had its effect on the new commander in chief. At any rate, on 11 January 1874 a medical survey found him unfit to continue in command by reason of "general neuroses" which had caused mental and physical deterioration. Enoch Parrott's flag was hauled down the next day, and he returned to the United States to be retired for physical disability.

The *Hartford's* commanding officer, Captain Edmund R. Colhoun, succeeded the admiral as senior U.S. naval officer on the Asiatic Station, a position which he held for almost five months. During that time, Spanish-American relations were strained by an incident that occurred on the other side of the world. The steamer *Virginius*, flying American colors, was intercepted on the high seas off Cuba by a Spanish warship and taken into Santiago. Charging that she had been running arms to Cuban insurrectionaries, the authorities ordered the execution of her master and passengers, a number of whom were American citizens. The killings were halted when a British man-of-war arrived from Jamaica, and the U.S. government dispatched a strong note to Madrid, demanding redress. Pending the Spanish reply, units of the North and South Atlantic and European fleets were ordered to rendezvous at Key West, Florida, in readiness for hostilities.

News of the *Virginius* crisis reached Captain Colhoun in mid-January. He immediately directed the warships of his command to remain in ports which had telegraphic connection with Hong Kong; should the situation warrant further action, he intended to concentrate the vessels in the British colony's harbor. There, apparently, they would await orders from the Navy Department. In the event, no action was required, for Spain's release of the *Virginius*, which turned out to be owned by Cubans and had no right to fly the stars and stripes, and payment of an indemnity satisfied the American demands. On 2 February, the U.S. warships on the Asiatic Station were directed to resume their normal activities.

A minor uprising in Kyushu brought the *Lackawanna* from Shanghai to join the *Palos* at Nagasaki late in February. It was quickly put down by imperial forces, and a month later the screw-sloop spent several days in a vain search for an American steamer which had foundered while on passage from Nagasaki to Shanghai. Colhoun in the *Hartford* touched at Nagasaki in April and then went on to Yokohama where the *Idaho* was sold at public auction and the screw-sloops *Tuscarora* and *Kearsarge* arrived from the United States. The former was engaged in running lines of deep sea soundings across the Pacific. This seems to have been her sole appearance in the Far East; how her name came to signify the Yangtze gunboat, "with seven decks and a straw bottom," of later legend is not apparent. The *Kearsarge* was joining the squadron to relieve the *Iroquois*, which departed Hong Kong bound for the Mare Island Navy Yard early in May 1874.

The *Yantic*, requiring repairs after a cruise through the Philippines and to Singapore, came to an anchor off Shanghai on 3 May, just in time to combine with the *Ashuelot* and foreign gunboats in sending a force ashore to quell a riot. The international settlement sustained some property damage and several foreigners responded to Chinese stones with more lethal gunfire, but the sailors and marines cleared the streets and restored order without firing a shot.

Five days later, the *Ashuelot* steamed down the Hwangpoo from Shanghai and began an ascent of the Yangtze which ended two weeks later at Ichang, some 959 miles upstream. She was the first American warship to venture beyond Tung Ting Lake, and Commander Edmund O. Matthews found the navigation above the lake rather difficult: "The river here is much narrower, being generally about half a mile wide, with short bends and strong chow-chow water which is so powerful as, from time to time, to take control of the vessel out of our hands and force us to back to prevent striking the bank." Nor did backing always suffice—the *Ashuelot* was set ashore by wayward currents twice, but she escaped with no greater damage than some bent paddle buckets. Needless to say, the gunboat attracted considerable attention as she breasted the stream— "During the whole passage the river bank was lined with people as far ahead as one could see"—and the authorities at Ichang ordered the populace to treat the visitors civilly, even stationing an armed boat to prevent the swarms of small craft from annoying the Americans.[5]

Desiring to gain some knowledge of the Upper Yangtze before taking his command farther, Commander Matthews, accompanied by the U.S. consul from Hankow, several officers, interpreters, and guides, set out on "a toilsome march of eight days over mountains and through gorges in boats. . . ."[6] Chinese encountered along the way were invariably friendly and hospitable, but at Kweichowfu, 110 miles above Ichang, a French missionary informed the party that missions and tea houses had been forbidden to admit foreigners, while junks bound for Chungking were detained if their cargoes included any foreign goods. Feeling that his dress was not suitable for official visits, the commander sent his card to the local authorities and chartered a junk in which to return to Ichang. The passage through the gorges, hair-raising at times, convinced Matthews that a steamer with independently powered paddle wheels and capable of 14 knots should be able to proceed upstream from Ichang. The *Ashuelot* did not possess these characteristics and her coal supply was depleted; she dropped back down the river, obtaining small amounts of coal at Shasi and Hankow, and anchored off Shanghai on 21 July.

Meanwhile, Captain Colhoun's tenure as senior naval officer had ended. Rear Admiral Alexander M. Pennock, a veteran of Far Eastern cruises in the *Columbia* and the *Marion*, read his orders on board the *Hartford* at Yokohama on 29 May 1874. The new commander in chief, recently detached from the North Pacific Squadron which he had commanded since 1872, may have been pleased at the prospect of a squadron composed of eight ships, twice the number of his previous command. If so, his pleasure was short-lived; within six weeks he was complaining that only the flagship and the *Kearsarge* could be relied on in an emergency, while "the frequent repairs on the others are embarrassing to me and a source of very great expence to the Government."[7] A month later, the *Lackawanna*'s boilers were reported beyond repair, whereupon the Navy Department ordered that her screw and shaft be removed so that she could remain on the station as a sailing sloop of war. Captain Edward Y. McCauley found his vessel's performance under sail improved after she ceased to be a steamer, but the admiral thought her too leewardly to serve in any capacity except as guardship at Yokohama, whence she sailed for Mare Island in February 1875.

While the *Lackawanna* was stationed in Tokyo Bay, some of her liberty men ran afoul of the law while intoxicated and found themselves haled before a consular court, which fined them and then asked that Captain McCauley force them to pay the fines or withhold the proper amounts from their pay. Sailors had been tried by consular courts before, to the dismay of their commanding officers, and on this occasion McCauley referred the matter to Admiral Pennock, who ruled that consuls did *not* have jurisdiction over naval personnel if a vessel of the U.S. Navy were in the vicinity. Having issued this edict, Pennock asked the Navy Department to settle the question definitely. A Department solicitor held that civil and naval courts both had authority—indeed, a sailor could be tried and punished by both for a single offense—but that no one, consul or naval officer, could withhold a sailor's pay for any purpose without the man's explicit permission. Thereafter, the secretary of the navy referred the matter to the State Department with the request that consuls be advised to return sailors arrested for "breaches of the peace . . . or drunken follies on shore" to their ships for punishment.[8] Unfortunately, consuls were not likely to heed suggestions that they limit their authority voluntarily; more would be heard of this matter later.

A more complex problem arose when a *Lackawanna* sailor of British nationality was arrested for drunk and disorderly conduct and assaulting a Frenchman. The U.S. consul general refused to try him because of Mc-Cauley's intransigence in the matter of withholding fines, whereupon the Japanese police delivered the culprit to a British court which fined him $3.50. Captain McCauley demanded that the money be refunded because the court lacked jurisdiction, and ultimately the controversy was referred to the two governments. Almost a year later, Foreign Secretary Lord Derby and Secretary of State Hamilton Fish agreed that their respective authorities in China, Japan, and Siam would refrain from interfering with one another's citizens serving in foreign men-of-war "upon the principle that having taken service with a foreign State, they are for the time being under the protection of such foreign State. . . ."[9]

Admiral Pennock decided in January 1875 that the *Saco* could be sent to the southern portion of the station. The gunboat touched at Singapore and Penang before proceeding to the west coast of Sumatra where Netherlands troops and warships were fighting the native state of Achin. Commander Charles J. McDougal was greeted courteously by the Dutch flag officer, who loaned him charts and procured a pilot for the *Saco*. The Dutchman also warned of cholera ashore, so McDougal limited his visits to the former pepper ports, of which Mukkee had been burned to the ground yet again, this time for violating a supposed promise to accept Dutch rule. After assuring himself that no American interests were endangered and that the Dutch faced an arduous and costly campaign in their effort to control all of Sumatra, the commander departed for Batavia. The *Saco*'s track led thence to Singapore and along the coasts of Borneo and Palawan to Manila, whence she returned to Hong Kong early in May. McDougal's report that he had lost four men to Asiatic cholera brought orders from Pennock that the *Saco* repair to Yokohama to avoid the heat and humidity of the Hong Kong summer.

Several months earlier, the admiral had learned that his relief was about to leave the United States and that he himself should depart the station in the *Hartford* during the summer. Pleading ill health, the retiring commander in chief requested permission to sail to San Francisco in the Pacific Mail steamer while Commander David B. Harmony took the erstwhile flagship home by way of the Suez Canal. Pennock left the *Hartford* at Hong Kong in mid-June and hoisted his flag in the *Saco* at

Yokohama long enough to attend to official business there. Then he sailed for California in the mail steamer, leaving Commander Robert F. R. Lewis of the *Kearsarge* as senior U.S. naval officer.

The veteran *Hartford* took her final leave of the South China Sea soon afterward and sailed to Singapore to await the arrival of Pennock's relief, Rear Admiral William Reynolds, who was coming out in the screw-frigate *Tennessee*. A cholera epidemic in the British crown colony caused Harmony to consign the squadron records to the care of the U.S. consul, and the screw-sloop stood on to Aden. Learning that stokers frequently succumbed to the extreme heat in the firerooms of ships in the Red Sea, the commander decided to emulate the mail steamers and British and French naval vessels by employing Lascar coal heavers who were accustomed to work in those hellish temperatures. The total cost of utilizing them amounted to only $142, and Harmony recommended to the Bureau of Equipment and Repair that all U.S. men-of-war passing through the Suez Canal and the Red Sea be allowed to follow his example.

Within a week, another did. The USS *Tennessee* embarked twenty-three Lascars at Port Said before entering the canal and they apparently suffered no ill effects despite the 165 degrees recorded in her firerooms. Even the economy-minded Navy Department could appreciate the benefits of this practice, which came to be followed as a matter of course.

Admiral Reynolds, who found the passage through the canal a memorable experience—"certainly, there is no navigation in the world which can approach its utter novelty"[10]—assumed command of the Asiatic Station at Suez on 16 August 1875. This, however, was little more than a formality, for he would have no means of exercising his authority over any of his squadron's vessels other than the *Tennessee* until he arrived in Oriental waters.

To be sure, the flagship was an impressive vessel—the biggest U.S. warship in commission and the largest naval vessel in the Far East during her cruise, both British and French flagships being appreciably smaller. But the *Audacious* and the *Montcalm* were armored ships carrying rifled guns, while the American—a wooden vessel with a battery composed mainly of smoothbores—was their superior only in performance under sail and in the comfort of her senior officers' quarters. Nonetheless, the *Tennessee* increased her country's prestige in Oriental eyes.

Meanwhile, Commander Lewis was repeating the oft-heard complaints about the state of the boilers in the squadron's other ships, a complaint that Reynolds would echo when he fell in with them. The *Saco* was kept at Yokohama and the *Palos* at Shanghai, both almost useless, while the double-enders were in little better state.

It should be noted that ships of the U.S. Navy were not the only sufferers from chronic boiler problems during this period. Naval and merchant steamers of all flags were plagued by boiler corrosion; idle boilers corroded more rapidly than those in use, so warships were more seriously affected because they spent less time under steam and seldom utilized full boiler power except in an emergency. Engineers and scientists had a variety of opinions as to the cause of the corrosion; thus, specific remedies were largely ineffectual. Improved materials and designs for boiler construction led to a gradual diminution of the problem. Until these became available, there was no alternative to frequent repair.

Admiral Reynolds arrived at Woosung in November, and, finding that new boilers for the three iron gunboats had been shipped to Shanghai, he lost no time in ordering that they be installed immediately. The *Yantic* also was sent to Shanghai for boiler repair, but the *Saco*, deemed unworthy of further expenditure, continued as station ship at Yokohama. The flagship sailed to Nagasaki in December and spent several weeks having her decks and upper works recaulked by Japanese laborers. The *Kearsarge* was the only unit of the squadron which was not immobilized as 1875 ended.

The admiral took advantage of his sojourn at Nagasaki to evolve plans for operations by the Asiatic Squadron in the event that the United States became a belligerent. As he knew, the settlement of the *Virginius* crisis had not ended Cuban resistance to Spanish rule and the longer that the already protracted struggle dragged on, the greater the likelihood of American involvement. Thus, Reynolds assumed that Spain was the potential enemy and the Philippine Islands his obvious theater of operations. Should the United States be allied with a power with territorial holdings in the Far East, he foresaw few problems, but the neutrality of other nations would deprive the squadron of its bases. To rectify this impossible situation, he proposed to capture Subic Bay, a sheltered and reportedly unfortified anchorage on the coast of Luzon, only thirty miles northwest of Manila Bay. While transports laden with troops were en route from California to the newly acquired base, the warships would be operating against the Spanish Far Eastern naval forces, whose defeat would lead to Manila's surrender. Occupation of the area adjacent to the capital city by American soldiers could be expected to end hostilities in the Philippines— the admiral thought resistance elsewhere in the islands unlikely. Reynolds prefaced his war plan with a statement urging the necessity of speedy dispatch of coal, ammunition, and reinforcements to his squadron. He also needed timely intelligence of the passage of Spanish men-of-war southward through the Suez Canal, suggesting that "Larrabee's Cipher & Secret Letter & Telegraphic Code," a copy of which he had found in the squadron files, be used to communicate this and other information to him.

By mid-March of 1876, it seemed that Admiral Reynolds's war plan might be tested. Secretary of State Fish had invited European nations to join the United States in forcing Spain to concede self-government to Cuba some months earlier, and the mails from San Francisco informed the admiral that warships of three squadrons were being concentrated at Port Royal, South Carolina. "Under these circumstances, I shall move all the ships to the southern ports of China, so as to have them convenient, in case of need; and shall retain them in that quarter, for the present."[11] By "all the ships," Reynolds meant the *Kearsarge, Yantic, Ashuelot,* and *Palos,* the only units ready for service, although the *Tennessee,* which required docking to repair damage done to her stem by her anchor chain while at Woosung, probably could have joined them in the event of hostilities.

The *Kearsarge* paid a ten-day visit to Manila in April, ostensibly to gain information pertaining to the military campaign which the Spaniards were waging against the sultan of the Sulu Archipelago. She returned to report that the Spanish naval forces in the Philippines were even weaker than Reynolds had thought; the ships of his command should have been able to master them with relative ease.

However, there was no war. Secretary Fish's suggested multi-national intervention received scant support either at home or abroad, and Spain promised to reform its Cuban government. On 22 May, the admiral concluded that most of his vessels could be ordered to more northerly waters for the summer.

Some weeks earlier, the *Saco* had sailed from Yokohama bound for the Mare Island Navy Yard with the squadron's invalids and those whose enlistments had expired or who had been sentenced to confinement in the naval prison. The decrepit gunboat steamed well clear of the land before hauling her boiler fires and making sail. Soon afterward, she encountered swells which caused her to roll heavily and started serious leaks—within a few minutes ten inches of water surged over the fireroom floor plates as she rolled. Commander McDougal had the pumps rigged and all boiler fires lighted; by the time steam had been raised, the combined efforts of bilge pumps and the condenser bilge injection were required to keep the water down. The *Saco* had no choice but to return to Japan for docking and repair. She finally left the station three weeks later.

While the Asiatic Squadron was preparing for a war against Spain, General F. W. Partridge, the U.S. consul at Bangkok, had requested that a man-of-war be sent to Siam to force its government to honor treaty commitments. A subsequent letter indicated that the difficulties had been settled amicably, but the tone of the communications made it apparent to Admiral Reynolds that the consul had small respect for Siamese and none at all for Americans residing there. Later in the spring, a missionary wrote of Partridge's high-handed conduct which had upset plans for a Siamese exhibit at the United States Centennial Exposition. Thereupon, the *Ashuelot* was ordered to Bangkok to investigate. Commander Matthews listened to Partridge's account of the lack of respect shown him and his son, the vice-consul, and then insisted on hearing the other side of the story, to the consul's obvious annoyance. After sixteen days of audiences, conversations, and entertainment—including an elephant hunt for the naval officers—the gunboat sailed for Saigon, whence the commander dispatched a twenty-four page report which left little doubt that Partridge's behavior had been inexcusable or that his son had been engaged in illegal activities. On receipt of this document, the admiral sent the *Ashuelot* back to Bangkok to embark the Siamese exhibit; it was transshipped to a merchant steamer at Hong Kong and reached Philadelphia in time to be seen by thousands of Americans and other visitors to the Exposition. Nor did matters end there. The State Department, acting on the complaints and reports forwarded by the admiral, dismissed the Partridges from the consular service. The elder's successor soon restored the traditionally amicable relationship between the two governments, as Reynolds ascertained during a visit to Siam with the *Tennessee* and the *Ashuelot* in January 1877.

As the threat of war with Spain faded, the situation in China was attracting attention. The first railroad in the empire, linking Shanghai with Woosung, was nearing completion. Its construction had been delayed by the attitude of Chinese authorities who perhaps saw in it another means for the extension of Western, especially British, economic influence. Revision of Anglo-Chinese treaty provisions offered the potential for further difficulty, and a drought in northern China helped to stimulate anti-foreign sentiment among its inhabitants.

The flagship stayed in Japanese waters until early September when, hearing that Anglo-Chinese negotiations were reaching a critical state at Chefoo, the admiral got her underway to join the *Ashuelot* at that point, leaving the *Yantic* to show the flag at Yokohama. The *Palos* at Tientsin and the *Monocacy* at Shanghai were within easy steaming distance of Chefoo, but the *Kearsarge* at Vladivostok was out of reach. The Chefoo Convention, however, had already been signed when the *Tennessee* arrived, so Admiral Reynolds made a circuit of the Gulf of Pechihli, transferring his flag to the *Ashuelot* to visit Newchwang and Tientsin, and spending a week in Peking.

More Chinese ports, including Wuhu and Ichang on the Yangtze, were opened during the early months of 1877, furnishing employment for the *Monocacy*, *Palos*, and *Ashuelot* which conveyed officials from the nearest American consulates to take part in the ceremonies. Soon afterward, the iron screw-gunboat *Alert*, a unit of the squadron since the preceding autumn, was sent to succor survivors from a vessel said to have been lost in the Bismarck Sea off New Guinea. The *Alert* returned after ten weeks to report that no one in the vicinity had any knowledge of a shipwreck; obviously the report, attributed to a merchant mariner who had received it from a native using sign language, was false—or it had been garbled in transmission!

In July, Admiral Reynolds acknowledged orders to return to the United States in his flagship upon the arrival of his relief in the autumn. A few days later, however, the admiral was rendered insensible by "an attack of congestion of the brain" while at work in his cabin. Although his condition improved gradually thereafter, he doubted his ability to continue as commander in chief. A medical survey recommended that he return to the United States at an early date, so on 12 August 1877 Admiral Reynolds turned his command over to Captain Jonathan Young of the *Tennessee* at Yokohama and sailed for San Francisco in the mail steamer.

Two weeks later, the *Alert*'s sister *Ranger* reported for duty with the Asiatic Squadron, whereupon the *Kearsarge*, which had been on the station for more than three years, was ordered to Boston by way of the Suez Canal. The worn-out *Yantic* had been sent to Norfolk during the preceding northeast monsoon, so the squadron was reduced to six vessels, of which only the flagship and the two new gunboats were thought to be suitable for service as cruisers. However, this force was undoubtedly more efficient than that of three years before, if only because all units had new or virtually new boilers.

And there seemed to be no pressing need for a larger force. Six years after Admiral Porter had expressed his concern about the establishment of an effective Chinese navy, rivalry among provincial officials, insufficient funds, and a lack of organization remained apparently insuperable difficulties. No foreign naval officer seems to have taken the Chinese navy very seriously for some time to come.

CHAPTER THIRTEEN

Worn-out Ships and a Treaty with Korea

Rear Admiral Thomas H. Patterson, who succeeded Admiral William Reynolds, hoisted his flag in the *Tennessee* at Yokohama on 4 October 1877. Almost at once, he learned that cholera was reaching epidemic proportions in several Japanese ports, including Yokohama. The admiral and the fleet surgeon agreed on preventive measures, and then the outbreak subsided as quickly as it had begun; in Yokohama, its diminution was attributed to a typhoon which cleansed the atmosphere.

Turning next to the matter of logistics, Admiral Patterson found the inventory of stores in the depot at Nagasaki so small that he had to authorize the purchase of provisions on the open market. Although the danger of such a reliance on local sources was obvious, the admiral felt that the economies that could be realized by the acquisition of the bulk of the squadron's foodstuffs at Yokohama, Shanghai, and Hong Kong would justify the practice. The Bureau of Provisions and Clothing concurred, and as a result the importance of Nagasaki as the squadron's base declined markedly.

Leaving the *Alert* to show the flag at Yokohama, with orders to cruise about Tokyo Bay under sail periodically to exercise her company, Patterson touched at Kobe, Nagasaki, and Shanghai in the flagship before standing down the coast to Hong Kong in January 1878. A few weeks later, he boarded the *Ranger* for a visit to Canton and was received by the viceroy, who questioned him about the reported mistreatment of Chinese in the United States. The naval officer could only reply that he supposed

184

the incidents referred to had been at the hands of wayward persons who would be punished by his government.

The admiral took leave of the *Tennessee* early in March. He had hoped to retain her until a suitable flagship arrived, but peremptory orders from Washington led him to transfer his flag to the *Monocacy* and send the screw-frigate home. The *Monongahela*, another of the war-built screw-sloops, joined the admiral at Shanghai a month later. Unfortunately, her boilers were unfit to carry more than fifteen pounds of steam pressure, sufficient for 7 knots in smooth water. Patterson kept his flag in the *Monocacy* until the *Monongahela* completed boiler repairs eight months later.

Late in April 1878, Admiral Patterson read in a Shanghai newspaper that U.S. naval vessels had been directed to seize merchantmen of American ownership that were involved in the illegal transportation of coolies. Although he disclaimed previous knowledge of such a directive, the admiral sent the *Ranger* to ascertain if any American vessels were embarking coolies at Hong Kong, Whampoa, and Canton, while the *Alert* proceeded to Amoy and Swatow for the same purpose. The Navy Department's order authorizing their missions reached Patterson a month later. Ultimately, the admiral reported that, while no violations of the law had been discovered by the gunboats, he had evidence that the bark *H. N. Carlton*, which had cleared Hong Kong in December 1877, had subsequently embarked coolies at a Chinese port where no consul was stationed. In fact, it was the loss of this vessel on Molokai in the Hawaiian Islands, revealing the presence of fifty coolies who could not be legally accounted for, that had led to the seizure order. As Patterson stated, continued vigilance on the part of consuls and naval officers was essential for the implementation of the order.

By the autumn of 1878, the *Alert* had been in commission for more than three years, so the admiral sent her to Mare Island to ship a new crew, believing that "the system of maintaining the crews of our vessels by enlistments on the station . . . involving a mixture of all nationalities is detrimental to the best interests of the service."[1] Patterson also urged that the gunboat be overhauled at the California navy yard, pointing out that the corrosion of the *Monocacy*'s hull plating could likely be attributed to the carelessness of Oriental shipyard workers.

But the *Monocacy* was a long way from being unserviceable, as she proved when HMS *Iron Duke* grounded on a spit at Woosung on 7 May 1879. Although the British battleship was in no immediate danger, she had taken the ground on a spring tide and each succeeding flood was driving her farther onto the spit. Learning of her plight, the *Monocacy*'s commanding officer offered the services of his vessel and of the screw-gunboat *Palos*. During each high water for the next three days, British tars strained at the capstan bars in an effort to kedge off, while the *Monocacy*, her big paddle wheels churning the river's surface to muddy foam, and the *Palos*, reverting to the tugboat role for which she had been designed, pulled on hawsers leading from the battleship's bow. The *Iron Duke* was floated early on the morning of 11 May. When Vice Admiral Robert Coote's offer to pay for the coal consumed was declined, he insisted that a day be appointed when he and the battleship's captain could entertain the Americans' commanding and executive officers at dinner.

Former President Ulysses S. Grant, making a journey around the world, had arrived at Shanghai a few weeks earlier. The *Ashuelot* embarked his party there for passage to Tientsin, whence the general visited Peking. A former president was the nearest thing to royalty that the United States could provide, and the Chinese were suitably impressed, even inviting Grant to help to mediate a Sino-Japanese controversy regarding control of the Ryukyu Islands. On leaving the Pei Ho, the general boarded the newly arrived screw-sloop *Richmond*, which conveyed him to Yokohama.

Admiral Patterson lost no time in transferring his flag to the *Richmond* after General Grant had disembarked. One of the *Hartford*'s sisters, she was a much more satisfactory flagship than the smaller *Monongahela* and a good steamer, although the admiral thought her coal consumption excessive. The *Monongahela*, a private vessel once more, made a visit to Hakodate before sailing for Mare Island in accordance with Navy Department orders. The *Ranger* followed in November.

Thus, the coming of 1880 found the Asiatic Squadron reduced to five vessels, of which only the flagship was an efficient cruiser. This diminution of the squadron's strength simply reflected the situation of the U.S. Navy generally. The war-built vessels were almost completely worn-out, while a depression during the middle years of the decade coupled with partisan wrangling and public apathy limited the funds available to the Navy Department for construction of new vessels and maintenance of those in existence. Secretary of the Navy George M. Robeson had used some of the moneys appropriated for the latter purpose to build a few new warships under the guise of repairing old ones, but even their completion was often delayed for want of funds. The secretary's own complacency about the condition of the service, together with the uncertainty of his professional advisors as to the types of vessels needed and the purposes for which they were required, obviously did nothing to persuade the Congress that a major program to revitalize and enlarge the U.S.

Navy was necessary. Nor did the change of administration in 1877 bring about anything more significant than the substitution of Richard W. Thompson for Robeson in the Navy Department. Thompson's complacency seems to have equaled that of his predecessor, and his knowledge of naval matters was naturally much less.

The screw-sloop *Ticonderoga,* on "a diplomatic & commercial cruise around the world under the auspices of the State Department" and flying the broad pennant of Commodore Robert W. Shufeldt, reached Japan in April.[2] Her mission, exemplifying the role of the Navy as a promoter of American commercial interests, was Shufeldt's own concept, based partly on his experiences as master of merchant steamers and consul general at Havana, Cuba. While serving as chief of the Bureau of Equipment and Recruiting, he had gained influence with Secretary Thompson, who in turn helped to win the support of the State Department. Shufeldt's orders were reminiscent of those under which Captain John Percival had sailed in the *Constitution* in 1844, calling for an investigation of commercial opportunities in the lesser nations of Africa and in the Indian Ocean; but the commodore's mission was to conclude with a visit to "some port of the Corea with the endeavor to reopen by peaceful measures negotiations with that government."[3]

Renewed interest in Korea seems to have begun with a report from Peking in 1874 that a new ruler of the Hermit Kingdom might be less inclined to maintain the policy of seclusion than his predecessor had been. The Japanese government succeeded in gaining a treaty of commerce and amity after a show of force in 1876, and Admiral Reynolds had witnessed the embarkation of the first Korean embassy a few months later as it left Japan to return home. He described its members as having "an exceedingly uncivilized appearance," and added his belief "that progress will be very tardy, in any way, in opening intercourse with the Peninsula."[4]

Although the State Department shared Reynolds's opinion, it sent orders to Minister John A. Bingham to request that the Japanese government communicate with that of Korea in support of Shufeldt's endeavor. However, the Japanese foreign minister, explaining that Japan's relationship with Korea might be jeopardized by an endorsement of the American mission, provided no more than a letter introducing the commodore to the Japanese consul at Pusan on Korea's southeastern coast and authorizing the consul to offer such assistance as he could. Accordingly, Shufeldt sailed to Pusan in the *Ticonderoga,* arriving on 4 May, and the Japanese consul forwarded his official letter to provincial authorities, only to have them refuse to transmit it to Seoul. Having failed in this approach, the commodore returned to Japan, where he and Bingham finally were able to persuade the foreign minister that he should write a letter to accompany Shufeldt's and send both to Seoul by diplomatic mail. Shufeldt agreed to await a reply at Nagasaki rather than at Pusan or another Korean port.

Whiling away the summer months of 1880 in Nagasaki's pleasant harbor, Commodore Shufeldt attempted to attain another goal which he had set for himself—command of the Asiatic Squadron. At fifty-eight years of age, he realized that he was unlikely to reach the rank of rear admiral, normally held by officers commanding squadrons, many months before his retirement. Therefore, virtually his only opportunity lay in convincing the Navy Department that his success in negotiating a treaty with Korea would depend largely on his ability to appear in the role of commander in chief. Earlier efforts to get the desired orders through friends in Washington apparently had elicited no response, so Shufeldt suggested to Admiral Patterson that the latter might wish to turn the squadron over to him and return home in the *Ticonderoga*—with the Department's permission, of course. Patterson, who might have resented the presence of a junior flag officer in an independent command on his station, had treated Shufeldt very affably, but he responded that he had never failed to complete a cruise and did not propose to do so now.

Another possibility seemed to present itself through the agency of the Chinese consul at Nagasaki, whose assistance the commodore had sought in translating his letter to Korean authorities. With Shufeldt's permission, the Chinese sent a copy to Li Hung-chang, who, as commissioner of trade for the northern ports and viceroy of Chihli, was reputed to be the most powerful man in China. Li responded by inviting Shufeldt to visit him at Tientsin, an invitation which its recipient thought implied a desire to retain him to reorganize the Chinese navy, especially since Sino-Russian relations had reached a critical point after the Chinese government had rejected a boundary settlement desired by St. Petersburg. The commodore was not free to go to Tientsin until August, but in the meantime he did his utmost to demonstrate his friendship for China by such gestures as arranging to have the men-of-war in Nagasaki harbor dress ship and fire national salutes on the occasion of the emperor's birthday—the first time this honor had ever been accorded to the Chinese ruler outside of his own domain, wrote Shufeldt.[5]

The commodore's letter to Korea was returned early in August, unopened reportedly because it had been improperly addressed. This rebuff, together with the news that a more senior flag officer had sailed from San Francisco to relieve Admiral Patterson, was naturally depressing to Shufeldt. He thought that the Department had erred in not offering him the command "because I have reason to believe that my personal influence both in China & Japan is greater than that of any Naval officer of whatever grade or nationality." However, he might yet startle his superiors in Washington by announcing his elevation "to the grade of Admiral in Chief to H. C. M. the Emperor of China & the 'Son of Heaven'!"[6]

In quest of this appointment, Shufeldt sailed to Chefoo in the *Ticonderoga*, whence he proceeded to Tientsin for an interview with Li. Their conversation, which covered a variety of topics, lasted almost three hours, and the commodore returned to his flagship convinced that Li would help the United States to negotiate the desired treaty with Korea and that there would be no Sino-Russian conflict because Li and his fellows recognized their country's military weakness. The latter information was encouraging —if a war were likely, the U.S. government probably would not permit Shufeldt to accept the prominent and lucrative position which Li implied he would be offered. As soon as the danger of typhoons had diminished, the *Ticonderoga* got underway for San Francisco.

The threat of war between Russia and China had concerned Admiral Patterson as well. In April, he had queried the Navy Department about his proper course of action should a Russian fleet blockade one or more of the treaty ports, and by mid-summer he was relaying rumors that the Russians intended to seize a port in Korea as a base whence to conduct a campaign against China and that the French and German squadrons were to be reinforced. Anticipating that his force would be asked to cooperate in defending the foreign commercial community, Patterson requested instructions to cover such a contingency. The screw-gunboat *Swatara*, one of Robeson's "administratively rebuilt" vessels that had reached the station in April, was ordered to Hakodate and Vladivostok in an effort to ascertain Russian intentions. Commander William T. Sampson reported ostensible preparations for war at the Siberian naval base but thought local officials sincere in disclaiming any knowledge of plans for a movement against Korea.

Meanwhile, a three-man commission headed by James B. Angell, the new U.S. minister to China, had arrived at Yokohama, and, since all three were accompanied by their families, the *Richmond* and the *Ashuelot* were required to transport them to the Taku Bar, where the *Monocacy* relieved the flagship which drew too much water to reach Tientsin. The commissioners had been appointed to negotiate an amendment to the 1868 Sino-American treaty, which permitted free entry of Chinese into the United States. They succeeded in gaining Chinese acceptance of an agreement whereby the U.S. government could "regulate, limit, or suspend" the immigration of Chinese coolies.[7] Even this, however, did not satisfy anti-foreign elements in the United States; these were able to bring about virtual exclusion of Chinese laborers within a few years in spite of the fact that this contravened the Angell treaty.

Hardly had Angell reached his legation before he wrote the admiral that the diplomatic and consular communities at Peking and Tientsin thought war between China and Russia almost inevitable. But Patterson was not sufficiently impressed to leave Yokohama; the *Alert, Ashuelot,* and *Monocacy,* already in Chinese waters, could defend American interests should the need arise.

Admiral Patterson's equanimity during this time of alarm may have been due partly to the knowledge that his relief was en route to the station. His flag was hauled down and that of Rear Admiral John M. B. Clitz was hoisted in the *Richmond* at Yokohama on 11 September 1880.

The new commander in chief, who had sailed in the old *Mississippi* with Commodore Matthew Calbraith Perry a quarter-century earlier, found the vessels of his command in relatively good order. The *Ashuelot* and the *Palos* were exceptions—the former had damaged her rudder while turning in the narrow river at Tientsin, but she had to winter there in the *Palos's* stead because the smaller vessel required boiler and engine repairs.

The tendency of his commanding officers to undertake repairs to their vessels without reference to the admiral caused the latter to call this to Secretary Thompson's attention. Stating that he probably would have authorized the work had he been consulted, Clitz wrote: "If Senior Officers Present can make repairs ad libitum then there is not much necessity for a Commander in Chief."[8] This seems a curiously limited view of his role for an admiral to express.

Early 1881 found Clitz at Hong Kong, whence he went to Shanghai to speed work on the *Monocacy,* which he thought had been too long in dockyard hands. The *Swatara* visited Nagoya and Kagoshima with imperial permission, neither being an open port, while the *Alert* was preparing to undertake surveys in the Bonin Islands. The *Ashuelot* arrived at Shanghai late in March with four men suffering from smallpox contracted at Tientsin; fortunately, only one died and no further cases appeared.

Since the three-year enlistments of the *Richmond's* sailors would expire at the end of 1881, the Navy Department ordered that she proceed to the Isthmus of Panama to exchange crews with the old *Powhatan* during the autumn. Her decks had to be recaulked before she could undertake the transpacific voyage, so Clitz shifted his flag to the *Monocacy* in July. Like Patterson before him, the admiral found the double-ender too crowded to be an effective flagship, but neither the *Ashuelot* nor the *Swatara* could offer more suitable working space. He therefore asked that the Department authorize the expenditure of $60 per month to rent an office in

Yokohama in which the squadron's business might be transacted. Notwithstanding the secretary's refusal of this request, it seems that he and his staff resided ashore during most of the eight months before the *Richmond* returned to the station.

The *Swatara* was ordered to Chefoo to escape Shanghai's summer heat, and on arrival off the northern Chinese city, Commander Sampson decided to carry out an exercise which he and his officers had been planning for several months. To this end, he desired that a battalion of armed sailors and marines be permitted to spend four days ashore. The taotai thought the request too unusual to be granted in full; he allowed the force to stay two days, adding that it could be landed for daily exercise at any time.

On 13 July, 123 officers and men, of whom twenty were marines, embarked in the ship's boats, carrying with them all the necessary accouterments, provisions, ammunition, and two howitzers. The steam launch towed the flotilla to the beach, where a company of sailors was landed and deployed to protect the disembarkation; when it had been completed, the battalion was marched to the campsite with the marines serving as rear guard. By the time tents were being erected, curious Chinese were appearing on the scene in considerable number, so sentinels had to be posted to prevent theft and the sale of intoxicants. After maintaining wartime patrols and watches during a rainy night, the force carried out target practice with small arms and howitzers the next day, followed by a simulated attack on the camp. The second night was even wetter, but apparently it failed to dampen the spirits of the battalion—at any rate, the exercise concluded with a "friendly scuffle" between the marines and a company of sailors ordered to "capture" them. All hands were reembarked in ninety minutes after the *Swatara* fired the gun recalling the battalion.

Sampson thought this exercise, which seems to have been the most ambitious and realistic since the Korean expedition a decade earlier, a great success. He gave full credit to his subordinates, especially to Lieutenant Commander William M. Folger, the *Swatara*'s executive officer who commanded the force, and to its supply officer, Ensign William F. Fullam; perhaps the latter's subsequent efforts to have sailors assume the duties of marines had their genesis in this exercise.

During the autumn of 1881, the Navy Department called Clitz's attention to the fact that some time had elapsed since a warship of the squadron had cruised in the more southerly waters of the station. Clitz might with justice have muttered a salty oath on reading this letter—of his six vessels, the *Richmond* had not yet returned from Panama, the *Alert* and the *Palos* were engaged in hydrographic duties assigned by the Bureau of

Navigation, and the *Ashuelot* was preparing to return to Tientsin for the winter with her rudder still unrepaired because use of the dock at Nagasaki could not be obtained until it was too late for her to enter the Pei Ho. The *Swatara*, the only ship really suitable for distant service, could not be spared from the vicinity of the China coast. Within a short time, her services too were required—to convey Commodore Robert W. Shufeldt to Korea.

Shufeldt had found a supporter in Secretary of State James G. Blaine, at whose request the Navy Department ordered the commodore to join the diplomatic mission at Peking as naval attaché in the spring of 1881. This position, however, was mainly for appearance's sake, serving to explain his presence while he was actually engaged in preliminary negotiations toward a Korean treaty. On his own account, the commodore continued to hope that he might obtain profitable employment with the Chinese navy.

Accompanied by his daughter, Mary, who was to serve as his secretary and hostess, Shufeldt paused at Tientsin for an interview with Li Hung-chang before going on to Peking. The viceroy was mildly optimistic regarding the prospects for a treaty, but Shufeldt was made to understand that patience would be required because of the anti-foreign sentiment which remained important in Korea. On 7 July, the commodore reported to Minister Angell in Peking; only then was the true purpose of his mission revealed to the diplomat. To maintain his contact with Li, Shufeldt established himself at Tientsin, where he acted as an unofficial consultant to the Chinese navy while awaiting the reply to a letter that the viceroy had dispatched to the Korean government. Whether Li ever had any real intention of appointing Shufeldt to a prominent and lucrative position in the Chinese navy is not clear; at any rate, he did not do so, and Shufeldt attributed this unwillingness to intrigue on the part of jealous Europeans. Minister Angell and Chester Holcombe, who succeeded as chargé d'affaires in the autumn, advised the naval officer to abandon his quest for employment, but the latter was still at Tientsin in December when the news came from Li that the Korean government was indeed prepared to begin negotiations with the United States.

Commodore Shufeldt's appointment as special envoy empowered to conclude a treaty had been sent by the State Department in mid-November, as had Clitz's order to place a vessel at his disposal. These letters reached Tientsin two months later, but formal negotiations could not begin until March because of Li's absence from the city during the winter. In February, Shufeldt conferred with Holcombe in Peking, drawing up a draft treaty and ascertaining that the Chinese government would place no obstacles in the way of his efforts.

Negotiation of the treaty took place at Tientsin, with Shufeldt and Li the principals involved, for the Korean representative remained very much in the background. Blaine had cautioned the commodore not to ask too much—an agreement guaranteeing succor of American vessels and mariners was the first essential and could lead to an expanded treaty later—but Shufeldt and Holcombe had gone far beyond this in their draft, including diplomatic and consular representation, arrangements for citizens of each to reside and carry on trade in the other, tariff stipulations, prohibition of opium importation, most-favored-nation status for the United States, and extraterritoriality for its citizens. Apparently none of these subjects caused much difficulty; however, Li insisted that the treaty contain a statement recognizing China's suzerainty over Korea. Shufeldt refused to accept this, so the negotiations dragged on for weeks with each party seemingly obdurate. Finally, the commodore's threat to discontinue the talks led Li to agree that suzerainty need not be mentioned in the treaty if that document were accompanied by a letter to the president from the Korean monarch in which the Chinese position was noted. Since Li had accepted this compromise once before, only to denounce it subsequently, Shufeldt could not be certain that the Chinese acquiescence was final. Nonetheless, he summoned the *Swatara* to Chefoo, where he embarked after a brief visit to Shanghai.

The *Swatara*, preceded by three Chinese gunboats which sailed for Korea a day in advance, departed Chefoo in a dense fog on the morning of 8 May 1882. Fog, ordinarily the mariner's foe, was welcomed on this occasion, for it enabled Shufeldt to evade the scrutiny of those in HMS *Vigilant* and the German flagship who had been observing his movements with keen interest. It also hampered the *Swatara*'s progress; Commander Philip H. Cooper dared not to approach the rocks and islands off the Korean coast until the weather cleared on 11 May. The gunboat came to an anchor the next day at Chemulpo.

Korean commissioners visited the warship "in great state" on 14 May to arrange the formal meetings. The first of these took place on 20 May at a village five miles from the anchorage, and two days later Commodore Shufeldt and fifteen other naval officers in full dress, escorted by a marine guard, joined the Koreans in a large tent erected for the final ceremony. When the signatures had been affixed to the six copies of the treaty, the *Swatara* ran up a large Korean ensign (which her sailmaker had made for the occasion) and fired a national salute, followed by fifteen guns in honor of the admiral commanding the Chinese vessels. The Japanese gunboat *Banjo* took no part in the firing of salutes; her presence symbolized the Sino-Japanese rivalry for control of "the land of the morning calm."

Robert W. Shufeldt had accomplished his goal of obtaining an American-Korean treaty before any other Western nation had concluded a similar agreement; indeed, the treaties which Korea made with other major powers generally accepted that with the United States as a model. What of his ambition to command the Asiatic Squadron?

That too seems to have been within his grasp, for Admiral Clitz had already asked that he be relieved in September 1882, by which time he would have held the command for two years, and Shufeldt's friends in Washington thought that they had arranged the commodore's appointment. But while awaiting a response to his request to succeed Clitz, Shufeldt received a communication in which Secretary of the Navy William E. Chandler informed him that his future orders depended on a "satisfactory explanation of a letter 'reflecting in severe terms upon the Chinese people, their government, principal officers and the Empress.' "[9] Thereupon, the commodore withdrew his request and prepared to return to the United States.

The explanation, had he submitted one, would seem to be as follows. He was accustomed to correspond with his close friend, Senator Aaron A. Sargent of California, with the understanding that the latter might release certain letters to the press. On 1 January 1882, Shufeldt, no doubt discouraged by his failure to obtain the desired position with the Chinese navy and exasperated by the slow progress toward a treaty, had unburdened himself in an "extraordinary letter, brutal in its frankness," castigating Li Hung-chang and the Chinese generally.[10] Its heading, "Open Letter to Hon. A. A. Sargent," and its style led the recipient to release it to American newspapers in March 1882—which, according to Mary Shufeldt, was not the commodore's wish. Shufeldt confirmed this to Sargent, not blaming the senator, but "I have suffered for it more than any other act of my life. . . . I have been summarily recalled from China and my Corean work to a great extent nullified."[11]

However, neither the Korean treaty nor Commodore Shufeldt's career seems to have suffered as a result of this indiscretion. The exchange of ratifications of the Korean treaty was carried out in due course, while friends assured Shufeldt that Secretary Chandler would offer him a position greatly to his liking—the presidency of the Naval Advisory Board which was to advise the secretary on the design and construction of warships soon to be authorized by the Congress.

Shufeldt's negotiations during the spring of 1882 had no immediate effect on the Asiatic Squadron. The *Swatara* lay at Kobe while awaiting his orders, and the *Monocacy* continued to fly Admiral Clitz's flag at Yokohama until March, when the *Richmond* returned from Panama manned by a new crew and in need of a thorough overhaul. Clitz decided that both vessels should join the *Swatara* at Kobe while the necessary repairs were made to the screw-sloop. That city had better privately owned repair facilities and a more sheltered harbor than Yokohama, and artisans from the two gunboats could help the *Richmond*'s men, thus reducing the number of dockyard laborers who would have to be employed. The *Alert* and the *Palos*, released from their hydrographic duties, also came to Kobe in a few weeks.

The *Alert* was approaching the end of her second cruise on the station, so the admiral ordered her to Yokohama and thence to Mare Island for overhaul and a newly enlisted company. She departed Kobe on 18 April, only to return the next day heeled well over to port with a hole gaping in her starboard side. While steaming down the Kii Suido the night before, the gunboat had encountered the Japanese imperial yacht *Jingei Kan*, a slightly smaller paddle steamer. The night was clear and calm, and the two vessels had had each other's running lights in sight for an hour when the Japanese steamer inexplicably turned hard to starboard, ramming the American even as the latter maneuvered to avoid collision. Commander Louis Kempff and his men reacted promptly, rigging the pumps and running the *Alert*'s guns out to port in order to bring the hole in her side above the water. Eleven minutes after the impact, the badly damaged gunboat was put on a course for Kobe, the hole plugged with hammock mattresses which, together with her port list and a smooth sea, enabled her to reach the harbor without difficulty an hour before her assailant stood in.

The provincial governor called on Clitz to express his sympathy and then, admitting that the *Jingei Kan* was solely responsible for the collision, he proposed that his government pay for the *Alert*'s repairs. The admiral declined this offer, subject to the Navy Department's approval, but when the gunboat touched at Yokohama six weeks later, the governor of Hiogo insisted that she be docked at Yokosuka for an inspection of her repaired side before she began her transpacific passage.

Within a few months, Admiral Clitz was repaid in his own coin—the *Ashuelot* ran into a Japanese lighthouse steamer early in November, and the director of lighthouses refused to permit the United States to defray the cost of the latter's repairs.

In June the *Monocacy* paid a visit to Korea, the first since the treaty's signing. Leaving Nagasaki, she steamed through the Korea Strait and up the east coast of the peninsula in thick, rainy weather which prevented celestial observations and made the identification of landmarks very difficult. Sailing directions for the region were of little assistance, but deep water close inshore and the absence of uncharted outlying dangers combined to make the passage uneventful. The gunboat spent two days at

Wonsan, then known as Gensan or Port Lazaref, which Commander Charles S. Cotton reported to be a fine harbor. There was no town of any size in the vicinity, only straggling villages composed of "wretched mud huts crudely thatched with straw" from which virtually no provisions could be procured, "agriculture [seeming] to be among the lost arts there." Several officers visited these villages and "were objects of the most excited and even annoying and rude curiosity."[12] The numerous Koreans who flocked on board the *Monocacy* were equally curious. Cotton ascertained that they recognized her as an American warship and were aware of the Shufeldt treaty. From Wonsan, the double-ender stood down the coast to Pusan, where she replenished her bunkers from the supply of coal maintained by the Japanese government, and then sailed for Chefoo on 1 July.

A month later, news of an apparent anti-Japanese rising in Korea reached Admiral Clitz at Yokohama. Almost simultaneously, the Navy Department directed him to place a warship at the disposal of Minister to China J. Russell Young, and Minister Young recommended that a vessel be sent to Korea. The *Swatara*, which had been the squadron's most efficient cruiser, had sailed for the United States a few days earlier, so the admiral ordered Commander Cotton to take the *Monocacy* to Chemulpo.

Meanwhile, it became apparent that the Korean coup had been directed against the country's court, with the queen and other prominent members of the pro-foreign group being killed. The Japanese minister, who had escaped in a small boat, was picked up by a British survey vessel and brought to Nagasaki, whence his government decided that he should be returned to Seoul with a force sufficient to guarantee his legation's safety. Assurances that the Japanese did not intend to initiate hostilities were tempered by the fact that the Chinese government could be expected to send troops into Korea to counter the Japanese presence; thus, a Sino-Japanese conflict might result.

The *Monocacy* reached Chemulpo on Sunday, 13 August, and found four Japanese vessels with 1,200 soldiers embarked and two new Chinese cruisers. By custom, the quiet of the Sabbath was never disturbed by firing salutes, but Young's directive to Cotton emphasized the importance of maintaining an amicable relationship with the Japanese. The *Monocacy*'s saluting battery therefore boomed out the thirteen guns due a rear admiral and the Japanese flagship properly returned the salute gun for gun.

Official visits were exchanged the next day, with Cotton explaining his role: "to observe, report, counsel moderation on the part of the Japanese if opportunity offers, to remain neutral so far as acts of aggression are concerned, to see Korean authorities & give such moral support as may be possible."[13] The Chinese minister, who had helped to negotiate the Shu-feldt treaty, brought two Korean officials on board the *Monocacy* to confer with Cotton. They discouraged the commander from returning their visit at Seoul, nor did he insist, having some idea of the distance to the capital and of the quality of accommodations available there.

Chinese troops arrived and were landed at a point far enough from the Japanese forces to prevent a clash; not long afterward, the Chinese quietly abducted the Korean monarch's father, who was said to have led the rising, and sent him to China. The king, restored to full powers, agreed to a convention whereby the Korean government undertook to pay an indemnity and the expenses of the Japanese expedition, to send a diplomatic mission to Japan, and to permit the Japanese legation guard to remain in Seoul for one year. Cotton transmitted this information to his superiors and, judging that the Korean crisis had subsided for a time, got the *Monocacy* underway for Chefoo on 4 September.

A crisis of another sort emerged in China in the autumn of 1882. On 24 November, Minister Young wrote Admiral Clitz confidentially about a "succession of events in Shanghai seriously involving American and other interests."[14] These had to do with the efforts of foreign entrepreneurs to establish manufacturing enterprises in China, sometimes selling stock to Chinese. Initially, the viceroy of Nanking proceeded against an American, W. S. Wetmore, who had begun the spinning of cotton yarn and whose Chinese comprador owned stock in the company. The viceroy forbade Chinese to participate in such a venture on the ground that a Chinese company had been granted the sole right to produce cotton yarn. However, the foreign diplomatic corps agreed that Wetmore's business was a treaty right. Before this issue had been decided, the comprador was detained, to be tried for his reputed participation in the Taiping Rebellion, a charge obviously devised to justify his arrest. Another order forbade all Chinese residing in Shanghai to use electric lighting. In addition, an American firm, Russell and Company, which was manufacturing silk filaments for use in light bulbs, was ordered to cease their production. No monopoly was involved in this instance; the action seems to have been taken because the electric light had been introduced by foreigners.

Confronted by this obviously anti-foreign stance on the part of a powerful Chinese official, Young was uncertain about what Clitz should do. After stating that veteran diplomats held that this was the most serious threat to foreign interests in China since the signing of the treaties, the minister wrote that, while he would like a warship at Shanghai, he did not consider the situation sufficiently important to ask that one be sent. He was especially desirous of avoiding anything that might be interpreted as a show of force.

Some two weeks later, Young informed the admiral that the viceroy's harassment of foreigners seemed to have ended; however, the refusal of authorities at Swatow to recognize German ownership of an area adjoining the customhouse had resulted in the plot's occupation by armed sailors from SMS *Elizabeth*. The Chinese government had subsequently ordered the Swatow and Amoy taotais to desist from any interference with German holdings. But on 30 December, the minister wrote that Sino-German relations had been strained seriously by the Amoy taotai's refusal to heed the order. Clitz was told "that our flag should appear in Chinese waters in whatever force you can spare."[15]

In response, Clitz ordered the *Monocacy* from Nagasaki to Amoy and informed the minister that the *Richmond* and the two double-enders constituted the entire force at his command, for the *Palos* was under repair at Nagasaki.

A major squadron composed of only three effective vessels might seem ludicrous, yet it was not atypical for the U.S. Navy at that time. The Pacific Squadron, with six vessels including a sailing storeship, was the Navy's largest, while the North Atlantic Squadron, numbering five warships, was a close second. The European Squadron had three ships and that in the South Atlantic had two. In mid-February, however, the Asiatic Squadron was reduced even further.

Commander Horace E. Mullan had reported from Shanghai that the *Ashuelot* was no longer needed there, so she was ordered south early in February. The veteran double-ender sailed from Amoy on 17 February,

FIGURE 13–1.   The ill-fated *Ashuelot* at Yokosuka.

bound for Swatow. When fog caused her speed to be reduced soon afterward, her navigator plotted a track to a point well to the eastward of the Lamock Islands off Swatow, from which she could steam into the harbor if the visibility had improved enough by the next morning.

As the watch was relieved at 4 A.M. on 18 February, lookouts reported land abeam to starboard. The officer of the deck shouted "Hard astarboard!" and rang two bells to stop the engine. As she turned to port, the vessel heeled slightly and those on deck heard a "crunching noise" as a rock off East Lamock Island ripped her starboard bilge open beneath the fore rigging. Commander Mullan, who had been reclining on the chartroom transom, rejected his executive officer's suggestion that the gunboat be beached because "there was too bold water there and by doing so, we might lose lives."[16] Instead, he had the boats cleared for lowering and, when it became apparent that his command had suffered fatal damage, ordered that she be abandoned.

The *Ashuelot*'s abandonment should have been carried out with a minimum of confusion, for both watches were still on deck and the order to leave the vessel was given about a half-hour before she sank. But Mullan made no attempt to ascertain that all hands had actually come up from below, nor did he direct those on deck to don life preservers—indeed, he had to be dissuaded from abandoning ship himself while most of his men were still on board. When he finally did drop from a Jacob's ladder into his boat, the commander insisted that no one remained on board, yet at least four men followed him into the gig.

The boats made East Lamock Island without difficulty, and there a muster revealed that eleven men, of whom three were Chinese, had perished with the *Ashuelot*. Later in the day, the survivors sought such shelter as the lighthouse on nearby High Lamock Island could offer. All were embarked in a Chinese revenue steamer sent from Swatow on 19 February, and three days after the *Ashuelot*'s loss, her company boarded the *Richmond* at Hong Kong.

For the next month, what remained of the U.S. Asiatic Squadron was immobilized at Hong Kong while a court of inquiry heard the testimony of the late gunboat's officers and men, testimony which caused it to report that the conduct of Commander Mullan was sufficiently suspect to warrant his trial by general court-martial. Admiral Clitz telegraphed this information to the Navy Department, adding that the squadron did not have enough senior officers to constitute such a court. The Department responded by ordering two captains to the station for court-martial duty and directing Clitz to retain the "Ashuelots" on board the *Richmond* at Hong Kong.

This order forced the admiral to change his plans. The first U.S. diplomatic mission to Korea was expected in Japan shortly, and Clitz had intended to convey it to Chemulpo in the *Richmond*, thereafter returning to Yokohama to await his relief, Rear Admiral Peirce Crosby. Now he had no choice but to assign the *Monocacy* to the Korean mission; fortunately, the *Palos* was completing her overhaul and would be available to take the larger gunboat's place in Chinese waters.

But the *Palos* was showing the effects of age and service, too. While she was docked at Nagasaki, it had become apparent that much more than a routine overhaul would be required to make her seaworthy. This report was cabled to the Navy Department, where the bureau chiefs concerned agreed that the sometime tugboat was not worth the cost of extensive repairs and should be sold. Confronted with the problem of finding a replacement, Secretary William E. Chandler finally decided that not more than $10,000 should be spent on the *Palos*—as it turned out, that gave her an additional ten years of life!

With his flagship forced to remain at Hong Kong, the *Monocacy* required for the Korean mission, and the *Palos* incapable of any but limited service, Clitz must have been surprised to receive an order that henceforth Shanghai be visited frequently by vessels of his squadron and that the *Monocacy* be sent there for a reasonable length of time in the near future. This unwise interference in the admiral's disposition of his force stemmed from complaints by members of Shanghai's American community who were inclined to feel that they were paid too little attention by their country's naval forces. Clitz himself admitted that the complaints had some validity in this instance. More than a year earlier, he had disagreed with the consul general's actions in dealing with enlisted men who were absent over leave in Shanghai. The matter had been referred to the Navy Department and, receiving no response, the admiral had adopted a policy of sending vessels to Shanghai only if their presence was clearly required. On the Department's behalf, it must be added that this order was dated 7 February, eleven days before the *Ashuelot* sank.

By coincidence, the letter directing Admiral Crosby, commander in chief of the South Atlantic Squadron, to assume command of the Asiatic Squadron bore the same date. This fact is worth noting, for Clitz's relief has been attributed to the loss of the *Ashuelot*.

Actually, the admiral had twice applied for relief, in letters dated 5 May and 14 October 1882, and Crosby had been informed of his impending transfer at least as early as January 1883. This is not to suggest, however, that Clitz enjoyed the full confidence of the Navy Department as his cruise neared its end. Reports of intemperance among the squadron's officers had caused concern, and Admiral Clitz, himself reputed to be a heavy drinker, could hardly be expected to curb such tendencies on the part of his subordinates.

Yet too much can be made of this. Courts-martial for drunkenness were hardly unusual and John Mellen Brady Clitz was neither the first nor the last of the Navy's senior officers to display "an inordinate fondness for liquor."[17] Nor should Minister Young's opinion be ignored: "The Admiral did all in his power, with his limited forces, to impress upon the Chinese the fact that we were a government with power to maintain our rights under the Treaties."[18] Probably the most abstemious of Clitz's fellow flag officers could have done little more.

CHAPTER FOURTEEN

The Sino-French War

Rear Admiral Peirce Crosby, serving in the Far East for the first time, received a request for assistance soon after hoisting his flag in the *Richmond* on 21 April 1883. The consular agent at Swatow feared that Sino-German tension would lead to disturbances and asked that a warship be sent. With his flagship unable to leave Hong Kong while the *Ashuelot* courts-martial were in session, the *Monocacy* on her way to Korea, and the *Palos* under repair, the admiral could only explain his inability to comply and express the belief that the British and German gunboats already at Swatow would have a calming effect on the populace.

The court-martial of Commander Horace Mullan determined that his vessel's loss was directly attributable to his drunkenness—his written night orders had specified a course which headed the *Ashuelot* directly toward East Lamock Island! He was sentenced to be dismissed from the Navy, after which the court adjourned on 1 June.

Soon afterward, the *Richmond* sailed to Shanghai. Crosby found the international settlement there perturbed by the possibility that a Franco-Chinese war might develop as a result of the continuing French conquests in Annam. That crisis, however, was averted for a time. Therefore the flagship departed for Japan at the end of June; her company needed a change of climate, and the admiral had his own reason for wishing to visit Yokohama—his wife had accompanied him to the station and awaited him there.

The *Monocacy* joined the flag some weeks later after ferrying a diplomatic mission from Korea to Nagasaki, whence the Koreans sailed for the United States in the mail steamer. Minister to Korea Lucius H. Foote wished to keep a warship in Korean waters, so the double-ender returned to Chemulpo after completing minor repairs.

The first addition to the squadron since the *Ashuelot*'s loss, the screw-gunboat *Essex*, arrived at Yokohama on 11 August. The admiral allowed her a few days for boiler repair and then sent her to Chemulpo to relieve the *Monocacy*, so that the double-ender could convey Minister J. Russell Young on a round of visits to Chinese ports. Nor was the *Essex* the sole reinforcement; her sister *Enterprise* was making a long passage out by way of the Cape of Good Hope, running a line of soundings across the Atlantic and Indian oceans as she progressed, while the older screw-sloop *Juniata* came out by the more usual Suez route after pausing at Malta where Commander George Dewey had to be detached to undergo emergency surgery.

Both vessels reached the Netherlands East Indies early in September and there received telegraphic orders to offer their assistance to Dutch naval officers who were attempting to bring relief to devastated areas and restore aids to navigation in the aftermath of the cataclysmic eruption of Krakatoa on 27 August. The resulting tsunamis had claimed some 36,000 lives in the adjacent coastal areas of Java and Sumatra, and for a time thereafter masses of floating pumice impeded the passage of ships in Sunda Strait. Although nearly half of the island had simply disappeared, there was no assurance that its volcanic potential was spent, and approaching vessels had to be warned of the danger.

But the Dutch admiral did not desire the services of foreign warships nor could the *Juniata* and the *Enterprise* have lingered even had he wished them to do so, for in mid-September they received orders to proceed to China forthwith. Clashes between a few intoxicated Europeans and Chinese had led to a riot at Canton in August, and while Chinese police and troops brought this under control, a more serious outbreak was precipitated on 10 September by the drowning of a Chinese allegedly pushed overboard from a British steamer by a Portuguese watchman. This threatened the entire foreign community, and Admiral Crosby received a telegram from Washington directing him to take all measures necessary to protect American interests in China. Although he had heard unofficially that Chinese troops and British gunboats had the situation at Canton in hand, the admiral summoned the *Juniata* and the *Enterprise* at once and ordered the *Palos* up the Canton River when she completed her repairs at Hong Kong on 27 September. The *Juniata* arrived at Hong Kong early in October, to be joined by a new commanding officer who took the screw-sloop to Canton despite her 16-foot draft, altering the vessel's trim sufficiently for her to edge past the barrier without damage. The *Enterprise* reported two days later, by which time orders had reached Hong Kong for her to go on to Shanghai.

On 1 October 1883, Rear Admiral Peirce Crosby requested permission to return to the United States and retire, citing "urgent domestic reasons" as justification.[1] The Navy Department did not respond to his telegram at once, perhaps because of the critical situation at Canton, but on 30 October Crosby acknowledged an offer of immediate retirement so that a brother officer might be promoted to rear admiral before he too had to retire. Thus, Captain Joseph S. Skerrett assumed the title of senior naval officer on that date, and the *Richmond* left Kobe to convey Crosby and his wife to Yokohama, whence they sailed in the next mail steamer.

Receipt of a telegram directing him to cooperate with foreign naval forces in the event of a Sino-French conflict caused Skerrett to sail to Nagasaki a month later. There, on 19 December, Acting Rear Admiral John Lee Davis, who had last visited Nagasaki in the old *Preble* almost thirty-five years earlier, assumed command of the Asiatic Squadron. At fifty-eight years of age, Davis was reputed to be a fine seaman and a strict disciplinarian, qualities which would stand him in good stead in this assignment.

Conditions on the Asiatic Station certainly seemed to require a vigorous commander in chief at this time. The Franco-Chinese rivalry in Annam presented a more immediate danger than the Sino-Japanese competition in Korea in the eyes of foreign observers because it was generally believed that the Manchu dynasty could not survive a war with France. However, any conflict involving China was likely to be accompanied by widespread domestic disorder with consequent danger to the lives and property of foreigners, many of whom were already uneasy and prepared to demand the protection of a warship at the slightest pretext. With a squadron composed of six vessels, all in good condition except the *Monocacy* whose boilers were showing signs of weakness after eight years of service, Admiral Davis could respond to pleas for assistance more readily than many of his predecessors, yet it was clear that nothing short of international naval cooperation could provide effective protection to his fellow-countrymen in the event of civil war in China.

The *Richmond* sailed for Shanghai the morning after Davis assumed command, and there he found a letter from Vice Admiral George O. Willes, whom the British Admiralty had directed to work with his American counterpart to safeguard their nationals in the treaty ports. The Briton suggested that at least one U.S. warship be kept at Shanghai and another at Canton for the time being, to which Davis agreed, adding that the vessels under his command had been ordered to act in concert with those of Britain whenever the need should arise.

But the American flag officer also took care to caution his commanding officers with regard to this association, writing confidentially that their vessels were to cooperate with men-of-war under foreign flags "in the interests of humanity only," and that immediate protection was to be afforded to all foreigners who were attacked by Chinese. Officers commanding U.S. warships were forbidden to place themselves under the orders of any foreigner, nor were they to become involved in a confrontation with French forces that certain foreign powers inimical to the Gallic nation (most likely Britain and Germany) might attempt to bring about. Davis held that the situation of the United States in the Orient was unique: "The history of the European Powers in the East shows that it has been customary to bombard the native forts and towns upon the slightest provocation. With us a resort to such extreme measures has been seldom necessary."[2] This fact and the known absence of American territorial ambitions there gave the United States a greater moral influence in the Far East than powers with much larger fleets could exercise. The latter were thus the more desirous of involving American warships in combined operations for whatever purpose.

Admiral Davis spent three months at Shanghai; during this time a board composed of three of the squadron's officers, of whom Skerrett was the senior, prepared a plan for the defense of foreign lives and property. Davis transmitted their handiwork to the senior foreign naval officers for their approval and then to the Shanghai municipal council which undertook to raise 400 volunteers to assist the sailors and marines landed from the warships. The *Monocacy* and the *Juniata* were at Shanghai in January; the admiral had a battalion made up of the three ships' landing parties drilled ashore and then paraded through the streets to hearten the foreigners and impress the Chinese. The *Alert* also was ordered to Shanghai when she returned to the station.

While Davis was detained at Shanghai preparing for the defense of its international settlement, the situation at Canton required attention. The southern city's populace, which was considered much more turbulent than that of Shanghai, had been restive since the riots of the preceding autumn, and some regarded occasional incidents of mob violence against missionaries in the vicinity as evidence of a forthcoming effort to rid southern China of Christian influence. Moreover, the authorities had ordered the Canton River blocked at Whampoa Reach to prevent a French attack on the city itself. The foreign diplomatic and consular representatives protested that the Chinese had no right to close a treaty port in time of peace, and Admiral Davis ordered the *Essex*'s commanding officer to seek information pertaining to the proposed obstruction, taking care neither to offend the Chinese nor to allow his vessel to be trapped in the river. His report that a clearly marked passage would be left in the barrier alleviated the fears caused by its construction.

Davis himself went up to Whampoa early in April. There he transferred his flag to the *Monocacy*, and the *Richmond* dropped downstream to Hong Kong whence she sailed for New York after filling up with coal and provisions. The admiral found everything quiet at Canton; he met U.S. Consul Charles Seymour, reputed to be one of the ablest of the consular community, and Vice Admiral Sir William Dowell, Willes's relief, who was flying his flag in the tender *Vigilant*. Noting that British, French, and German gunboats were also moored off the city, Davis recommended that ships of the different nationalities take turns at guarding foreigners there.

Later in April, the *Enterprise* stood up the river with Minister Young on board, whereupon Davis shifted his flag to the newcomer. A week later, Young and Davis visited Macao and then proceeded to Hong Kong, where the USS *Trenton*, newly arrived from the United States with the Korean diplomatic mission embarked, saluted both. Davis ordered her to convey the Koreans to Chemulpo; he would join her after visiting the treaty ports in the *Enterprise*.

The *Enterprise* and the *Trenton* joined the *Juniata* and the *Essex* at Nagasaki at the end of June. Admiral Davis transferred his flag to the *Trenton*, the most impressive flagship to show the stars and stripes on the Asiatic Station since the *Tennessee*'s departure. To be sure, she was another wooden ship with full sail rig, but her battery of muzzle-loading rifled guns and her 12-knot speed made her the most formidable American warship of that time. And her ram bow, while adding little to her offensive power, at least gave the *Trenton* the aggressive appearance typical of the latest foreign men-of-war.

Admiral Davis planned to take all four ships to sea, and, after detaching the *Essex*, which was under orders to return to the United States, he would visit Kobe, Yokohama, Hakodate, Vladivostok, and Korean ports with the remaining vessels. Events to the southward, however, kept these plans from being carried out. In May, the Chinese government had agreed to relinquish its suzerainty over Annam, leaving France a free hand in that area. Chinese forces were to be evacuated, but their departure was not rapid enough to satisfy French officers on the scene, whose impetuosity led to a clash late in June in which the greatly outnumbered force of Frenchmen suffered heavy losses.

Reports of this incident reached Nagasaki by telegraph within a few

FIGURE 14–1. The *Trenton* making sail.

days, so Davis awaited developments there until 12 July. With the excitement apparently having subsided, his three vessels made a leisurely passage to Kobe, where the latest information from China indicated that the difficulties growing out of the Annam clash would be settled amicably. The warships continued on their way to Yokohama, with the admiral drilling them in squadron tactics under sail and steam en route.

Arriving at Yokohama on 21 July, Admiral Davis found telegrams from the *Monocacy*'s Commander Francis J. Higginson and from Minister Young that indicated that the situation was exceedingly grave. But Davis did not depart at once. A court-martial had been convened to try a paymaster in accordance with a Navy Department order, and it would have to be postponed indefinitely should the vessels sail before its deliberations had been completed. Therefore, the admiral required more specific information about the nature of events in China before leaving Yokohama. Commander Higginson informed him that Foochow, downstream from which the Chinese had their principal naval arsenal and one of their four fleets, was the critical point, for Rear Admiral Amédé A. P. Courbet had ascended the River Min with French naval forces while others menaced Keelung, just across the Formosa Strait.

By 27 July, the *Enterprise*'s officers had completed their testimony before the court, so she was ordered to Shanghai to relieve the *Monocacy*, whose draft would permit her to ascend the Min to Foochow. The flagship and the *Juniata* followed two days later, but their passage to the Yangtze Kiang was prolonged by the necessity to spend one night at anchor in the Inland Sea while machinery repairs were made; in steaming through the Strait of Shimonoseki the *Trenton*'s commanding officer chose to pass on the wrong side of a buoy with the result that the flagship grounded and was not refloated until the next day. Thereafter, she pressed on at her maximum sustained speed, coming to anchor at Woosung on 5 August, one day before the *Juniata* arrived.

Meanwhile, Admiral Davis's detention in Japanese waters had evoked consular criticism. Seymour wrote from Canton that a single British gunboat was off that city (the *Palos* having gone to Hong Kong to give her company liberty), while "the foreign war fleets, as usual are enjoying their summer in Japan; and possibly protecting the bathers at Chefoo occasionally."[3] His counterpart at Chefoo, Consul A. R. Platt, complained that no U.S. warship was among those anchored there, and Consul Edwin Stevens at Ningpo stated bluntly: "It seems like an utter impossibility to keep an American man-of-war very long out of those seductive [Japanese] ports."[4] Minister Young responded by explaining the arrangements for international naval cooperation and praising Admiral Davis for his "zeal, energy, and promptitude. . . . Considering the paucity of his force and the extent of his command he has done most meritorious work."[5]

At Shanghai, Davis received a full account of the Sino-French imbroglio from Young. The minister reported that the imperial government had refused to accept responsibility for damages occurring in disturbances resulting from French belligerency, although he was sure that it would do its utmost to protect all foreigners, including Frenchmen, residing in China. Nonetheless, the diplomatic corps at Peking agreed unanimously that the foreign governments must undertake to defend their nationals. To this end, Young felt that a vessel of war must be kept at each treaty port, whether coastal or on the Yangtze.

A dispatch from Admiral Dowell explained to Davis the arrangements the Briton had made to carry out the diplomats' wishes. A total of twenty-four gunboats and larger vessels, including the *Monocacy* and the *Palos* and thirteen under the British white ensign, were listed, and Dowell hoped that Davis might send other ships of his command to specified points, especially on the Yangtze, and to Tientsin. Davis replied that the *Trenton*, which was undergoing engine repair, and the *Juniata* would remain at Shanghai; the *Monocacy* was at Foochow and would be reinforced by the *Enterprise*; and the *Alert* had been ordered to relieve the *Palos* at Canton, whereupon the latter would go to Tientsin. The screw-sloop *Ossipee*, en route to the station, would be assigned as necessary on arrival.

Davis next turned his attention to Foochow, where Higginson had indicated that he planned to land forces to protect the Americans' property. By officer-messenger, the commander was ordered to furnish his fellow-countrymen refuge on board the *Monocacy*, but not to send armed men ashore. A telegram from Young urging the same restraint was received by the admiral soon afterward; however, Higginson argued that Davis's order had upset all his plans and would result in loss of life as well as property. Thereupon the admiral cabled: "Land if necessary to save life"; he transferred his flag to the *Enterprise* preparatory to sailing to the Min at high water the next day, 10 August.[6]

The River Min was the scene of considerable activity when the *Enterprise* approached on 12 August. The French armored cruiser *Triomphante* was anchored off the bar, discharging unessential equipment into a transport to reduce her draft sufficiently to ascend the river; a corvette was moored two miles upstream; and a squadron of ten vessels, including two torpedo boats and the cruiser *Volta* flying Courbet's flag, was lying in the Pagoda Anchorage, beyond which only light-draft craft could proceed. Eleven Chinese gunboats, less formidable than their potential opponents, and some junks and fire boats were moored abreast and above the French squadron. Admiral Dowell was there as well, with the British screw-corvettes *Sapphire* and *Champion*.

Admiral Davis paid official visits to the senior naval officers, foreign and Chinese, and to the imperial commissioner before setting out for Foochow by small boat, leaving orders for Commander Albert S. Barker to be prepared to send one hundred of the *Enterprise*'s men upstream to join him. Off the city, he boarded the *Monocacy* and noted with satisfaction that HMS *Merlin*, crowded with eighty men from the *Champion* in addition to her own sixty, was riding at anchor nearby.

Commander Higginson could add little to the admiral's understanding of the situation. Obviously the French could not threaten Foochow itself —Courbet had too few shallow-draft vessels to undertake that—but news of a clash between his squadron and the Chinese men-of-war or of an assault on the naval arsenal just above the Pagoda Anchorage was expected to loose a tide of turbulence that would endanger all foreigners in the city. However, the landing of foreign sailors might have the same result. Thus, when the taotai assured Davis of his intent to protect the foreign settlement, the American promised that the gunboats' men would be kept on board until it became apparent that the Chinese efforts to guarantee the safety of foreigners were actually insufficient.

So far as the likelihood of a battle in the Pagoda Anchorage was concerned, the admiral concluded that something decisive must occur within a short time and summoned the *Enterprise*'s men to reinforce the *Monocacy*'s company. The mandarins commanding the fleet and fortifications were reported to be urging their superiors at Peking to permit offensive action, which the latter apparently were unwilling to do in the absence of a formal declaration of war. Days passed. The French warships, cleared for action, kept their guns manned and prepared to slip their cables at a moment's notice. Chinese troop units marched about the shores, and laborers worked feverishly at the arsenal, although foreigners could not decide whether they were preparing it for defense or demolition. The days of waiting in the heat of the South Chinese summer must have been extremely trying for all, not least for those in the badly overcrowded *Monocacy* and *Merlin*. By 18 August, Admiral Davis had begun to doubt that there would be any fighting; on the same date, Chinese officers were informed by Peking that war could not be avoided.

Three days later, British and American warships and the few foreign merchantmen steamed to anchorages well clear of the probable belligerents. Admiral Courbet seems to have notified the consuls at Foochow that he would engage the Chinese on 23 August. The availability of the *Triomphante* may have decided the date—the armored cruiser stood up to the Pagoda Anchorage at high water just before 2 P.M., and as soon as the ebb had begun, swinging the anchored Chinese vessels stern-on to the French, the latter opened fire. Almost simultaneously, a torpedo exploded against the side of the Chinese senior officer's ship, which drifted away to sink. Such a beginning might have disheartened the stoutest of sea-fighters; it certainly added nothing to the efficacy of the Chinese resistance which lasted for a period variously reported as from seven to twelve minutes. In that short time, the Chinese vessels were sunk or beached, with the exception of two which fled in good season. Thereafter, small boats from the British and American warships plied the waters of the anchorage, picking up swimming survivors and removing others from floating wreckage, while their surgeons attended the wounded, including those in a French torpedo boat. Unfortunately, boats and surgeons alike were too few to succor all who required assistance—the Chinese casualties included many missing in addition to 521 killed and 150 wounded. Admiral Courbet reported that his victory had cost the French six killed and twenty-seven wounded.

Later in the afternoon, the French ships engaged the Pagoda Anchorage forts and arsenal, repeating the bombardment the next day. On 25 August, Courbet led his ships down the Min, taking the downstream forts from the rear with little difficulty and demolishing them in turn. Ironically, those same forts might very well have prevented the French warships from ascending the river at all, had their garrisons been permitted to oppose Courbet's advance without a declaration of war.

The sounds of battle were plainly audible at Foochow, but no outbreak followed. Attempts by the Chinese authorities to explain to the populace that the French alone were the enemy and that no Frenchmen resided there may have been responsible; at any rate, an American missionary held that "vagabonding thieves and pirates and disorganized soldiers" presented the only danger to foreigners a week after the engagement.[7]

On 30 August, Admiral Courbet notified Dowell that he planned no further operations in the vicinity of the Min, and the Briton forwarded this information to Davis. The detachments from the *Champion* and the *Enterprise* were returned to their vessels within a few days, and Admiral Davis hoisted his flag in the latter on 6 September. That afternoon HMS *Zephyr* arrived at the Pagoda Anchorage to report that a battery covering Kinpai Pass eleven miles downstream had fired into her, wounding three men. The Chinese authorities apologized promptly. Apparently she had been mistaken for a French gunboat of similar appearance. Davis immediately wrote an order requiring the commanding officers of his vessels to communicate with local officials before standing into any Chinese port or stream. Informing Minister Young of his action, the admiral suggested that the Chinese government be urged to establish signal stations at harbor and river mouths to which ships could identify themselves and make known their desire to enter. The *Enterprise* was not molested when she steamed down the Min the next day. Those in her noted that the Chinese were hard at work rebuilding the forts that the French had destroyed, and the works at Woosung were also being strengthened when she stood up the Yangtze. At Shanghai, the admiral returned to the *Trenton* and ordered the *Enterprise* to Chefoo.

The ensuing weeks were relatively quiet. Admiral Courbet proclaimed a blockade of Formosa, but it was not enforced strictly and caused little inconvenience. The *Ossipee* reported for duty and was ordered to Shanghai, whence the *Trenton* and the *Juniata* sailed late in October bound for Nagasaki, there to survey and dispose of the stores remaining in the squadron's supply depot. The Navy Department and Davis agreed that the storehouse should be returned to its owner at the expiration of the lease; they disagreed, however, on an alternate site. Probably influenced by the State Department, the Navy Department wished to lease a suitable storehouse at Yokohama, while Davis, supported by several of his subordinates, argued that stores could be purchased at the major ports on the station readily and often at lower cost than that incurred in shipping them from the United States. Moreover, supplies, especially provisions, tended to accumulate in a depot, often deteriorating before they could be issued to vessels. If, in spite of these objections, the Navy Department was determined to maintain a storehouse, the officers recommended that it be at the more centrally located Shanghai or Hong Kong. The prospect of saving money carried the day.

On 5 December, the admiral reported that all was quiet on the China coast, nor did he indicate any concern about affairs elsewhere on the station. On the same day, however, Minister Foote wrote from Seoul that a revolution had occurred in Korea and that a gunboat should be sent at once. Foote's letter reached Nagasaki on 13 December, whereupon a cable was sent to Commander Barker at Shanghai, directing him to order the *Ossipee* at Chefoo to fill up with coal and proceed to Chemulpo. Meanwhile, the *Trenton's* black gang was lighting boiler fires and raising steam; the flagship weighed anchor and stood out that night, lashed by gale-force winds as she cleared the harbor.

Arriving at Chemulpo four days later, Admiral Davis found that British and Japanese gunboats had preceded him. At Foote's request, a small guard was sent to Seoul the next morning. The *Ossipee* and the German gunboat *Iltis* steamed into the harbor on 22 December, bringing the number of warships present to seven, and Minister Foote and his wife boarded the *Trenton* that evening, having left the legation under the care of Ensign George C. Foulk, the naval attaché.

From the minister and others, Davis learned that the revolution had begun with attacks on anti-foreign officials of the Korean government. As disorder spread, the Japanese minister had ordered his legation guard to protect the king. This action enraged the Chinese present, who then joined the Korean mob in unsuccessful assaults on the Japanese soldiery; when the king's safety had been assured, the Japanese troops formed a hollow square, with the wives and children of Japanese residents inside, and fought their way to Chemulpo. Although their losses were light, a number of Japanese civilians had been killed in Seoul, for which the Japanese government was certain to hold the Chinese responsible.

Minister Foote had offered to mediate the Japanese-Korean difficulty. When negotiations began on 24 December, he transferred to the *Ossipee*; the *Trenton*, with Mrs. Foote on board, departed for Nagasaki on Christmas Day. Early in January 1885, the *Ossipee*'s Commander John F. McGlensey reported from Seoul that a Japanese-Korean agreement had been reached, including an indemnity and the building of barracks in Seoul to house Japanese troops. The Sino-Japanese problem, on the other hand, was to be settled by direct negotiation between Peking and Tokyo.

While her larger consorts were keeping a watchful eye on Sino-French and Sino-Japanese developments, the *Palos* was spending the winter at Newchwang, thirteen miles up the Liao Ho from the Gulf of Liaotung, northern extremity of the Gulf of Pechihli. The old gunboat was not exactly a stranger to Newchwang, having first visited the city in 1871, but no American warship had wintered there before. The essential difference between the Pei Ho, in which the *Palos*, the *Monocacy*, and the late *Ashuelot* had been accustomed to spend an occasional winter, and the Liao Ho was that the ice on the latter often reached a thickness which made it impossible for vessels to remain at Newchwang unless they were secured in docks excavated in the mud of the river bank. Getting the gunboats into and out of these docks was a difficult evolution, not least because of the 4-knot current in the river. The first British vessel to winter there, the little gunboat *Grasshopper* in 1870, had broken her back entering the dock; she was sold and broken up without leaving it. The *Palos*, on the other hand, seems to have been docked without untoward incident, but the experience of spending the harsh winter months in an isolated Chinese city can hardly have been a pleasant one for her company. Before many weeks had elapsed, her chief engineer took his own life.

Early March 1885 brought a telegram from Minister Young announcing that the government of France had declared war on China. Understandably having taken the Pagoda Anchorage engagement as a hostile act, China had declared war on 26 August 1884; now, some six months later, France had declared war. The situation was the more serious because Admiral Dowell, warned of Anglo-Russian differences in Afghanistan, began to withdraw British warships from Chinese treaty ports in order to concentrate the China Fleet at Hong Kong. Russian and French vessels were unavailable for obvious reasons, so responsibility for the protection of foreigners in the Far East devolved on the seven American, three German, and one Italian men-of-war on the station. Fortunately, the Chinese showed no disposition to take advantage of the absence of the British gunboats, to whose presence they had become so accustomed.

The *Trenton* and the *Enterprise* stood on up the coast to the Min, where the latter relieved the *Juniata* to which the admiral transferred his flag. The *Trenton* was ordered to Nagasaki, while Davis went on to Shanghai in the hope that he might expedite the *Monocacy's* repairs. There, he found the foreign residents quite optimistic, with some reason as it turned out, for negotiations between Chinese and French emissaries were well advanced, and hostilities ceased on 15 April. Anglo-Russian tension seemed to be easing as well. Dowell had sent some of his gunboats back to the Chinese treaty ports, although his big ships were kept at Nagasaki whence they could counter any Russian squadron leaving Vladivostok.

By mid-May, however, Anglo-Russian differences had been resolved amicably, and the Sino-French armistice was still in effect. The *Palos*, freed from her virtual imprisonment at Newchwang, came south to be inspected by the admiral, who sent her to Canton as the *Alert's* relief until the *Monocacy* had completed her post-repair trials, after which the double-ender steamed up to Canton and the *Palos* went to Foochow. The *Alert* was docked at Nagasaki where she was joined by the *Juniata* and the *Ossipee*. For two weeks the admiral kept their companies engaged in a variety of drills, and early in June he took them to sea for tactical maneuvers under sail and steam. When he was satisfied with their proficiency, the force dispersed—the *Alert* to Chemulpo, the *Ossipee* to Shanghai, and the *Juniata* to Nagasaki to await the *Trenton*, which had taken the *Ossipee's* place in Korean waters.

The Sino-French treaty, virtually repeating the agreement of a year earlier, was signed in June. Ironically, Vice Admiral Amédé A. P. Courbet, whose conduct of the naval war against China had won him acclaim in France, died of cholera only hours after receiving this news. The U.S. Asiatic Squadron was reduced when the *Enterprise* was ordered home by way of Australia, continuing her earlier deep-sea soundings as she proceeded. The *Juniata* also was detached, with orders to investigate the situation in Madagascar where French expansion might be injurious to American trade. However, the screw-sloops *Marion* and *Omaha* were en route to the station, so the squadron's diminution was of short duration. With the international scene apparently tranquil, Admiral Davis found time to give some attention to the discipline and efficiency of the ships under his command. Two general orders issued on board the *Trenton* in July indicated the admiral's displeasure with some of the practices he had noted in the various vessels which had flown his flag or had been in his company. Generally, the irregularities were those to be expected in warships accustomed to spending lengthy periods in Oriental ports with little supervision by the flag officer—small craft from the shore allowed to crowd alongside; their occupants engaging in noisy conversation with man-of-warsmen and with one another; such boats being utilized by officers and men going ashore at all hours in preference to awaiting the regular departure of a ship's boat; inattention to proper uniform and to smoking regulations; officers whose wives came out to the station being allowed to spend much of their time ashore; liberty being granted at the commanding officers' whims—these and similar slovenly practices were to cease, and ships' companies henceforth would observe the daily routine to be expected of a properly regulated naval vessel. Yet John Lee Davis was not simply a martinet—he forbade "noises disturbing the good order and quiet of a well disciplined ship, except after sundown, when the crew should be allowed every enjoyment consistent with propriety."[8]

The *Ossipee* was ordered to Yokohama in August, there to meet the new U.S. minister to China, Charles Denby. She put in at Nagasaki to coal and was steaming through the Inland Sea when cholera afflicted a number of her seamen. Commander McGlensey set a course for Kobe, the nearest port which could offer medical assistance, and in accordance with the surgeon's recommendation, sterilized the berth deck by admitting steam from the main boilers. Three men had died by the time the *Ossipee* let her anchors go off Kobe, where two more expired in the hospital to which her sick were transferred. After her crew had been landed, the entire vessel was disinfected with chloride of lime, and the berth deck was twice fumigated with sulphur. News of the *Ossipee*'s plight was telegraphed to Admiral Davis, who sent a surgeon from the flagship to help the screw-sloop's medical officers.

Commander McGlensey at first inclined to the view that the cholera germs had been brought on board in clothing which had been laundered at Nagasaki. Later, however, he pointed out that, while taking on coal, "the deck of this ship was crowded by a number of the dirty filthy, lowest class of Japanese, who do the coaling of ships, [and] I think that it is very likely that they left the seeds of the disease behind."[9]

Owing to recurrent outbreaks of diarrhea, the *Ossipee's* men were still on the beach when, on 28 September, seven destitute American seamen were brought to Kobe. They had abandoned the bark *Cashmere* after she had been wrecked in a typhoon on 12 September, leaving five shipmates who thought a sinking hulk preferable to a small boat. The surgeons considered the *Ossipee* still unsafe for her crew so an appeal was made to the captains of Russian and French warships at Kobe. Both declined to undertake a search for the five, the former because he was under secret orders and the latter on the ground that the bark must have already foundered. Thereupon, McGlensey ordered his healthy men to prepare the *Ossipee* for sea, and she sailed on 30 September, leaving sixteen sailors with weak bowels in the hospital. For a week, gales and heavy seas frustrated the search, but the commander persisted—"I think anything is better than that it should be said that five men were allowed to perish without any effort being made to save them."[10] The screw-sloop returned to Kobe in mid-October to find that the five, who had reached the northernmost of the Ryukyus on a raft, had already joined their fellows. But at least there had been no recurrence of cholera among her company—the *Ossipee* could resume her interrupted passage to Yokohama.

The remainder of 1885 passed without notable incident. The *Monocacy* was ordered to winter at Tientsin, and Admiral Davis continued his practice of shifting his other vessels from one port to another as regularly as possible, while the *Alert* was ordered to the more southerly waters of the station, which had perforce been neglected for some time.

On 5 January 1886, the day before the *Alert* was to sail from Shanghai, the acting consul general received a report that American Methodist missionaries at Chinkiang had been "outraged" by Chinese carpenters whom they had employed. The taotai declined to punish the carpenters until he had investigated the incident thoroughly, so the local consul asked that a warship be sent. One might have expected the consul general to cable the request to Admiral Davis at Nagasaki to learn if the *Alert* should go up to Chinkiang before beginning her southerly cruise. Instead, HMS *Wanderer* ascended the Yangtze immediately and the *Marion* followed a week later, whereupon the taotai ordered that the desired punishment be inflicted without further investigation.

Vice Admiral Richard V. Hamilton, who had succeeded Sir William Dowell as commander in chief of Britain's China Station in November 1885, was understandably critical of the *Wanderer's* response to an American appeal for assistance at a time when a U.S. warship was also at Shanghai, ready for sea. He went on to condemn the traditional international cooperation in such incidents and doubted "if any United States official would look on the question in the same light if a British man-of-war were to assist a Chinese Consul in obtaining redress for the 'gross outrage' perpetrated on Chinese Citizens in California."[11]

Hamilton's letter was forwarded to the British Foreign Office, which responded that, while restraint in the use of gunboats for the protection of foreigners was desirable, "the position of Europeans in China cannot fairly be compared with that of foreign residents in more civilized countries."[12]

Whether the United States could be included among those "more civilized countries" must have seemed debatable in 1886, for anti-Chinese outbreaks in that nation had reached their peak with the Rock Springs, Wyoming, massacre of September 1885 in which twenty-eight Chinese lost their lives and fifteen more suffered serious injury at the hands of a mob. During the ensuing months, hundreds of other Chinese were driven from their homes, had their property destroyed, and endured various indignities elsewhere in the American West. Efforts on the part of the U.S. government to deal with these disgraceful incidents were halting and ineffectual, nor did that government respond promptly to Chinese demands for an indemnity. Indeed, the solution to the problem, as most Americans seemed to see it, was to ban all Chinese from the United States, regardless of treaty provisions to the contrary, which perhaps could have been more nearly justified had all citizens of the United States been recalled from China and the vessels of the Asiatic Squadron forbidden to touch at any of that nation's ports.

The squadron, including the *Alaska*'s sister *Omaha* which reported for duty in January 1886, spent much of its time in Japanese waters, although Davis took care that Canton, Shanghai, and Chemulpo were not left unattended. The cruises of three vessels came to an end in 1886—the *Trenton* departed Yokohama for Norfolk in May, the *Alert* sailed for San Francisco in July, and the *Ossipee* left Nagasaki bound for New York in October. The first was most sorely missed, for none of the remaining ships could provide office space for the conduct of squadron business, stowage for records, or adequate quarters for the flag officer and his staff. The elderly *Brooklyn*, another of the *Hartford*'s sisters, had been ordered to the station to replace the *Trenton*, but she did not sail from New York until mid-August and required more than seven months to reach Yokohama, in part because the Navy Department decided that she should show the flag at Muscat, Bombay, and other ports along the way. Meanwhile, Admiral Davis listed the *Marion* as his flagship while overseeing most of his squadron's activities from Yokohama's Club Hotel, a course which he may have found the less trying because his health was showing the effects of nearly three years in the Orient.

On 22 November 1886, Rear Admiral Ralph Chandler assumed command of the Asiatic Squadron. Describing his arrival, Chandler wrote that Davis "was like a school boy let loose after his three years of service here."[13]

Well he might have been, for few commanders in chief had held the command in more trying times. Nor had any of Davis's predecessors done more to shape the squadron into an efficient force—he had flown his flag in even the least of its warships in order to see for himself the conditions of life and discipline therein and conducted tactical maneuvers or exercises ashore whenever he could bring a sufficient number of vessels together. John Lee Davis had proven himself an unusually competent commander in chief. Unfortunately, his health had been permanently impaired, and he died little more than two years after returning home.

CHAPTER FIFTEEN

The Last Years of the Old Navy

When Rear Admiral Ralph Chandler assumed command of the Asiatic Squadron in November 1886, it was considerably weaker than it had been a year earlier, consisting as it did of the screw-sloops *Omaha* and *Marion* and the gunboats *Monocacy* and *Palos*. Even the arrival of the *Brooklyn* and the *Essex*, both on their way from the United States, would leave the Asiatic Squadron below its former strength, reflecting the absence of any imminent crisis on the station.

Nor were all of the ships in good condition. Half of the *Essex*'s boilers were unreliable when she arrived in January 1887; in April, Chandler had to report that the hull repairs necessary to make the *Monocacy* seaworthy would cost $24,000. The *Brooklyn*, which had to have her decks and upper works recaulked at Yokohama on arrival, also required boiler and other repairs estimated at $15,000 to make her an effective cruiser.

The *Brooklyn* reached Yokohama on 31 March only because Chandler, impatient for a proper flagship, had ordered her to Japan from Batavia, thus preventing the visits to Netherlands East Indies ports which the Navy Department had included in her itinerary. For this assumption of Departmental authority, Secretary of the Navy William C. Whitney called the admiral to account. The latter defended himself by pointing out that the *Brooklyn* was not assigned to special service—she had been designated as his flagship, and had he understood that she was not intended to be available for that purpose until six months after he had assumed the command, he would not have accepted the assignment. After promising to

219

transfer his flag to the *Omaha* in the autumn so that the *Brooklyn* could carry out the remaining visits, Chandler offered to relinquish his command immediately if Whitney should so desire. This misunderstanding ended with Whitney's decision that the admiral himself should visit the Netherlands East Indies and the Philippines in his flagship during the next winter.

Admiral Chandler spent the first seven months of his tenure at Yokohama where the *Brooklyn* was refitting and the *Monocacy* was awaiting a decision about her future. The *Palos* also arrived for repairs, which cost less because the fleet engineer found that the *Essex*'s damaged boiler tubes could be cut down to fit the smaller vessel's boilers.

During the spring, Minister Hugh A. Dinsmore wrote that the naval attaché, Ensign George C. Foulk, was facing possible expulsion from Korea because of his supposed authorship of news stories offensive to the government. Chandler replied that a naval attaché could be forced to depart only if his own government recalled him, surely an arrogant view even for a Westerner in the Orient, and ordered the *Marion* to Chemulpo in mid-May. After discreet inquiries, her commanding officer reported that Chinese officials at Seoul were Foulk's true enemies—they thought him pro-Japanese and were jealous of his influence with the king. The admiral forwarded this report to the Navy Department together with his own opinion that the powers jointly should notify the Chinese government that it must either make Korea a part of its empire or allow the Korean monarch to govern his kingdom entirely without interference. Chandler favored the latter course, thinking that American trade would benefit, although he must have realized that the United States was unlikely to participate in such international action.

George C. Foulk was recalled by the U.S. government in June 1887, but the *Marion* remained at Chemulpo until relieved by the *Essex*, after which she departed for Panama to embark a new crew. The admiral himself visited Korea during the summer, and, although he thought the foreigners there perfectly safe, he ordered the *Omaha* and the *Essex* to alternate between Chemulpo and Chefoo for the next several months and authorized the former's Captain Frederick V. McNair to act at discretion in any emergency.

The year ended without untoward incident, and January 1888 found the *Omaha* exchanging crews at Panama, the *Essex* repairing boilers at Kobe, and the *Palos* wintering at Chemulpo, while the *Monocacy* continued to be little more than a station ship at Yokohama. The *Juniata* would arrive in mid-March; until then, the *Brooklyn* was the only vessel available to answer requests for assistance. Nonetheless, she had to sail to the southward in accordance with the Navy Department's orders.

The flagship stood out of Kobe on 25 January, paused at Hong Kong for recaulking and at Singapore to fill her coal bunkers, and then went on to Batavia, where Chandler learned that Java's other harbors were either too shallow or too exposed for a vessel of the *Brooklyn*'s size. Thereupon, she made her way to Celebes and through the Moluccas, touching at ports that no U.S. warship had visited in a decade or more, before putting in at Manila at the end of March. Admiral Chandler reported that the cruise had been very pleasant and the Dutch officials uniformly courteous; he added that none of the ports after Batavia had U.S. consular representatives, nor, in the absence of American residents or trade, were any needed. Perhaps with a touch of sarcasm, he concluded his report by stating that the 6,500 miles of almost constant steaming had been very trying for the *Brooklyn*'s old boilers. Well might the admiral have been critical, for the Navy Department certainly had erred in sending the flagship on an utterly pointless mission at a time when she was the only serviceable cruising vessel on the station.

Seoul was the scene of some excitement in June. French and American missionaries in the Korean capital had been active in recruiting children for instruction in the mission schools, and the anti-foreign party was said to have spread a rumor that these youngsters were actually being killed and boiled for the manufacture of medicines and photographic supplies. Koreans accused of kidnapping children for sale to the missions were assaulted by a mob, whereupon Minister Dinsmore relayed the king's request that the *Essex*, which had relieved the *Palos* at Chemulpo, send a small guard to the city. Commander Thomas F. Jewell was reluctant to comply without direct orders from his superior, suggesting instead that the missionaries and other Americans who might be endangered seek refuge in the gunboat. Within a few hours, however, Dinsmore sent another dispatch, stating that the foreign diplomatic representatives agreed that a force must be sent. Rapid communication with Admiral Chandler was impossible, and men were being landed from French and Russian gunboats; therefore, Jewell sent a force of twenty-five sailors and marines ashore that night with strict orders that it be kept at the U.S. legation and act only to protect life. Guided by an American resident who knew the road, they marched most of the thirty miles in darkness, thus avoiding both the sun's heat and the Koreans' notice. The *Juniata* arrived from Shanghai within a week, by which time the disturbances had been quelled by Korean authorities. Admiral Chandler commended the *Essex*'s detachment on its efficiency and good behavior; when it had been reembarked, the gunboat was ordered to Yokohama by way of Vladivostok and Hakodate.

The *Marion* returned to the station in early summer, and, after she had been docked at Yokosuka, Chandler transferred his flag to her so that the *Brooklyn* could depart for the United States upon completion of her boiler repairs. The latter left Yokohama early in August and a week later, forty miles from Nagasaki, her engine was disabled by a broken crank. When the breeze proved too light to give the *Brooklyn* steerageway, her steam launch and pulling boats attempted to tow the ship, only to find their efforts thwarted by tide rips. Thus, the erstwhile flagship was drifting aimlessly in the East China Sea when the Russian man-of-war *Bobr* hove into sight. Although her commanding officer was under orders to proceed to Vladivostok with dispatch, he passed a hawser and towed the *Brooklyn* into Nagasaki before continuing on his course. Chandler recommended that she be sent home under sail and, the Navy Department concurring, had the *Juniata* and the *Palos* tow her to a point well offshore whence the old vessel began her final passage to New York by way of Honolulu and Cape Horn.

The *Juniata* too was approaching the end of her career. After bidding the *Brooklyn* bon voyage, she went on to Hong Kong and then sailed for New York, pausing at Singapore to repair damages suffered in a Gulf of Tonkin typhoon.

As the year ended, the three effective American warships—the *Marion*, *Omaha*, and *Essex*—were at Shanghai, whence the last sailed for New York early in January 1889. The flagship soon followed her as far as Hong Kong, and the *Omaha* was sent to Nagasaki to return Minister Dinsmore to Korea.

Arriving at Chemulpo on 8 February, Captain McNair received a cable from Chandler: "Proceed utmost dispatch Chinkiang Yang-tse river serious riots."[1] Dinsmore was put ashore with some haste, and the *Omaha* sailed the next morning. She took a pilot off the mouth of the Yangtze Kiang two days later and ran aground in the river that afternoon. Backing off undamaged at midnight, the screw-sloop continued upstream, exchanging salutes with Chinese batteries as she proceeded. She anchored off Chinkiang near the British *Mutine* and *Firebrand* and a small Chinese gunboat on the afternoon of 12 February.

From the U.S. consul, McNair learned that the rioters had burned the police station and continued their work of destruction in the foreign settlement until Chinese troops arrived to put an end to the disorder— before either of the British warships had appeared on the scene. No lives had been lost, but the British and American consulates and buildings of the American Baptist and Methodist missions had been burned or looted. Local authorities were held to be blameless and had indicated their willingness to make compensation for the damages.

The *Omaha* remained a week and then, with her bunkers almost empty, dropped down to Shanghai where McNair learned that he was now the senior U.S. naval officer on the Asiatic Station. Rear Admiral Ralph Chandler's telegram to McNair at Chemulpo seems to have been the last order which he issued as commander in chief of the Asiatic Squadron. Just three days later, on 11 February 1889, the fifty-nine-year-old flag officer died suddenly at Hong Kong. He was buried in Happy Valley Cemetery on 13 February after the colony's civil authorities together with officers of the Royal Navy and the British Army had joined the *Marion*'s officers and men in extending military honors to "a model Naval officer and a dignified and courteous gentleman."[2]

News of the admiral's demise was at once cabled to the Navy Department and to Captain McNair. There was little for McNair to do save to take his vessel to Japan in due course to meet a new commander in chief. While waiting for him at Kobe in March, however, McNair did have the distinction of greeting the first warship of the "new" U.S. Navy to visit the Far East.

This "new" Navy may be said to have had its beginning almost eight years earlier, when Secretary of the Navy William H. Hunt had convened an advisory board composed of line and staff officers headed by Rear Admiral John Rodgers to consider the condition of the service's vessels and to recommend a building program to satisfy its immediate needs. When the board reported that no wooden warship should be retained if she required repairs amounting to 30 percent of the cost of a replacement, the Congress agreed; but the board's concomitant recommendation that thirty-eight small cruisers (of which twenty would be described more accurately as gunboats) and thirty torpedo vessels and rams for coast and harbor defense be built as soon as possible elicited little enthusiasm among congressmen. Secretary Hunt's successor, William E. Chandler, had refused to allow the matter to rest. He summoned a second, smaller, advisory board in July 1882, with Commodore Robert W. Shufeldt as its president (Admiral Rodgers had died two months earlier). The work of the two boards, together with the support of Secretary of the Navy Chandler and President Chester A. Arthur, led the Congress to authorize in 1883 the construction of four small warships, of which three were to be cruisers and the fourth a "dispatch boat." Succeeding Congresses appropriated money for additional men-of-war and by 1889, no less than twenty-five had been authorized. However, design and construction presented unforeseen problems, so that only the small cruisers *Atlanta* and *Boston* and the dispatch vessel *Dolphin* had been commissioned before the end of 1888.

The *Dolphin*, making a voyage of circumnavigation intended to test her durability and performance under varying conditions, steamed into Kobe

FIGURE 15–1.   Stephen C. Rowan and Robert W. Shufeldt.

harbor early in March, and Captain McNair decided that she should visit Shanghai and then ascend the Yangtze, spending a day at each of the principal ports likely to be accessible at that season. The appearance of a modern warship would enhance American prestige with both Chinese and foreigners and also satisfy the desire of Charles Denby, U.S. minister to China, that a gunboat touch at these ports periodically.

The new commander in chief, Rear Admiral George E. Belknap, hoisted his flag in the *Omaha* at Yokohama on 4 April 1889. A veteran of the attack on the barrier forts below Canton in 1856 and commander of Rear Admiral Henry Bell's punitive force which landed on Formosa eleven years later, Belknap had last visited Asiatic waters in command of the *Tuscarora* in 1874.

The *Marion* and the *Monocacy* were also at Yokohama, and the *Palos* had steamed over to Chemulpo from the Pei Ho in mid-March. The *Dolphin* had carried out McNair's orders to show the flag on the Yangtze and then stood down the coast to Hong Kong, where she was preparing to sail for New York by way of the Suez Canal.

Sending the *Marion* to Nagasaki, the central point whence she could be ordered at need, the admiral planned to cruise to the station's treaty ports as soon as his flagship could be readied for sea. However, the *Monocacy*'s future was still uncertain, and he felt that he should remain at Yokohama to await the Department's decision with regard to her. Authorization to repair the old double-ender at Yokosuka was received in due course, and Belknap stayed to supervise the work. Thus, almost six months elapsed before he and the *Omaha* left Japan; when they did, it was only to touch at Chemulpo and Chefoo before returning to Nagasaki to oversee the *Palos*'s machinery repairs.

Canton and Hankow were the scenes of riots during the summer of 1889, and Minister Denby wrote the State Department to urge the necessity of a return to "the inevitable gunboat policy."[3] Secretary of the Navy Benjamin F. Tracy forwarded a copy of Denby's letter to Belknap in the autumn, to which the admiral replied that he had only the deep-draft *Omaha* and *Marion* immediately available for duty, for the newly arrived *Swatara* had been strained in a South Atlantic gale and the *Monocacy* was awaiting ordnance stores and a new crew.

The double-ender was ready in December, and the admiral, reporting that she had weathered a gale "as well as any vessel could have done" while en route to Shanghai, stated that the addition of Hotchkiss revolving cannons and Gatling guns to her armament had made the old gunboat a much more effective warship. The *Monocacy* ascended the Yangtze to Chinkiang, whence she steamed to Canton after the *Palos* relieved her later in the spring of 1890. The *Marion* spent a short time at Chemulpo before sailing for San Francisco in March, and the *Swatara* went to Shanghai upon completion of hull repairs at Nagasaki. Meanwhile, Admiral Belknap in the *Omaha* remained in Japanese waters although there seems to have been no reason why he should not have cruised about the station as he had planned to do a year earlier.

In mid-April, he reported that the Japanese fleet and a large military contingent had held maneuvers which no foreigners save those in the imperial service were permitted to observe. Following these exercises, the fleet moored off Kobe, and that evening the governor of Hiogo, the U.S. consul, and the Japanese and Russian admirals and their staffs were Belknap's guests at a dinner in the *Omaha*'s cabin. The next morning all of the warships present manned their yards and fired national salutes as the emperor reviewed the fleet. A reception for flag and commanding officers followed, at which the emperor personally thanked the American admiral for having the *Omaha*'s marine guard paraded and her band playing Japan's "national hymn" as the imperial flagship steamed past.

In a sense, this review might be said to have been Japan's "coming-out party" as a modern naval power, for the nineteen warships, "homogeneous in composition, well disciplined and thoroughly drilled," rivaled even Britain's China Fleet in force and number, and Admiral Belknap reported that they performed evolutions "with celerity and precision."[4] The U.S. Navy certainly could not have mustered a fleet comparable in any way to that of the Imperial Japanese Navy in 1890. And perhaps the Japanese themselves were aware of their power; in May, Belknap wrote confidentially of his concern lest assaults on British and American missionaries in Tokyo portend serious anti-foreign outbreaks throughout Japan.

But Korea was the immediate problem. In mid-May, Secretary Tracy cabled that Belknap was to "act in concert" with the Korean monarch to deal with unrest expected to follow the demise of the dying dowager queen. The *Swatara* was ordered to Chemulpo from Shanghai, touching at Nagasaki en route to receive the admiral's instructions. The queen died early in June, whereupon the U.S. minister to Korea, Augustine Heard, asked Commander Philip H. Cooper to bring his vessel's battalion to Seoul. The fifty sailors and marines were kept in the vicinity of the legation for nine days and returned to their ship when it became apparent that they had responded to a "false alarm."

In July, Vice Admiral Nowell Salmon informed Belknap that henceforth British men-of-war on the China Station would fire salutes only once every six months—on the first occasion of meeting the flag officer being saluted—and that official visits would be exchanged with the same frequency. Admiral Belknap heartily concurred in this arrangement, issuing orders to his subordinates that they adhere to a like schedule. Indeed, this order was long overdue, for the firing of salutes had reached ridiculous proportions with some of the gunboats of newer "naval powers" banging away with apparent delight on the slightest pretext without regard to the protocol of salutes. So noisy had these greetings become that some communities, most notably the international settlement at Shanghai, simply banned them. The French, Russian, and German squadrons agreed to similar limitations, presumably with equal relief.

The summer of 1890 passed without notable incident. In October, Belknap transferred his flag to the *Swatara*, which was repairing at Yokohama, so that the *Omaha* could go on a cruise "for the exercise of her crew at sea, for target practice at Chemulpo," and to bring back from the *Monocacy* and the *Palos* those men whose enlistments would soon expire. The *Omaha* remained at Chemulpo until after the funeral of the dowager queen and then returned to Yokohama to embark the admiral once more. The time-expired men were transferred to the *Swatara*, which sailed for Mare Island on 29 October, there to be laid up until she was sold six years later. However, the screw-gunboat *Alliance*, absent on a visit to the Caroline Islands since reaching the station a few weeks earlier, returned from that mission to keep the squadron's strength at four vessels.

The *Palos* departed Chefoo for Tientsin at the end of October. Like most of her kind, she was accustomed to cross the Taku Bar on a flood tide, which carried her up the Pei Ho to the city. In 1890, however, her old engine was working badly and her bottom was foul; she failed to keep pace with the tide and was tied up to a tree on the river bank to await the next flood. By that time, offshore winds had lowered the river level to the extent that her commanding officer had to hire a cargo boat into which to discharge the *Palos*'s supplies and equipage except a small amount of coal and her guns, the latter retained as ballast. When it became apparent that the venerable gunboat required further assistance, a tug helped her to negotiate a shoal and several difficult bends in the river. Thereafter, dense fog delayed her progress, but the *Palos* was finally moored to the Tientsin Bund a short distance from the French *Aspic*.

In December Admiral Belknap found time for a visit to Shanghai—his first in almost two years on the station—and then returned to Yokohama, where he acknowledged an order to send the *Omaha* to Panama. The *Monocacy* became the flagship; she had better accommodations than the *Alliance*, which was sent to China and Korea. The squadron's third vessel, the *Palos*, was ordered to Canton upon leaving Tientsin despite her need of docking and overhaul.

The parlous state to which the Asiatic Squadron had been reduced in the spring of 1891 was attributable in part to the efforts of the United States to save the Bering Sea fur seals from extinction. After the arrest of Canadian sealing schooners on the high seas as early as 1886 had incurred the displeasure of the British government, attempts at a compromise dragged on for several years until 1891, when Britain and the United States agreed to a *modus vivendi* whereby pelagic sealing in the area was forbidden pending a definitive settlement. As a result, vessels which otherwise would have been sent to the Asiatic Station had to be diverted to the Bering Sea to enforce the prohibition.

On 21 May, Minister Denby telegraphed his suggestion that a warship be sent up the Yangtze at once. Belknap sought further information from the consul general at Shanghai and learned that, while riots had been suppressed at several Chinese cities, more trouble was expected at Nanking, Chinkiang, and Hankow. Five foreign gunboats were reported to be in the vicinity; the *Alliance* and the *Palos* were ordered to join them forthwith.

The *Palos* had an eventful passage. On getting underway at Canton, she had to drop an anchor to keep from going ashore when her engine failed to reverse. As the gunboat swung to the ebb tide, her counter grazed a yacht moored nearby. Lieutenant Commander Joseph Marthon quickly had the yacht's damage surveyed and dropped down to Hong Kong, whence he reported the incident before putting to sea. Little more than a week later, the *Palos* was in trouble again. Standing up the South Channel into the Yangtze estuary on a flood tide, she collided with the Kiutoan light vessel, which was torn from her mooring and badly damaged. Beyond crushing her own wood stem, the *Palos* was not injured, but she ran aground three hours later and was not refloated until the next day.

On her way up the river, the *Palos* paused off each of the open ports to communicate with local officials, and at Kiukiang on 6 June the British consul came on board to inform Marthon that an outbreak had occurred the night before at Wusueh, some twenty-five miles upstream. The German gunboat *Iltis* at Kiukiang was not ready for service and the French *Inconstant* had not yet arrived, so the *Palos* pressed on and came to anchor off Wusueh's customhouse that evening. From a Chinese customs official, Marthon learned that the trouble had begun with a rumor that missionaries were removing children's eyes for use in photography. Thereupon, a mob had attacked the mission school, looting the building and killing a missionary and the customs commissioner, both Englishmen. Order had since been restored, and the surviving missionaries had departed for Hankow before the *Palos*'s arrival. Marthon asked that a party from his gunboat be permitted to attend the inquest scheduled to be held by mandarins from Hankow on the morrow. The inquest passed without incident, and the *Palos* returned to Kiukiang.

Fifteen minutes after she dropped anchor there, a riot was reported ashore. The *Inconstant* and the *Iltis* landed armed men to defend their nationals, and Marthon sent a lieutenant with twenty-two sailors to protect Americans and Britons who fled the city. However, he refused an appeal that he send a party into Kiukiang itself on the ground that the *Palos*'s few men could neither help others nor defend themselves in a large Chinese city. Within two hours, the Chinese themselves had quelled the riot and the foreign sailors were reembarked.

The situation along the Yangtze remained tense but calm during most of the summer. The *Palos* spent the remainder of June at Kiukiang while her black gang patched her boilers as best they could. When HMS *Alacrity*, flying the flag of Vice Admiral Sir Frederick Richards, came to anchor off the city, Marthon prepared to make an official call on the British commander in chief. To his surprise, Richards paid the first visit, boarding the *Palos* to express his appreciation of the American's willingness to act on behalf of British subjects at Wusueh. This courteous gesture—a vice admiral ordinarily would not visit a foreign lieutenant commander in the latter's decrepit gunboat—was probably the high point of Joseph Marthon's career.

Late in July, the *Palos* was sent from the Yangtze to the Min in response to the U.S. consul's fear of unrest at Foochow. Marthon found that his command could not venture beyond the Pagoda Anchorage because the Chinese had blocked the river; however, he visited the consulate and took steps to provide for its defense in case of trouble. Since the viceroy had an army of 8,000 men in the vicinity, Marthon thought the danger from discontented elements of the population exaggerated.

While the *Alliance* and the *Palos* were enduring the Chinese summer heat, the *Monocacy*, flying Admiral Belknap's flag, lolled at anchor in the comfort of Yokohama's cooler clime, and frequent rumors of impending crises in China had no discernible effect on the admiral. Minister Denby's report of imminent trouble at Canton in August led Secretary of the Navy Tracy to inquire rather pointedly whether the *Monocacy* could not proceed there from Yokohama, to which Belknap replied that she could not safely go before the end of October because "no convoy could render aid in event typhoon."[5] He had no vessel to accompany the *Monocacy* in any event, but a better day was ahead; Tracy cabled the welcome information that the new cruiser *Charleston* would depart Mare Island for the Orient in mid-August while the *Marion* and the *Alert* were to join the squadron from the Bering Sea within a few weeks.

Early September brought news of a riot at Ichang in which foreign missions and property were destroyed. Belknap ordered the *Palos* from the Min and the *Alliance* from Chefoo to Shanghai; en route the latter picked up eight Chinese who had survived the sinking of their junk only to face a lingering death from thirst had the *Alliance* not sighted their raft. The *Palos* was sent up the Yangtze to join the one Russian, two French, and four British gunboats stationed at the various treaty ports, but none could reach Ichang because of insufficient water at that season.

The first of the promised reinforcements stood into Yokohama on 21 September. A steel vessel with armored protective deck, heavy armament, and 18-knot speed, the *Charleston* was mainly notable as the first of the Navy's ocean-going warships to dispense with sail entirely. Admiral Belknap lost no time in transferring his flag to her and sent the *Monocacy* to Yokosuka for docking before taking both ships to Shanghai in mid-October. The *Alert* reported for duty before the admiral left Yokohama— she had come from Unalaska by way of Petropavlovsk—but the *Marion*, unable to obtain enough coal at Unalaska to chance the possibly stormy northern track, had to take the much longer route via Honolulu.

Admiral Belknap was not permitted to enjoy his modern flagship for long. On 29 October, he received a confidential order to send the *Charleston* home at once. She got underway on 4 November and ran over to Yokohama, where the admiral learned that the United States was on the verge of war with Chile as the result of a Valparaiso tavern brawl in which two sailors from the USS *Baltimore* had been killed. The *Charleston* spent ten days adjusting her machinery, after which Belknap boarded the *Marion*, and the cruiser headed for Honolulu and Callao.

The *Palos*'s Lieutenant Commander Marthon contracted cholera in November. The doctors felt that he was too ill to be transferred to a faster vessel for transportation to the hospital at Shanghai, so the old gunboat raised steam and lumbered down the Yangtze at her pathetic maximum speed. The sick man was taken on board the harbor master's steam launch even before the *Palos* moored at Shanghai, but the efforts at haste were vain—Joseph Marthon died two days later, by which time the *Palos* was on her way back to her post.

But she was not to spend the winter on the Yangtze. Minister Denby and Consul General J. A. Leonard informed Admiral Belknap that Manchuria and Mongolia were in a state of rebellion against the Chinese government and asked that a gunboat be sent to Tientsin. The old *Palos* was recalled to Shanghai, whence she sailed on 2 December. One day out, she encountered a gale against which no headway could be made, so she was hove to on the port tack. During the next two days, the gunboat's upper works leaked so badly that her officers' and crew's quarters were almost uninhabitable, and as "all steam-pumps were unable to clear the ship, the hand pumps had to be worked almost continually, the limbers having been [choked] by the working of the ship; all the battens forming the inner skin of the ship worked off and fell into the bilge."[6] When the weather moderated, the *Palos* was put back on her course, only to heave to again five hours later because of a condenser casualty. Reporting this, her chief engineer wrote: "In fact the 'Palos' seldom, if ever, makes a run of any length, without a stoppage of the Engines being rendered necessary by some accident, as the carrying away of a valve, the bursting of a pipe, leakage of the boilers or similar causes—"[7] Lieutenant Commander John C. Rich finally got her across the Taku Bar with the assistance of a tug six days after she left Shanghai, only to find the Pei Ho choked with ice. Making the best of a bad situation, he moored his vessel at Tangku, just inside the Pei Ho entrance; from there, a landing force could be transported to Tientsin by rail if necessary. Rich also had the *Palos* surrounded by a boom of logs to protect her from the ice, a necessary precaution because a hole had already been punched through the badly rusted plates at the waterline on her starboard bow.

As 1891 neared its end, Admiral Belknap was looking forward to the arrival of his relief, Rear Admiral David B. Harmony, who, for reasons best known to the Navy Department, was coming out by the Cape of Good Hope route in what must have seemed the proverbial "slow boat to China," in this case the elderly USS *Lancaster*, the last of the famous *Hartford*'s sisters to serve on the Asiatic Station. Arriving at Hong Kong late in January 1892, Harmony was ordered by Belknap to assume the command at Yokohama. The leewardly *Lancaster* was incapable of making such a passage against the northeast monsoon so Harmony had to sail in a mail steamer. He relieved Belknap on 20 February 1892.

Rear Admiral George E. Belknap was considered an able officer, yet it is difficult to avoid criticism of his performance as commander in chief. To be sure, the squadron under his command usually numbered only a few aged and infirm vessels, but this does not explain his apparent unwillingness to leave Yokohama. During his tenure of nearly three years on the station, he visited Korea once and China twice, for a few days only on each occasion, nor did his flagship touch at other Japanese ports except when she was en route from or to Yokohama. Strangely enough, there were few consular complaints of the admiral's inattention—perhaps those officials had learned the futility of efforts to bestir an immobile flag officer.

CHAPTER SIXTEEN

The Sino-Japanese War

Rear Admiral David B. Harmony, who had last served in the Far East seventeen years earlier, remained at Yokohama only until the *Alliance* could be summoned to convey him to Hong Kong. To his embarrassment, his temporary flagship grounded on the submerged end of a breakwater while standing out in clear weather, a mishap later attributed to her navigator's color blindness. Tugs working nearby came to her assistance, as did the commanding officer of HMS *Mercury*, who brought an anchor and a cable in his steam launch, and the *Alliance* was floated without damage at high water.

Harmony ordered the *Marion*, which had spent her entire six months on the station riding at anchor off Yokohama, to Nagasaki for docking and then to Chemulpo. The *Alert* was kept at Kobe and the *Alliance* at Nagasaki, both ready for sea at short notice although active cruising was limited by a Bureau of Equipment directive that coal consumption be kept to a minimum. The *Monocacy* remained on the Yangtze, where she was joined in April 1892 by the steel gunboat *Petrel*, another of the vessels of the "new" Navy. Called the "baby battleship" because of her heavy armament—four 6-inch guns, of which two could bear on any target—the *Petrel* was handicapped by her 11-knot speed and poor performance under sail. Nonetheless, she was to spend the next twenty years on the Asiatic Station, with time out for brief periods on Bering Sea patrol.

The *Palos*, the squadron's lame duck, was still on the Pei Ho, and Lieutenant Commander John C. Rich reported that her boilers could no longer produce enough steam to turn her engine. Noting that a vessel so decrepit ought never to have been sent to the Pei Ho, the admiral ordered the *Marion* to tow her to Nagasaki for survey as soon as the danger of storms on the Yellow Sea had passed.

Almost immediately upon hoisting his flag, the new commander in chief began to receive reports pertaining to the situation along the Yangtze. He was not especially concerned, holding that American business interests in China were almost entirely in the hands of foreign and Chinese merchants, none of whom could claim the protection of the United States, and that American-flag shipping had almost disappeared from Chinese waters.

The protection of missionaries, however, was his responsibility, and the missionary community was hardly insignificant in terms of numbers. The treaties forced on China in 1858 and 1860 had introduced religious toleration to that nation, and the thirty years following had brought a steady increase in Christian missionary activity. By 1890, there were 513 American missionaries representing nineteen denominations in China; only the British supported a greater number. And, while foreigners generally resided at one or another of the relatively few treaty ports, missionaries were wont to range far into the hinterland "only controlled by their own interpretation of the wishes of the Almighty."[1] Thus, to afford them even a modicum of protection taxed the resources of naval officers, many of whom undoubtedly agreed with the *Monocacy's* Commander Francis M. Barber that all entitled to and claiming the U.S. government's protection should be brought more directly under that government's control.

But 1892 was a quiet year throughout the Orient. Even Korea was so tranquil that the State Department agreed that a warship need not be kept at Chemulpo. The *Marion*, which towed the *Palos* to Nagasaki in mid-June, thereafter cruised in northern Japanese waters, and the *Alliance* sailed for Mare Island in August. A few weeks earlier, the *Palos's* fate had been decided by a board of survey which found that thorough repair of her hull and machinery would require expenditures far beyond the old gunboat's worth. Admiral Harmony recommended that she be decommissioned and sold. The Navy Department concurred, so the veteran *Palos*, literally worn-out after twenty-two years on the Asiatic Station, was stripped of usable fittings and sold for scrap on 25 January 1893.

The spring of 1893 found Admiral Harmony concerned about the Chinese reaction to exclusion legislation recently passed by the U.S. Congress. Considering the Yangtze Valley the area most likely to experience anti-foreign turbulence, he assigned the *Marion*, *Monocacy*, and *Petrel* to spend the summer shuttling between Shanghai and the river's treaty ports, while the *Alert* in Japanese waters would respond to developments elsewhere on the station. The admiral himself was nearing the statutory retirement age, so the *Lancaster* steamed to Yokohama to await his relief, Rear Admiral John Irwin, who assumed command of the Asiatic Squadron on 7 June.

Irwin's tenure of command was uneventful and unexpectedly brief. The *Petrel* was ordered to the Bering Sea for the summer, and the *Alert* departed for San Francisco in mid-August. The steel gunboat *Concord*, larger and faster than the *Petrel*, was en route to the station, and the protected cruiser *Baltimore* was under orders to relieve the aged *Lancaster*, so the commander in chief could look forward to a proper flagship. These vessels had yet to reach the station when, on 11 October, Admiral Irwin received a confidential telegram informing him that he was to be relieved of his command on 27 October, on which date he and his staff would take passage in the mail steamer to Honolulu, there to hoist his flag in the protected cruiser *Philadelphia* as commander in chief of the Pacific Squadron. A day earlier, somewhat similar orders had been sent to Acting Rear Admiral Joseph S. Skerrett, commander in chief of the Pacific Squadron, who was to take Irwin's place.

Such a "swap" of commands was not usual for the U.S. Navy, and it obviously requires some explanation. For this, one must look to Honolulu where, a few months earlier, a bloodless revolution had occurred. The last Hawaiian monarch, Liliuokalani, had been dethroned by American Hawaiians who seem to have triumphed mainly because of the presence of the U.S. cruiser *Boston*, which landed an armed force ostensibly to protect American interests. A provisional government, quickly formed and as quickly recognized by the U.S. minister, sent commissioners to Washington to arrange American annexation of the islands. A treaty to this end was drawn up and signed without difficulty, but the Senate delayed action on it at the request of President-elect Grover Cleveland. After his inauguration, Cleveland withdrew the treaty and ordered an investigation, which revealed that native Hawaiians generally preferred the deposed queen. The provisional government, however, refused to give way, nor would American opinion permit the use of force to restore a monarch. Thus, Hawaii remained independent under a government which intended that it become a part of the United States as soon as possible, while President Cleveland, who would not countenance annexation, was determined that foreign influence must not supplant that of his nation at Honolulu.

Admiral Skerrett had assumed command of the Pacific Squadron on 9 January 1893, one week before the Hawaiian revolution. Arriving in Honolulu soon after the event, he reported that the provisional government was incapable of gaining the public support necessary to win an election. His subsequent communications, however, indicated that Skerrett was being won over by that government, leading Navy Secretary Hilary A. Herbert to warn that his course should be one of complete neutrality toward both governmental and royalist factions. Soon thereafter, Skerrett managed to bring about the dispatch of a British warship to Hawaiian waters—which the United States was anxious to avoid—by indiscreetly telling the British minister that the vessels of the Pacific Squadron were not authorized to protect foreigners in the islands. This indiscretion, which the admiral himself reported, convinced Herbert that Skerrett must leave Honolulu. A simple removal from his command was out of the question, for the naval officer would almost certainly demand a court-martial which might be embarrassing to the government, so the secretary ordered him to exchange commands with the somewhat senior and presumably more perceptive John Irwin.

Joseph Skerrett, of course, was no stranger to the Far East, having commanded the flagship *Richmond* for some three years and served as the squadron's senior officer after Peirce Crosby's sudden departure in 1883. Skerrett hoisted his flag in the *Lancaster* on 9 December 1893, hoping perhaps that the Asiatic Station would prove a less taxing command than that which he had relinquished. However, it was not to be.

For a time, all went well. The *Concord* and the *Petrel* had reported for duty before the admiral's arrival, and the *Baltimore* steamed into Hong Kong later in December. The *Lancaster* and the *Marion*, the last of the U.S. Navy's old wooden warships to serve on the Asiatic Station, both departed in mid-February. The *Lancaster*, sailing from Hong Kong to New York by the Suez route, made a routine passage, but not the *Marion*.

The *Marion* stood out of Yokohama bound for Mare Island with fine weather and a fair wind. One day out, Commander Charles V. Gridley ordered her boiler fires burned down and her screw uncoupled. She made good progress under sail the next day, but on 22 February the wind increased gradually until it reached hurricane strength. The *Marion* was hove to under storm canvas, and boiler fires were lighted; but she labored so violently in mountainous seas that several boilers began to work loose in their saddles and all leaked badly. Water was pouring into the vessel through deck and side seams, while waves breaking on board carried away a boat and several gunport covers. Gridley had the prisoners released so that they could take a turn at the deck pumps, assist in the stokehold, or, if necessary, abandon ship. But the *Marion* and her men were equal to this occasion. The boilers were chocked in place, and half were made tight enough to provide steam to pumps and engines. Oil streamed from the weather bow exerted its calming effect on the troubled waters, lessening the impact of the waves. The gale diminished markedly the next day, and

FIGURE 16–1. The screw-sloop *Marion*, last wooden ship of the "Old Navy" on the Asiatic Station.

on 24 February Commander Gridley set a course for Yokohama, whence he reported that his vessel owed her survival to her own seaworthiness, adding that the service still had topmen capable of hazardous work aloft. After being docked and repaired, the *Marion* took her final departure from the station on 10 April.

The *Concord* and the *Petrel* sailed for the Bering Sea in mid-May, leaving only the flagship *Baltimore* at Nagasaki and the *Monocacy* at Shanghai to cope with any emergency. And the emergency was not long in coming. A rebellion by the reactionary Tonghak cult in Korea during the spring led the king to request Chinese assistance, and Japan, which seems to have encouraged the Tonghaks in order to bring about a confrontation with China, also decided to send troops. As the Tonghak forces approached Seoul late in May, the new U.S. minister to Korea, John M. B. Sill, agreed with Dr. Horace N. Allen, veteran medical missionary and confidant of the king, that naval support should be requested. The State Department transmitted Sill's report to the Navy, whereupon Skerrett was ordered to take the *Baltimore* to Korea. She departed Nagasaki on 3 June, one day after the telegram had been received and deciphered.

The U.S. flagship found Japanese, Chinese, and French men-of-war in the Chemulpo anchorage, and Sill soon came on board to inform Admiral Skerrett of the situation. The minister doubted that Korean troops would be able to defeat the rebels and warned that the *Baltimore* would probably have to furnish a guard to protect the legation from the Seoul mob in the event of a Tonghak victory. Skerrett forwarded Sill's statement to the Navy Department together with his own desire that one of the gunboats be sent back from the Bering Sea. Notwithstanding the minister's prediction, the Tonghak rebellion was quelled by the Koreans themselves within a few days, before any foreign troops had been landed. But the king's request for assistance from China had set in train events of far greater import than a mere insurrection.

Admiral Skerrett had an audience with the king in Seoul on 12 June and later reported that the monarch had voiced his pleasure that the flagship had come to Chemulpo to aid the Koreans. In response, the admiral stated that he was authorized only to protect American citizens and to act with Minister Sill. Indeed, he was powerless to do more; for the vanguard of the Japanese force, 300 sailors and marines, had arrived in Seoul a day earlier and, even as Skerrett conferred with the king, transports laden with 1,000 Japanese soldiers and their accouterments steamed into Chemulpo harbor. These troops shortly relieved the sailors and marines in Seoul, and on 16 June, another 3,000 soldiers—infantry, cavalry, and artillery—were landed at Chemulpo as seven Japanese warships stood by.

Nine days later, Sill wrote Skerrett that Japanese troops had occupied strategic locations surrounding Seoul, that 5,000 Chinese soldiers were en route to Chemulpo, and that Japan was expected to initiate hostilities if China refused to surrender her claim to suzerainty over Korea. On the next day, 26 June, the minister sent word of his intention to put the missionary property adjoining the legation under his protection so that asylum could be offered to all who might desire it. The twelve marines whom Skerrett had suggested as a legation guard would be too few to patrol such an area, so Sill was pleased to learn that the *Baltimore* would provide as many as 120 if necessary.

Even as the minister was congratulating Skerrett on his decision to remain at Chemulpo, the admiral concluded that the *Baltimore* would have to depart because her crew had little more than a week's provisions and the troops and companies of ships in the vicinity had already consumed most of the victuals normally available at Chemulpo. On 25 June, he asked that the *Monocacy* be allowed to relieve the flagship and the Navy Department agreed, whereupon Skerrett cabled her to proceed to Chemulpo immediately. But telegraphic communication with Shanghai had been interrupted, so the double-ender, which was expected on 1 July, failed to appear. Instead, the next day brought a telegram from Secretary Herbert: "Keep Baltimore Chemulpo until further orders."[2] Nonetheless, the cruiser stood out of the Korean anchorage on 3 July, bound for Nagasaki. Dense fogs encountered en route slowed her progress to the extent that her men had to be put on short rations before she finally reached Nagasaki.

The admiral attempted to explain his direct disobedience of orders in a letter written as his flagship was departing Chemulpo. He pointed out that provisions could be obtained more cheaply at Yokohama than at Nagasaki; therefore, those consumed while the *Baltimore* was at the latter port had not been replenished. The cruiser had had enough food for one month when she was ordered to Chemulpo and, because of the peremptory tone of the telegram, he had not felt justified in delaying to fill her storerooms. Steamer connections between Yokohama and Chemulpo were too uncertain to allow him to order supplies from Yokohama, and he did not know whether his telegram had ever reached the *Monocacy*. Thus, he had no alternative to disobedience.

Skerrett must have been aware that several questions remained unanswered: Why had he not arranged to have supplies shipped to the *Baltimore* at Chemulpo before she sailed, leaving the paymaster at Nagasaki to complete the arrangements if necessary? Why had he not attempted to purchase provisions immediately upon arrival in the Korean harbor? Why had he waited so late to summon the *Monocacy*, which might have been instructed to obtain supplies for the flagship at Shanghai before sailing? A court of inquiry could be expected to conclude that the admiral had failed to ensure that his squadron's only effective cruising vessel was prepared for duty, and, when that duty was thrust upon her, he had failed to take timely steps to ensure her endurance. He could expect little charity from a secretary of the navy who had already removed him from one command, so, with his flagship shrouded by a thick fog which must have depressed his spirits even further, Rear Admiral Joseph S. Skerrett decided to request early retirement on arrival at Nagasaki.

The *Baltimore* steamed into the Japanese harbor on 8 July, and command changes followed in rapid succession. Skerrett's flag was hauled down three days later, with the cruiser's commanding officer assuming the position of senior naval officer on the Asiatic Station. Captain Benjamin F. Day, who had been ordered to command the *Baltimore*, relieved him on 12 July; thus a newcomer who had no previous service in the Far East became senior naval officer at a very critical time.

Day got his cruiser underway on 14 July, and she made a three-day passage to Chemulpo. The anchorage was crowded with British, French, German, Russian, Chinese, Japanese, and American warships on her arrival. Commander Robert E. Impey came on board to report that the *Monocacy* had been at Chemulpo for the past ten days. The situation ashore seemed unchanged, and in his first communication to Minister Sill, Captain Day expressed the opinion that the Americans in Seoul would be in no danger so long as they attended to their own business and did not meddle in politics. However, on 23 July the minister wrote that a guard was required at once, for Japanese soldiers had abducted the king and Seoul was in a state of turbulence. After arranging their safe transit with the Japanese consul, Day ordered twenty marines under Captain George F. Elliott to make a night march to the legation while his two vessels' steam launches towed small boats laden with thirty sailors and tents, equipment, and a month's provisions up the river.

The Japanese seizure of the Korean monarch marked the beginning of a Sino-Japanese war. Chinese troops numbering 8,000 had been landed at Asan, an anchorage some thirty miles to the southward of Chemulpo, during the *Baltimore's* absence, while reinforcements had brought the Japanese army to somewhat more than 10,000 men. On 25 July, Japanese warships left Chemulpo hastily after hearing heavy gunfire from the direction of Asan. Captain Day supposed that Chinese men-of-war were helping to defend their troop encampment against a land assault, but the firing was actually that of a naval engagement in which superior Japanese forces drove off or destroyed Chinese warships coming to the assistance of a chartered transport carrying 1,100 infantrymen. The latter was sunk with heavy loss of life within a short time.

Thereafter, the Chinese leaders, Li Hung-chang and Admiral Ting Ju-ch'ang, concluded that their major responsibility was to protect the Chinese coast from the Yalu River (the boundary between Manchuria and Korea) to Weihaiwei on the northern side of the Shantung Peninsula. Essentially, this amounted to an abandonment of Korea, and of the Chinese army there, to Japan. But the imperial government at Peking neither ordered a more aggressive strategy nor combined China's other three fleets with Ting's Peiyang (northern) fleet to assure naval superiority.

Meanwhile, the Navy Department was taking steps to strengthen the Asiatic Squadron. The *Concord* and the *Petrel* were ordered back to the station, and a new commander in chief, Acting Rear Admiral Charles C. Carpenter, sailed from San Francisco in the mail steamer on 7 August. With less than three months' seniority as a commodore, Carpenter was hardly a veteran flag officer, and his only previous experience in the Far East—a three-year cruise in the *Hartford* and the *Wyoming* under Rear Admiral Henry H. Bell—was more than a quarter-century in the past. Nonetheless, he proved equal to the demands of an unexpectedly arduous command.

Carpenter hoisted his flag in the *Monocacy* at Nagasaki on 28 August and sailed for Chemulpo in the double-ender two days later, leaving orders for the *Concord* to join him as soon as she had filled up with provisions and coal. He transferred to the *Baltimore* on 3 September, after which the *Monocacy* went on to Tientsin for the winter.

Hostilities continued in August and September. Japan's fleet penetrated the northern part of the Yellow Sea for ineffectual bombardments of Weihaiwei and Port Arthur, the principal Chinese bases, while the Japanese army in Korea moved northward with sufficient rapidity to convince the Chinese government that troops would have to be sent by sea to reinforce the garrison at Pyongyang, through which the major road to Manchuria ran. The Peiyang fleet was ordered to escort five troop transports from Talienwan (Dairen) to the mouth of the Yalu, which it did on 16 September, but the Japanese army had routed the defenders of Pyongyang on the preceding day.

The Peiyang fleet was at anchor in the Yalu estuary on 17 September—a fine, clear day—when clouds of smoke were sighted on the southwestern horizon. Admiral Ting ordered his twelve warships to raise steam, and they stood out to meet a like number of Japanese vessels under Vice Admiral Ito Sukenori. Ting's two second-class battleships (built in Germany ten years earlier) and two armored cruisers gave him the advantage in heavy guns and armor, for protected cruisers of English or French design were Ito's most formidable ships. The Japanese ships, however, were generally newer, were capable of higher speeds, and had an overwhelming superiority in quick-firing guns. And perhaps most important, their companies boasted a standard of leadership and discipline which the Chinese could not match. After some four hours of hard fighting, during which four Chinese cruisers were destroyed and several Japanese vessels damaged, Ito broke off the engagement, leaving both battleships, which had fired away virtually all of their ammunition, and several smaller ships to limp into Port Arthur.

News of the Battle of the Yalu—one of the earliest in which armored fleets were engaged—reached the West in a short time, and governments that were spending large sums of money to construct modern navies were anxious to obtain information with regard to the effectiveness of the various types of armament and systems of protection embodied in the warships that had survived the action. Secretary Herbert instructed Admiral Carpenter to afford the squadron's intelligence officers every opportunity to inspect the damaged vessels. But when the admiral requested that an officer be allowed to accompany the Japanese army marching toward Manchuria, the secretary declined, pointing out that the Navy wanted information on the extent and type of damage suffered by the veterans of the Yalu fight. A few days later, Herbert suggested that permission for officers to visit Japanese and Chinese navy yards might be had upon application to the respective legations, to which Carpenter replied that the Japanese at least would not welcome such application— they had discharged all foreigners from their Nagasaki dockyard in order to ensure secrecy.

The *Concord*, which had been delayed by an engineering casualty, reached Chemulpo late in September, and the admiral ordered her to send men to relieve the *Baltimore*'s legation guard at Seoul. As soon as her sailors and marines had been reembarked, the flagship stood out for Nagasaki, there to replenish her supplies and be docked for bottom cleaning.

At Nagasaki, Carpenter received a telegraphic order to station vessels at Chinkiang and Newchwang, and a letter of the same date directed him to consider the protection of American citizens, especially missionaries, as his responsibility and to keep the "fighting lines" and areas of particular interest to the United States under careful surveillance. The Asiatic Squadron was obviously too weak for such manifold duties, so the admiral was to arrange cooperation (similar to that of a decade earlier) with foreign commanders in chief, and the *Charleston*, the smaller cruiser *Detroit*, and the gunboats *Yorktown* and *Machias* had been ordered to the station. "The arrival of these vessels will place you in command of a large squadron, from which the Department expects energetic and efficient work."[3]

The *Charleston*, the first of the promised reinforcements, actually arrived at Yokohama early in October, before Herbert's letter announcing her arrival reached the admiral. She required two weeks for machinery repair, however, and then her steering gear was found to be deranged, so Carpenter had to take the *Baltimore* back to Chemulpo at the end of the month in order that the *Concord* could be sent up the Yangtze to Chinkiang.

The *Baltimore* ran over to Chefoo early in November and then steamed up to Port Arthur with the signal flags required by the Chinese government prominently displayed. On signal from the nearest fort, she stopped three miles offshore and awaited a torpedo boat which brought permission for her to anchor there and for the admiral to visit the Chinese flagship. Leaving his vessel in readiness to get underway and with a searchlight prepared to illuminate her colors, Carpenter boarded the battleship *Ting Yuen* hoping to be allowed to examine her battle damage and that of the other Chinese warships. Admiral Ting was not on board, but his second in command pointed out that the fleet went to sea every night—Carpenter could inspect the ships on their return the next day. They did not return on 8 November, however; instead Japanese torpedo boats reconnoitered the area, and when the Chinese forts opened fire on them at dusk, Carpenter concluded that the *Baltimore* should depart for Chefoo.

In accordance with the Navy Department's order, Admiral Carpenter had already written his foreign counterparts regarding cooperation to protect their respective nationals during the Sino-Japanese War. Vice Admiral Edmund R. Fremantle responded that he had received similar instructions from the British Admiralty and, while the French, German, and Russian senior officers did not have specific orders to this effect, all were willing to join in such an endeavor. As might have been expected, Admiral Fremantle took the initiative, informing his fellow flag officers of his dispositions in order that they might station their vessels most advantageously.

The *Petrel* steamed up the Liao Ho early in November, and Lieutenant Commander William H. Emory at once contracted to have a mud dock excavated so that she could winter at Newchwang. Coolies laboring around the clock, with the gunboat's searchlights providing illumination at night, completed the dock in less than two weeks. A veteran river pilot then took the vessel a short distance upstream before turning to make an approach to the dock entrance, which she missed by eight feet, driving her bow into the soft bank. A kedge on a wire rope was carried out into the stream and the gunboat was refloated the next morning, only to have the rope part and foul her screw. The pilot assured Emory that a vessel of the *Petrel*'s size could never be docked there, and departed. The gunboat's men spent the remainder of that day removing the wire from her screw, and on 16 November, two days after the first attempt, she tried again without a pilot. That effort failed, as did another, but on her fourth attempt, the *Petrel*, drawing four inches of water in excess of the depth on the dock sill, was forced through the mud into the dock.

Ironically, the Navy Department, which must have learned that there were no Americans among the one-hundred foreigners at Newchwang, had already revoked its order that a vessel be kept there. But Admiral Carpenter, who had gone to some trouble to assure a supply of coal for the *Petrel* throughout the winter, decided that she should remain in her dock nonetheless. The foreigners at Newchwang, already alarmed by reports of the Japanese advance, would have only the little British *Firebrand* to look to if the *Petrel* were withdrawn, and the presence of an American gunboat in an area which had no American residents would be a clear example of international cooperation. So the *Petrel*'s men mounted Gatling guns in commanding positions around the dock and spent much of the winter watching Chinese troops straggle past.

News of Port Arthur's fall reached Chefoo on 23 November, whereupon Carpenter sailed for the captured city. The Japanese commanders were quite willing to permit foreign observers to land and provided officers to guide those who wished to examine the fortifications or visit the battlefield. Thereafter, the flagship returned to Chefoo, whence she steamed to Nagasaki to obtain coal, money, and mail.

Almost a month earlier, Charles Denby, U.S. minister to China, had recommended that fifty marines be quartered in the *Monocacy* at Tientsin so that they could be ordered to Peking in case of need. Admiral Carpenter received this suggestion coldly, responding that the old gunboat lacked adequate accommodations for so many men and that it would be unwise to send a small force into "the heart of a country rent by internal contention. . . ."[4] Nonetheless, the Navy Department ordered the marines sent, and Carpenter was directed to arrange international cooperation in protecting the legations at Peking, without offending either of the belligerent governments.

The *Baltimore* had only forty-two marines ready for duty and the *Charleston*'s were required for the legation guard at Seoul, so the admiral ordered Commander Impey to add eight marines from the *Monocacy*'s complement and hold the fifty in readiness to proceed to Peking. Impey was also to inquire about the possibility of sending them in company with guards from foreign men-of-war. Whether the marines marched as part of an international force or alone, they should depart for Peking only after permission for their transit had been sought from the proper authorities; failing that, the commander had discretion to decide whether or not they should be sent, while Denby was urged to use his influence with the Chinese authorities to gain the desired permission.

Admiral Carpenter responded to a Department order that his vessels be kept in Chinese waters by pointing out that the British, French, and Russian flag officers would leave a single ship from each of their fleets off Chefoo while they retired to Woosung or Nagasaki for the winter. He himself had planned to make Nagasaki his headquarters because of its central location and excellent communication facilities, while "Chefoo, at best, is but a poor anchorage, and with the advent of the winter gales, for a vessel the size of the Baltimore is most undesirable."[5] But at Chefoo the *Baltimore* remained, dragging in the December gales which swept the anchorage with discomforting frequency until the admiral had her shifted to a berth off the lighthouse. It was secure, but its distance from the landing made communication with the shore even more difficult.

The *Concord*'s sister *Yorktown* joined the flagship off Chefoo in December, enabling the *Baltimore* to relieve the *Charleston* at Chemulpo during the following month, so that the latter could be docked as ordered by the Navy Department. While at Chemulpo, Captain Day was directed to investigate the reported misbehavior of the flagship's legation guard some months earlier. According to a private letter written in Seoul on 13 October 1894, "We have had to blush for our American soldiers and some of the officers from the 'Baltimore.' They get beastly drunk and carouse about the streets in a most disgraceful manner, frightening and surprising the Japs and Koreans."[6] The marines, of course, were beyond reach at Tientsin, but Day queried the naval officers who had been with the guard and then reported realistically that "men who do not get drunk are not plentiful in the Navy and Marine Corps."[7] Nonetheless, the captain thought that the men had behaved unusually well and that the report of officers carousing in the streets was unfounded. Meanwhile, Minister Sill had been making his own inquiry at Carpenter's request. He traced the letter to a missionary's wife, who was unable to substantiate her statements or even to name her informants. Sill added that he had found no evidence to support the allegations made in the letter. With that, the incident was closed, although Admiral Carpenter asked that all correspondence relative to the matter be sent to the mission board concerned.

Meanwhile, the war continued. Japanese warships shelled Tengchow, to the westward of Chefoo, on 18 January 1895, and the Reverend Dr. Calvin W. Mateer, head of Tengchow's Presbyterian mission, cabled a request that the Japanese commanders be informed of the mission's presence and the absence of any Chinese troops. To this, the *Yorktown's* Commander William M. Folger responded that a belligerent had the right to fire on an enemy city and that he would evacuate any Americans who wished to leave Tengchow. Another bombardment was reported the next day. The *Yorktown* was off Tengchow on 20 January, but a snowstorm prevented communication with the shore until the following morning, when she embarked seventeen members of missionary families, leaving Dr. Mateer and eight fellows to look after the mission and aid the inhabitants so far as they could.

Upon hearing of the bombardments and of a Japanese landing near Weihaiwei, the Peiyang fleet's base, Admiral Carpenter decided that he should concentrate his available force off Chefoo. Leaving orders that the *Charleston* join him on her return from Nagasaki, he got the flagship underway and steamed across the Yellow Sea on 22 January. Ten foreign warships, half flying Britain's white ensign, were anchored off the Chinese city on the *Baltimore's* arrival, while Admiral Fremantle, with four vessels of his fleet, was observing the Japanese operations in the Weihaiwei vicinity. Commander Folger reported that each of the men-of-war off Chefoo had contributed an officer and fifteen men to a force landed to police the international settlement.

The problem of the missionaries remained. Several missions were located along the road between Chefoo and Weihaiwei, a road that would be crowded by refugees and fleeing troops as Weihaiwei's fall became imminent. Missionaries who had spent years—sometimes decades—attempting to win the trust of the Chinese, feared that their work would be undone should they abandon their stations to seek shelter at Chefoo; indeed, some saw in the approaching crisis a unique opportunity to prove their devotion to the Chinese.

Admiral Carpenter, on the other hand, had been ordered to protect the missionaries, and, while the latter might not complain if he failed to do so, their brethren in the United States and the Cleveland administration, which was deeply interested in missionary activities, were unlikely to understand the situation. Yet it was obviously impractical to provide a guard for each mission station, so the admiral could only assure the missionaries that they would be safe from mob violence if they came to Chefoo.

But what if Chefoo itself were attacked? When Field Marshal Count Oyama apprised Admiral Fremantle of his intention to send a force to Chefoo's foreign concession area to guarantee order, the Briton replied that such a measure was unnecessary and then sought Carpenter's opinion as to whether the Japanese could legally capture a treaty port or occupy its international settlement in the event of the city's surrender. The American had no hesitation in affirming the right of a belligerent to capture and occupy any enemy city in its entirety, adding that foreigners residing therein did so at their own risk.

Dr. Mateer continued to believe that Tengchow might be spared if the Japanese could be made aware of its defenseless state. Through the consular agent at Chefoo, he asked Carpenter to inform Count Oyama and Admiral Ito of his willingness to negotiate with them. The admiral properly refused to do this, pointing out that he had no authority to act as mediator and that Mateer would very likely incur Chinese hostility should it become known that the missionary had proposed to provide information regarding the city's defenses, or lack thereof, to the enemy. Carpenter did promise that if the opportunity occurred, he would suggest to the Japanese commanders that the missionaries be treated as noncombatant residents; beyond that he would not go.

Although Weihaiwei, invested by land and sea, was still holding out as January ended, the growing hopelessness of the situation led missionaries farther to the westward to decide that at least their families should be evacuated. The *Charleston* was sent to embark a group from the shore of Laichow Wan, the southern extremity of the Gulf of Pechihli, on 7 February. The cruiser encountered ice as she approached the coast, but her boats found a lead through which Captain George W. Coffin forced his ship to within three miles of Sansan Saddle, the prominent hill near which the missionaries were waiting. Fourteen persons, of whom only four were American and half were children, were embarked, after which the *Charleston* found that the lead had vanished. She made little headway with four of her six boilers on the line, so Coffin resorted to backing down as far as possible and then ramming the ice at full speed. A few such thrusts sufficed to free the cruiser, which anchored in the bay until morning and then returned to Chefoo.

The *Yorktown*, which was sent to evacuate another group from the south coast of the Shantung Peninsula, also had some difficulty in completing her mission. Fog slowed her progress, and as she closed the shore, the Chinese fishing junks scattered, fearing that she was a Japanese man-of-war. It took some time to identify the embarkation site, from which a small boat returned bringing the message that the lack of carts and the illness of a missionary had made it impossible for the party to reach that point. Thereupon, the *Yorktown* stood on to Kiaochow Bay, off which she waited for three days, until seven women and six children were brought on board. Although gales made the return passage uncomfortable, the gunboat anchored off Chefoo on 21 February, nine days after her departure.

Weihaiwei fell on 12 February, the day on which the *Yorktown* sailed on her rescue mission. With his base's fortifications being systematically reduced and with vessels of his fleet falling victim to torpedo boat attacks

FIGURE 16–2. The *Yorktown* rigged for Christmas, Shanghai, 1895.

and bombardment, Admiral Ting Ju-ch'ang surrendered the city and then committed suicide. The victorious army behaved in exemplary fashion, in marked contrast with its reported excesses at Port Arthur, and foreign observers were soon examining damaged forts and hulks to glean information that their own armed forces could put to use.

Minister Denby became concerned upon learning of this defeat of the Chinese. He asked Carpenter's advice as to whether the marines in the *Monocacy* should be ordered to Peking—troops of other nations were already there and the policy of international cooperation seemed to require that the United States should be represented. He feared, however, that public opinion at home would not support a possibly provocative step. But the admiral refused to become involved. He had opposed the idea of a legation guard from the beginning; the marines were at Tientsin nonetheless and Commander Impey had orders to send them to Peking at the minister's request. Hence Denby would have to accept the responsibility.

The surrender of Weihaiwei and the remnant of the Peiyang fleet relieved much of the tension at Chefoo. Foreign commanders in chief began to disperse their squadrons within a short time, leaving one or two vessels to look after their respective nationals. A telegram of 12 January had authorized Admiral Carpenter to distribute his force as he saw fit, so on 27 February the *Baltimore* weighed anchor and shaped a course for Nagasaki, leaving the *Charleston* off Chefoo and the *Yorktown* to proceed to Chemulpo.

In March, the Asiatic Squadron was finally brought up to the strength promised by Secretary Herbert five months earlier. The *Detroit* was sent to relieve the *Yorktown* at Chemulpo, while the *Machias* was ordered to Amoy to cope with an emergency which failed to develop. A few weeks later, however, the gunboat's presence turned out to be beneficial; her fire and rescue party took the lead in extinguishing a fire raging on board a kerosene-laden German steamer.

Admiral Carpenter saw in the *Yorktown*'s departure from Chemulpo the occasion for withdrawing the legation guard from Seoul. When Minister Sill demurred on the ground that Seoul's American community, composed mainly of missionaries, was larger than that of any other foreign nation, the admiral had Commander John S. Newell send fifteen marines from the *Detroit* to relieve the *Charleston*'s contingent, which had been at Seoul for five months. He protested to Herbert against the practice of sending guards "to places distant from base. . . ."[8] A month later the State Department instructed Sill to warn the missionaries in Korea that they could not be assured of protection unless they were willing to seek refuge at points accessible to warships or at Seoul, so long as a legation guard remained there. Commander Newell was able to reembark the *Detroit*'s marines in mid-June, but the admiral thought it well to keep a vessel at Chemulpo.

The Sino-Japanese War ended with the signing of the Treaty of Shimonoseki on 17 April 1895. The victorious Japanese gained possession of the Liaotung Peninsula in the north and of Formosa and the Pescadores Islands off China's south coast, although European pressure subsequently caused them to relinquish the first. China was forced to recognize Korea's independence, to agree to a new commercial treaty with Japan, and to pay an indemnity, which was increased when the Japanese yielded their claim to the Liaotung Peninsula.

The relatively harsh peace terms intensified fears that the Chinese defeat would be followed by widespread disorder throughout the empire, and when a mutiny among Chinese troops in Formosa was reported, Minister Denby appealed to Admiral Carpenter for assistance. The *Concord*, about to sail for Chefoo after completing her refit, was dispatched to Formosa immediately. On arrival at Taipak on the Keelung River, the site of the disturbance, she found neither American citizens nor American property in need of protection—indeed, the U.S. consular agent was an Englishman who also represented several other nations. Under the circumstances, there was no reason to linger, so the *Concord* proceeded on her way to Chefoo. In mid-May, she and the *Yorktown* embarked the flagship's marines, who had come from Tientsin by commercial steamer, and ferried them to the *Baltimore* at Nagasaki.

Early in August, members of the "Vegetarian" secret society, which had been terrorizing an area of Fukien province to the northwestward of Foochow, became infuriated when a Christian convert sought protection from the local authorities after his shop in a village called Huashan had been looted. Chinese troops were therefore sent to the village. Blaming a British missionary for this action, the Vegetarians retaliated by attacking the missionary settlement; eleven Britons, of whom a number were women, were killed and others were injured, including the only American present. The consul general at Shanghai heard of the massacre two days later and cabled the State Department: "Can go near scene in small boats. Urge Admiral land Marines and shoot the murderers of our ladies."[9] Carpenter, who learned of the assault on 4 August, ordered Commander Folger, the senior officer at Shanghai, to send the *Detroit* to the Min if the situation warranted any action. Apparently the commander thought it did not; he recommended only that the *Yorktown* and the *Detroit* be kept at Shanghai (despite an outbreak of cholera in the city) to await further developments. When Minister Denby telegraphed a request that a vessel be sent, the admiral asked the consul at Foochow if Americans there were

FIGURE 16–3.   The flagship *Baltimore* at anchor.

in any danger. The answer was affirmative, so the *Detroit* departed Shanghai on 10 August, nine days after the Huashan massacre had occurred.

The cruiser, in company with French and British men-of-war, spent ten weeks sweltering in the Pagoda Anchorage while a party of sailors and marines accompanied Consul James C. Hixson and Commander Newell, both of whom participated in the investigation of the massacre and of the Vegetarians' activities generally.

Carpenter's delay in ordering the *Detroit* to the Min was due partly to a Navy Department directive that squadron commanders gather their vessels annually for tactical maneuvers. His plans for assembling the squadron off Chefoo were well advanced when he was informed of the Vegetarian atrocities. The *Charleston*, laid up in a Nagasaki dockyard while awaiting a new piston that had been ordered from her builder, could not take part, so the admiral was the more reluctant to send the *Detroit* to the southward unless she were really needed. With the *Charleston* at Nagasaki, the *Detroit* in the Pagoda Anchorage, the *Machias* on the Yangtze, and the *Monocacy* at Chemulpo, the Asiatic Squadron that spent the third week in September maneuvering in company consisted only of the *Baltimore* and three gunboats, one of which, the *Petrel*, was so slow that she was excused from the final two days' evolutions.

Following the maneuvers, the *Yorktown* relieved the *Monocacy* so that the double-ender could be docked at Shanghai, the *Concord* ascended the Hwangpoo for docking before taking the *Detroit*'s place in the Min, and the flagship returned to Nagasaki. There the admiral received news of a coup in Korea. Japanese and Koreans, supported by the formers' minister in Seoul, had overthrown the government and assassinated the queen. A few members of the "King party" sought asylum in the American legation, to which Commander Folger sent a small marine guard, and the admiral ordered the *Petrel* from Chefoo to join the *Yorktown* at Chemulpo. The U.S. government, however, showed no inclination to stand in the way of Japan's domination of Korea, at least so long as the latter remained nominally independent, so the Asiatic Squadron's involvement in Korean affairs diminished markedly after 1895, although one or another of its vessels was often at Chemulpo.

Admiral Carpenter had planned to spend the autumn in southern Chinese waters. He visited Shanghai in early November, leaving the *Baltimore* at Woosung, and there received news which led him to change his plans—his wife was seriously ill, and, since there were no immediate crises on the station and he was but a few months from statutory retirement, the admiral asked to be relieved of his command. The *Baltimore* steamed to Yokohama, where his flag was hauled down on 16 November

1895, and Captain Day became senior naval officer on the Asiatic Station for the second time in little more than a year.

Rear Admiral Charles C. Carpenter's fourteen months in command of the Asiatic Squadron had not been an easy time, but he had performed his duties in a very capable fashion, winning the approbation of the secretary of the navy. The approval was certainly merited.

CHAPTER SEVENTEEN

To Manila Bay

The Asiatic Squadron received a new flagship as well as a new commander in chief late in 1895. The two did not come out together—Rear Admiral Charles C. Carpenter found the former, the new protected cruiser *Olympia*, awaiting him at Yokohama, while his relief, Rear Admiral Frederick V. McNair, arrived in the mail steamer six weeks later.

The *Olympia* had encountered her first gale after sailing from Honolulu, and her commanding officer reported enthusiastically on her behavior, stating that she would be able to fight her guns even in heavy seas. Like most U.S. cruisers of her generation, however, she was afflicted by overcrowded and inadequately ventilated engineering spaces. As she was weathering the gale, coal in bunkers over her after fireroom ignited. Her seamen, sweating profusely and gagging on the smoke and gas that rendered bunkers, wing passages, and berth deck almost uninhabitable, extinguished the fire and removed the smoldering coal, tasks made none the easier by the ship's motion in the seaway.

Admiral McNair, a veteran of three cruises in the Far East, found the vessels of his command scattered as usual: the *Detroit* at Hong Kong, the *Concord* in the Pagoda Anchorage, the *Yorktown* and the *Petrel* at Shanghai, the *Machias* at Chemulpo, the *Monocacy* spending yet another winter at Tientsin, and the *Charleston* still laid up at Nagasaki. The *Baltimore* had sailed for Mare Island before the admiral's arrival.

This disposition of the squadron is noteworthy because even as McNair assumed command, the United States and Britain seemed to be on the verge of hostilities as a result of the intervention of President Grover Cleveland in the Venezuela–British Guiana boundary controversy. One might expect that the commander in chief would have received timely orders to concentrate his force, yet only on 29 January 1896 did Navy Secretary Hilary A. Herbert direct McNair to keep his vessels "fully coaled, in readiness for service and well in hand."[1] By that time, Britain, less pugnacious than the United States, had decided to agree to arbitration, so the danger had passed.

The one incident involving squadron personnel and possibly related to the controversy occurred at Shanghai. Lieutenant Commander William H. Emory was walking the *Petrel*'s quarterdeck one evening when a searchlight on board HMS *Spartan*, moored nearby, was trained on him repeatedly. Emory protested the discourtesy to Commander Charles H. Stockton of the *Yorktown*, who forwarded the complaint to the cruiser's commanding officer, Captain Alfred L. Winsloe, adding "I am quite sure that you will agree with me that, under existing circumstances, it is advisable that the officers and men under our respective command should be instructed to avoid anything that, purposely or inadvertently, gives offence or causes irritation." Winsloe sent an officer to apologize to Emory and explained to Stockton that enlisted men had been practicing with the light—"I hope that you will attribute their eccentricities to a want of knowing better, rather than a wish to offend."[2] That should have ended the matter, but brawls ashore between British and American sailors finally led to a conference in the *Yorktown* at which Winsloe and Stockton agreed that liberty should be granted only on alternate nights until tempers had cooled.

Another example of Anglo-American cooperation, the joint investigation of the Vegetarian massacre in Fukien province, had ended after the execution of twenty-four leaders of the society; but U.S. Consul James C. Hixson believed that many more of the secret society had escaped punishment and continued to seek evidence of their guilt. When the viceroy at Foochow refused either to receive the consul or to respond to his letters, Minister Charles Denby protested, whereupon an audience was granted. The *Concord*'s commanding officer, who accompanied Hixson, demanded on behalf of his government that greater respect be shown the consul. This demand was not approved by Admiral McNair, for it implied the threat of military action. In fact, of course, all of those murdered by the Vegetarians were Britons; since Britain had indicated satisfaction, there was little reason for the United States to press the issue.

In mid-February, the *Machias* was called on to send a legation guard to Seoul. Ice made the river impassable, so twenty-two sailors and marines made a forced march to protect the legation against an insurrectionary mob that was protesting decrees issued by the Japanese-dominated government. The arrival of such a force a decade earlier might have hinted at an attempt to exert pressure on the Korean government; in 1896 it did not, but the *Machias* and her successors at Chemulpo had to maintain a guard at Seoul until the end of July.

During the spring, the *Concord* and the *Petrel* departed for overhaul at Mare Island, and the newly arrived protected cruiser *Boston* joined the *Olympia, Detroit,* and *Yorktown* at Woosung for inspections and drills. The four ships' companies had an unexpected opportunity to demonstrate their proficiency at life-saving early on the morning of 30 April, when the passenger steamers *Newchwang* and *On Wo* collided near their anchorage. The former, her bow badly crumpled, was run ashore without loss of life, but the *On Wo* sank a few minutes after the collision. The men-of-war immediately turned their searchlights on the disaster scene and lowered small boats which picked up forty-five of the sunken vessel's people; some 250 others were trapped below decks or swept away into the darkness by the swift current.

The *Olympia* led the squadron to sea on 9 May and it steamed northward, maneuvering in response to the flagship's signals as it went. The *Charleston* joined the force off Chefoo, after which she was ordered to California for decommissioning, and the remainder of the squadron was dispersed.

The admiral had hoped to find the *Monocacy* awaiting him at Chefoo, but abnormally low water in the Pei Ho kept her imprisoned long after her usual April departure date. She was not even afloat until 28 June, and then she could not traverse the shoals downstream until November. McNair did not think it advisable to expose the old double-ender to the Yellow Sea's autumnal gales, especially since a typhoon had driven the German *Iltis* onto rocks off the Shantung Promontory in July with the loss of sixty-eight lives, yet he certainly had no desire to send her back up the Pei Ho. He finally decided that she should spend the winter at Tangku, just above the river mouth, before going to Shanghai for overdue repairs.

The tranquility that had prevailed on the station throughout 1896 was disturbed slightly as the year came to an end. Minister to Siam John Barrett had been urging that a gunboat be sent to Bangkok—"I must submit that the Legation flag is becoming very lonesome and longs for the sight of colors on a man-of-war"; but he could provide no convincing evidence that a warship was needed there until the Siamese government foreclosed on a teakwood concession which had been granted to an American medical missionary.[3] The missionary charged that this action violated his rights under the Siamese-American treaty, and Barrett sent a vice-consul to look after the disputed estate, where he was forcibly arrested by Siamese soldiers. The minister made the most of this incident in his reports, to which the State Department added its recommendation that a vessel be sent. The *Machias* was dispatched from Canton and arrived at Bangkok on 23 January 1897, no doubt to Barrett's great satisfaction. This show of force led to the vice-consul's release, and the gunboat lingered in the Menam River until early March in order to impress upon the Siamese government the grave view that the United States took of this affair. The dispute regarding the teakwood concession had been submitted to an arbitrator who found for the missionary (since the latter had died in the meantime, it was rather a hollow triumph).

The *Monocacy* made what appeared to be her final sea passage in the spring of 1897, steaming from Tangku to Shanghai. McNair intended to have her repaired there, but the Navy Department refused to authorize any further expenditure on the veteran side-wheeler, directing the admiral to retain her for service on the Yangtze only until a new shallow-draft gunboat could be completed and sent out to replace her. McNair accepted this directive reluctantly, nor was the *Monocacy's* sea-going career yet at an end; she survived to return to the Taku Bar during the Boxer Rebellion of 1900–1901.

Japanese-American relations were strained during the summer of 1897 as a result of the Hawaiian government's refusal to admit additional Japanese immigrants or to repeal discriminatory laws relating to the one-quarter of the archipelago's inhabitants who were of Japanese birth or ancestry. The Japanese cruiser *Naniwa* was ordered to Hawaii, where-upon Honolulu turned to Washington for support. When President William McKinley obligingly sent a treaty of annexation to the Senate with a message urging its approval, the Japanese government made a formal protest to the State Department. Although the Senate failed to act on the treaty before adjourning late in July, the administration continued to hope that the agreement might yet be ratified and steadfastly refused to concede that the Japanese had a valid reason for opposing the annexation. Meanwhile, the Japanese government accepted a Hawaiian proposal that the immigration matter be submitted to arbitration. In December, Tokyo formally withdrew its opposition to the American annexation of Hawaii, which took place some eight months later.

Other than an order that he provide timely information regarding "significant movements" of Japanese warships, Admiral McNair received no instructions from the Navy Department regarding this crisis. Nonetheless, anti-American feeling in Japan caused him some concern. In July, *Yorktown* sailors on liberty in Kobe clashed with townspeople, causing the gunboat and the *Boston* to be withdrawn from that port, and later in the year authorities at Nagasaki seemed very perfunctory in their investigation of the apparent murders of seamen from the *Olympia* and the *Yorktown.*

As 1897 ended, Frederick V. McNair undertook to acquaint his successor with the situation on the Asiatic Station. The squadron was described first—it consisted of four vessels, the *Detroit, Yorktown,* and *Machias* having sailed for the United States during the year. The flagship was at Nagasaki, the *Boston* at Chemulpo, the *Petrel* at Canton, and the *Monocacy* at Shanghai. Reinforcements had been ordered—the protected cruiser *Raleigh* had just steamed through the Suez Canal on her way from the European Station, the new shallow-draft gunboat *Helena* was approaching Madeira en route to the Orient, and the *Concord* was preparing for sea at Mare Island.

Turning to matters on the station, the admiral mentioned "the distinct lack of friendliness on the part of the Japanese."[4] But he thought the recent German occupation of Kiaochow Bay a more serious occurrence. The murder of two German missionaries in the Shantung Peninsula during the autumn had been the pretext for this action, with Vice Admiral Otto von Diederichs announcing that the bay would be held until the Chinese government had satisfied a series of demands, including punishment of the murderers and provincial officials, payment of an indemnity, and the grant of economic concessions in Shantung to Germans. Within a short time, however, the British commander in chief had noted that the Germans were busily developing a naval base and "all visible signs prove that they have every intention of remaining in the Shantung promontory."[5] This was hardly surprising—the German East Asiatic Squadron had been increased in size and number of ships and in 1895 Berlin had sought to lease a naval base site on the Chinese coast without success. Admiral McNair had heard rumors to the effect that Britain, France, and Russia were preparing to acquire segments of China's territory for themselves; although these were unconfirmed, "it will be seen that a general state of inquietude prevails in affairs on the Station; this may be expected to continue until some definite action of the European powers more clearly shows the attitude that they intend to maintain in Asiatic affairs."[6] The Philippine Islands received little notice in McNair's report—he had no official knowledge of the rebellion said to be occurring there, and American interests seemed not to be endangered.

Admiral McNair's lack of curiosity with regard to the Philippines seems inexplicable. An insurrection had begun in Cuba almost three years earlier, and many of his fellow-countrymen were demanding that Spain be forced to relinquish the island even before he sailed from San Francisco in the autumn of 1895. Spanish-American relations had deteriorated steadily since that time, as he must have been aware, and the war plan drawn up by a naval intelligence officer in 1896 included offensive operations against Manila. But there is no evidence of any effort on the admiral's part to gain information about the city's defenses or the Spanish squadron's strength and efficiency.

McNair's indifference was not shared by Commodore George Dewey, the sixty-year-old Vermonter whose broad pennant was hoisted in the *Olympia* at Nagasaki on 3 January 1898. Dewey's only previous assignment to the Far East had been terminated by illness while his command was en route to the station; nonetheless, his reputation for aggressiveness had recommended him to Theodore Roosevelt, the firebrand assistant secretary of the navy, who was instrumental in having him ordered to relieve McNair.

Commodore Dewey's initial actions as commander in chief were quite routine. The *Olympia* steamed to Yokohama in mid-January so that he could confer with the minister to Japan and be presented to the emperor. There he received telegraphic orders to retain the squadron's time-expired seamen, and another dispatch informed him that the *Helena* had been directed to join the European Squadron at Lisbon. The *Concord* and the *Raleigh*, however, were still en route to the station—the former stood in from San Francisco on 9 February, and Dewey ordered her to relieve the *Boston* at Chemulpo, after which the flagship departed for Hong Kong. She arrived on 17 February, to be welcomed by the *Petrel*; the *Raleigh* steamed in from the southward on the next day.

A telegram announcing the destruction "by accident" of the USS *Maine* with heavy loss of life in Havana harbor reached Dewey soon after his arrival. The American men-of-war half-masted their colors upon receipt of the news; strangely enough, the official mourning period was abruptly terminated by another telegraphic order only three days later.

A more important telegram, this one from Roosevelt, was deciphered for the commodore on 26 February: "Order the Squadron except Monocacy to Hong Kong. Keep full of coal. In the event of declaration of war Spain, your duty will be to see that the Spanish squadron does not leave the Asiatic coast and then offensive operations in Philipine Islands. Keep Olympia until further orders."[7] Most of his vessels were already at Hong Kong, so Dewey had only to order the *Boston* and the *Concord* from Chemulpo; he did this at once.

Meanwhile, the Navy Department was belatedly arranging the transportation of an additional supply of ammunition to the Asiatic Squadron. On 3 March, Secretary of the Navy John D. Long asked the Mare Island commandant if a merchant steamer could be engaged to embark forty tons of projectiles and powder charges for shipment to Hong Kong; if not,

FIGURE 17–1. The *Olympia* at Hong Kong, firing a salute in honor of Washington's Birthday.

the elderly screw-gunboat *Mohican* was to convey the munitions to Honolulu for transshipment to the Pacific Squadron flagship *Baltimore*. The *Mohican* sailed a week later and steamed into the Hawaiian harbor on 19 March. Transferring both the ammunition to the *Baltimore* and Rear Admiral Joseph N. Miller's flag to the old gunboat required six days, after which the cruiser stood out for Hong Kong. The *Baltimore*'s steel plating had gathered a profuse growth of weeds and barnacles during the 4½ months she had spent at anchor off Honolulu, and her commanding officer ultimately concluded that, even at her most economical speed, his command's coal supply was inadequate for the 5,000-mile passage. Six days out, he ordered steam for her maximum sustained speed and set a course for Yokohama, where orders from Commodore Dewey awaited her—she was to fill up with provisions and coal before joining the squadron. No time was wasted. As soon as the empty lighters had been towed away, the cruiser's anchor was weighed and she resumed her passage to Hong Kong on 15 April.

While ammunition was undeniably important, Dewey was probably more anxious about fuel for his vessels. On 26 February, he cabled that coal should be shipped from San Francisco because of its "great scarcity" on the station. Secretary Long's reply was not very helpful; he authorized the commodore to order 5,000 tons of coal from England if it could not be obtained in the Far East.

Dewey surmounted his fuel problem before the end of March. Bunkers in all his vessels were filled with coal, and he had contracted for 3,000 tons of Cardiff in a collier approaching Hong Kong. Indeed, the squadron was ready for almost any eventuality. Storerooms and lockers contained provisions and stores, including tobacco, for three months. To be sure, magazines were not yet filled to capacity, but the *Concord* had embarked a quantity of 6-inch ammunition that had been shipped to Yokohama too late for the *Yorktown*'s use—it was divided among her consorts except the *Olympia* which carried no guns of that caliber—and the *Baltimore* was known to be en route with an additional supply of ammunition.

Recognizing the importance of continued logistic support, the commodore chartered the *Nanshan*, in which the squadron's coal was embarked, on her arrival and asked that he be permitted to buy her and another cargo steamer. Almost simultaneously, Secretary Long ordered him to procure two merchant vessels, so the two-year-old *Nanshan* and the smaller and older *Zafiro* were quickly acquired from their British owners. Long directed that the crews of both ships be enlisted in the U.S. Navy for a year's special service, that naval officers be put in command, and that both be armed. Dewey, however, had the *Nanshan* and the *Zafiro* registered as American merchantmen and cleared for the Bonin Islands, hoping thus to avoid their preclusion from Nagasaki, where he planned to obtain the additional supplies of coal and provisions that would be required in the event of a protracted conflict. A telegram from the minister at Tokyo dispelled the commodore's naive assumption that any Japanese port would be open to his ships during a war. Thereupon, he turned to Shanghai, assuming more realistically that the Chinese government would not enforce strict neutrality. The *Monocacy*'s commanding officer, excluded from active participation in the forthcoming strife by his gunboat's obsoleteness, made arrangements for lading the squadron's supply vessels at Shanghai and also sent three officers and fifty men from the old double-ender to Hong Kong, where an officer and four men were assigned to each of the purchased steamers and the remainder ordered to fill vacancies in the warships' complements.

Preparations for hostile action occupied the companies of the American men-of-war at Hong Kong as the days passed. The white and buff "livery" worn by ships of the "new" Navy disappeared under coats of lead grey, and the *Boston* and the *Petrel*, the only fully rigged vessels among them, were directed to send their lower and topsail yards to the *Nanshan*—they retained their topgallant yards for use in making flag hoists.

The new revenue cutter *McCulloch*, en route from her builder's yard on the Atlantic coast to her station at San Francisco, stood in on 17 April. Larger and faster than the *Petrel*, the composite-built cutter would have been a valuable addition to the squadron but for her armament; where the "baby battleship" mounted 6-inch guns, the *McCulloch* had 6-pounders; nor were the 3-inch field pieces contributed by the *Raleigh* and later by the *Baltimore* of much use, lashed as they were to the cutter's deck.

The eagerly awaited *Baltimore* made her appearance on the morning of 22 April. Forewarned of her condition, the commodore had the cruiser docked less than twenty-four hours after her arrival. Dockyard workers began to scrape her bottom plating as the dock was being pumped dry, while sailors applied a "coat of war paint" to her topsides and upper works. The work continued throughout the night; by 7 A.M., Sunday, 24 April, the *Baltimore*'s underwater body had received two coats of anti-corrosive paint and one of anti-fouling compound; her stern glands had been repacked, her screws polished, and her valves overhauled.

The feverish activity continued through the Sabbath. As soon as the ship had been warped out of the dock and towed to a mooring buoy, coal lighters were brought alongside to starboard and port, and coolies spent eight hours transferring their contents to her bunkers. Meanwhile, dockyard artisans worked on her secondary gun mounts until the early hours of 25 April.

There was need for haste. Her Majesty's secretary of state for colonies had cabled the governor of Hong Kong that a state of war existed between the United States and Spain, and the governor had formally notified Commodore Dewey of this fact during the afternoon of 23 April, adding "be good enough to leave the waters of the Colony with all ships under your command not later than 4 P.M. on Monday the 25th instant."[8]

The *Boston* led the squadron's gunboats and auxiliaries to sea the next day, to Mirs Bay, the anchorage just to the eastward of Hong Kong's territorial waters. The three larger cruisers joined them on 25 April, the *Raleigh* limping on one shaft because parts of her port circulator pump had had to be left at the dockyard.

That evening a tug brought cipher dispatches for Dewey, the most important of which ordered him to proceed to the Philippines and capture or destroy the Spanish squadron. In another message of the same date, Secretary Long stated rather plaintively: "I do not know what arrangement has been made to keep in communication with you."[9] Dewey replied that telegrams sent to Hong Kong would be delivered to him so long as the squadron remained in Mirs Bay, from which it would sail as soon as Oscar F. Williams, lately U.S. consul at Manila, joined him.

After the tug had departed, the commodore summoned his commanding officers to the flagship, and later that night the Ardois lights suspended from the *Olympia*'s main truck blinked an order that secondary batteries be kept manned and sentries armed.

Final preparations were made on 26 April. Boats from the squadron went alongside the *Baltimore* in turn to embark their ships' allotments of ammunition. Dewey ordered one of the cruiser's lieutenants to the *McCulloch* as senior officer of the "auxiliary squadron"; he was accompanied by four armed sailors lest the standard of discipline in the revenue cutter be found wanting. The *Raleigh* received her circulating pump parts from Hong Kong later in the afternoon, and machinists from the *Olympia* helped the smaller vessel's engineers to reassemble the pump. Both of the *Raleigh*'s engines were ready for service the next morning.

Consul Williams and *New York Herald* correspondent Joseph L. Stickney, a former naval officer, arrived in a tug from Hong Kong soon afterward. Dewey conferred with the former and then assigned him to quarters in the *Baltimore*, while Stickney, who had Long's permission to accompany the squadron if the commodore agreed, remained in the flagship.

Soon after noon, all vessels hove their anchor chains in to short stay, and at 1:55 P.M. flag hoist 121 was hauled down from the *Olympia*'s yardarm. Capstans and windlasses began to revolve; links of chain crept upward through the hawsepipes, were hosed down, and clanked into the chain lockers. In cruiser and gunboat, cutter and cargo ship, anchors were reported aweigh and the Asiatic Squadron put to sea under overcast skies, forming into a single column of warships, the flagship in the van, with the *McCulloch* leading the *Nanshan* and the *Zafiro* on a parallel track abeam to starboard.

The passage to Luzon was devoid of incident. The light airs and smooth sea typical of the change of monsoon prevailed, nor was the heat unduly oppressive for those laboring in the stokeholds because the squadron's 8-knot speed required only a portion of the ships' boiler power. Crews were exercised at battle stations daily, and the warships made final preparations for hostile action. All had been partially stripped for action at Hong Kong except the *Baltimore*; her wake was littered by inflammable fittings that had contributed to her comfort in peacetime but were considered potentially hazardous in war.

The commodore possessed fairly complete knowledge of the Spanish naval forces and of the fortifications in the vicinity of Manila Bay. He had sent this information to the Navy Department a month earlier, concluding: "I believe I am not over-confident in stating that with the squadron now under my command the vessels could be taken and the defenses of Manila reduced in one day."[10] What he could not know was the location of the Spanish squadron, for Consul Williams reported that Rear Admiral Don Patricio Montojo y Pasaron might have taken the men-of-war under his command to a station in Subic Bay, 30 miles northwest of the Manila Bay entrance. This is what Montojo had done, but he found that work on the shore defenses there had hardly begun, so his vessels returned to an anchorage off the naval arsenal at Cavite, five miles south of Manila, on 29 April.

Lookouts in the *Olympia* made out Cape Bolinao on Luzon's west coast before dawn on 30 April, and the *Boston* and the *Concord* increased speed to reconnoiter Subic Bay. They rejoined the squadron that afternoon, passing the *Baltimore* as she sent a small boat to a Spanish schooner that had been brought to by a shot across the bow. After interrogating the schooner's master, the *Baltimore* caught up with her consorts, whereupon the flag signaled all to stop and send their commanding officers to the *Olympia* for a final conference. At 6:20 P.M., the squadron started ahead once more, forming a single line led by the flagship, with the auxiliaries bringing up the rear.

Dewey chose to enter Manila Bay through the Boca Grande between Corregidor and Caballa islands on the one hand and El Fraile on the other, because the batteries on either side were unlikely to command its 3½-mile width as effectively as those defending the narrower Boca Chica north of Corregidor, which was generally used by steamers. He was not concerned about the possibility of encountering mines, holding that the channel's depth and currents would render any attempt at mining nugatory. Nonetheless, watertight doors below decks were closed, causing temperatures to soar.

The men went to general quarters as the column approached the Boca Grande, each ship following the screened stern light shown by her next ahead. Corregidor, its lighthouse darkened, loomed up dimly to port and fell slowly astern, its garrison apparently unaware of the Asiatic Squadron's passage. Even the flames streaking upward from the *McCulloch*'s funnel when soot therein ignited, attracted no notice on Corregidor, but gunners on El Fraile to starboard fired several ineffectual shots, to which the *Raleigh, Concord, Boston*, and the cutter responded with a few rounds as they steamed out of range.

With his force's presence already revealed to the enemy, Commodore Dewey could use the *Olympia*'s red-and-white Ardois lights to order a reduction of speed to 4 knots and to direct the auxiliaries to take station on the port side of the line of warships. As the *McCulloch* drew abeam of the flagship, she signaled that her chief engineer had collapsed and her surgeon wished to discuss his condition with other doctors. The flag's response was a curt "Impossible," nor would a consultation have helped, for the elderly engineer died twenty minutes later.[11]

Manila's lights were sighted at 3 A.M., Sunday, 1 May, and at daylight the squadron was close enough to determine that none of the sixteen vessels anchored off the city was a warship. Dewey directed the *McCulloch* to see her charges to a location beyond the range of enemy guns; then the *Olympia* headed for Cavite at 6 knots, followed in distant order by the *Baltimore, Raleigh, Petrel, Concord,* and *Boston,* each with battle ensigns streaming from her mastheads and sailors waiting tensely for the action to begin.

It began with several shots from Manila's shore batteries, all of which fell short and to which only the *Concord* replied. The batteries on Sangley Point to the northward of Cavite opened fire before the squadron was within range—it stood onward as its officers picked out Montojo's vessels in Canacao Bay between Sangley Point and Cavite. They numbered seven, not one even a match for the *Concord* except the flagship *Reina Cristina* which, with six 6.3-inch guns and a speed of 14 knots, was only slightly superior. Nor were the shore batteries markedly formidable, consisting as they did of a half-dozen modern guns and a number of antiquated pieces. Although Manila's fortifications contained a more impressive array of artillery, Admiral Montojo had chosen not to avail his ships of their protection because of the likelihood that the city itself would suffer the effects of American gunfire.

The *Olympia* fired ranging shots from her forward turret and turned west when some two miles separated her from the enemy. Commodore Dewey made his celebrated remark: "You may fire when you are ready, Gridley," and Captain Charles V. Gridley passed the order to his division officers.[12] The *Baltimore* and the vessels astern of her unleashed their batteries as they turned in succession. Within a few minutes a hail of American projectiles was falling on and about the Spanish ships and batteries, which were replying in kind. A launch, mistakenly thought to be a torpedo boat, steamed out from Cavite and drew an inordinate amount of fire without fatal result before she drifted ashore on Sangley Point. With the point well abaft her beam, the flagship reversed course, followed in turn by the rest of the squadron, while the *McCulloch*, waiting to tow any disabled vessel to a safe anchorage before replacing her in the line of battle, emulated the evolution somewhat farther out in Manila Bay.

Dewey had stressed the importance of conserving ammunition—to little avail, for most of the American gunners seemed determined to crush the enemy by sheer weight of shells, and few division officers showed any inclination to restrain them. Ordnance equipment, experiencing its first test in combat, limited the expenditure of ammunition more effectively— electrical firing circuits generally failed to withstand repeated shocks, forcing gunners to use slower percussion primers; breech lock wedges swelled and jammed; and primer and shell cases often had to be extricated from the guns forcibly. Nonetheless, the volume of fire was impressive, especially when the range permitted the rapid-firing 6-pounders to be used.

The master of the British merchant ship anchored nearest to Sangley Point deposed later that he and his company "could see the shots striking many of the Spanish ships, and also striking right into the fort, and we could not help but notice that the Americans had much better marksmen than the Spaniards."[13] In fact, the Asiatic Squadron's gunnery was extremely inaccurate. With no attempt at target distribution or salvo-firing, spotting the fall of shot was impossible even before clouds of brown powder and coal smoke, which the breeze was too light to dispel, reduced the visibility. The primitive fire-control devices were of little use—smoke and powder grains smudged the *Olympia*'s telescopic sights, and what seem to have been the squadron's only range finders, experimental instruments installed in the *Baltimore*, were quickly disabled by the concussion of her guns. The *Petrel*'s Lieutenant Bradley A. Fiske, the inventor of the range finders, was perhaps more effective, shouting ranges obtained with a stadimeter of his own design to the "baby battleship's" commanding officer from a platform rigged on her foremast.

But at least some of the American shots did find Spanish targets— several of Montojo's ships were afire at one time or another, and an apparent attempt by the *Reina Cristina* to close the *Olympia* ended with the Spanish flagship in flames and grounded off the arsenal at Cavite; but very few rounds from Spanish guns hit anything other than the surface of Manila Bay. The high-sided *Baltimore*, the best target in the American column, seems to have attracted the greatest amount of fire, but she counted only five hits; these disabled a 6-inch gun, caused a minor leak, and wounded eight of her company slightly. The *Boston*, at the end of the line, was struck by four shots, one of which went through her foremast; 6-pounder projectiles did unimportant damage to the *Olympia* and the *Raleigh*; the *Petrel* was scarred by a shell fragment; and the *Concord* was not even grazed.

This happy state of affairs was not apparent to the commodore. So far as he could see, his vessels had steamed past a greatly inferior Spanish force five times at relatively close ranges without inflicting serious damage. A report that the flagship's ammunition supply was dangerously

FIGURE 17–2. The *Boston* engaging Spanish warships and batteries in Manila Bay, 1 May 1898.

depleted led him to break off the action at 7:35 A.M. in order that more effective tactics could be decided on.

The squadron steamed out into Manila Bay and stopped barely beyond the range of the city's batteries, which kept up an intermittent and useless fire. Commanding officers were summoned to the flagship, and their reports did much to cheer Dewey, as did the revelation that the ammunition shortage was less acute than at first stated. The hands were piped to breakfast, and as they ate, the pall of battle smoke over Cavite lifted, revealing the Spanish squadron in a deplorable state. The *Reina Cristina*'s magazines exploded a short time afterward, and other vessels were seen to be burning, fleeing, or abandoned.

The Asiatic Squadron returned to finish the action at 10:45 A.M., with the *Baltimore*, which had been ordered to speak an approaching steamer and so was closest to Cavite, leading the line. The shore batteries which returned her fire were quickly silenced, the *Concord* and the *Petrel* steamed inshore to destroy the remaining Spanish vessels, and at noon white flags were hoisted over the arsenal. Fifty minutes later, the *Petrel* signaled: *"Everything surrendered."*[14] The Battle of Manila Bay was over.

CHAPTER EIGHTEEN

Retrospect

Although Commodore George Dewey's cheering sailors and marines cannot have realized it—and probably would not have been impressed if they had—the Battle of Manila Bay was a turning point in the history of the squadron in which they served. During most of the nineteenth century, the U.S. Navy had maintained a force on the station primarily for the purpose of protecting the persons and interests of American citizens in the Far East, especially in China, Japan, and Korea. Territorial acquisition had tempted some naval officers, but heretofore the United States had avoided this form of imperialism. After 1 May 1898, the Philippine Islands became a major responsibility of the Asiatic Squadron, which had to help first with their conquest, then with their pacification, and finally with their defense. American attitudes toward the Far Eastern situation in general reflected the fact that the U.S. flag flew over something more than legation and consulate, and the squadron's role changed accordingly.

Opinions about the importance of the U.S. Navy in Asian waters during the nineteenth century must vary, nor can any be conclusive because of the presence of foreign warships, especially those of Britain's Royal Navy, which helped to provide the degree of security necessary to encourage the establishment and expansion of trade. On the whole, the American men-of-war carried out their duties in a pacific fashion. With the exception of the destruction of Sumatran villages, the affair at the barrier forts, and the 1871 expedition to Korea, belligerent action was undertaken very reluctantly and on a small scale, in marked contrast with the records of some of the foreign navies during the same period. To offset the hundreds of Oriental lives lost as a result of these attacks, one may mention the numerous distressed mariners and others assisted by U.S. naval vessels and personnel. Were a list of these compiled, it might approach that of the casualties in length.

U.S. policy vis-à-vis the Far East, which was concerned principally with the extension of trade, owed much to the Navy. Naval officers— Matthew Calbraith Perry and Robert W. Shufeldt—negotiated treaties with Japan and Korea, while others had a lesser part in bringing about treaties with China. American diplomats, with the obvious exception of Humphrey Marshall, generally seemed satisfied with the support accorded them by successive commanders in chief; if members of the consular service sometimes found cause for complaint, it must be remembered that these officials usually had little regard for the health of warships' companies or for conditions elsewhere on the station. Japan and Korea, however, do seem to have received an undue amount of attention from the Asiatic Squadron. While orders from the Navy Department were responsible for the almost constant presence of an American man-of-war at Chemulpo, the commanders in chief themselves preferred Japan to China, largely because of the former's more salubrious climate.

The squadrons on distant station were also intended to provide active service for officers and men. To this end, the Navy Department urged commanders in chief to employ their ships actively in cruising about the station, but this requirement ran counter to that of keeping vessels in the principal treaty ports and to the frequent admonitions to observe strict economy in coal consumption. There is no evidence, however, that the standards of seamanship and military preparedness in the Asiatic Squadron were inferior to those in other squadrons or navies. Of the three American warships lost on the station, the *Porpoise* almost certainly succumbed in a typhoon and the *Oneida*'s sinking may be attributed to the poor judgment of a British merchant mariner. Only the wreck of the *Ashuelot* reflected unfavorably on the Asiatic Squadron. Other vessels ran aground or suffered storm or collision damage—almost all were saved solely through the exertions of their own people. Nor was the squadron's military record unimpressive. With the exception of the Formosa expedition ordered by Rear Admiral Henry H. Bell, the belligerent operations in which American man-of-warsmen participated invariably ended with the dispersal of the turbulent mob or the pirate fleet, or with the capture and destruction of the offending forts and villages.

No matter that they were few in number and occasionally somewhat decrepit, that they were manned by sailors and marines of diverse origin and morality, that their officers frequently imbibed too freely—the warships that displayed the stars and stripes in Asian waters during the nineteenth century provided an interesting chapter in their Navy's history, a chapter of which any sea service might be proud.

NOTES

Chapter 1

1. Secretary of the Navy, *Annual Report, 1831*, p. 38. Hereafter cited as *Annual Report* with year.

2. *Annual Report, 1832*, p. 42.

3. Woodbury to Geisinger, confidential (copy), 6 January 1832, Levi Woodbury Papers, #11 (1st Series), Library of Congress Manuscript Division.

4. Woodbury to Secretary of State Edward Livingston, confidential (copy), Wednesday evening [probably 7 December 1831], ibid.

5. Livingston to Woodbury, 3 January 1832, ibid.

6. Quoted in Charles O. Paullin, *Diplomatic Negotiations of American Naval Officers, 1778–1883*, p. 175. Hereafter cited as Paullin, *Diplomatic Negotiations*.

7. Quoted in Charles O. Paullin, *American Voyages to the Orient, 1690–1865*, p. 32. Hereafter cited as Paullin, *American Voyages*.

8. "Notes on Two Cruises (Peacock)," Geisinger Papers MS. 1283, Maryland Historical Society.

9. *Annual Report, 1837*, p. 4.

10. Dickerson to Kennedy, 26 January 1835, Letters Sent by the Secretary of the Navy to Officers, 1798–1868, Record Group 45 (RG 45), National Archives.

11. Lieutenant Sylvanus W. Godon to Lieutenant Garrett J. Pendergrast, Bombay, 29 October 1835, Area 10 File, RG 45.

12. Kennedy to Dickerson, New York, 20 April 1835, Letters Received

by the Secretary of the Navy from Officers Commanding Ships of War, RG 45. Hereafter cited as Captains' Letters.

13. Kennedy to Secretary of the Navy, Honolulu, 30 September 1836, ibid.

Chapter 2

1. 24th Congress, 1st Session. House of Representatives Document 785, p. 10.

2. Bridgman [probably to Dr. Rufus Anderson], Canton, 15 May 1839, American Board of Commissioners for Foreign Missions, South China Mission, ABC 16.3.8, Houghton Library, Harvard University. Hereafter cited by ABC number and mission locality.

3. Williams to Anderson, Canton, 17 May 1839, ibid.

4. Read to Secretary of the Navy James K. Paulding, Macao Roads, 10 June 1839, Captains' Letters.

5. Downes to Badger, 4 May 1841, ibid.

6. *Canton Register*, 5 April 1842, copy in Letters from Officers Commanding Squadrons, 1841–1886, East India Squadron, RG 45. Hereafter cited as East India Squadron Letters.

7. Viceroy Ke to Kearny, Canton, 15 October 1842, quoted in Carroll S. Alden, *Lawrence Kearny: Sailor Diplomat*, pp. 147–48. Hereafter cited as Alden, *Kearny*.

8. Snow to Kearny, Canton, 20 October 1842, East India Squadron Letters.

9. Henry Pinkney to Eliza Pinkney Williams, Boca Tigris, 1 November 1842, Manuscript Vertical File, Maryland Historical Society.

10. Kearny to Secretary of the Navy, Amoy, 19 May 1843, East India Squadron Letters; card published by the Crew of the U.S. Ship *Constellation*, quoted in Alden, *Kearny*, p. 210.

Chapter 3

1. Parker to Secretary of the Navy, Bombay, 27 November 1843, East India Squadron Letters.

2. Bridgman to Anderson, Macao, 18 July 1844, ABC 16.3.3, Amoy.

3. Hunter Miller, ed., *Treaties and Other International Acts of the United States of America*, 4:569. Hereafter cited as Miller, *Treaties*.

4. Cochrane to Parker, Hong Kong, 27 July 1844, East India Squadron Letters.

5. McKeever to Parker, Macao Roads, 19 October 1844, ibid.

6. Parker to McKeever, Boca Tigris, 2 November 1844, ibid.

7. Russell, Wetmore, Olyphant et al. to Parker, Canton, 26 November 1844, ibid.

8. Henshaw to Percival, 22 January 1844, Record of Confidential Letters, No. 1, RG 45. Hereafter cited as Confidential Letters with volume number.

9. Quoted in Percival to Secretary of the Navy, 21 June 1845 (copy), Subject File VD, RG 45.

10. Endorsement on Percival to Secretary of the Navy, 21 June 1845, ibid.

11. Biddle to Secretary of the Navy, Canton, 21 January 1846, East India Squadron Letters.

12. Secretary of the Navy George Bancroft to Biddle, 22 May 1845, Confidential Letters, No. 1.

13. Biddle to Secretary of the Navy, off the coast of Japan, 31 July 1846, East India Squadron Letters.

14. Quoted in ibid.

15. Geisinger to Glynn, Whampoa, 31 January 1849, ibid.

16. W. G. Beasley, *Great Britain and the Opening of Japan, 1834–1858*, pp. 90–91.

17. Memorandum of conversation with Matsmora Schal, Nagasaki, 22 April 1849, East India Squadron Letters.

18. Memorandum of conversation with high military chief named Hagewara Matasak, Nagasaki, 26 April 1849, ibid.

19. Ogden to Geisinger, at sea, 27 June 1849, ibid.

20. Geisinger to Secretary of the Navy, Macao Roads, 26 November 1849, ibid.

21. Voorhees to Secretary of the Navy, Hong Kong, 20 July 1850, ibid.

22. Voorhees to Secretary of the Navy, Hong Kong, 23 July 1850, ibid.

Chapter 4

1. Aulick to Secretary of the Navy, Rio de Janeiro, 15 September 1851, East India Squadron Letters.

2. Graham to Aulick, 17 and 18 November 1851, Confidential Letters, No. 2.

3. Aulick to Secretary of the Navy, Hong Kong, 17 February 1852, East India Squadron Letters.

4. Graham to Aulick, 18 November 1851, Confidential Letters, No. 2.

5. Welles to Senior Naval Officer, Hong Kong, 31 August 1861, Confidential Letters, No. 5.

Chapter 5
1. Lieutenant John R. Goldsborough to Commander Louis M. Goldsborough, Hong Kong, 28 December 1852, Area 10 File.

2. DeSilver to Perry, 28 April 1853, East India Squadron Letters.

3. Perry to Commodore William B. Shubrick, Shanghai, 15 May 1853, ibid.

4. Abbot to his wife, quoted in Samuel Eliot Morison, *Old Bruin: Commodore Matthew Calbraith Perry*, pp. 341–43.

5. Marshall to Perry, Shanghai, 22 [?] September 1853, East India Squadron Letters.

6. 36th Cong., 1st Sess., Sen. Doc. 39, p. 3.

7. Pontiatine [Putiatin] to Perry, Shanghai, 12 November 1853 (copy), East India Squadron Letters.

Chapter 6
1. Dobbin to Abbot, 17 November 1854, Confidential Letters, No. 3.

2. Abbot to Secretary of the Navy, Whampoa, 9 January 1855, East India Squadron Letters.

3. Abbot to Secretary of the Navy, Hong Kong, 12 November 1855, ibid.

4. Armstrong to Secretary of the Navy, Hong Kong, 3 July 1856, ibid.

5. Surgeon William M. Wood, *Fankwei; or, The San Jacinto in the Seas of India, China, and Japan*, p. 275.

6. Foote to Armstrong, off the Barrier Forts, 26 November 1856, East India Squadron Letters.

7. Parker to Armstrong, 13 December 1856, ibid.

8. Dobbin to Armstrong, 27 February 1857, Confidential Letters, No. 3.

9. Journal kept by Davenport, 1856, copy in Subject File HL, RG 45.

10. Spooner to Armstrong, 16 January 1857, East India Squadron Letters.

11. Perry to Parker, Macao, 21 January 1857 (copy), ibid.

12. Assistant Surgeon A. L. Gihon to Fleet Surgeon William M. Wood, Shanghai, 14 April 1857, ibid.

13. Quoted in Armstrong to Secretary of the Navy, Hong Kong, 9 May 1857, ibid.

Chapter 7

1. Miller, *Treaties*, 7:796.
2. Tattnall to Toucey, Shanghai, 1 September 1858, East India Squadron Letters.
3. Toucey to Tattnall, 10 December 1858, Confidential Letters, No. 4.
4. First Assistant Engineer R. C. Potts, "Journal on board of U.S.S. Pohatan," Logs, Journals, and Diaries of Officers of the United States Navy at Sea, RG 45.
5. Quoted in Tattnall to Toucey, 4 July 1859, East India Squadron Letters.
6. Tattnall to Hope, 7 July 1859, China Question, IV, Admiralty Records 125/100, Public Record Office, p. 569. See also Tattnall to Captain Hand, RN, 20 August 1859, ibid., p. 679. Hereafter cited as Adm 125 with relevant number and volume title if any.
7. Journal of Tattnall's flag lieutenant, Stephen D. Trenchard, quoted in Edgar S. Maclay, *Reminiscences of the Old Navy*, p. 83.
8. Miller, *Treaties*, 4:566.
9. British consul, Nagasaki, to Hope, 24 September 1859, Adm 125/115.
10. Toucey to Stribling, 10 June 1859, Confidential Letters, No. 4.
11. Ibid.
12. Stribling to Toucey, Shanghai, 3 October 1860, East India Squadron Letters.
13. *Saginaw* folder, ZC File, Naval Historical Center, Washington Navy Yard.

Chapter 8

1. McDougal to Welles with enclosures, Yokohama, 23 July 1863, *Official Records of the Union and Confederate Navies in the War of the Rebellion*, Series 1, Volume 2, pp. 393–99. Hereafter cited as *ORN* with volume number.
2. Commander in chief to Secretary of the Admiralty, 29 July 1863, Adm 125/117.
3. Commander in chief to Secretary of the Admiralty, 15 September 1864, Adm 125/118.

Chapter 9

1. *Annual Report*, 1865, pp. xiv–xv.
2. Welles to Bell, 31 July 1865, *ORN*, 3:575–76.
3. Bell to Welles, Macao Roads, 7 February 1866, Asiatic Squadron

Letters. The East India Squadron was not officially renamed until 23 April 1866, but the collection of letters is so titled after 31 December 1865.

4. Bankhead to Bell, Foochow, 23 March 1866, ibid.

5. Bell to Welles, Hong Kong, 9 March 1866, ibid.

6. Bell to Welles, Yokohama, 25 August 1866, ibid.

7. *Annual Report, 1886*, p. 14. Each of the squadrons officially became a "fleet" at this time, but "squadron" describes the force on Asiatic Station much more accurately and will continue to be used.

8. Shufeldt to Bell, Hong Kong, 3 October 1866, Letter Book— *Wachusett*, September 1866–January 1868, Robert W. Shufeldt Papers, Naval Historical Foundation (NHF), Library of Congress Manuscript Division.

9. Shufeldt to Bell, Amoy, 22 November 1866, Asiatic Squadron Letters.

10. Schufeldt to Bell, at sea, 30 January 1867; Shufeldt memorandum, 25 January 1867, ibid.

11. Bell to Welles, Shanghai, 19 June 1867, ibid.

12. Ibid.

13. LeGendre to Bell, 28 November 1867, ibid.

14. Bell to Welles, Shanghai, 18 July 1867, ibid.

15. Carter to Bell, Hong Kong, 10 September 1867, ibid.

16. Commodore John R. Goldsborough to Welles, Hiogo, 16 January 1868, ibid.

17. E. Mowbray Tate, "Admiral Bell and the New Asiatic Squadron, 1865–1868," *The American Neptune*, 32 (April 1972):134.

Chapter 10

1. Robley D. Evans, *A Sailor's Log*, p. 110.

2. Rowan to Welles, Yokohama, 24 July 1868, Letters of S. C. Rowan, U.S.N., Comd'g Asiatic Squadron, to the Navy Department from October 1867 to November 1870, RG 45. Hereafter cited as Rowan Letter Book.

3. Rowan to Welles, Nagasaki, 24 October 1868, ibid.

4. Samuel P. Boyer, *Naval Surgeon: The Revolt in Japan, 1868–1869*, p. 54.

5. Rowan to Keppel, Hong Kong, 8 January 1869, Asiatic Squadron Letters.

6. General Order No. 19, 14 January 1869, ibid.

7. Rowan to Welles, Nagasaki, 27 October 1868, Rowan Letter Book.

8. Charles W. Clift's Journal, Log #426, 29 May 1869, Mystic Seaport, Inc.

9. William B. Burtis, "Private Journal of a Cruise to China and Japan in the years of 1867, 1868, 1869 and 1870 in the Flag Ship Piscataqua," Manuscripts and Archives Division, The New York Public Library, Astor, Lenox and Tilden Foundations.

10. Rowan to Robeson, Yokohama, 16 April 1870, Rowan Letter Book.

11. Rowan to Borie, Nagasaki, 5 June 1869, ibid.

12. Rowan to Robeson, Hong Kong, 4 January 1870, ibid.; Rowan to Robeson, Hong Kong, 3 January 1870, Asiatic Squadron Letters.

13. "Official Notes and Evidence in the Proceedings of the Naval Court of Inquiry as to the collision between the U.S. Corvette *Oneida* and the P. & O. Stmr. *Bombay*," China Station, XV, Adm 125/15, p. 609.

14. Belknap to Secretary of the Navy, Yokohama, 10 May 1889, Area 10 File.

Chapter 11

1. Blake to Rodgers, Woosung, 24 November 1870, Letter Book, 1869–72, Homer C. Blake Papers, New-York Historical Society, Manuscript Section.

2. Fish to Low, 20 April 1870, Diplomatic Instructions of the Department of State, 1801–1906—China, RG 59.

3. Tilton to "Nannie," 20 May 1871, in Carolyn A. Tyson, comp., *Marine Amphibious Landing in Korea, 1871*, p. 8.

4. Blake to Rodgers, 17 June 1871, *Annual Report, 1871*, p. 286.

5. Tilton to Rodgers, 16 June 1871, ibid., p. 305.

6. Schley to Kimberly, 14 June 1871, ibid., pp. 296–97.

7. General Order No. 32, copy in Silas Casey Papers, NHF.

8. Edward B. Drew to Li, guardian-general, *Papers Relating to the Foreign Relations of the United States Transmitted to Congress with the Annual Message of the President, Dec. 4, 1871*, p. 194.

9. Rodgers to Robeson, Chefoo, 5 July 1871, Asiatic Squadron Letters.

10. Excerpt from the diary of Captain James, chief pilot with the Japanese squadron, in Plunkett to Vice Admiral Alfred P. Ryder, 6 March 1876, Adm 125/122.

11. Quoted in Rodgers to Anne Rodgers, 26 October 1871, Rodgers Collection, NHF.

12. Rodgers to Anne Rodgers, at sea, 8 December 1871, ibid.

13. Quoted in Rockwell to Low, Tientsin, 30 November 1871, Charles H. Rockwell, Letter Book—*Palos*, Letter Books of Officers of the United States Navy at Sea, March 1778–July 1908, RG 45.

Chapter 12

1. *Annual Report, 1871*, p. 41.
2. Jenkins to Low, Calcutta, 20 December 1872, Asiatic Squadron Letters.
3. Jenkins to Robeson, Nagasaki, 11 September 1873, ibid.
4. Jenkins to Robeson, Shanghai, 26 November 1873, ibid.
5. Matthews to Rear Admiral Alexander M. Pennock, Shanghai, 22 July 1874, ibid.
6. Ibid.
7. Pennock to Robeson, Kobe, 13 July 1874, ibid.
8. Endorsement on Pennock to Robeson, Nagasaki, 2 October 1874, ibid.
9. Confidential Correspondence respecting Consular Jurisdiction over British subjects serving on board Foreign Ships of War, China Station, XXII, Adm 125/22, p. 193.
10. Reynolds to Robeson, Suez, 15 August 1875, Asiatic Squadron Letters.
11. Reynolds to Robeson, Shanghai, 14 March 1876, ibid.

Chapter 13

1. Patterson to Thompson, Yokohama, 23 October 1878, Asiatic Squadron Letters.
2. Manuscript entitled "The Treaty with Korea," Washington, D.C., 1898, Subject File, Shufeldt Papers.
3. Quoted in Paullin, *Diplomatic Negotiations*, p. 295.
4. Reynolds to Robeson, Yokohama, 9 July 1876, Asiatic Squadron Letters.
5. Shufeldt to "Moll" (Miss Mary A. Shufeldt), Nagasaki, 13 August 1880, Shufeldt General Correspondence, Shufeldt Papers.
6. Ibid.
7. Immigration Treaty, 17 November 1880, in Paul H. Clyde, ed., *United States Policy toward China: Diplomatic and Public Documents, 1839–1939*, pp. 152–54.
8. Clitz to Thompson, Shanghai, 24 December 1880, Asiatic Squadron Letters.
9. Quoted in draft, Shufeldt to Chandler, San Francisco, 30 July 1882, Subject File, Shufeldt Papers.
10. Sargent to Shufeldt, New York, 20 April 1882, General Correspondence, ibid.

11. Shufeldt to Sargent, San Francisco, 15 October 1882, ibid.
12. Cotton to Clitz, Chefoo, 7 July 1882, Asiatic Squadron Letters.
13. Cotton to Clitz, off Roze Island, 13 August 1882, ibid.
14. Young to Clitz, confidential, 24 November 1882, ibid.
15. Young to Clitz, 30 December 1882, ibid.
16. Quoted by Lieutenant A. J. Iverson, Record of General Court-Martial 6415, RG 125.
17. Kenneth J. Hagan, *American Gunboat Diplomacy and the Old Navy, 1887–1889*, p. 119.
18. Young to Crosby, 8 May 1883, Asiatic Squadron Letters.

Chapter 14
1. Crosby to Chandler, Yokohama, 1 October 1883, Asiatic Squadron Letters.
2. Davis to commanding officers, confidential, Shanghai, 30 January 1884, ibid.
3. Seymour to Young, 19 July 1884 (copy), ibid.
4. Consul Edwin Stevens to Commander Francis J. Higginson, 29 July 1884 (copy), ibid.
5. Young to Seymour, 4 August 1884 (copy), ibid.
6. Davis to Chandler, Foochow, 15 August 1884, ibid.
7. Rev. Caleb C. Baldwin to Langdon S. Ward, Foochow, 1 September 1884, ABC 16.3.5, Foochow.
8. General Order No. 27, Nagasaki, 21 July 1885, Asiatic Squadron Letters.
9. McGlensey to Davis, off Hiogo, 18 September 1885, ibid.
10. McGlensey to Davis, off Hiogo, 29 September 1885, ibid.
11. Hamilton to Secretary of the Admiralty, [17 April 1886], China Station, XXX, Adm 125/30.
12. P. W. Currie (Foreign Office) to Secretary of the Admiralty, 23 June 1886, ibid.
13. Quoted in James M. Merrill, "The Asiatic Squadron, 1835–1907," *The American Neptune*, 29 (April 1969):114.

Chapter 15
1. Quoted in McNair to Secretary of the Navy, Shanghai, 20 February 1889, Area 10 File.
2. Biographical sketch of Ralph Chandler, Z File, Naval Historical Center.

3. Denby to Secretary of State Thomas F. Bayard, 2 March 1889 (copy), Area 10 File.

4. Belknap to Secretary of the Navy, Kobe, 13 April 1890, ibid.

5. Belknap to Secretary of the Navy, Yokohoma, 11 August 1891, ibid.

6. Rich to Belknap, Taku, 7 December 1891 (copy), ibid.

7. Passed Assistant Engineer W. C. Eaton to Rich, enclosure in ibid.

Chapter 16

1. Barber to Harmony, Shanghai, 5 March 1892 (copy), Area 10 File.

2. Herbert to Skerrett, 29 June 1894, Translations of Cipher Messages Sent, RG 45. Hereafter cited as Cipher Messages Sent.

3. Herbert to Commander in Chief, 24 September 1894, Area 10 File.

4. Carpenter to Denby, Chefoo, 19 November 1894 (copy), ibid.

5. Carpenter to Secretary of the Navy, Chefoo, 7 December 1894, ibid.

6. Quoted in Day to Ensigns G. N. Hayward, H. G. McFarland et al., Chemulpo, 11 January 1895 (copy), ibid.

7. Day to Carpenter, Chemulpo, 12 January 1895, ibid.

8. Carpenter to Secretary of the Navy, Nagasaki, 13 April 1895, ibid.

9. Consul General Thomas R. Jernigan to Acting Secretary of State Edwin F. Uhl, 3 August 1895, Subject File VI, RG 45.

Chapter 17

1. Herbert to McNair, 29 January 1896, Area 10 File.

2. Stockton to Winsloe, 21 December 1895; Winsloe to Stockton, 21 December 1895; ibid.

3. Barrett to Secretary of State Richard Olney, 17 August 1896 (copy), ibid.

4. McNair memorandum, 31 December 1897, ibid.

5. Vice Admiral Sir Alexander Buller to Secretary of the Admiralty, 10 December 1897 (confidential), China Station, LII, Adm 125/52, p. 434.

6. McNair memorandum, 31 December 1897, Area 10 File.

7. Roosevelt to Dewey, 25 February 1898, Cipher Messages Sent.

8. Major General Wilsone Black to Dewey, 23 April 1898, Area 10 File.

9. Long to Dewey, 24 April 1898, Cipher Messages Sent.

10. Dewey to Secretary of the Navy (Bureau of Navigation), 31 March 1898, Area 10 File.

11. *Olympia* log, 1 May 1898, Logs of United States Naval Ships and Stations, 1801–1946, RG 24. Hereafter cited as Ships' Logs.

12. Quoted in Richard S. West, Jr., *Admirals of American Empire*, p. 203.

13. Affidavit by A. W. Robbins, master, *Buccleuch*, subscribed before U.S. consul, Liverpool, 19 November 1898, Area 10 File.

14. *Baltimore* log, 1 May 1898, Ships' Logs.

BIBLIOGRAPHY

List of Abbreviations

LC	Library of Congress Manuscript Division, Washington, D.C.
MdHS	Maryland Historical Society, Baltimore, Md.
NA	National Archives, Washington, D.C.
NHF	Papers of the Naval Historical Foundation, deposited in the Library of Congress Manuscript Division
N-Y HS	Naval Historical Society Collection, New-York Historical Society
NYPL	Manuscripts and Archives Division, New York Public Library, Astor, Lenox and Tilden Foundations
SL	East India or Asiatic Squadron Letters

This book is based mainly on manuscript materials, of which the most important are the collections of Letters Received by the Secretary of the Navy from Officers Commanding Ships of War (Captains' Letters); Letters from Officers Commanding Squadrons, 1841–1886, East India Squadron (after 1 January 1866, Asiatic Squadron); and the Area 10 File, which contains papers relating to the Pacific Ocean west of longitude 180°, extended westward to include the Indian Ocean. All are included in the Records of the Office of Naval Records and Library, Record Group 45, NA, as are Letters Sent by the Secretary of the Navy to Officers, 1798–1868 (Secretary's Letters, 1789–1868); Letters Sent by the Secretary of the Navy to Officers, 1861–1886 (Secretary's Letters, 1861–1886); Records of Confidential Letters; Translations of Cipher Messages; Logs, Journals, and Diaries of Officers of the United States Navy at Sea, March 1778–July 1908 (Officers' Journals); and Letter Books of Officers of the United States Navy at Sea, March 1778–July 1908 (Officers'

282

Letter Books). Logbooks of specific vessels are found in Logs of United States Naval Ships and Stations, 1801–1946, Records of the Bureau of Navigation, Record Group 24, NA. The personal papers collected by the NHF include many of value to this work. The British Admiralty Station Records, China: Correspondence (Adm 125), in the Public Record Office, London, contain useful information on the Royal Navy's cooperation with U.S. naval forces and some observations on the latters' activities. Other manuscript collections are cited in the sections to which they are most relevant.

Among published sources, the *Annual Reports* of the secretaries of the navy list the vessels assigned to the various squadrons and comment briefly on the major events on each station. The *Dictionary of American Naval Fighting Ships* (6 vols. to date, Washington, D.C.: Government Printing Office for Naval History Division, 1959–76), is an invaluable source of information on U.S. naval vessels and their service. Howard I. Chapelle, *The History of the American Sailing Navy* (New York: W. W. Norton and Company, 1949) is superb for the characteristics of sailing warships, while Frank M. Bennett, *The Steam Navy of the United States* (Pittsburgh: Warren and Co., 1896), and John D. Alden, *The American Steel Navy* (Annapolis, Md., and New York: Naval Institute Press and American Heritage Press, 1972), are very useful for steam-propelled vessels. Sir Edward J. Reed and Rear Admiral Edward Simpson, *Modern Ships of War* (New York: Harper and Brothers, 1888) is an interesting contemporary comment on warships of the United States and on other navies.

A number of sources provided biographical data on naval officers, including Thomas H. S. Hamersly, ed., *General Register of the United States Navy and Marine Corps* (Washington, D.C.: Thomas H. S. Hamersly, 1882); Lewis R. Hamersly, comp., *The Records of Living Officers of the U. S. Navy and Marine Corps* (Philadelphia: J. B. Lippincott and Co., 1870, and 5th ed., L. R. Hamersly & Co., 1894); *The National Cyclopedia of American Biography* (56 vols., New York: James T. White & Co., 1898–1975); and *The Dictionary of American Biography*, Allen Johnson and Dumas Malone, eds. (20 vols., New York: Charles Scribner's Sons, 1928–37). Peter Karsten, *The Naval Aristocracy* (New York: The Free Press, 1972), has information on officer attitudes —many of his impressions are rather unfavorable.

For background information on the Far East and U.S. policy thereto, the following works have been used: Tyler Dennett, *Americans in East Asia* (1922; reprint ed. New York: Barnes and Noble, Inc., 1941); John W. Foster, *American Diplomacy in the Orient* (Boston: Houghton Mifflin Co., 1903); and Paul H. Clyde, ed., *United States Policy toward China:*

Diplomatic and Public Documents, 1838–1939 (1940; reprint ed. New York: Russell and Russell, Inc., 1964). The essays by Edward D. Graham, John K. Fairbank, Kwang-ching Liu, and Robert S. Schwantes in *American–East Asian Relations: A Survey*, Ernest R. May and James C. Thompson, Jr., eds. (Cambridge, Mass.: Harvard University Press, 1972), were especially helpful. Texts of treaties negotiated before 1863 and information pertaining to them are found in D. Hunter Miller, ed., *Treaties and Other International Acts of the United States of America* (8 vols., Washington, D.C.: Government Printing Office, 1931–48); for later treaties, William M. Malloy, ed., *Treaties, Conventions, International Acts, Protocols, and Agreements between the United States of America and Other Powers, 1776–1937* (4 vols., Washington, D.C.: Government Printing Office, 1910–38), was used. Foster R. Dulles, *The Old China Trade* (Boston: Houghton Mifflin Co., 1930), and Samuel Eliot Morison, *The Maritime History of Massachusetts, 1783–1860* (Boston: Houghton Mifflin Co., 1921), discuss merchant shipping. Dudley W. Knox, *A History of the United States Navy* (New York: G. P. Putnam's Sons, 1936), and Harold Sprout and Margaret Sprout, *The Rise of American Naval Power, 1776–1918* Princeton, N.J.: Princeton University Press, 1939), remain the best of the U.S. Navy's operational and policy histories, respectively. Two works by Charles O. Paullin, *Diplomatic Negotiations of American Naval Officers, 1778–1883* (Baltimore: The Johns Hopkins Press, 1912), and *American Voyages to the Orient, 1690–1865* (Annapolis, Md.: U.S. Naval Institute, 1971, originally published as articles in the U.S. Naval Institute *Proceedings*, 1905–14), were of great assistance to me. James M. Merrill, "The Asiatic Squadron, 1835–1907," *The American Neptune*, 29 (April 1969):106–17, is a brief survey. James B. Wood, "The American Response to China, 1784–1844: Consensus Policy and the Origin of the East India Squadron" (Ph.D. dissertation, Duke University, 1968), differs from my account in some particulars.

No prudent navigator would think of sailing into Asian waters without charts and sailing directions, nor should the historian. Both of these indispensable aids to navigation were in almost constant use during the writing of this book.

Chapter 1

For the attack on Quallah Battoo, see Downes's report in Captains' Letters and also Midshipman James L. Parker, "U.S. Frigate Potomac: Journal of a Pacific Cruise, 1831–33," N-Y HS. Correspondence relating to the Roberts mission is in the Levi Woodbury Papers, #11 (1st Series),

LC, and in the Geisinger Papers, MdHS. Statistics on American trade with China are from 26th Cong., 1st Sess., H. Ex. Doc. 248. The origins of the U.S. Navy's distant-station policy are discussed in Robert G. Albion, "Distant Stations," U.S. Naval Institute *Proceedings*, 80 (1954): 265–73; for its effects and problems, see Robert E. Johnson, *Thence Round Cape Horn: The Story of United States Naval Forces on Pacific Station, 1818–1923* (Annapolis, Md.: U.S. Naval Institute, 1963), Chapter 1. The *Peacock*'s first cruise is described succinctly in "Notes on Two Cruises (Peacock)," Geisinger Papers MS. 1283, MdHS; and Maurice Collis, *Foreign Mud: The Opium Imbroglio at Canton in the 1830s and the Anglo-Japanese War* (1946; reprint ed. New York: W. W. Norton and Co., 1968), has good accounts of Macao, Canton, and conditions of trade with China. The *Vincennes*'s cruise is described in Aulick's reports, Captains' Letters, while Kennedy's letters in the same collection are the best source for the *Peacock*'s second cruise. Her stranding is also described in Lieutenant Sylvanus Godon's letter of 29 October 1835, Area 10 File, and by Edmund Roberts in a letter to his children dated 22 October 1835, typescript in Subject File HG, Box 149, RG 45, NA.

Chapter 2

Read's reports in Captains' Letters are supplemented by the "Journal of a Cruise in the U.S. Frigate Columbia, Bearing the Broad Pennant of Com. G. C. Reed," kept by Midshipman J. J. Guthrie, Officers' Journals. A number of books were published by individuals making the cruise, of which Fitch W. Taylor, *The Flagship, or, A Voyage around the World* (2 vols., Boston: Little, Brown, 1840), is the best known. Letters from missionaries in South China in the papers of the American Board of Commissioners for Foreign Missions, in Harvard University's Houghton Library, describe the situation in the vicinity of Canton on Read's arrival, as does Collis, *Foreign Mud*. Kearny's sailing orders are in Secretary's Letters, 1789–1868, and his cruise is described in Carroll S. Alden, *Lawrence Kearny: Sailor Diplomat* (Princeton, N.J.: Princeton University Press, 1936), which quotes extensively from his reports in SL and presents a very favorable view of its subject. Henry Pinkney's letters in the Manuscripts Vertical File, MdHS, provide an interesting view of life on board the *Constellation*. For Downes's rebuttal to Kearny's report of the frigate's condition, see Captains' Letters.

Chapter 3

SL include Parker's and McKeever's reports. Percival's sailing orders are in Records of Confidential Letters; his reports in Captains' Letters are supplemented by materials in the John Percival Papers, N-Y HS, and by "Journal of a Cruise in the U.S. Frigate Constitution," kept by Midshipman M. Patterson Jones, Officers' Journals; Midshipman J. E. Hopson, "Journal of the U.S. Ship Constitution," N–Y HS; and former Midshipman D. H. Lynch, "Cruise of the old U.S. Frigate Constitution around the World, 1844, 1845, 1846," typescript in Subject File OM, RG 45, NA. Written long after the cruise, the last is of doubtful reliability; it contains many of the anecdotes about "Mad Jack" Percival. Commodore Biddle's sailing orders are in Records of Confidential Letters, and his cruise is most adequately described by his own reports, SL. For early contacts with Japan as well as Biddle's cruise, see Samuel Eliot Morison, *Old Bruin: Commodore Matthew Calbraith Perry* (Boston: Little, Brown and Co., 1967), and W. G. Beasley, *Great Britain and the Opening of Japan, 1834–1858* (London: Luzac and Co., 1951). The former is especially critical of Biddle's conduct; Richard A. von Doenhoff, "Biddle, Perry, and Japan," U.S. Naval Institute *Proceedings*, 92 (Nov. 1966): 78–87, is somewhat less so. Geisinger's official reports are supplemented by his private papers in MdHS. Voorhees's reports are in SL; Graham's criticism of his premature departure is in Records of Confidential Letters.

Chapter 4

The Aulick Expedition Papers, MdHS, add little to the account of Aulick's difficulties with the Navy Department given in Paullin, *Diplomatic Negotiations of American Naval Officers*. The correspondence between Aulick and Inman is in SL, as is everything pertaining to the *Robert Bowne* incident. For the subsequent career of Walter M. Gibson, later "the Mormon king of Hawaii," see his biographical note in *Dictionary of American Biography*.

Chapter 5

Perry's reports of the Japan Expedition in SL may be supplemented by the journals kept in the *Macedonian* by John R. C. and Lawrence F. Lewis and by J. Glendy Sproston, NYPL. Francis L. Hawks, comp., *Narrative of the Expedition of an American Squadron to the China Seas and Japan, Performed in the Years 1852, 1853, and 1854 under the Command of Commodore M. C. Perry, United States Navy* (3 vols., Washington, D.C.: Beverly Tucker, Senate Printer, 1856–58), is the official account, based on records kept by the squadron's officers and others. Other published works dealing with the Japan expedition are myriad. The most recent and among the best is Morison, *Old Bruin*, while

Arthur Walworth, *Black Ships off Japan: The Story of Commo. Perry's Expedition* (New York: Alfred A. Knopf, 1946), is also worth perusing. For the North Pacific Surveying Expedition under Ringgold, see Letters of Surveying Expedition, Bering Strait, North Pacific, and China Seas, October 1852–January 1855, in RG 45, NA, which also has Records Relating to the United States Exploring Expedition to the North Pacific, 1854–1856, for Rodgers's tenure of command; the latter, edited by Allan B. Cole, were published as *Yankee Surveyors in the Shogun's Seas* (Princeton, N.J.: Princeton University Press, 1947). Officers of the squadron kept numerous journals and letter books, many of which are in Officers' Journals and Officers' Letter Books, RG 45, NA. None is more valuable than Acting Lieutenant Francis A. Roe, "Journal of a Cruize in Porpoise," in the Francis A. Roe Papers, NHF. Lieutenant Alexander W. Habersham, who sailed in the *John P. Kennedy* and the *John Hancock*, wrote of his experiences in *My Last Cruise, or, Where We Went and What We Saw* (Philadelphia: J. B. Lippincott and Co., 1857). George M. Brooke, Jr., "John Mercer Brooke, Naval Scientist" (Ph.D. dissertation, 2 vols., University of North Carolina, 1955), is based on the papers of the expedition's astronomer. Ringgold's removal from command is discussed in Robert E. Johnson, *Rear Admiral John Rodgers, 1812–1882* (Annapolis, Md.: U.S. Naval Institute, 1967). The *Plymouth's* action at Shanghai is the topic of George E. Paulsen, "Under the Starry Flag on Muddy Flat: Shanghai, 1854," *The American Neptune*, 30 (1970):155–66.

Chapter 6

Abbot's and Pope's reports are in SL, as is Preble's account of the *Queen's* engagements with pirates. A copy of Pegram's report of the later attack on Khulan is in Subject File OO, Box III, RG 45, NA. Armstrong's cruise is described in SL; in Assistant Surgeon R. P. Daniel, "Medical Journal aboard the USS San Jacinto, October 1855–August 1858," Officers' Journals; and in Surgeon William M. Wood, *Fankwei; or, The San Jacinto in the Seas of India, China, and Japan* (New York: Harper and Brothers, 1859), which is laudatory of the commodore and his subordinates. For the attack on the barrier forts, see the Andrew Hull Foote Papers, NHF, which contain Foote's private journal as well as copies of reports and correspondence. See also Fred B. Rogers, *Montgomery and the Portsmouth* (San Francisco: John Howell Books, 1958). Davenport's opinions of Armstrong and Foote are expressed in his journal, copy in Subject File HL, RG 45, NA.

Chapter 7

In addition to Tattnall's reports in SL, the journal-letters written by Captain Du Pont to his wife, now in the Samuel Francis Du Pont Papers, Eleutherian Mills Historical Library, Greenville-Wilmington, Del., provide an interesting account of the *Minnesota*'s cruise and the 1858 attack on the Pei Ho forts. The British gunboats are described by Antony Preston and John Major in *Send a Gunboat: A Study of the Gunboat and Its Role in British Policy, 1854–1904* (London: Longmans, Green and Co., Ltd., 1967). My account of Admiral Hope's assault on the Pei Ho forts and the *Toey-wan*'s part therein is based on the British Admiralty records in Adm 125, many of which are published in D. Bonner-Smith and E. W. R. Lumby, eds., *The Second China War, 1856–1860* (London: Navy Records Society, 1954); First Assistant Engineer R. C. Potts, "Journal on board of U.S.S. 'Pohatan,'" in Officers' Journals; a letter written by John S. Lürman, a member of Ward's suite, to Gustav W. Lürman on 2 July 1859, typescript in Manuscripts Vertical File, MdHS; Edgar S. Maclay, *Reminiscences of the Old Navy* (New York: G. P. Putnam's Sons, 1898); and Charles C. Jones, Jr., *The Life and Services of Commodore Josiah Tattnall* (Savannah, Ga.: The Morning News Steam Printing House, 1878), which is nineteenth-century biography of the most laudatory sort. Edith Roelker Curtis, "Blood Is Thicker Than Water," *The American Neptune*, 27 (1967):157–76, is an uncritical biographical essay on Tattnall. Stribling's reports are in SL. For details of the *John Adams*'s detention at Rio de Janeiro, see the Brazil Squadron Letters and Captain Alfred T. Mahan, *From Sail to Steam: Recollections of Naval Life* (New York: Harper and Brothers, 1907). Lieutenant Henry A. Wise chronicled the *Niagara*'s visit to the Far East in his "Private Journal on Board Frigate Niagara, 1860," Officers' Journals. Stribling's general order on the outbreak of the Civil War is in SL and is printed in full in Paullin, *American Voyages to the Orient*. Engle's reports are in SL, and for the *Saginaw*'s condition, see the ZC File, Naval Historical Center, Washington Navy Yard.

Chapter 8

McDougal's and Price's reports are in *Official Records of the Union and Confederate Navies in the War of the Rebellion* (31 vols., Washington, D.C.: Government Printing Office, 1894–1927). For the *Alabama*'s itinerary, see Charles G. Summersell, ed., *The Journal of George Townley Fullam, Boarding Officer of the Confederate Sea Raider Alabama* (University, Ala.: University of Alabama Press, 1973). The deterioration of

Anglo-American relations in the Far East may be traced in Adm 125, which also contains accounts of the conferences involving foreign naval officers and of the Dutch, American, and French engagements in the Strait of Shimonoseki, and Admiral Kuper's reports of the bombardment of Kagoshima and the joint operation against Shimonoseki. Preston and Major, *Send a Gunboat*, has brief descriptions of the two latter battles.

Chapter 9

For the effects of the Civil War on the American merchant marine, see George W. Dalzell, *The Flight from the Flag* (Chapel Hill, N.C.: University of North Carolina Press, 1940), and Robert G. Albion and Jennie Barnes Pope, *Sea Lanes in Wartime* (New York: W. W. Norton Co., Inc., 1942). Bell's reports can be found in SL; his cruise is also the subject of E. Mowbray Tate, "Admiral Bell and the New Asiatic Squadron, 1865–1868," *The American Neptune*, 32 (April 1972):123–35, which is favorably inclined toward Bell. Shufeldt's mission to Korea is described in his reports in SL, which should be supplemented by the Robert W. Shufeldt Papers, NHF. John Haskell Kemble describes the Pacific Mail Steamship Company's transpacific service in "A Hundred Years of the Pacific Mail," *The American Neptune*, 10 (1950):123–43. Grace E. Fox, *British Admirals and Chinese Pirates, 1832–1869* (1940; reprint ed., Westport, Conn.: Hyperion Press, Inc., 1973), is the standard work on anti-piratical activity; it does less than justice to the U.S. Navy's role but explains Keppel's policy. The opening of Osaka and Bell's drowning were described by several who were in the vicinity; Lieutenant Commander Alfred T. Mahan in a letter dated 13 January 1868, Robert Seager II, and Doris D. Maguire, eds., *The Letters and Papers of Alfred Thayer Mahan* (3 vols., Annapolis, Md.: Naval Institute Press, 1975), and Commander J. Blakeley Creighton, 12 January 1868, in Letter Book 15, Henry Aug. Wise Papers, N-Y HS, are especially valuable. The funeral description is based on Mahan's letter, which is reprinted almost verbatim in *From Sail to Steam*.

Chapter 10

"Letters of S. C. Rowan, U.S.N., Comd'g Asiatic Squadron, to the Navy Department from October 1867 to November 1870, RG 45, NA, duplicate his reports in SL. Fleet Captain's Clerk William B. Burtis, "Private Journal of a Cruise to China and Japan in the years of 1867, 1868, 1869 and 1870 in the Flag Ship Piscataqua," NYPL; Charles Clift's Journal, Log #425 and 426, G. W. Blunt White Library, Mystic Seaport,

Inc., Mystic, Conn.; Francis A. Roe Papers, NHF; Samuel P. Boyer, *Naval Surgeon: The Revolt in Japan, 1868–1869*, ed. Elinor Barnes and James A. Barnes (Bloomington, Ind.: Indiana University Press, 1963); Robley D. Evans, *A Sailor's Log* (New York: D. Appleton and Co., 1908); Mahan, *From Sail to Steam*; and Robert Seager II, *Alfred Thayer Mahan* (Annapolis, Md.: Naval Institute Press, 1977), are all very useful for this chapter. Dr. Boyer, *Naval Surgeon*, provides the gruesome details of the venereal disease problem. The *Cayolte* incident is described therein and by Mahan in Seager and Maguire, eds., *Letters and Papers*. Burtis, "Journal," and Boyer, *Naval Surgeon*, confirm the Duke of Edinburgh's rudeness and Rowan's reaction thereto. The *Idaho*'s ordeal was related by one of her company in "A Night in a Typhoon," *Atlantic Monthly*, 25 (March 1870):343–48—Bennett, *Steam Navy of the United States*, identifies Medical Director A. L. Gihon as the author. My account of the *Oneida*'s loss is based on the records of the British court of inquiry, which are in Adm 125 and are reprinted, together with the records of the American court, in 41st Cong., 2nd Sess., H. Ex. Doc. 236.

Chapter 11

Rodgers's reports in SL may be supplemented by his letters to his wife and others in the John Rodgers Collection, NHF. This account of the Korea expedition, with the exception of a few changes, first appeared in Johnson, *Rear Admiral John Rodgers*. Most of the officers' reports relevant to the operation were printed in Robeson's *Annual Report, 1871*, while Low's are in *Papers Relating to the Foreign Relations of the United States Transmitted to Congress with the Annual Message of the President, Dec. 4, 1871* (Washington, D.C.: Government Printing Office, 1871). Marine Captain McLane Tilton's letters to his wife are in Carolyn A. Tyson, comp., *Marine Amphibious Landing in Korea, 1871* (Washington, D.C.: Naval Historical Foundation, 1966). The Homer C. Blake Papers, N-Y HS, and the Silas Casey Papers, NHF, have relatively little on the expedition. Lieutenant Charles H. Rockwell, Letter Book—*Palos*, Officers' Letter Books, and his journal, Officers' Journals, have details of the gunboat's visit to Newchwang and her winter at Tientsin. The opening of telegraphic communication with the Far East is discussed in Robert G. Albion, "Communications and Remote Control," U.S. Naval Institute *Proceedings*, 82 (August 1956):832–35.

Chapter 12

John L. Rawlinson, *China's Struggle for Naval Development, 1839–1895* (Cambridge, Mass.: Harvard University Press, 1967), is the standard work on its subject. For officers' indulgence in strong drink, see Boyer, *Naval Surgeon*; Seager, *Mahan*; and Karsten, *Naval Aristocracy*. Rear Admiral Kemp Tolley, *Yangtze Patrol: The U.S. Navy in China* (Annapolis, Md.: Naval Institute Press, 1971), describes some of the early warship ascents of the river. The boiler problem is discussed in Chief Engineer Richard Sennett, RN, *The Marine Steam Engine* (London: Longmans, Green, and Co., 1882), and in Engineer Captain Edgar C. Smith, RN, *A Short History of Naval and Marine Engineering* (Cambridge: Babcock and Wilcox, Ltd., 1937).

Chapter 13

The essential source for Shufeldt's negotiation of the treaty with Korea is the Shufeldt Papers, NHF, which also have full details on the indiscreet letter to Sargent. See also Shufeldt's letter books in the *Ticonderoga*, RG 45, NA. Kenneth J. Hagan, *American Gunboat Diplomacy and the Old Navy, 1877–1889* (Westport, Conn.: Greenwood Press, 1973), emphasizes naval officers' interest in the extension and protection of trade. Clitz's reports in SL reveal the paucity of resources open to him, and this account of the *Ashuelot*'s loss is based on the testimony at Commander Mullan's court-martial, Record of General Court-Martial 6415, RG 125, National Record Center, Suitland, Md.

Chapter 14

Davis's reports and copies of consular complaints are in SL. For the Sino-French War and its background, D. W. Brogan, *The Development of Modern France* (New York: Harper and Brothers, 1940), and Frederick L. Schuman, *War and Diplomacy in the French Republic* (New York: Whittlesey House—McGraw-Hill Book Co., Inc., 1931), are useful. Rawlinson, *China's Struggle for Naval Development*; H. W. Wilson, *Ironclads in Action: A Sketch of Naval Warfare from 1855 to 1895* (3d rev. ed., 2 vols., London: Sampson Low, Marston and Co., 1898); and E. H. Jenkins, *A History of the French Navy* (Annapolis, Md.: Naval Institute Press, 1973), have accounts of the Pagoda Anchorage battle. Davis's general orders directed at improving the discipline and efficiency of his squadron are in SL.

Chapter 15

With the discontinuance of the Squadron Letters in 1886, the Area 10 File became the depository for reports and correspondence of commanders in chief. The Z File, Naval Historical Center, has a description of Chandler's funeral. The George E. Belknap Papers, NHF, have some material on the assignment of new ships to the Asiatic Station and on the Japanese maneuvers of 1890.

Chapter 16

Paul A. Varg, *Missionaries, Chinese, and Diplomats: The American Protestant Missionary Movement in China, 1890–1952* (Princeton, N.J.: Princeton University Press, 1958), discusses the growth of American missionary activity in the Orient for this period. Irwin's and Skerrett's exchange of stations is explained most adequately in Hugh B. Hammett, *Hilary Abner Herbert: A Southerner Returns to the Union* (Philadelphia: The American Philosophical Society, 1976), although Hammett states that Skerrett was ordered home from Honolulu. Johnson, *Thence Round Cape Horn*, inexplicably omits any mention of the incident or of Skerrett's brief tenure as commander in chief, while Walter R. Herrick, Jr., *The American Naval Revolution* (Baton Rouge, La.: Louisiana State University Press, 1966), has Skerrett relieved by Rear Admiral John G. Walker, who actually relieved Irwin. William R. Braisted, *The United States Navy in the Pacific, 1897–1909* (Austin, Texas: University of Texas Press, 1958), gives the sequence of command changes correctly. Rawlinson, *China's Struggle for Naval Development*; Wilson, *Ironclads in Action*; and Admiral Sir Reginald Custance, *The Ship of the Line in Battle* (Edinburgh: William Blackwood and Sons, 1912), have accounts of the Sino-Japanese War. Jeffrey M. Dorwart, *The Pigtail War* (Amherst, Mass.: University of Massachusetts Press, 1975), shows little understanding of the Asiatic Squadron's activities or of nautical matters generally; his "The United States Navy and the Sino-Japanese War of 1894–1895," *The American Neptune*, 34 (1974):211–18, is no better. The murder of the missionaries in Fukien province is investigated by Salvatore Prisco III, in "The Vegetarian Society and the Huashan-Kut'ien Massacre of 1895," *Asian Forum*, 3 (1971):1–13.

Chapter 17

The Alfred Moore Scales Papers, East Carolina Manuscript Collection, East Carolina University, Greenville, N.C., include letters from Ensign Scales on board the *Machias* and with the legation guard sent to Seoul in 1896. For the Siamese teakwood concession incident, see Salvatore Prisco III, *John Barrett, Progressive Era Diplomat: A Study of a Commercial Expansionist, 1887–1920* (University, Ala.: University of Alabama

Press, 1973). Braisted, *The United States Navy in the Pacific, 1897–1909*, has a good introductory chapter on the Asiatic Station in the 1890s. The account of Dewey's preparations for belligerent operations in the Philippines is based mainly on the Area 10 File, Translations of Cipher Messages, and logs of the individual ships. Much of this material was printed in *Naval Operations of the War with Spain: Appendix to the Report of the Chief of the Bureau of Navigation, 1898* (Washington, D.C.: Government Printing Office, 1898). Rear Admiral French E. Chadwick, *The Relations of the United States and Spain: The Spanish American War* (2 vols., New York: Charles Scribner's Sons, 1911), remains the best work on its subject; it differs from my account in some minor details. Dewey's most recent biography, Ronald Spector, *Admiral of the New Empire: The Life and Career of George Dewey* (Baton Rouge, La.: Louisiana State University Press, 1974), adds little on this portion of its subject's career that is not in Richard S. West, Jr., *Admirals of American Empire* (Indianapolis, Ind.: The Bobbs-Merrill Company, 1948). Accounts of the Battle of Manila Bay are myriad; this one is taken principally from the ships' logs and reports by commanding officers and others.

Index

Aulick, John H.: commands the *Vincennes*, 11; commander in chief, 50–55, 57–58, 60
Azuma. See Kotetsu

Badger, George E., secretary of the navy, 23
Balestier, Joseph, diplomatic agent, 47
Ballard, Henry C., commander in chief, Pacific Squadron, 16
Baltimore, protected cruiser, 230, 234–40; visits Port Arthur, 241–42; reported misconduct of legation guard, 243–44, 247, 248, 250, 252; brings ammunition to Dewey, 258–59; docked at Hong Kong, 260, 261–62; in Battle of Manila Bay, 263–66
Banjo, Japanese gunboat, 193
Bankhead, John P., 126–27
Barber, Francis M., 233
Barker, Albert S., 210, 212
Barrett, John, diplomat, 254–55
Baseball game, 146
Belknap, George E.: commands Formosa landing force, 132, 134; report of Buddhist ceremony, 152; commander in chief, 224; reports on Japanese maneuvers, 225, 226, 227, 229, 230; evaluated, 231
Bell, Henry H.: commands the *San Jacinto*, 84, 86, 87; commander in chief, 125–27; prefers Nagasaki as base, 128, 129; desires to capture Seoul, 130–31; and Formosa expedition, 132, 134, 135; death of, 137; mentioned, 138, 139, 143, 168, 173, 224, 239, 268
Belliqueuse, French ironclad, 143
Benicia, screw-sloop, 154–56, 159–60, 167, 170
Bering Sea patrol, 227, 229, 234, 236
Biddle, James, commander in chief, 37–38, 40; visits Japan, 41–42, 43, 45, 63
Bingham, John A., diplomat, 187
Blaine, James G., secretary of state, 192, 193
Blake, Homer C., 155; commands Korea landing force, 158–61, 163
Boat-racing, 152–53

Bobr, Russian warship, 222
Boiler problems discussed, 180
Bombay, Peninsular and Oriental steamer, collides with the *Oneida*, 150–52
Borie, Adolph E., secretary of the navy, 147
Boston, sloop of war, 23–25, 27
Boston, protected cruiser, 223; at Honolulu, 234, 254–57, 260, 262; in Battle of Manila Bay, 263–64
Bowring, Sir John, governor of Hong Kong, 80, 83, 91, 95
Boxer, schooner, 2, 6–9
Boxer Rebellion, 255
Brandywine, frigate, 31–33, 35–36
Bridgman, Elijah C., missionary: on opium traffic, 20, 25; on Treaty of Wanghia, 33, 38
Broad, George E., British commander, 132
Brooke, John M., 105
Brooklyn, screw-sloop, 217, 219–22
Brown, George, 142
Bruce, Sir Frederick, British diplomat, 102
Buchanan, Franklin, 57
Buchanan, James, president, 105
Buddhist ceremony in memory of the *Oneida*, 152
Bustard, British gunboat, 120

Campbell, Archibald, death of, 15
Canton, China: regulations governing trade, 3; factories in, 7; trade stopped in 1839, 19–22; 1842 riots in, 28; capture of barrier forts in, 83–90; captured in 1858, 96; 1883 riot in, 203; 1889 riot in, 225
Caprice, chartered merchantman, 62
Carpenter, Charles C., commander in chief, 239–42; opposes sending marines to the *Monocacy*, 243, 244–45, 247; and Huashan massacre, 248, 250–51
Carter, Samuel P., 136
Cashmere, merchant bark, 216
Cayolte, Peruvian merchantman, 145
Cecille, Jean-Baptiste, French commander in chief, 43

last passage of, to the Pei Ho, 230, 232; condemned and sold, 233

Parker, Foxhall A., commander in chief, 31–33; prefers Macao to Hong Kong, 34, 35–36, 60

Parker, Peter, missionary and diplomat, 38, 40, 43, 54, 81; on capture of barrier forts, 90, 91, 92

Parkes, Harry, British consul, 82

Parrott, Enoch G., commander in chief, 174–75

Partridge, F. W., consul, 181, 182

Patterson, Thomas H., commander in chief, 184–85, 188–90

Paulding, James K., secretary of the navy, 23

Peacock, sloop of war of 1813, 3

Peacock, sloop of war of 1828, 2, 5–8; significance of first cruise of, 9, 11, 12; stranded, 13, 14–18, 106

Pearson, Frederick, 120, 122

Pegram, Robert B., 79

Peiyang fleet, Chinese, 239; in Battle of Yalu River, 240, 244, 247

Pellew, Sir Fleetwood, British commander in chief, 67

Pembroke, merchant steamer, 116

Peninsular and Oriental Steam Navigation Company, 52, 75, 150

Pennock, Alexander M., commander in chief, 177, 178

Penobscot, screw-gunboat, 136

Percival, John, 36–37, 187

Perry, Jane Slidell, 59

Perry, Matthew C., commander in chief, 43, 53, 59; selects bases, 60–61; first visit to Japan by, 63–65; and Humphrey Marshall, 66, 67; second visit to Japan by, 68–71; and North Pacific Expedition, 73; relinquishes command, 74–75, 76, 77, 137, 158, 190, 268

Perry, Oliver H., consul, 83, 91

Perry, brig, 32, 33, 35

Perseus, British screw-sloop, 122

Petrel, steel gunboat, 232, 233, 235, 236, 239; winters at Newchwang, 242, 250, 252; and Shanghai incident, 253, 254, 256, 257, 260; in Battle of Manila Bay, 263–66

Philadelphia, protected cruiser, 234

Philippine rebellion, 256

Pierce, Franklin, president, 71, 79

Piracy, 47, 76, 129, 135

Piscataqua, screw-frigate, 140, 142, 143, 146; renamed *Delaware*, 147

Platt, A. R., consul, 208

Plover, British screw-gunboat, 102, 103

Plymouth, sloop of war, 44, 46–48, 53, 56, 61–62; with Japan expedition, 63–64, 65, 68; at Shanghai, 73–74

Pope, John, senior naval officer, 78, 80–81

Popoff, A. A., Russian commodore, 105

Porpoise, brig, 72; lost, 73, 268

Port Arthur, China, 240, 241; fall of, 242, 247

Port Hamilton, Kŏmun Do, 131

Port Lazaref (Wonsan), Korea, 196

Porter, David D., 147, 167, 170, 183

Portsmouth, sloop of war, 81, 82; attacks barrier forts, 84–88; to Singapore, 91; and Japan, 93–94, 95

Potomac, frigate, attacks Quallah Battoo, 1–2, 3, 5, 6, 8, 11, 23

Pottinger, Sir Henry, British general, 27

Powhatan, paddle frigate: with Perry, 65, 68, 69, 72, 76, 79–80, 98–100; off the Taku forts, 102, 104, 106, 109

Preble, George H., 76–78

Preble, sloop of war, 44; at Nagasaki, 45–46, 204

Price, Cicero, 117–20, 123

Princeton, screw-sloop, 65

Pruyn, Robert H., diplomat, 116, 120, 123

Putiatin, E. V., Russian admiral and diplomat, 67, 96–99

Quallah Battoo, Sumatra: Downes attacks, 1, 6, 11; Read bombards, 18, 36

Queen, British paddle steamer: chartered by Perry, 67–68, 72; fights pirates, 76–77; captured and burned, 92

Qui Nhon, Cochin-China, 109, 112

Radford, William, 109
Raleigh, protected cruiser, 256, 257, 260, 262; in Battle of Manila Bay, 263–64
Ranger, iron screw-gunboat, 183, 184, 186
Rattler, British screw-sloop, 79
Read, George C., commander in chief, 17; attacks Quallah Battoo and Mukkee, 18–19, 20–22
Reed, J. H., drowned off Osaka, 137, 138
Reed, William B., diplomat, 95–98, 100
Reina Cristina, Spanish cruiser, in Battle of Manila Bay, 263–66
Relief, storeship, 125, 126
Reynolds, William, commander in chief, 179; plans for Philippines attack, 180, 181–84; describes Korean embassy, 187
Rice, Elisha E., consul, 145
Rich, John C., 230, 232
Richards, Sir Frederick, British commander in chief, 228
Richmond, screw-sloop, 186, 189–91, 194–95, 198–200, 202, 204, 206
Ringdove, British screw-gunboat, 167
Ringgold, Cadwalader, 72–73
Robert Bowne, merchantman, seized by coolies, 53–54, 57
Roberts, Edmund, diplomatic agent, 2, 6–8; urges establishment of squadron, 9, 11, 12–14; death of, 15
Robeson, George M., secretary of the navy, 147, 155, 166, 169, 186–87, 189
Rock Springs, Wyoming, massacre, 217
Rockwell, Charles H., 161, 168–69
Rodgers, John: with North Pacific Surveying Expedition, 72–73; commander in chief, 154; and Korean expedition, 155–56, 158–60, 165–66, 167–69; president, Naval Advisory Board, 223
Rodney, British screw-ship of the line, 137, 144
Roe, Francis A., 151–52
Rolando, Henry, 79

Roosevelt, Theodore, assistant secretary of the navy, 257
Rover, merchant bark, wrecked on Formosa, 132, 134
Rowan, Stephen C., commander in chief, 140–42; and venereal disease problem, 143–45; snubbed by duke of Edinburgh, 147, 148, 149; convenes *Oneida* inquiry, 151, 152–54, 168
Roze, Pierre G., French commander in chief, 130, 156, 165
Russell and Company, 91, 92, 96, 197

Saco, screw-gunboat: boiler problem of, 170, 172, 174; southern cruise of, 178, 179–80; nearly founders, 181
Saginaw, paddle gunboat, 106–8; ascends Yangtze, 109; at Qui Nhon, 109, 112, 113, 114
St. Louis, sloop of war, 31–33; visits treaty ports, 34; and Australia and New Zealand, 35–36
St. Mary's, sloop of war, 47, 55–56
Salmon, Nowell, British commander in chief, 226
Saluting, limitation of, 226
Sampson, William T., 189, 191
San Jacinto, screw-frigate, 80; disabled, 81; at Shimoda, 82; sends force to attack barrier forts, 84–88, 91–93, 95, 125
Sapphire, British screw-corvette, 210
Saratoga, sloop of war, 52; stranded, 54; in typhoon, 56, 59; with Japan expeditions, 63, 65, 66, 69, 71
Sargent, Aaron A., senator, 194
Satsuma, Japanese daimyo, 115, 118
Schenck, J. Findley, 108; at Qui Nhon, 109, 112, 113
Schenck, Robert A., 51–53
Schley, Winfield S., 165
Scurvy, 22
Semiramis, East India Company steamer, 54
Sémiramis, French screw-frigate, 117, 121
Semmes, Raphael, Confederate commander, 119
Sepoy Mutiny, 95

Sources of Illustrations

Estate of Col. Fred B. Rogers: Figure 6–1
Evans, Robert D., *A Sailor's Log* (New York, 1908): Figure 4–2
Heinl, Robert D., Jr., *Soldiers of the Sea* (Annapolis, 1962): Map 6–1
Mystic Seaport Photograph: Figure 2–1
National Archives: Figures 11–1, 14–1, 16–2
Naval Historical Foundation: Figure 17–1 (Doutreaux Collection); Map 11–1
Naval Photographic Center: Frontispiece; Figures 3–1, 4–1, 6–2, 8–1, 9–1, 10–1, 11–2, 13–1, 15–1, 16–3, 17–2
Peabody Museum: Figure 12–1
Reed, Sir Edward, and Simpson, Edward, *Modern Ships of War* (New York, 1888): Figure 16–1